Classical Ethics: East and West

Classical Ethics

East and West

Ethics from a Comparative Perspective

ROBERT B. ZEUSCHNER

ECHO POINT BOOKS & MEDIA, LLC

Published by Echo Point Books & Media
Brattleboro, Vermont
www.EchoPointBooks.com

ISBN: 978-1-62654-851-0

Interior illustrations by Ronald Jimenez

Cover images from top to bottom:
Plane tree with wide branches in autumn misty park, unknown photographer;
Buddha, Stephanie Carter;
St. Augustine and Four States of a Fraternity, Pietro Perugino;
Confucius, unknown artist {{PD-1923}};
Section from *The School of Athens,* Raphael {{PD-1923}};
John Stuart Mill, London Stereoscopic Company {{PD-1923}}.

Cover design by Adrienne Núñez,
Echo Point Books & Media

Editorial and proofreading assistance by Christine Schultz,
Echo Point Books & Media

Additional credits are located on page 293.

*Dedicated to
David, Danae,
Jennifer, and Scott*

Foreword

Everyone wants to be happier. Some take that desire more seriously than others, studying what wise thinkers have said, paying close attention to their own life and past, or trying psychotherapy or spiritual practices in the hopes of achieving greater inner peace. As a philosophy major in college, I was drawn to this quest, and in my senior year I started a dedicated Zen meditation practice. I tended to focus on big existential questions, and, I'm embarrassed to say, I hoped for some big breakthrough from meditation that would make my inner struggles disappear in a flash.

What I overlooked was the importance of ethical or moral focus and behavior. That is not to suggest I blatantly mistreated others, but I did not bring the same kind of intensity or curiosity about ethical actions as I did to mindfulness practices. What I didn't see is that ultimately the two cannot be separated. Consider this, for example: before meditating one afternoon, you decide to steal your neighbor's stereo system and slash his truck tires. You then sit down to meditate, hoping for peace of mind. Obviously that makes no sense. But in much more subtle ways, we do similar things all the time. For instance, we might trash someone with gossip and then do not notice the effect it has on us (let alone how it may eventually hurt that person's feelings). We may tell small fibs now and again and wonder why we feel anxious. If you want to see the power of ethical actions on your state of mind, commit to only telling the truth in a kind way for a week or even a few days. You will see that it affects your whole state of mind.

Of course, this is not a how-to book, but an academic text. I believe one's studies can be more engaging when you know why it matters. *Classical Ethics: East and West* does not tell the reader how to behave, but engages us in the exploration of essential questions of ethics. Introducing his book to me, Professor Zeuschner asked:

> How do we distinguish good from evil? Is it the result of critical thinking, or emotion, or reliance on supernatural beings? Do morally correct actions produce pleasure or happiness as a consequence? Or consider, what is the role of God in ethics? Is it possible to have ethical

values and not believe in God? Does an ethical theory based upon the will of God have any conceptually puzzling features? How do other (non-Christian) cultures understand the foundation for ethical judgments? What is the role of conscience? Do we have a duty to do what is right? If so, is moral behavior determined by duty? Is what is right merely whatever action produces the greatest happiness for the greatest number? Is it possible to define "good" or is the term indefinable? Are ethical judgments relative, or absolute?

When I discussed this foreword with Zeuschner, he noted that:

The goal of this book is to provide you with the tools to think about difficult ethical issues yourself, and arrive at your own conclusions. You will read the writings of the best philosophers and are invited to think carefully about their solutions to some of the more interesting problems that have arisen in the field of ethics. For example, can we knowingly do something wrong, or is all wrong behavior committed out of ignorance? What is the basis of being moral: is it following a list of rules, is it something we do on the basis of reason or on the basis of emotion, or is it developing a certain sort of personal virtue? How does our character affect our morals, and can we develop a moral character—if so, how?

Dr. Zeuschner also pointed out that this is a philosophy textbook:

In philosophy the approach is that of critical philosophical analysis— using our ability to reason. Nothing is assumed to be true; every claim is open to rational challenge. We do not accept something as true just because someone else said so. We must ask "why" and we must ask "how do you know?" It's important to have the courage and skill to use your own intelligence. By discussing a number of different answers to the questions above, we hope to stimulate thinking on a number of the basic questions which all human beings confront at one time or another in their life.

Ethical inquiry deals with our lives as we really live them. By studying what some of the greatest minds of history have thought about ethical behavior, you not only build your ability to think clearly but also increase the understanding and wisdom that will bring greater awareness to your own ethical life. This in turn can lead you to greater happiness. So in that light, I hope you appreciate and soak in the genius, fortitude, and creativity of the thinkers profiled in Professor Zeuschner's wonderful book. Their ideas can both inform and develop wisdom. Learn well and enjoy.

—Marshall Glickman, publisher of Echo Point Books & Media and author of *Beyond the Breath: Extraordinary Mindfulness Through Whole-Body Vipassana Meditation*

Brief Contents

Part IV
ETHICS IN CHINA DURING THE CLASSICAL PERIOD
(5TH–2ND CENTURY B.C.E.): CONFUCIANISM AND TAOISM

Part V
WESTERN ETHICS FROM THE RENAISSANCE
TO THE NINETEENTH CENTURY

Detailed Contents

Part I
ETHICS IN ANCIENT GREECE
(5TH–2ND CENTURIES B.C.E.)

PART III
BUDDHIST ETHICS IN INDIA (5TH CENTURY B.C.E.)

Part V
WESTERN ETHICS FROM THE RENAISSANCE TO THE NINETEENTH CENTURY: THE BEGINNINGS OF MODERN ETHICS

Preface

Classical Ethics: East and West is designed to serve as an introductory textbook in ethics. It includes explanatory analyses of the writings of the very best of the classic Western philosophers, and several of the most important philosophers of Asia and the Far East, stressing India and China.

The texts in this book represent a broad range of ideas concerning ethical choices, spanning two millennia and several continents. They include the ethical teachings of historic philosophical traditions as well as particular religious traditions (Christianity, Indian Buddhism, and Chinese Taoism).

In the recent past, "philosophy" has come to mean a specialized approach that is critical, logically rigorous, and analytical and generally focuses on careful systematic analysis of fundamental concepts. However, this approach, as valuable as it is, is not typical of all traditional Western or non-Western philosophers. The traditional approach includes a greater willingness to engage in speculative philosophy, a willingness to attempt to create a complete system that can explain the fundamental and enduring questions about nature and humanity. The majority of the philosophers in this anthology pursue the traditional approach to philosophy.

The purpose of this volume is to help students reason about ethical principles as they occur in different cultural contexts, gain insight into the foundations of morality in Western contemporary civilization, and enrich their thinking with a perspective provided by cultures that do not share the same presuppositions of the Greek and Christian traditions.

Organization

Within the text's five sections are the most important standard classical Western theories in ethics, including theories of self-realization, egoism, utilitarianism, God-based "Divine Command" ethics, and several major Eastern perspectives, some of which have very different presuppositions than the Western views. These include ethics grounded in the experience of enlightenment, and a rather radical form of ethical relativism.

Each section is arranged chronologically. We begin in Part One with a remarkably creative period in human history, the period from the fifth century B.C.E.

to the third century B.C.E. We'll read the ideas of the Greeks as Western philosophy took shape under the hands of Socrates, Plato, and Aristotle. In Part Two, we focus on the two philosophers who had the most influence on traditional Christian ethical theories, St. Augustine and St. Thomas Aquinas. In Part Three, we discuss the ethical theory of one of India's greatest philosophical traditions, Buddhism. In Part Four, we analyze two of the great philosophers of China's classical period, Confucius and Lao-tzu. These two ways of looking at the world laid the basic shape for all subsequent Chinese thought about ethics and the world and profoundly influenced Japanese and Korean civilization as well.

The Western selections in Part Five include the newer ethical theories that originated after the period of the Middle Ages and culminated in the ethical arguments of Joseph Butler, Immanuel Kant, David Hume, and John Stuart Mill.

The Eastern selections in this anthology are not exhaustive of the broad range of Eastern ethical theories, but they do include the most important thinkers in India and China. The range of ethical theories in the East is at least as varied as Western theories, and it is a profound error to think that the majority of the thinkers in India can be described with just one worldview. The same is true for China, Korea, Japan, and Southeast Asia. This book could easily be doubled in size and still not encompass each differing viewpoint. However, there was a serious attempt to ensure that none of the most influential ethical theories have been omitted.

In the twentieth century, ethics has had a tendency to move away from general theories to rather technical metaethical questions. For reasons of consistency and length, I have restricted the selections in this text to traditional classical ethical theories and do not include any philosophers after John Stuart Mill. Because the text is designed as an introduction, more recent theories of scholars like George E. Moore, William D. Ross, Charles Stevenson, William Frankena, Kurt Baier, John Rawls, Philippa Foot, R. B. Brandt, or A. I. Melden are not included.

Pedagogical Features

This textbook includes several special features. (1) Presented first is a brief historical background and biography of the philosopher under discussion, including references to contemporaneous developments in art, politics, and science, to locate the historical perspective for the benefit of the student. It has been my experience that today's student does not have a solid grounding in historical periods, and even supplying a date such as 470–399 B.C.E. means very little. For some students, the difference between the times of Socrates and that of Darwin are very hazy. (2) Next a summary overview of the relevant arguments occurs, which precedes the quotations from the actual philosopher. Thus, the student begins the section with an idea of where the discussion is going to go, and the most important conclusions are outlined before the detailed examination of the ideas. (3) Additional explanations of technical passages are provided. The writings of philosophers are not easily accessible, and for students who have never read philosophy, the intellectual content can be quite intimidating and opaque.

Consequently, extended discussions of these arguments are found in each chapter, sometimes using examples that are more contemporary. (4) Key technical terms and names encountered in the readings occur in **boldface** and are defined in the end-of-chapter glossaries. The glossaries will often contain explanations of other references. Teachers of philosophy sometimes overlook the technical vocabulary, and even words that are a part of the vocabulary of an average well-educated person are often troublesome for the college student. A selected bibliography also follows each chapter. (5) Critical remarks and questions on potential difficulties in each tradition are discussed. It is important for students to understand that none of the systems presented in this book are perfect, answer all questions, and have no difficulties. An objective person will encounter these various theories, and certain questions are absolutely appropriate. I do not intend to suggest that these objections cannot be answered; rather, the Problems to Ponder sections are intended to provoke the student into taking a more critical stance on each topic. Just because Aristotle wrote down some insight of his does not mean that the student should memorize it and take it as the final truth.

Each selection has been carefully edited to make it accessible to the beginning student, but not at the price of oversimplifying the author's ideas.

There is considerable opportunity for the teacher to do some comparative philosophy in classroom discussion. For example, the Greeks have a very different view of the nature of reality than the biblical Christian, or Taoist, or Kantian way of thinking about reality. One particularly fertile topic for discussion is the range of behaviors considered virtuous in these different systems. For example, pride is a virtue for Aristotle, and a vice for the biblical Christian view. Devotional faith is not a virtue for the Buddhists, Taoists, or Greeks but is one of the most important virtues for the Christians. Meditation is a virtue for the Buddhists, but not for the others. Some of these systems consider consequences relevant to morality, others do not, and this is another topic rich in possibility for comparative discourse. Student papers can be assigned on comparative issues, and it is an excellent place for essay examination questions.

Acknowledgments

Writing a book is a complex process and the range of my indebtedness is quite wide. Many people contributed to this work, including all of the students whom I have taught over the years. I owe much to the professors who taught me when I was taking philosophy classes several decades ago, especially Abraham Kaplan, Hans Meyerhoff, John Hospers, David Kalupahana, and Chang Chung-yuan.

I must also thank Brian Kirby, without whom this book would never have been finished. His advice was always appropriate, his encouragement always appreciated, and his friendship deeply valued. I want to thank the talented artist, Ron Jimenez, who produced the insightful sketches of each philosopher found at the beginning of each chapter.

There are many people at McGraw-Hill who have helped to shepherd this book from its initial beginnings to the finished manuscript. I gratefully acknowledge the following for their assistance in preparing this book for publication and for many helpful suggestions: Dorothy Raymond, Kay Brimeyer, Laurie McGee, Sarah Moyers, Bill Mclane, Alexis Walker, Vicki Nelson, Monica Eckman, and Dan Loch.

I also wish to thank the anonymous reviewers for McGraw-Hill for reading earlier versions of chapters and offering suggestions for their improvement.

Despite all the scholars whom I have relied upon for the contents of this volume, all errors and omissions are, of course, solely the responsibility of the author.

Introduction

Most of us have a general understanding of the word *ethics*. We know that ethics is concerned with judging things to be good and bad, and with separating right actions from wrong actions. But it is even more than that. Ethics explores *what* makes certain actions right or wrong, and *why* we think those actions are right and others are wrong.

In general, there is fair agreement on the kinds of people who are considered good. For example, good people tend to be concerned with others rather than being self-centered, they tend to be helpful, patient, and do not inflict needless suffering upon anyone. You may believe that it is good to keep your promises, but still be puzzled about *why* we think promise keeping is good. There are many other questions as well. You may wonder about what makes a person good. Which of our goals are good, and why? When you have two alternatives, how can you tell which one is morally best? Is the right action always the most rational choice? Is our intuition or our conscience always trustworthy?

People who are concerned with questions like these are doing ethics. **Ethics** is the study of the moral attitudes and aspirations of human beings, and the study of the processes by which human beings make decisions on questions of moral behavior and moral conduct. Whenever we study or analyze ideas about what is good and what is not good, or whenever we study questions relating to our duty, we are doing ethics. And these questions are intimately connected to our idea of human nature.

In general, philosophers try to think critically about ethical questions. That is, philosophers think carefully about the fundamental concepts and theories of ethics and subject their findings to careful examination. Is the ethical theory internally consistent, or does it contradict itself somewhere? Do the implications of one theory offer a better solution to a moral dilemma than other theories? Does the position make claims that go contrary to human experience? Are there claims for which no evidence is offered? Are there claims for which it is impossible to provide evidence?

Claims that lack sufficient justification are rejected by philosophers, because in the absence of justification, we have blind belief. If there is no objective evidence, then we must wonder what could possibly make one blind belief preferable to any other blind belief. There must be some reason if you prefer one system over another. That reason is open to examination.

In this book we will critically read the writings of numerous philosophers and several religious leaders. The critical analysis of philosophical claims is standard and causes no problems for most people, but some students interpret a philosopher's critical analysis of religious claims about moral behavior as evidence of a hostile attitude toward religion. If you think that your religious beliefs are reasonable, that there are good reasons for accepting those beliefs, then you should be willing to embrace a rational investigation of those beliefs. By nature and by training, philosophers are independent and suspicious whenever someone claims that something is the *Truth*. Claims are not accepted as true simply because someone says so; they require evidence to support them. If I claim that you owe me $50, you do not blindly accept the claim. You demand evidence. Similarly, we cannot accept as true the strongly held beliefs of followers of particular religious traditions just because people feel passionately about them, any more than we can accept at face value the popular polemics of the opponents of particular religious traditions.

Every philosopher, whether arguing for a general theory or merely offering an answer to an ethical conundrum, must provide reasons that support the position, and it is evaluated by asking questions such as "What do you mean by your key terms?" and "How do you know your premises are true?" We ask if there are *good* reasons to support the position, and if the logical structure of the various arguments is cogent or sound.

It is only missionaries or moralists who argue the superior truth of one tradition or the falsehood of others based on faith. A philosopher is not a missionary, not a moralistic crusader urging people to adopt his or her particular moral values. Rather, a philosopher attempts to analyze each claim independently based on the quality of the evidence offered and the cogency of the reasoning behind the arguments.

Ethics Is a Branch of the Theory of Value

Philosophers usually classify ethics as belonging to a larger area of philosophy called **theory of value,** or **axiology.** If you think about it, human beings can make several different kinds of statements. Among them are *statements of fact* and *statements of value.*

> The novel *Tarzan of the Apes* was written by Edgar Rice Burroughs in 1911 (fact).

> The novel *Tarzan of the Apes* is a great novel (value).

Statements of fact (factual judgments) are descriptive statements about the world, about qualities, or about relations between qualities, and they are publicly testable. However, statements of value (also called value judgments) appraise the worth of actions, objects, feelings, and so on.

When we "appraise the worth" of something, we judge it to be good or bad, beautiful or ugly, and so on, and we judge almost everything: physical objects, experiences, social institutions, forms of government, and so on. We make judgments about things like this school, about education in general, about types of shoes, about specific automobiles, about films, books, TV shows, art, music, and dance.

When we study the processes and principles by which we judge artistic endeavors like art, music, dance, and film, this generally falls under the heading of *aesthetics* (or *esthetics*). But when we study the underlying principles that we rely on to justify our judgments of human actions and human beings, this falls under the heading of *ethics*. We may try to figure out what is right or wrong for us to do in some particular situation, or, we may try to judge whether a human being is a good person or a bad person; when we do things like this, we are making a *moral appraisal*. It is only human behavior that is subject to moral appraisal, but not all human behavior—it must involve choice as well. There must be some sense in which the person did *choose* the action that we are judging. Normally I am not judged as having done something immoral or wrong if I trip and fall upon you and hurt you (although I may be chided for being careless and not paying attention to what I was doing), because this was not something that I chose to do.

However, we do not apply moral judgments to all behavior involving choice; there must be some moral rule or moral principle that is relevant to the behavior in question. For example, there isn't any moral rule governing my choice of breakfast cereal; there isn't any moral rule governing the choice of clothing colors (I am not immoral for mixing two colors that clash, but I may be accused of having bad taste). Although there are no moral rules about my clothing colors, there are moral rules governing which parts of my body the clothing should cover!

Some Key Concepts in Ethical Discourse

A distinction is sometimes made in ethical philosophy between "morals" and "ethics." Although they are often treated as synonyms, we shall not do so in this text. **Morals,** or morality, will be used to refer to conduct or actions; we speak of a "moral act" or "moral behavior." On the other hand, ethics, or ethical, will be used to refer to the *study* of the underlying principles guiding moral conduct, which might be the study of the moral codes that people actually do follow, or perhaps the moral codes that people ought to follow. Thus, *ethics can be defined as the study of morality.*

Note that we have many terms that describe people who are interested in ethics. A *moralist* is not the same as an ethical philosopher. The term *moralist* often refers to persons who strongly hold to values that they consider worthwhile, and they are certain that other persons should adopt their values. These people are in the business of *persuading* others and *prescribing* behavior to others. Some of us are comfortable following tradition, and most of us are encouraged to simply do what we are told. A moralist or religious leader may simply tell us how we ought to act, and tell us to follow the "right" way, which corresponds to his or her *belief* about what is right. In this case, you are not encouraged to use your own ability to reason, or use your own mind—the implication is that the moralist's mind is better than yours, or that the issues are too difficult for you to reason about, or perhaps that others simply know better than you do.

The moralist is not much interested in understanding the fundamental questions (e.g., "How do you know these principles are true?") or asking *why* anyone ought to follow his or her prescriptions. In contrast, the ethical philosopher undertakes the systematic questioning and critical examination of the underlying principles of morality without blind preconceptions that decide the answers before we have asked the important questions.

In general, each philosopher in a tradition is aware of the writings and ideas of those who came before; perhaps the philosopher can deepen the insights of the past, or come up with ideas that go against those who came before—but the philosopher always argues for his or her conclusions using *reason*. Philosophers are not much concerned with what another philosopher *believes*, but rather, what evidence is offered to support the conclusions. If you think your own position is rational, then you must have good reasons for your conclusions.

Ethical philosophers explore issues such as the nature of morality, the justification of moral judgments, the appeal to human flourishing as the foundation for ethics, the investigation into the nature of the good life, and whether morality is simply relative to one's culture or group, or actually objective and the same for everyone at all times. When undertaking such explorations, ethical philosophers tend to fall into two separate approaches to justify their conclusions and reasoning.

Two Approaches to Ethics

Often, ethical philosophers distinguish between **normative ethics** and **critical ethics**. Normative ethics are concerned with the *norms* of human behavior. What sorts of behavior are right, and what are wrong? For example, is abortion morally permissible or not? Under what conditions? What about euthanasia? Civil disobedience? Is it ever permissible to take a human life? Is war ever justified? Under what conditions? Is capital punishment morally permissible? Under what conditions? Are human beings justified in destroying entire species when profits or jobs are at stake? Why, or why not?

Critical ethics (which is also known as metaethics, because *metaethics* means "about ethics") is a careful analysis of the *language* and *concepts* of ethics. Notice that a metaethical theory does *not* ask whether a particular action is right or wrong—that is the approach of normative ethics. Instead, in critical ethics we analyze the language used in moral appraisal, we clarify moral concepts and moral questions; we analyze the meaning of ethical terms. If you say to the critical philosopher, "It is good to keep one's promises," the critical philosopher will ask what the term "good" refers to when you say that "It is good to keep one's promises." From the standpoint of critical ethics, the answer to this question can take many different forms. For example, I might claim that "good" means:

I am expressing my personal approval of such behavior [I personally approve of promise keeping].

I am trying to influence your behavior [I want you to keep your promises].

I am saying that society in general approves of promise keeping.

I am saying that keeping one's promises will generate the maximum amount of pleasure or happiness for each human being involved.

I am saying that promise keeping has a property or quality that belongs to it—if that quality is present, we call it "good," and when absent, we say "not good."

I am saying that God approves of promise keeping, or perhaps God commands promise keeping.

I am saying that promise keeping is in accord with the inner essence of human nature.

I am saying that keeping your promise will tend to decrease the total amount of human suffering.

If we focus on the specific question of "what makes this a good act," it is often possible to divide ethical theories into two different categories: **teleological** (also called consequentialist ethics) and **deontological** (also called nonconsequentialist ethics). Many ethical theorists can be distinguished from one another by whether they think that the consequences of actions are the single most important element in determining whether an action is moral or immoral, or whether they minimize the importance of consequences for determining morality. A consequentialist ethical theory (teleological theory) holds that people's actions or motives are to be judged solely or primarily by the consequences of the act, particularly the production of some good. Any ethical theory that considers the *consequences* of an action to be most important for determining whether the act is right or wrong is a teleological (or consequentialist) ethical theory.

Nonconsequentialist ethical theories (deontological theories) are those which argue that people's actions or motives are to be judged primarily by their conformity to moral rules and not judged directly by their consequences. In general, a deontological theory claims that the moral value of an act is *not* entirely dependent on its consequences. Consequences may play a role, but consequences are not what is most important. Sometimes consequences are considered important when they coincide with certain moral rules. What the rules are varies according to the theory. For example, an ethical theory of duty (such as that of the German philosopher Immanuel Kant) might claim that an action has moral worth only insofar as it is in accord with one's duty, and one cannot consider the consequences of the action. Another deontological example: many people interpret traditional Christian ethics as asserting that you must act in accord with the will of God, and if you know the will of God, you need not consider the consequences.

A Brief Survey of Types of Ethical Theories

In the history of Western philosophy, there tend to be several different approaches that justify how we arrive at and defend the moral decisions we make. The traditional philosophers offer different standards of conduct and use different assumptions to support their conclusions. And, not surprisingly, many similar approaches are found among the Eastern philosophers as well. However, there are also some Eastern approaches to ethics that are not found in the mainstream of Western philosophers.

Among the most common approaches to ethics we find the following:

1. **Virtue ethics:** A person's character traits, habits, and virtues determine the proper standard of conduct. An individual who has the proper character traits makes a judgment, and an action taken by someone with those desirable character traits will be a good act. Aristotle is the most famous of the philosophers who argued for this position.

2. **Divine command theory of ethics:** The proper standard of moral conduct is determined by the commands and prohibitions of a divine being. An action is morally right if commanded by the deity, and wrong if forbidden or condemned by the deity. Variants on this theme are typical of many who have offered a philosophical justification for Christian ethics, especially St. Augustine.

3. **Egoism:** The proper standard of moral conduct is whatever is in one's own personal self-interest, usually whatever promotes pleasure for the individual. If the action produces pleasure (or happiness) for the individual, the action is right; if it produces pain (or unhappiness), the action is wrong. The Greek Sophists argued for this sort of position.

4. **Formalism (deontological ethics):** The proper moral standard is acting in accord with rules that are rationally derivable; following an abstract rational rule or procedure for conduct makes one's choice right. The German philosopher Immanuel Kant is probably the most famous of the philosophers who offered a deontological ethical system.

5. **Utilitarian theory:** An action is right if it maximizes the total amount of happiness for all the people affected by the choice. This approach to ethics, which is still very important today, is typically associated with John Stuart Mill.

6. **Natural behavior theory:** The proper standard of moral conduct is to put your choices in accord with patterns that describe all of nature; trust yourself; an action is correct if it is in accord with the "flow" of Nature, if the action is spontaneously drawn from the unselfish egoless self. The poetic writings of the ancient Chinese Taoists suggest this approach.

7. **Human nature theory:** We can understand our moral duties by understanding human nature. Some of the human nature theories argue that human beings are fundamentally good in their nature, and if uncorrupted by external influences or if the agent can return to his or her originally uncorrupted self, all choices will be morally correct when made from such a standpoint. Variations on this position are associated with the great Chinese teachers, Confucius and Mencius, but also Western thinkers as well, such as Joseph Butler.

8. **Relativism in ethics:** Whether Eastern or Western, the relativist argues that no objective moral judgments are possible, that moral choices may depend on the culture, the period, the group, or a subgroup. Some relativists argue

that all knowledge is impossible, and thus there can never be certainty in any moral judgment. In Greece, the Sophists held to such a position, and in China, the humorous and insightful Taoist Chuang-tzu seems to be an ethical relativist.

9. **Ethics of equanimity:** Accepting what cannot be changed, and recognizing that the peaceful mind can produce a life of peace, happiness, and harmony with other persons and the world. The Stoics in Greece held such a view, and we find echoes of it in Buddhism and Taoism.

Eastern Thought and Western Thought

Eastern philosophy is not just an oriental variation upon standard Western philosophy. The questions asked in the two traditions are often similar, but just as often they are dissimilar. The fundamental presuppositions of oriental thought generate different understandings of the main philosophical questions in general. In fact, there is no single term in *classical* Indian or Asian thought that translates exactly to the Western term *philosophy* (this is a Greek word that means, literally, "love of wisdom").

The classical systems of Eastern thought discussed in this book are complete, self-contained intellectual and spiritual traditions that arose out of their own presuppositions, uninfluenced by traditional Western assumptions. Like Western philosophy, the oriental systems contended with one another, modified their own positions, and took up new questions as historical periods changed.

Often, the Eastern philosophical systems tend to be better described as "paths" that require action to solve life's ultimate problems rather than abstract "philosophies" whose purpose is to lead to an intellectual understanding of fundamental concepts. This can make many Westerners uncomfortable, for it tends to break down the historically recent Western emphasis on the separation of philosophy and religion.

Although Westerners have a tendency to think of all oriental philosophers as generally saying the same basic sorts of things, this is an error. A rich variety of positions could be included under the label "oriental philosophy," including **materialism, idealism, hedonism, pantheism,** forms of utilitarianism and **atheism,** as well as several varieties of **theism** and even **nihilism.** The Eastern traditions are at least as immense and complex as those found in Western philosophy. The impulse for philosophical clarity is found for the past twenty-five hundred years in both East and West. That is a lot of time for each generation to analyze the ideas of the previous one and use those to avoid pitfalls and errors and to develop new insights.

Similar sorts of questions arise in both East and West, such as questions of ethical wisdom, questions of what constitutes the good life for a human being, ideas about what constitutes fundamental human nature, questions on how one's character ought to be shaped or developed, and questions on whether ethics is primarily a private matter (personal insight), a public and social phenomenon (rules of society) and perhaps relative to one's culture, or a divine matter (ethics as commands of a Divine Being). However, equally interesting are the questions of differences. Several questions arise in Eastern ethical theories that are not discussed in the West, and questions arise in Western ethics that are not considered important in the East.

Consider some of the following questions. What is the true nature of the self? Is the goal of life to understand the self, or to *liberate* the self? That the goal is liberation tends to be an unstated Eastern presupposition. But this raises further questions that tend not to be important in Western philosophy, such as "Is the self capable of liberating itself, or does liberation require an intermediary, a priest, a god incarnate, or even a philosopher?"

Common to both East and West are questions about human nature. Are human beings fundamentally flawed, depraved, and condemned? Christian philosophy has tended to find human beings flawed, and this flaw is the cause for a gulf between the divine and humanity. However, in the East, a more common assumption is that of enlightenment ethics, i.e., all human beings are innately enlightened with no gap or gulf between the divine and the secular. Consequently, investigation into the reasons for the existence of evil (**theodicy**) tend not to preoccupy non-Western philosophers.

What ought to be the goal of life? Happiness? Pleasure? Success? Wisdom? Enlightenment? Liberation? Peace of mind? To live in accord with divinely imposed purposes? To understand that there is no fundamental difference between the self and the world? Some of these responses are found commonly in the West, and uncommonly in the East, and vice versa. For example, understanding the fundamental nonduality of self and world is not a common Western goal of life.

What Is Comparative Ethics?

Do Westerners have anything to learn from China or India? The selections discussed in this volume will help to answer this question. We will see that we can view the fundamental questions of ethics from several different perspectives. It is my personal belief that the more perspectives from which one can view the fundamental questions of philosophy, the better one can understand these questions. If we have only the perspective of the Judeo-Christian tradition, we run the risk of falling into two traps.

The first is thinking that any alternative to our own worldview must be fundamentally erroneous, because from our perspective, our presuppositions, and our worldview, the alternative position doesn't seem compelling. As a result, we conclude that the non-Western philosophers must be somehow fundamentally foolish, adopting a view that does not make sense.

The second trap is the assumption that Eastern perspectives are merely variations on the identical positions found in Western religion and philosophy, and therefore there is no point in studying them because we cannot learn anything new.

Even worse, it is tempting to assume that the categories we use to compare East and West derive from our privileged tradition, such as Christianity, and all other philosophies will have to answer questions couched in the presuppositions and categories of Christian thought. A question such as "What is God's purpose for our life?" is simply not meaningful in the early Buddhist, Taoist, or Confucian context and trying to force it on these Asian systems distorts the philosophy beyond recognition. Even if our motivation were a genuine intention not to overlook the non-Western, our procedure in the end would be ethnocentric. Non-Western traditions are not Western, and we must be careful not to ignore that fact.

GLOSSARY

atheism Atheism is the position that no good evidence supports the claim that a supreme being, deity, or God exists. The *theist* believes that there is a god who answers prayers and cares about human beings; the *atheist* (the *a* means "no" or "not") sees no good reason to think that such a being exists.

axiology Axiology is also referred to as theory of value; study of what humans value, and why. This includes ethics as well as philosophy of art and beauty.

critical ethics Critical ethics is a careful analysis of the language and concepts of ethics; it is not concerned with what particular actions are morally correct or immoral. Thus, critical ethics is also known as metaethics, because *metaethics* means "about ethics." Modern ethical philosophy tends to be predominantly critical ethics; these philosophers analyze the language used in moral appraisal, they attempt to clarify moral concepts and clarify moral questions, and they focus on the analysis of the meaning of ethical terms.

deontological ethics Deontological ethics is also called "nonconsequentialist" ethics. A deontological ethical theory argues that to determine whether an act is moral or immoral, one does not need to check the consequences of the act. Formal rules are sufficient (see also formalism). The opposite position is called a **teleological** ethical system, or a consequentialist ethics.

divine command theory of ethics The proper standard of conduct is determined by the commands and prohibitions of a divine being. An action is right if commanded by the deity, and wrong if forbidden or condemned by the deity.

egoism Egoism is an ethical position that argues that the proper standard of moral conduct is whatever is in one's own personal self-interest, usually whatever promotes pleasure for the individual. If the action produces pleasure (or happiness) for the individual, the action is right; if it produces pain (or unhappiness), the action is wrong.

enlightenment ethics Several moral systems are based on the idea that human beings are capable of attaining a deeply spiritual state called enlightenment. In these systems, the moral value of an action depends on whether or not it contributes to the spiritual enlightenment of a human being. The ultimate foundation or justification for morality is that moral behavior flows naturally from people who are enlightened, and our moral rules are simply attempts to describe the natural behavior of the enlightened person. This, and several variations of this position, are associated with the early Buddhist philosophers.

ethics Ethics is the study of moral behavior; the study of the fundamental principles underlying morality.

ethics of equanimity Equanimity simply means peacefulness, a mind at balance. An ethical system of equanimity would argue that peace of mind is the goal of morality, and it is achieved by peacefully accepting what cannot be changed, and striving for a mind in balance. A mind like this is the key to a life of peace, happiness, and harmony with other persons and the world. The Stoics in Greece held such a view, and we find echoes of it in Buddhism and Taoism.

formalism   Ethical formalism claims that there are formal rules for deriving ethical behavior, and one does not need to check the consequences of one's choices (see also **deontological ethics**). For example, if a philosopher argues that the proper moral standard is determined by following an abstract rational rule or procedure and doing so makes one's conduct or choice right, then the philosopher holds a formalist position.

hedonism   Hedonism is the philosophical position that maintains that pleasure is the highest good for human beings, and pleasure is the thing that we value just for itself, not as a tool or means to obtain some other goal or object.

human nature theory   This is an ethical system that says that all of our moral duties can be made clear if we just understand human nature. Morality is what is in accord with human nature; vice is what deviates from human nature. Some of the human nature theories argue that human beings are fundamentally good in their nature, and if uncorrupted by external influences or if the person can return to his or her originally uncorrupted self, all choices will be morally correct when made from such a standpoint. Variations upon this position are associated with the great Chinese teachers Confucius and Mencius, but also with Western thinkers such as Joseph Butler and St. Thomas Aquinas.

idealism   Idealism is any philosophy that argues that the fundamental nature of all reality is mind or consciousness. An idealist might argue that there is no matter whatsoever anywhere, or an idealist might argue that there is matter, but it is created by minds or consciousness, and therefore mind is fundamental.

materialism   Materialism refers to any philosophy that argues that the fundamental building block of all reality is matter. There are not two different kinds of fundamental stuff that make up all of reality. There isn't matter and mind, but just matter.

morals   The term *morals* or *morality* will be used to refer to value judgments concerning human conduct or actions covered by moral rules; we speak of a "moral act" or "moral behavior."

natural behavior theory   This is an ethical system that argues that the proper standard of moral conduct is to put your choices in accord with patterns of nature. An action is correct if it is in accord with the "flow" of Nature, if the action is spontaneous, and if it is the natural reaction of the unselfish egoless self. The poetic writings of the ancient Chinese Taoists Lao-tzu and Chuang-tzu suggest this approach.

nihilism   Briefly, the philosophical position that nothing is important, that nothing has any value or meaning beyond those temporary values we assign to things.

normative ethics   Normative ethics is that branch of ethics concerned with the *norms* of human behavior, concerned with exploring what sorts of behavior are right and what are wrong. For example, are people ever justified in disobeying the laws of the land (civil disobedience)?

pantheism   Pantheism means "all is God," and for a pantheist, everything in nature is divine or holy. Many pantheists equate God with the forces and laws of the cosmos.

relativism in ethics   The position of relativism in ethics, whether Eastern or Western, argues that objective or absolute moral judgments are not possible. A relativist might argue that moral choices depend on the culture, the period, the group, or a sub-group. Some relativists argue that all knowledge is impossible, and thus there can never be moral knowledge or certainty in any moral judgment.

teleological ethics A teleological ethical system, also known as a consequentialist moral theory, argues that morality is determined solely or primarily by the consequences of the act, particularly the production of some good. Any ethical theory that considers the *consequences* of an action to be most important for determining whether the act is right or wrong is a teleological (or consequentialist) ethical theory.

theism Briefly, theism is the view that one or more divinities (gods) exist and those divine beings care about human beings, answer prayers, and perform miracles. *Monotheism* is the belief that just one supreme being exists who cares about humans and answers prayers.

theodicy Briefly, theodicy refers to the theistic puzzle concerning the existence of evil, or apparent lack of justice in the world: How is it possible for evil to exist in a world created by a divine being who is the only creator of all that exists, and is perfectly good (therefore opposed to evil), infinitely powerful (therefore able to eliminate evil if it wishes to do so), and infinitely knowledgeable (therefore knowing that evil would result from the creation of the world)? How could a perfectly good being create evil? If that being didn't create evil, then it must be false that God is the only creator of all that exists.

theory of value   see **axiology.**

utilitarian theory The utilitarian principle, also known as the Greatest Happiness Principle, argues that an action is right if it maximizes the total amount of happiness for all the people affected by the choice.

virtue ethics A person's character traits, habits, and virtues determine the proper standard of conduct whenever there is a need to make a moral decision. Any moral action taken by an individual who has the proper moral virtues and character traits will be a good action.

PART ONE

Ethics in Ancient Greece (5th–2nd Centuries B.C.E.)

Scholars generally date the beginnings of Western philosophy from the Greek period of about 700–300 B.C.E. This time was important in other parts of the world as well. It was the time of the Buddha in India, of Zoroaster in Persia, of the Jewish Prophets, and of Confucius (K'ung-fu tzu) and Lao-tzu in China. In Greece, it was the time of Thales, Pythagoras, Heraclitus, Socrates, Plato, Aristotle, and Epicurus.

What set these Greeks apart from their ancestors is that they began to seek rational explanations for things that happened instead of answering all questions by referring to myth, custom, edict, revelation, and priestly authority. To understand natural phenomenon, these Greeks sought mechanisms, rather than divinities. The result was great advances in astronomy, geometry, logic, science, and philosophy (in this time, science was not distinguished from philosophy). Philosophy (as mentioned earlier, the word *philosophy* comes from the Greek and means "love of wisdom") was conceived of as a general *rational* inquiry into the nature of things intended to reveal ultimate truths of reality. The Greeks argued that it was reason which set human beings apart from the other animals, so rational thinking should be the guide for our lives. From this period on, Greek philosophers tended to try to produce a general theory that explained the ultimate nature of everything, obtaining new insights and truths by relying on observations and definitions, combined with deductive principles. Conclusions required good reasons to support them.

For example, Thales (around 600 B.C.E.) argued that water must be basic to all existence, and thus the fundamental nature of all of reality could be understood if we could understand the nature of water. As a result, Thales and his students studied all the forms of moisture including evaporation and condensation.

The Greeks took the earlier insights into geometry developed in Egypt and applied geometrical principles to all natural phenomena, including light and sound as well as the sun, moon, and stars. Later, the Greek mathematician Euclid (who flourished around 300 B.C.E.) was able to figure out and write down most of the fundamental theorems of geometry.

The world could be rationally understood using geometry! The Greek use of geometry rendered the cosmos accessible to examination. The Greeks reached conclusions that could be *proven* to be true, unlike the claims of myth and religion, which could not be proven true but were accepted on faith. This combination of logic and geometry became a model that later generations of Western thinkers used to understand the world, and as the basis for clear reasoning.

13

Socrates (470–399 B.C.E.) and Plato (427–347 B.C.E.) lived in this exciting period. During their lifetimes, the Acropolis in Athens was rebuilt, and Sophocles and Euripides were writing their tragedies. Hippocrates, the famous Greek physician, was about thirty years old when Plato was born. Socrates was over forty when the great statesman Pericles died.

Plato was born when Socrates was about forty-three years old. The playwright Aristophanes was writing and performing plays in Athens when Plato was ten and Socrates was in his fifties. Democritus, the Greek philosopher famous for his theory of atoms, was born twelve or thirteen years before Plato died.

The Peloponnesian War between the two Greek city-states of Athens and Sparta raged sporadically from 431 to 404 B.C.E., and Plato was about twenty-three years old when his home, Athens, finally lost the war. With its energy and resources drained, Athens began to decline. After the defeat of the Athenians, the Spartans set up a small group of aristocrats to rule, thereby overthrowing the Athenian democracy set up by Pericles just a few years before the birth of Plato. These political events profoundly affected both Plato and Aristotle, and all later Greek thought.

Another group of Greek philosophers was the Sophists (the Greek term *sophia* means "wisdom," but in this context perhaps should be translated "wit"[1]), a group of itinerant professional teachers who traveled from city to city, for a fee, giving instruction and training in grammar, poetry, mythology, and religion, but especially rhetoric, the art of persuading an audience. Skill in rhetoric is essential for a politician. The Sophists taught their students how to win at argumentation or debate. Budding politicians found this to be a very useful skill, particularly if it allowed them to convince others that they were right even when they were wrong. With the skills that the Sophists taught, a young man learned to sway an audience to vote for him or his pet projects. He could win a debate in the Greek Senate, or win a lawsuit and convince a judge to rule in his favor, even when the evidence was *not* in his favor.

There was more to Sophism than just skill at rhetoric. The Sophists had a theory of human nature as well. They claimed that every person seeks whatever is to his or her own advantage, and every person seeks power. They concluded that what you and I call "truth" is not absolute, but is subservient to power. What is considered true depends on what the people in authority want to be true.

The Sophists identified the highest human good with pleasure (a position that we call *hedonism*). They argued that pleasure is what we always actually desire and is the ultimate goal in human life. According to the Sophist, good and bad are simply a matter of custom and preference; nothing is either good or evil by nature. The rules of morality are just arbitrary conventions. There are no absolutes, no such thing as the right way to live; in other words, everything is relative. After all, the Greeks were trading with numerous different societies, and they knew that the moral rules and codes differed in the various parts of the known world.

You would probably agree with some of the Sophist positions. For example, Sophists argued that the Greeks were not naturally superior to the barbarian non-Greeks, that men were not naturally superior to women, and that freeborn people were not superior to slaves.[2]

This is the background for the world of Socrates, Plato, and later, Aristotle and Epicurus.

CHAPTER 1

Socrates and Plato: The Vision of "the Good" Solves All Ethical Problems

THE LIFE OF SOCRATES (470–399 B.C.E.)

If you had lived in Athens in the fifth century B.C.E., you might have been one of the approximately fifty thousand citizens, or you might have been one of the hundred thousand slaves (captured in the various wars conducted in the Mediterranean area). Either way, while visiting the city it is very likely that you would have passed a short, muscular, heavyset balding man with a distinctive blunt upturned nose. Most likely, he would have been barefoot and wearing a simple garment. He was Socrates. Socrates may have been trained as a sculptor; if so, he abandoned sculpture to begin a lifelong search for Truth, relying on his ability to reason to guide him. His bravery was legendary, and he followed his convictions arrived at by reasoning, no matter how unpopular they might be.

Socrates did not write down his ideas, because his method for attaining wisdom was to think out loud, to engage in philosophical dialogue with others around him. He had a strong commitment to establishing what could be known, and distinguishing it from what could not be known. He looked at each issue from all sides in a search for Truth. He was especially annoyed by smug people who, in their ignorance, thought that they had all the right answers. In his probing dialogues with them, he demonstrated to them that they did not know as much as they thought they did. Socrates had a skillful way of reasoning from general claims to conclusions, and he made himself very unpopular because he challenged most of the accepted beliefs of the time. He was not gentle when he encountered stupidity or ignorance, whether among philosophers or politicians. Socrates consorted with the most distinguished men of Athens, and the result was that he made enemies among many politically powerful people.

The method of reasoning used by Socrates is called the "Socratic Method." Socrates would begin his dialogues with someone who believed that he knew what was true. Socrates would ask a series of probing questions, refining and revising the various claims as he went along, requiring definitions for all key terms. The line of questioning invariably revealed logical inconsistencies on the part of the other person, and then Socrates would offer his own suggestions for a resolution.

Socrates attracted many students, and he taught those students the same techniques of questioning authorities. He had many good pupils, but one student was quite extraordinary—his name was Plato.

THE LIFE OF PLATO (427–347 B.C.E.)

Plato's family was wealthy and well connected. On his father's side, he was related to the last king of Athens, and, on his mother's side, he was related to the founder of Athenian law, Solon. Because of his position, Plato received an excellent education and was free to pursue whatever interested him. According to tradition, he excelled at music, logic, debate, math, poetry, and wrestling. He also served in the Greek army.

Plato is sometimes called the greatest Western philosopher, but that is not because he had all the right answers to the questions that people found puzzling. Rather, Plato's greatness is in his clear understanding of precisely what questions must be asked, combined with his acute awareness of the many errors to be avoided in resolving the questions, and his own creative exploration of the possible answers available for each problem. It has been said (with some truth) that much of the history of Western philosophy is a series of footnotes to questions and solutions originally posed by Plato.

Plato is part of the Greek recognition that *knowledge* is not simply repeating what the people in the past said and did. When we say we *know* something, we must be able to supply good reasons that support our conclusions. Similarly, when we make a claim about what is right and good, we must be able to support our moral judgments with reasons, and we also need to become clear about how we use our key moral terms. Like Socrates before him, Plato often asked, "What do you mean?" and "How do you know?"

In 407 B.C.E., when he was twenty, Plato became a student of Socrates. From Socrates, Plato learned how to think critically and carefully, and to analyze claims in the method perfected by Socrates, the Socratic Method.

Plato opposed the moral relativism of the **Sophists.** He was sure that the rules of morality were objective and absolute. Plato also was occupied with politics; he applied himself to trying to devise a form of government guided by goodness and truth. The solution that Plato came up with was a form of government in which a specially trained, wise, gifted minority controlled everything and made all decisions rationally, guided by their special understanding of perfect Goodness itself.

Plato did not have a very high opinion of the Greek form of democracy. He saw Greek democracy as a form of government controlled by those who pursued politics for the sake of power, wealth, or fame. The way it seemed to work in Athens, democracy was not in the interests of everyone. Instead, Athenian democracy allowed a few to rule by irrationally swaying the votes of the many by manipulating their fears and emotions. Plato also thought that democracy was controlled by an emotional and uncritical mob of voters.

Plato thought that there were objective and absolute values, but that these were not easy to comprehend, and thus it took a special few well-trained people to genuinely grasp those truths. In 403 B.C.E., democracy was restored in Athens. Nevertheless, it was still the case that a few people ruled Athens. In theory, the people ruled through elected representatives, but the ones who ruled were the few with charisma who could sway an uncritical mob, convincing them to vote for things that were immoral, impractical, or foolish. Plato saw the breakdown of tradition under democracy; he saw the Sophists' use of debating tricks and fallacies to sway the mob. He saw the rule of passion and emotion instead of reason. Plato saw that the cleverest, the most persuasive, the most attractive speakers could control the state.

Later, in 399 B.C.E., his worst fears were realized. The Athenian democracy voted to condemn the seventy-year-old Socrates to death because he was "a curious person, searching into things under the earth and above the heaven; and making the worse appear the better cause, and teaching all this to others."[3] Socrates supported the democratic form of government, and so he accepted the death sentence. When the time came, he calmly drank the poison (hemlock) and then sat with his friends in philosophical conversation. Socrates died as he had lived—with honor and courage. Plato described him as "the wisest, most just and best of all the men I have ever known." Plato was twenty-eight years old when Socrates was executed by the Athenian state.

Plato saw that the democracy of Athens condemned its most virtuous and intelligent citizen to death because he questioned complacency and he challenged conventional traditional wisdom. The trial and death of Socrates showed Plato what could happen when "justice" is reduced to a majority vote, and the majority makes emotional choices based on personal gain and sentiment, instead of rational choices based on an objective long-term view of what is genuinely good for society. This affected Plato deeply, and when his mature philosophy emerged, his philosophical ideas of morality and justice in the individual were intimately connected with Plato's image of justice in the state.

After the death of Socrates, Plato was too disgusted to remain in Athens, and he spent the next twelve years traveling in Egypt, Italy, and the other countries surrounding the Mediterranean.

Plato eventually returned to Athens, and about 388 B.C.E. he established a school called the **Academy** and taught there for forty more years until his death at about age eighty. For several centuries, the Academy was famous for the quality of its training in mathematics and philosophy. One of Plato's students discovered solid geometry,[4] and legal and political philosophy were stressed. The success of Plato's Academy is clear when we realize that it endured for almost nine hundred years, closing down in 529 C.E. only when, with the advent of the Dark Ages, the Christian government made it illegal for a non-Christian to teach in any educational institution.

PLATO'S PHILOSOPHY

Plato wanted to rectify the moral confusion of the times: he argued for the validity of absolute rules of morality, and he rejected the government of the rabble in favor of a government ruled by "philosopher-kings."

Plato wrote in elegant Greek using a dialogue form. The major character in Plato's dialogues is Socrates, although the words Plato put in the mouth of Socrates are not a faithful representation of the philosophy of Socrates. The early dialogues of Plato probably represent a fairly accurate impression of the teachings of Socrates, but the later dialogues are Plato's own ideas using Socrates as a spokesperson.

If you want to do further study in Plato's theory of ethics, the most important of the dialogues are the *Gorgias*, *Protagoras*, and *Republic*.

The Theory of Ideas or Forms

Plato asked questions about the ultimate nature of reality and attempted to find out why the world is the way it is (in philosophy, we call this **metaphysics**). Plato began by arguing that what is really true must always be true. He reasoned that if something is really true, it can never become false. If it is true one day and false another day, it is not really true. That the value of *pi* to ten places is 3.1415926536 is always true; that it is raining today is true sometimes and false sometimes. Therefore, whatever is relative and changing cannot be really true—only what is eternal and unchanging is truly real. Plato concluded that we can have knowledge of what is eternal, but we can have only beliefs and opinions about what is changing (and note that in the world that you and I live in, *everything changes*). On this basis, Plato introduced a distinction between the world that we know using our five senses, and a theoretical realm of eternal and unchanging **Forms,** or Ideas.

It seemed to Plato that corresponding to each general term in our language there is one Form that is the essence, a sort of "master blueprint." For the general term "cat," there exists an eternal unchanging Form of *catness*, which is the essence of *cathood* of which each individual cat is an imperfect copy. It is because each individual shares that common essence that we can apply the common term "cat" to it. Similarly, for "animal" there is the Form of animalness. The fact that each animal partakes in the Form animalness is what allows us to group them all into one category of "animal."

Consider a perfect circle—we use the concept of circularity to identify circular objects, but no human being has ever experienced a perfect circle. No matter how carefully you try to draw it, even using a compass or a computer, it will not be truly perfect. *Every* point on the circumference of the circle will not be *exactly* as far from the center as every other point. It can be close, but not perfect. Nevertheless, we understand perfect circularity. How can we understand it if it doesn't exist in this world?

It seemed clear to Plato that all words have meaning because they name things, so the term "circularity" must name something. We use the term, but we cannot point to circularity, we cannot hold it, we cannot bring circularity to class. You and I use the concept of perfect circle to compare this circle to that circle over there, but we cannot find circularity anywhere in this world. We use it, we know it, we recognize it, so it must exist. But where? Not in our world. If circularity does not exist in this world, it must exist somewhere else, in a timeless spaceless realm. This Plato called the realm of Forms. It is the highest level of reality, which consists of timeless essences. These Forms are more permanent, and ultimately, more *real* than anything in our world, although we cannot know them by our senses. Knowledge of Forms produces absolute knowledge. Plato argued that there must be Forms for Truth, for Beauty, for Justice, as well as for circularity and catness.

Unchanging truths are available to those who know the Forms. The highest knowledge is knowledge of the Forms, and this is attained by reason and intuition, not by the senses. Our senses know only the inferior realm of the changing and changeable, and this is the realm of imperfect copies of what is truly real. Our world and all the things in it are *less real* than the realm of Forms. The world of our senses corresponds to opinion or belief, but not true knowledge (because we have true knowledge only of those things that are truly real and unchanging, i.e., the Forms).

The Forms are arranged in a hierarchy, with some Forms higher than others. Plato argued that the highest Form, which caps the pinnacle of the pyramid of Forms, is the Form of the Good. The Good is the final goal that all things in the universe are seeking to realize. As the highest Form, it also serves as the ultimate source of all reality, truth, and goodness.

The higher the Form, the more real it is; thus, Forms define reality, and it follows that individual things are real only insofar as they partake in the Form of the Good (the more goodness in things in the empirical world, the more real they are). It would also follow that the less good in a thing, the less real it is. Ultimately, when we know the Form of the Good, we can compare ourselves to it and try to get our behavior to conform to it. Thus, the Form of the Good sets objective moral standards. We can know for certain what sorts of actions are right and which are wrong.

There is no way to avoid the next conclusion: the good life must include knowledge of the Forms, especially the Form of the Good. However, that is not enough. We also must have understanding of the "second-class" realm of ever-changing objects in our daily experience, those things that are just inferior copies of the perfect Forms. But we must be careful not to mistake the rough approximations we encounter here in this world for the highest ultimate knowledge of the Forms themselves.

The human intellect is capable of attaining genuine certain knowledge about the universe, about morality, about the goals of human life and human society because human beings can know the Forms (and thus the Sophists were wrong when they argue that morality is relative!).

The World of Goals and Purposes in Plato's Philosophy

In general, the Greeks thought that everything in the universe has a purpose or a proper function, and these all work together, each connected with and leading toward another higher goal, a final good. To explain individual things and understand things is to understand their separate purposes within a larger hierarchy of purposes.

For the Greeks in general, to understand an event was to understand the reason for its occurrence, to understand *why* it is. Socrates and Plato were not as concerned with the question of *how* it happens.

Every element of Plato's ethical theory is related to some consistent conception of final ends and purposes. Plato's understanding of the universe was modeled on human beings: we understand a human being's actions when we understand why he or she acted a particular way, when we understand what his or her purpose was in doing any action.

Suppose my purpose is to be the author of an exciting story. I need to accomplish several preliminary goals. My first goal is to find an idea. Using that idea, I develop it into a plot, devise characters, and then write a novel. Now I have a new goal based on what I've accomplished: my goal is to get the novel published. I find an agent and the story is published; the critics acclaim it as exciting. Clearly, I have fulfilled all of my purposes well. I've done a *good* job. I am a *good* novelist. Similarly, for the Greeks in general, how well a human being fulfilled his or her function (or purpose) determined the value of that human being.

Plato argued that happiness is the result of human beings conforming to their own natural function. Happiness is the result of functioning in an excellent manner. Thus, every element of his ethical theory is related to some consistent conception of final ends and good.[5]

PLATO'S ETHICS

For the Greeks, the key question in ethics concerned the good life. The Greeks wondered, "What is it that, when you possess it, results in a good life?" Some might have answered "Money, when it is possessed, results in a good life." The Sophists argued that the good life is a life filled with lots of pleasures. Plato (and Socrates) disagreed. They answered, "No, it is *wisdom,* which when possessed, results in a good life."

Plato argued that the wisest life is a well-rounded life, and a well-rounded life is a life guided by reason. Reason is the highest development of a person's personality and produces the happiest and best life for a human being. Using reason, one attains knowledge, and knowledge produces a harmonious person.

Plato also argued that only knowledge can lead to **virtue;** when people are ignorant, their personalities are not under control and irrational desires and passions control people. Plato was especially concerned with clearly defining the virtues, and then showing their relationship to happiness and goodness. For the Greeks in general, there were several key virtues. The morally virtuous person is wise, temperate or moderate, just, courageous, and pious (piety might be defined something like doing the good in service with the divine). However, for the Greeks, the term "virtue" did not have the exclusively moral connotation that it has in contemporary English. For the Greeks, virtue was understood as "excellence of function"; thus, the important human moral virtues are essential, basic functions that are excellently adapted for their purpose. As we shall see, one's purposes can best be achieved when desires and passions function harmoniously under the control of reason.

Plato also explored another important question: why should any person be morally virtuous? The Sophist answer was very straightforward: people are just or virtuous because they are forced to be so by society; the reason that people do not steal things is because if they take what is not given, they will be punished by the laws. However, if people had the power or ability to successfully be unjust, to get away with immoral activities without being caught, they would be unjust because injustice produces more pleasure than justice.

Plato thought that this was completely wrong, although persuasive, and he used a story about a magical ring as a starting point to lead to the ultimate conclusion that it is a mistake to behave unjustly, even if injustice does produce the most pleasure. To argue successfully against this Sophist position, Plato needed to show two things: (1) that good is not identical with pleasure, and (2) even though being just may not produce the most amount of pleasure, nevertheless being just is good. If he could do this, Plato (in the persona of Socrates) could show the Sophists to be wrong.

Pleasure Is Not the Standard of Morality

In his book *The Republic,* Plato tells the story of the magical ring of a shepherd named Gyges. This story is important because it raises the question: who is happier, the just person who follows moral rules, or the unjust person who gets away with injustice? Is justice good only because of the consequences of being just (people will not imprison you), or is justice something good in itself? If you could evade all bad consequences for behaving unjustly, would you behave unjustly? The story of the magical ring of the shepherd Gyges goes as follows:

> Even those who practice justice do so against their will because they lack the power to do wrong. . . . The story is that he [Gyges] was a shepherd in the service of the ruler of Lydia. There was a violent rainstorm and an earthquake which broke open the ground and created a chasm at the place where he was tending sheep. Seeing this and marveling, he went down into it . . . he . . . caught sight of a corpse which seemed of more than human stature, wearing nothing but a ring of gold on its finger. The ring the shepherd put on and came out. He arrived at the usual monthly meeting which reported to the king on the state of the flocks, wearing the ring. As he was sitting among the others he happened to twist the hoop of the ring towards himself, to the inside of his hand, and as he did this he became invisible to those sitting near him and they went on talking as if he had gone. He marvelled at this and fingering the ring, he turned the hoop outward again and became visible. Perceiving this he tested whether the ring had this power and so it happened: if he turned the hoop inwards he became invisible but was visible when he turned it outwards. When he realized this, he at once committed adultery with the king's wife, attacked the king with her help, killed him, and took over the kingdom.[6]

Making himself invisible, Gyges becomes above the law and the reach of society—he cannot be caught or punished. He can get away with anything he wants to do. What should he do? The Sophists claim that the only rational way for Gyges (and all human beings) to behave would be to *maximize his own self-interest.** It would be *irrational* to have the power to get anything we wanted, and then *not* use that power; it would be irrational to refuse to use the ring to gratify our desires, if we knew that we would never be caught or punished.

On the other hand, if justice were truly good in itself, then it would be better to refrain from using the ring. The Sophists argued that we evaluate justice on the basis of the *consequences* of being just, and it is obvious that happiness comes from injustice because this produces personal advantages (pleasure) in political, economic, and moral affairs. Injustice gives a person "the most profitable life."

So, the Sophists argued a course of action is rational only if the consequences of that action are in your long-term self-interest, and being unjust is in your long-term self-interest. If people could be unjust and *get away with it*, there would be no point in limiting themselves to what justice prescribes. What's worse, individuals who had this power to satisfy their own egocentric desires, and did not do so, would not be admired by others—rather, they would be looked upon as fools! The truly good life would be one of injustice.

Consider the politicians of Athens: if you commited minor theft and violence, you were disgraced when caught; but if someone like Gyges succeeded in overthrowing the government, robbing the entire body of citizens, and es-

---

*This position is called "psychological egoism" or "ethical egoism." The position called psychological egoism says that human nature is such that we cannot help but act this way. Another position, called ethical egoism, asserts that we *ought* to maximize our own self-interest; any other behavior would be irrational.

tablishing himself as ruler, the people envied him and called him happy and fortunate. Obviously, injustice was to be preferred to justice. The Sophists argued that justice is merely that which is in the interests of the stronger party, and thus not absolute. Justice does not exist except as defined by the rulers, and then it is what is in their best interests. In fact, injustice is what is in the interest and profit of yourself, and this is *good* judgment! This is why injustice is to be preferred over justice! Not only did the Sophists argue that injustice is better than justice, they also argued that justice is merely an artificial human convention.

In a text called the *Gorgias*, Socrates first inaugurates a step to prove that the highest good is not identical with pleasure. Plato engages in a dialogue with a youthful politician named Callicles, who represents the cynical person who doubts that there is any intrinsic justification for virtue or morality. Callicles believes that the good is simply whatever produces pleasure, evil is simply whatever produces pain. In the *Gorgias* dialogue, Socrates says, "Callicles of Acharnae has declared that pleasure and good are the same thing, but that knowledge and courage are different both from each other and from the good." Callicles asks whether Socrates agrees with this, and Socrates replies, "He [Socrates] does not; nor do I believe Callicles will either, when he takes the true view of himself."[7]

Here, Plato pursues a clever strategy to show that good is not the same as pleasure, and that evil is not the same as pain. He begins by arguing that a person *cannot* have both good and evil at the same time, because they are opposed to one another, and exclude one another.

If a thing is good, then it is not evil;

if a thing is evil, then it is not good.

Good and evil cannot exist simultaneously because they contradict each other. It follows that any pairs which can exist simultaneously cannot be identified with good and evil. This seems reasonable enough. Callicles agrees. But, once the Sophist admits this, Plato shows him that this logically implies that good is not the same as pleasure, and evil is not the same as pain. First Plato gets Callicles to see that you can have both pleasure and pain simultaneously:

SOCRATES: You have admitted that it is possible to feel pleasure while in pain.
CALLICLES: It looks that way.
SOCRATES: Then to feel pleasure is not to fare well, nor is to feel pain to fare badly. And the result of this is that what is pleasant is different from what is good.[8]

In other words, Callicles agrees that:

If a thing is pleasurable, it can simultaneously be painful;
if a thing is painful, it can simultaneously be pleasurable.
But, if a thing is good, it *cannot* simultaneously be evil;
if a thing is evil, it *cannot* simultaneously be good.

Callicles has trouble seeing why the conclusion follows, so Socrates summarizes the argument:

> The consequence, my friend, is that good is not the same as pleasure, or bad the same as pain. One pair of them ceases simultaneously, the other does not, for its members are different. How then could pleasure be the same as good, or pain as bad? . . . Yet consider: those that you call good, don't you call them good because of the presence of goodness in them, just as you call beautiful those in whom beauty is present?[9]

Let's summarize Plato's argument:

Good contradicts evil;

Pleasure does *not* contradict pain.

It follows that pleasure and pain are not related to one another the way good and evil are related.

Therefore, it must be false that good = pleasure, and that evil = pain.

In addition, in the dialogue called the *Protagoras*, Plato has another argument against the position of **hedonism** asserted by the Sophists. In this dialogue, Plato explores the relationship between virtue and pleasure. This is a dialogue between Socrates and a skilled Sophist named Protagoras. Here Plato argues that knowledge is essential to virtue, not pleasure, because knowledge is needed in order to choose pleasures wisely.

If one is a hedonist, how can we tell which action will produce the greatest amount of pleasure? We cannot use the standard of pleasure to tell which action will produce the best pleasures, because some pleasures are better than others. Plato, using Socrates as a character in his dialogue, argues that it is some sort of *knowledge* that is the standard.

If it were true that pleasure is itself good, then the strongest tyrant should allow his desires and passions unlimited play without restraint. Putting his ideas in the mouth of Socrates, Plato points out that, by the hedonist standard, the morally ideal person (or ruler) should pursue nothing but constant pleasure (because pleasure is identified with goodness), but as we know from human experience, such a person would never be satisfied and would never say "I've had enough pleasure"; rather, such a person will continue searching out more physical pleasures. Plato concludes that if pleasure is the same as good, then the best ruler or king should be a glutton for physical pleasure. Does the Sophist agree with this?

The Sophist does not want to hold up as the ideal ruler the person who constantly gorges himself on physical sense pleasures. The Sophist wants to say that some pleasures are *more valuable* than other pleasures. For example, we call a pleasure evil when it robs you of greater pleasures than it gives. If I rob a bank to get some money to pay for a new car, and I have thirty minutes of pleasure driving, followed by the loss of the pleasures of growing older with my spouse and children because I am in prison, what can I conclude? That pleasure was evil! Thus, Plato concludes that it is not the person who chooses any pleasure whatsoever, the intemperate person, who is truly happy; it is the temperate person who uses knowledge and reason to choose the best pleasures who is truly good and happy. The intemperate person does harm (evil) to herself or himself. A logical conclusion follows from this: pleasure is not the standard of good, because you declare the pleasure itself can be evil! Protagoras agrees, reluctantly.

Socrates quickly points out that this means that the sheer quantity of pleasure alone is *not* the standard; obviously we must use reason to judge which pleasures are superior and which are inferior. Yet, if pleasure is the only thing that is intrinsically valuable, what standard can we use to judge one pleasure *better than* another? Plato forces Protagoras to admit that this standard is *knowledge:*

> . . . you have agreed that when people make a wrong choice of pleasures and pains—that is, of good and evil—the cause of their mistake is lack of knowledge . . . you know yourselves that a wrong action which is done without knowledge is done in ignorance.[10]

When judging pleasures, the good choice is the one where the pleasure is not exceeded by painful consequences. It is a bad choice where the pain exceeds the pleasure. When you *know* that the pain will exceed the pleasure, you avoid that option. If you don't realize that the pain will exceed the pleasure, you go ahead and make an ignorant choice. Socrates discusses this:

> You say that a man often recognizes evil actions as evil, yet commits them, under no compulsion, because he is led on and distracted by pleasure; and on the other hand that, recognizing the good, he refrains from following it because he is overcome by the pleasures of the moment.[11]

Next, Socrates points out that the Sophist position is to equate good and pleasure, and evil and pain:

> The absurdity of this will become evident if we stop using all these names together—pleasant, painful, good and evil—and since [according to you Sophists] they have turned out to be only two, call them by only two names—first of all good and evil, and only at a different stage pleasure and pain. Having agreed on this, suppose we now say that a man does evil though he recognizes it as evil. Why? Because he is overcome. By what? We can no longer say "by pleasure," because it has changed its name to good. "Overcome," we say. "By what?" we are asked. "By the good," I suppose we shall say. I fear that if our questioner is ill-mannered, he will laugh and retort: "What ridiculous nonsense, for a man to do evil, knowing it is evil, and that he ought not to do it, because he is overcome by good."[12]

Plato has demonstrated that if good is taken as a synonym for pleasure, then one cannot say that a person does evil because he or she is overcome by pleasure; that would be equivalent to claiming that one does evil because he or she is overcome by good. There must be some other reason to explain how it is that people do things that they recognize as evil. Socrates has an answer. People do not act this way because they are overcome with pleasure; instead they act this way because they are *ignorant!* There is something important that they do not know.

You . . . who maintain that pleasure often masters even the man who knows, asked us to say it is not being mastered by pleasure. If we had answered you straight off that it is ignorance, you would have laughed at us, but if you laugh at us now, you will be laughing at yourselves as well; for you have agreed that when people make a wrong choice of pleasures and pains—that is, of good and evil—the cause of their mistake is lack of knowledge . . . and you know your-selves that a wrong action which is done without knowledge is done in igno-rance. So that is what "being mastered by pleasure" really is—ignorance, and most serious ignorance.[13]

This inaugurates the next step in Plato's critique of Sophistic hedonism. Is injustice intrinsically bad, or is it immoral because of the consequences of being unjust? Plato argues that to commit injustice damages one's character, it dam-ages one's soul, and this is the greatest evil a person can suffer. In fact, merely to suffer injustice is not as evil as to commit injustice. Socrates concludes, "Then it must follow that no one willingly goes to meet evil or that which he thinks to be evil,"[14] and the person who does evil is someone who is acting out of ignorance. Ultimately, *virtue is knowledge.*

Plato argues that when someone chooses evil, he or she does so under the mistaken impression that it is really good (but in fact it is evil). If we fully rec-ognize an act as evil, we will never deliberately choose it. Instead, we choose something that we think is good [for ourself], because we do not recognize it as evil. The thief is not consciously willing an evil deed, but instead is willing something that appears to be good, that is, the pleasure he/she will obtain when he/she has all that money . . . but the pleasure is sought in a way that lacks goodness.

The question we began with was "Why be just?" The Sophists argued that being unjust produces more pleasure, and so that is how we would live if we knew that we would not be caught and punished. Plato wanted to show that jus-tice is of value in and of itself, and not merely because its consequences produce pleasure.

To show this, Plato tried to show that being just is of value because it is the only way to be genuinely happy. Plato argued that to do or commit injustice se-riously damages one's character (or soul) and this is the greatest evil a person can suffer; to merely suffer injustice is not as evil as to commit injustice. In other words, what is evil is ultimately harmful to ourself; and no one knowingly harms himself or herself.

What Is the Real Nature of the Human Self?

What is it that separates humans from other living things? After an extended discussion of the topic, Plato outlines a psychological theory of the nature of the human self. He concludes that the human self (in Greek, **psyche,** or life force, soul, consciousness) has at least two clearly different faculties: reason (or intel-lect), and desire (or appetite). Appetite or bodily desire motives a person; it is the energy that drives the person—wanting things makes you do actions (this includes all the physical desires, such as hunger, thirst, and sexual desire). For

Plato, the appetite (or desire) aspect of the self is connected to the senses. We have experienced pleasurable sensations in the past, and we want to experience them again. Desire does not consider right or wrong; thus, desire can prompt us to act against our overall conception of how we ought to behave or ought to live.

In addition to desire and reason, Plato argues that human beings also feel emotions like indignation and anger. Plato writes:

> It is therefore not unreasonable for us to say that these are two distinct parts, to that with which it reasons the *rational part* of the soul, and that with which it lusts and feels hungry and thirsty and gets excited with other desires the irrational and *appetitive part,* the companion of repletions and pleasures—That is a natural way for us to think. Let these two then be described as two parts existing in the soul. Now is the spirited part by which we get angry a third part, or is it of the same nature as either of the other two?[15]

Plato asks, is indignation and anger (the spirited part of the personality) merely a variation on the reason part of the self, or is it actually a third part of the soul? Plato argues that it is independent of reason because we see indignation in children long before they develop the ability to reason. Anger and indignation are not desire or appetite, so it follows that the spirited aspect of the self is separate from both reason and desire. Spirit, passion, or emotion is what supplies enjoyment to life; it supplies pride and satisfaction when we perform our functions well, and it is the source of indignation and anger when we judge that something does not perform its function well. So, Plato concludes the soul consists of three elements: reason, appetite, spirit.

We have already seen the task of the appetite and spirited parts of the self. What is the task of the rational part of the character or self? Plato argues that the task of the rational part of the self is to make judgments and to pursue wisdom—and reason performs this task with excellence when it judges wisely, in accord with knowledge. Reason allows us to reflect on our desires, to assess or evaluate our desires, and to transform our desires. Reason actively moderates and regulates desires. He goes on to conclude that an individual's character depends on the highest element, reason, controlling the other two lower aspects:

> To produce health in the body is to establish the parts of the body as ruler and ruled according to nature, while disease is that they rule and are ruled contrary to nature. [Reason is fit by nature to rule]. . . . Therefore to produce justice is to establish the parts of the soul as ruler and ruled according to nature, while injustice means they rule and are ruled contrary to nature.
>
> Excellence then seems to be a kind of health and beauty and well-being of the soul, while vice is disease and ugliness and weakness.[16]

Reason must be in control of desire and passions, the way the chariot driver must control the twin stallions pulling the chariot. The horses move the chariot; similarly, appetite and desire motivate a person—wanting things makes you do something. When knowledge and reason are in control (like the chariot driver), a just, orderly, and well-balanced personality results. Intellectual pleasures and physical pleasures (in moderation) are both important.

When not under rational control, the horses won't run together but may attempt to go in two separate directions. The result is disaster. If reason is not controlling desires and passions, then desires and passions can sweep us along in a mad rush to obtain that which merely *appears* to be good. The bad horse overpowers the resistance of the chariot driver, and "passion darkens reason."

The Relationship between the Parts of the Self and the Greek Virtues

Plato found correspondences between the various parts of the self and four of the five Greek virtues mentioned earlier: wisdom, temperance, courage, justice, and piety. The moral virtue corresponding to reason, when reason carries out its proper function governing the soul, is wisdom (*sophia*). Thus, *wisdom* is the virtue appropriate to the rational part of the self. Rational regulation of *bodily* desire (appetite) constitutes *temperance*. The support of reason by the *passions/spirit* constitutes *courage*. Plato accounted for *justice* by declaring it a general virtue resulting from every part of the self (personality) performing its proper task or purpose in due harmony. Just people have a harmonious soul; unjust people have the three parts out of balance. The just person is harmoniously integrated. Thus, the good life for a human being is the one in which each part of the soul performs its functions excellently. The good and happy person is the one who is internally harmonious; internal harmony is what we all want most, for it is the only way to be happy.

Mental health is the result of the harmonious integration of the parts of the soul, and social health is the harmonious integration of the parts of society. Good practices lead to virtue; evil practices lead to vice.

We can relate this to Plato's claim that no one intentionally does evil, because to do or commit injustice seriously damages one's character (or soul) and this is the greatest evil a person can suffer; to merely suffer injustice is not as evil as to commit injustice. In other words, what is evil is ultimately harmful to ourself; it upsets the mental health of the parts of the soul being in balance, and this makes one an unjust person. This is harmful to the self, and no one knowingly harms himself or herself.

If reason is dominant in our personality, then knowledge is our goal; if desire is dominant, then gain and greediness describe our character; if spirit is dominant, then our goal tends to be success. Each aspect of the soul has its part to play, but the ideal is harmonious agreement with reason in control.

> . . . he is master of himself, puts things in order, is his own friend, harmonizes the three parts [of his character] like the limiting notes of a musical scale, the high, the low, and the middle, and any others there may be between. He binds them all together, and himself from a plurality becomes a unity. Being thus moderate and harmonious . . . he thinks the just and beautiful action, which he names as such, to be that which preserves this inner harmony and indeed helps to achieve it, wisdom to be the knowledge which oversees this action, an unjust action to be that which always destroys it, and ignorance the belief which oversees that.[17]

Why Be Virtuous?

> It is left for us to enquire, it seems, if it is more profitable to act justly, to engage
> in fine pursuits and be just, whether one is known to be so or not, or to do wrong
> and be unjust, provided one does not pay the penalty and is not improved by
> punishment.[18]

We return to the original question raised by the Ring of Gyges: which is the
more profitable, to be just and act justly and practice virtue, whether seen or un-
seen of gods and men, or to be unjust and act unjustly, if only unpunished and
unreformed?

Plato has an answer based on his prior analysis: virtue is the health and
well-being of the soul, and vice is the disease and weakness and deformity of
the soul.

> Therefore to produce justice is to establish the parts of the soul as ruler and
> ruled according to nature, while injustice means they rule and are ruled con-
> trary to nature.
> Excellence then seems to be a kind of health and beauty and well-being of
> the soul, while vice is disease and ugliness and weakness. . . . Then do not fine
> pursuits lead one to acquire virtue, ugly ones to acquire vice?[19]

In a dialogue with Glaucon, Socrates says to Glaucon that they need to in-
quire if it is more profitable to engage in justice or injustice. Glaucon says:

> But Socrates, he said, this enquiry strikes me as becoming ridiculous now that
> justice and injustice have been shown to be such as we described. It is generally
> thought that life is not worth living when the body's nature is ruined, even if
> every kind of food and drink, every kind of wealth and power are available; yet
> we are to enquire whether life will be worth living when our soul, the very thing
> by which we live, is confused and ruined, if only one can do whatever one
> wishes, except that one cannot do what will free one from vice and injustice and
> make one acquire justice and virtue.[20]

If you acquire gold and power, and enslave the best part of yourself (your
reason), how can that *really* be of benefit to you, how can it be a good life? If you
enslave the most divine part of yourself (reason) to the animal part of your self,
to the part of yourself that you share with the beasts (emotion, desire), then this
is to have an ugly diseased self, a terrible thing. It is not more profitable to do
wrong and then not be discovered; doing so, you become more vicious, less divine, and more wretched.

> Can it benefit anyone, I said, to acquire gold unjustly if when he takes the gold
> he enslaves the best part of himself to the most vicious part? Or, if by taking the
> gold he should make a slave of his son or daughter in the house of wild and evil
> men, it would certainly not benefit him to acquire even a great deal of gold on
> those terms.
> If then he enslaves the most divine part of himself to the most ungodly and
> disgusting part and feels no pity for it, is he not wretched and is he not accept-
> ing a bribe of gold for a more terrible death than Eriphyle [21] when she accepted
> the necklace for her husband's life?

. . . Therefore, in order that such a man be ruled by a principle similar to that which rules the best man, we say he must be enslaved to the best man, who has a divine ruler within himself [his intelligence]. It is not to harm the slave that we believe he must be ruled, . . . but because it is better for everyone to be ruled by divine intelligence.

. . . How then, and by what argument can we maintain, Glaucon, that injustice, licentiousness, and shameful actions are profitable, since they make a man more wicked, though he may acquire more riches or some other form of power? We cannot.

Or that to do wrong without being discovered and not to pay the penalty is profitable? Does not one who remains undiscovered become even more vicious, whereas within the man who is discovered and punished the beast is calmed down and tamed; his whole soul, settling into its best nature, as it acquires moderation and justice together with wisdom [Greek virtues], attains a more honoured condition than a strong, beautiful, and healthy body, in so far as the soul is to be honoured more than the body. [22]

Plato is arguing that if you do wrong and are discovered and punished, the ugly deformed beast within you is calmed down, tamed, and the parts of the soul regain some of their balance and harmony—and the harmonious soul is a kind of an image of (or analogous to) justice itself.

Plato's final answer to the question, "Why be just?" is simple. It may not produce more pleasure to be just than to be unjust, but it is better to be just than unjust because injustice invariably involves a disfigurement of the soul—and that is unhappiness, imbalance, disharmony, disease. Even if you get away with injustice, you cultivate disease within your very soul. If you are not caught, you get worse. If you are caught, the brutal part of your nature is pacified and the gentler, more human part of your nature is encouraged. The soul is perfected (harmonized), and you acquire justice, temperance, wisdom, and mental health.

Why be just? Because to be just produces health and well-being of your own deepest self; to practice injustice is to produce disease of the self, it is to corrupt and undermine "the very essence of the vital principle," and then life will not be worth living. With a diseased character or personality, one can never attain happiness. If reason is in control (which results in wisdom), and the parts of the soul are in harmony (which results in justice), the final result is human happiness.

The Role of the Forms in Plato's Theory of Ethics

Plato previously established that moral virtue is based on knowledge, but what is it that we have knowledge of? This leads us to the Forms in Plato's metaphysics, and their role in ethics. There is a Form of Justice, but as important as justice is for morality, there is a higher Form: the Form of the Good. And, the highest possible knowledge must be knowledge of the highest Form: knowledge of Goodness itself. Clearly, it is knowledge of the Form of the Good that is the basis of moral virtue.

The Good itself is so exalted it cannot be explained by any direct statement. Plato uses an analogy to indicate the importance of the Form of the Good; it functions like the sunlight our eyes use to see. The sun is the source of light: the soul is like the eye, and when we look at things illuminated by sunlight, we see clearly. But, when we look at things seen only in the twilight "of becoming and perishing" (our empirical world, imitations of the Forms), we have opinions but *not* knowledge.

> Say that what gives truth to the objects of knowledge, and to the knowing mind the power to know, is the Form of Good. As it is the cause of knowledge and truth, think of it also as being the object of knowledge. Both knowledge and truth are beautiful, but you will be right to think of the Good as other and more beautiful than they. As in the visible world light and sight are rightly considered sun-like, but it is wrong to think of them as the sun, so here it is right to think of knowledge and truth as Good-like, but wrong to think of either as the Good, for the Good must be honored even more than they.[23]

Plato's question is "Do you think that the possession of all other things like power and wealth are of any value if we do not possess the Good?" His answer is obvious: Without the Good, all other things are pale and insignificant.

Thus, Plato concludes that moral virtue is ultimately based on knowledge of the Supreme Form of the Good.

How Do Humans Come to Know the Good?

Plato argued that it is not easy to know the Form of the Good, yet anyone who wants to act rationally in public or private life must remember that the Form of the Good is the source of knowledge; it is like the sunlight that our eyes need in order to know anything. To know the Good, we must turn our attention *away* from the world of becoming (our empirical world) and instead turn toward the realm of the Forms. Of course, we cannot do that physically, but we can do it mentally—by focusing our *reason* on the source of all truth and knowledge. Next, Plato inquired as to who in the population is trained in the use of reasoning skills?

If there is such a thing as absolute Truth, and if there is truth about how we ought to live, then those who are willing and able to learn that truth are the ones who ought to lead society. Reason reveals knowledge of the Form of the Good, and philosophers are especially good at reasoning (by training and natural inclination), and thus they are able to *know* what is morally virtuous. It is only the philosopher who can have true knowledge of what is good for human beings, although the Good is so exalted, it cannot be explained by any direct statement.

Recall that virtue is knowledge; knowledge is knowledge of the Forms. Virtue, which is knowledge, involves knowing the Form of the Good, but it also involves knowledge of how to live a good life, and this is a matter of intellect and knowledge, not just a matter of opinion or belief as the Sophists had argued.

The task of the rational part of the soul is to pursue wisdom, and to make judgments—and reason performs this task with excellence when it judges wisely, in accord with knowledge, and the highest knowledge is knowledge of the Forms.

Someone who is capable of knowing the Form of the Good is in the ideal position to rule the state. Plato called this person the "philosopher-king." For the philosopher-king, the purpose of the state is the common good for all, not the good of any individual person or of any particular class of people. That perfect state is knowable by reason because there is a Form for the perfect political system. The pattern (Form) of the ideal state is available to those who are skilled in the use of their reason. The Philosopher-King can know it rationally and use that model to govern the state in perfect benevolence.

PROBLEMS TO PONDER

These are questions that any thoughtful person should think about if he or she were considering adopting Plato's view of ethics. Perhaps Plato can answer these questions. How would you answer them?

1. Why assume that there is any Form at all, much less a Form of the Good? The entire theory of Forms is problematic. Is there any other explanation for "catness" or "perfect circularity" other than Forms? If there are no Forms, then the entire ethical theory that claims that morality is objective (because it is based on eternal unchanging Forms) collapses.

2. When two people each claim to have insight into the Form of the Good, yet they disagree, how can we determine which person has the genuine insight? Suppose we ask a third person who claims to have apprehended the Form of the Good. What standard can we use to judge whether the third person has that insight? Is there any rational way of showing which of them is correct? What method is there for settling disagreements? Plato seems to assume that the overwhelming certainty that comes from insight into the Form of the Good will make such disagreements impossible— Plato assumes that two "visions" of the same Form cannot be different. If two people believe they each have had the proper vision, but still disagree, what is left to settle the matter? Violence? Intolerance? Throughout history, when human beings have believed that they are in possession of absolute truth, they have had a tendency to be intolerant of those who disagree, and have had a tendency to want to impose their "absolute truth" upon others, even using force if necessary (because they cannot be wrong).

3. For Plato, the Form of the Good yields absolute and objective moral truth; yet human experience seems to suggest that there may be no universally true answers to moral questions and political questions. There is clear variation from society to society. Even within the same society, there is great difference of opinion on what is right, what is good. Plato may be wrong that all moral issues are objective; morals may just be a matter of taste, of preference.

4. What about the soul, or seat of consciousness (*psyche*)? Plato argues that it has three parts, but what is this thing? How can the soul be nonmaterial? How can we know that we have such a nonmaterial substance? How can

something nonmaterial be said to have parts? Are there only three aspects to the soul? Or are there more? Or are there fewer? Where does emotion fit in? How does a nonmaterial consciousness affect a physical body, or come to know anything about the world?

5. What about Plato's politics? Plato argues that a "wise elite" composed of perfect philosopher-kings should have absolute power. Plato is certain that those who love the absolute truth will be above the temptation of power, above greed and political success—such persons will value happiness that comes from knowledge, the happiness of a right and rational life.

   What possible guarantee is there that any educational system could be so perfect as to guarantee that the rulers will not abuse their total power? Plato wants to give the philosopher-king absolute power, corresponding to his knowledge of the absolute truth (Forms). Isn't this very dangerous?

   Plato might respond that this objection is begging the question, that it is assuming that the philosopher-king is *not* in possession of absolute knowledge. This attitude that perfect knowledge exists is quite different from that of Plato's teacher. Socrates was deeply aware of how much he did *not* know; in fact, Socrates once remarked that his only superiority over other men was due to the fact that he was aware of his own ignorance, and they were not.

6. What educational system can produce a perfect human being? Isn't it naive and overly optimistic to assume that the perfect philosopher will be so in love with truth that he or she could never misuse his or her absolute power?

GLOSSARY

Academy   The Academy was the educational institution founded by Plato.

Form   A Form can be thought of as a master blueprint, an abstract ideal, which exists beyond time and space. The word *Form* is often translated as "Idea." Consider a master luthier (someone who builds classical guitars and lutes). That person has the ideal instrument in her mind: an instrument that will project its sound evenly, no matter where a string is pressed on the fretboard. The luthier builds an instrument, and the luthier knows that she is getting closer to the ideal instrument, but this is still not perfect. The ideal instrument is constructed on the basis of the idea in the mind of the luthier. The idea in the mind of the luthier exists—but only as a Form. Everything made of matter is an imperfect copy of the ideal Form.

hedonism   Hedonism is the philosophical claim that the ultimate good for a human being is pleasure, and it is pleasure that humans seek in life, or any position that holds that what is intrinsically desirable in human life is pleasure. Pleasure is the standard we use to measure how valuable other things are in our lives. Pleasure is the highest good for a human being. Clearly, an ethical hedonism is a teleological (or consequentialist) theory, because if the consequences of a choice produce pleasure, then the choice is right.

metaphysics   The branch of philosophy that attempts to study the ultimate nature of reality is called metaphysics. It discusses such topics as: Is reality basically made of matter, or matter plus mind (or spirit), or something else? Is reality ultimately comprehensible by humans, or impossible to understand?

psyche   This term is usually rendered "soul" in English. For the Greeks, the soul is where thoughts and sensations arise from, and having a psyche is what allows any thing to feel, respond, or be alive. Thus *all* living things that have any consciousness must have a soul.

Sophists   The Sophists were a group of Greek wandering teachers who taught students a number of basic skills, but stressed rhetoric, the ability to win at argumentation or debate. They claimed that every person seeks whatever is to his or her own advantage, especially power, and that what is considered "true" depends on what the people in authority want to be true. The Sophists identified the highest human good with pleasure and argued that moral distinctions and rules are just arbitrary conventions.

virtue   Virtue is the quality of performing an assigned function with excellence; the virtue of exercise is that it makes you healthy. For Plato, four of the virtues are connected to the three parts of the soul, when each part functions with excellence in proper harmony with the other parts. The most important virtues include piety, courage, wisdom, justice, and temperance (or moderation).

A GUIDE TO FURTHER READINGS

Cornford, F. M. *Before and After Socrates* (London: Cambridge University Press, 1932). A good introduction to Plato and Socrates.

Field, G. C. *Plato and His Contemporaries* (London: University Paperbacks, 1967). The Greek worldview in the time of Plato.

Grube, G. M. A. *Plato's Republic* (Indianapolis: Hackett Publishing, 1974). An easy-to-read translation of Plato's most influential book.

——. *Plato's Thought* (London: Methuen, 1935). A good study of the main structure of Plato's philosophy.

Gutherie, W. K. C. *Plato: Protagoras and Meno* (Baltimore, Md.: Penguin Classics, 1956). Good scholarly translations of important dialogues of Plato.

Helmbold, W. C. *Gorgias: Plato* (Indianapolis: Bobbs-Merrill Library of Liberal Arts, 1952). Good translation of another important Platonic dialogue.

Shorey, Paul. *What Plato Said* (Chicago: University of Chicago Press, 1933). Overview of Plato's philosophy.

Taylor, A. E. *Plato: The Man and His Work* (London: Metheun, 1960). Excellent source for Plato's life and philosophy.

——. *Socrates: The Man and His Thought* (New York: Doubleday, 1952). An attempt to separate out the historical Socrates from the Socrates who appears so often in Plato's dialogues.

Vlastos, Gregory. *Plato II: Ethics, Politics, and Philosophy of Art and Religion* (New York: Doubleday Anchor, 1971). Good academic essays and analyses of aspects of Plato's thought.

CHAPTER 2

Aristotle: The Foundation of Ethics Lies in Character and Virtue

THE LIFE OF ARISTOTLE (384–322 B.C.E.)

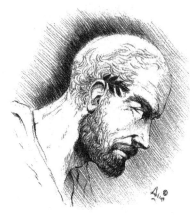

Aristotle was the last in the extraordinary line of teacher-pupils that began with Socrates, the teacher of Plato, and Plato, the teacher of Aristotle. Aristotle never knew Socrates; he had been dead for fifteen years before Aristotle was born. However, Plato and his Academy in Athens had been flourishing for more than twenty years before Aristotle's arrival in Athens as a young man. Unlike Socrates and Plato, Aristotle was not born in the city-state of Athens, but rather was born in an area of northern Greece called Macedonia.

Aristotle's father, Nichomachus, was the personal physician for the King of Macedonia, whose son would become known as Philip the Great. Philip the Great was the father of Alexander the Great, the military conqueror of much of the known world.

Aristotle was brought up in an atmosphere of science and scholarship, and the wide range of his father's interests accompanied Aristotle throughout his later life. When Aristotle was eighteen, his father died, and Aristotle went to Athens and studied under Plato at his Academy. Plato was sixty years old. Aristotle was Plato's brightest student, but he was not blindly devoted to Plato. Aristotle disagreed with Plato when he found flaws in his reasoning. For example, in Aristotle's *Nichomachean Ethics*, he criticizes Plato's theory of Forms, but first he remarks that he values truth more than blind devotion to his friend, Plato.[1] This attitude may have cost Aristotle a career as official successor to Plato at the Academy. We know that Aristotle was with Plato at the Academy for twenty years, first as a student, then as a researcher, and finally as a teacher. When Plato died in 347 B.C.E., Aristotle was passed over as head of Plato's Academy. Plato's nephew, a more devoted but intellectually inferior man, was put in charge.

After that, Aristotle traveled the Greek islands for several years, doing biological research involving marine life. Then, at age forty-two, he accepted an invitation by Philip the Great to return to Macedonia and be a tutor to his thirteen-year-old son, Alexander. How much influence Aristotle had over the young Alexander the Great is unclear.

At age forty-nine, Aristotle returned to Athens and opened a rival philosophical institution to Plato's Academy, called the **Lyceum.** He attracted many talented students and directed wide-ranging research in a broad range of science areas (stressing botany and zoology) in addition to philosophy.

Aristotle's tenure at the Lyceum lasted for only twelve years, ending when he was sixty-two years old. In the interim, his former student, Alexander the Great, had conquered most of the known world, including Athens, and had been elevated to the status of a deity.[2] After extraordinary military successes, Alexander died in 323 B.C.E., and anti-Macedonian feelings swept Athens. It seems likely that Aristotle was in physical danger; he left Athens after he was accused of "dangerous teachings" (just like Socrates seventy-six years earlier). He died of a stomach disease one year later in 322 B.C.E., at age sixty-three.

ARISTOTLE'S PHILOSOPHY

Aristotle wrote about metaphysics (questions about the ultimate nature of reality), physics, astronomy, biology, taxonomy, psychology, politics, aesthetics, rhetoric, poetics, and logic. It was said of Aristotle that he knew all that there was to be known. He certainly attempted to systematize all areas of knowledge.

Unlike Plato, who had a tendency to seek the solutions to human existence in an unchanging realm beyond human existence (the Forms), Aristotle did not look somewhere where eternal truths reign. Aristotle was fascinated by the world, and he treated the starfish and the snails as real, just as real as the sun and the moon and the truths of mathematics. Aristotle was more down-to-earth than Plato; he looked for ultimate truths in the world of human experience and was certain that human senses can know what is true and good. The scientist in Aristotle was curious about the world, and he realized that human knowledge has to accommodate a world where things constantly change. For Aristotle, natural science was more interesting than the abstract mathematics that Plato preferred. This attitude accounts for the profound difference between Aristotle and Plato when it comes to ethics.

ARISTOTLE'S ETHICS

The first genuinely systematic analysis of ethical questions in Western philosophy was carried out by Aristotle in the text that we know as the *Nicomachean*

Ethics.[3] Other references to issues of ethical importance are found throughout the writings of Aristotle.

The ethics of Aristotle have been described in several different ways by historians of philosophy. Sometimes the Aristotelian ethical theory is described as an "ethics of self-realization" or "self-perfection," because it bases itself on developing what is best and most excellent within us as human beings. It is also called an ethical system based on human virtues. Aristotle thought Plato was wrong when Plato sought the origin of morality in some otherworldly realm, divorced from our everyday experiences. Morality is based in human character, not Forms.

Aristotle does not ask "what moral rules should I follow?" For Aristotle, an appropriate question is "what sort of person should I be in order to lead the good life?" The phrase "what sort of person should I be?" is a reference to human character and the way you live your life on a daily basis. If you can find out what the human ideal is, that will provide a standard to aim at, a standard for the kind of person you want to become. Obviously, for Aristotle, questions of character, virtue, and human nature play an important role in moral growth.

Ethics is not a purely theoretical study for Aristotle; it is practical: "we are inquiring not in order to know what virtue is, but in order to become good, since otherwise our inquiry would have been of no use."[4]

Aristotelian ethics does not involve any supernatural dimension, such as the Realm of Forms of Plato, or divine commands of some deity. Rather, Aristotle is most interested in observable facts about a human being's character, those properties of character that provide for a good life. He wants to know the goal that human beings naturally incline toward attaining or achieving.

Aristotle agrees with Plato that all things have a purpose or function, and understanding those purposes, goals, or functions is how to understand things themselves. However, for Aristotle, our moral principles and behavior fit into a hierarchy of goals and purposes that are innate to human nature. For example, the alarm goes off and we get up and go to school. Why do we do that? Our immediate goal is to attend classes so that we can get a good grade. Why do we want that? Our larger goal is to graduate. Why do we want to do that? Our goal based upon good grades and graduation is to get a good job. Why do we want that? The next higher goal may be providing for our family, our children. Does this list of goals and choices go on endlessly, or is there some final goal? There would be no point to anything if there were an infinite series of goals. For our lives to have any meaning, the process must stop somewhere. Aristotle argues that if we can find the ultimate overall purpose or goal, we have found the Good itself, and the justification of all morality.

Like Plato, Aristotle attempts to understand ethics in terms of the question: "What is the good life?" But Aristotle rejects the idea that we can tell what is good by comparing it to the Form of the Good. Aristotle argues that the action which is opposed to the attainment of a human being's true good will be a "wrong" action. Whatever is conducive to the attainment of one's end (good) will be a "right" action on a person's part.

What Is the Good?

What is *the Good?* For Aristotle, the answer lies in human nature, in what people want to attain, in a person's ultimate goal. The good is whatever is aimed at; the good is that which humans are actually seeking. Thus, Aristotle begins his search for the chief good by asking: *what is the ultimate end or goal that people desire?* He concludes that it must be what he calls *well-being,* or **happiness (eudaimonia,** the condition of fulfilling one's function well or with excellence; something like *flourishing*), because (1) happiness is intrinsically desirable, (2) it is not a means to attain anything else, (3) by itself it satisfies human beings, and (4) wise people are able to attain it. The chief good is that for whose sake everything else is done, that for the sake of which all men do whatever they do.

> Every art and every inquiry, and similarly every action and pursuit, is thought to aim at some good; and for this reason the good has rightly been declared to be that at which all things aim. (1094a)
>
> If, then, there is some end of the things we do, which we desire for its own sake (everything else being desired for the sake of this), and if we do not choose everything for the sake of something else (for at that rate the process would go on to infinity, so that our desire would be empty and vain), clearly this must be the good and the chief good. Will not the knowledge of it, then, have a great influence on life? Shall we not, like archers who have a mark to aim at, be more likely to hit upon what is right? If so, we must try, in outline at least to determine what it is, and of which of the sciences or capacities it is the object. (1094a18–27)

Next, he asks "what is the nature of happiness?" Aristotle argues that *human happiness must be explained in terms of that unique function or activity which distinguishes human beings from other animals.* For Aristotle, that function is being able to *reason.* Aristotle stresses reason and the virtues of moderation, justice, and courage. He agrees with Plato that such virtues can be rationally justified and that the virtuous person is the happy person.

Next, Aristotle wants to know what science studies the ultimate goal, the Good, and his answer may surprise you: the science that studies the Good is social and political science. The state and the individual have the same good, although the Good as found in the state is greater and more noble than for the individual.

For Aristotle, what he calls the science of politics has as its proper end the Good for humankind. Individual or personal ethics is concerned only with the more limited goal of the good life for a particular person. Aristotle concludes that politics includes ethics and social philosophy as subcategories. It is the duty of the statesman to create for the citizens the best possible opportunity for living the good life. The person who studies politics must study virtue more than anything else, because the politician wishes to make his or her fellow citizens good and obedient to the laws. Thus, for Aristotle, ethics is regarded as a branch of political or social science.

Since virtue is an activity of the soul, the politician also must know about souls and their activity. There must be a chief good, or else there is an infinite series of goods that never comes to an end, an infinite regress. This chief good includes all the other theoretical pursuits, and this chief good is also the end or goal of political science.

> [The chief good] . . . would seem to belong to the most authoritative art and that which is most truly the master art. And politics appears to be of this nature; . . . politics uses the rest of the sciences, and since, again, it legislates as to what we are able to do and what we are to abstain from, the end of this science must include those of the others, so that this end must be the good for man. (1094a29–1094b8)
>
> The true student of politics . . . is thought to have studied virtue above all things; for he wishes to make his fellow citizens good and obedient to the laws. . . . By human virtue we mean not that of the body but that of the soul; and happiness also we call an activity of soul. But if this is so, clearly the student of politics must know somehow the facts about soul. . . . The student of politics, then, must study the soul. . . . (1102a6–22)

Because politics is not precise, and because ethics is a branch of politics, it follows that ethics is not precise. Think about justice. Just actions vary quite a bit and are influenced by social conventions, so we cannot be precise. However, the more we know about a subject, the more precise we can be in our evaluation and discussion of the topic. The more educated we are, and the more life experience we have had, the more we know about a lot of subjects; young people know less than older, more experienced people. The more experiences we have had with life, and the more ethical problems we have met with in our life, the deeper our understanding of morality. Aristotle concludes that the more mature one is, the more clearly one can discuss ethics.

For Aristotle, because ethics is a subgroup of politics, it is a practical enterprise, not purely theoretical. What follows? Aristotle concludes that we can never have total certainty in our ethical judgments. Every ethical judgment is concerned with judgment of actions, it is concerned with human character, it is concerned with making choices based on incomplete knowledge.

> Our discussion will be adequate if it has as much clearness as the subject-matter admits of, for precision is not to be sought for alike in all discussions, any more than in all the products of the crafts. Now, fine and just actions, which political science investigates, admit of much variety and fluctuation of opinion, so that they may be thought to exist only by convention and not by nature. And goods also give rise to a similar fluctuation of opinion, so that they may be thought to exist only by convention, and not by nature. And goods also give rise to a similar fluctuation because they bring harm to many people for before now men have been undone by reason of their wealth, and others by reason of their courage. . . . It is the mark of an educated man to look for precision in each class of things just so far as the nature of the subject admits. . . . (1094b15–25)

If you are mature enough to discuss ethics, you agree that the ultimate good is happiness, but there are still different opinions about its precise nature. People agree that happiness is the most important good for a human being, but they disagree about exactly what happiness is. Consider all the possible ways in which ordinary human beings pursue happiness. Ordinary people think happiness is a function of things like wealth, pleasure, honor, success, possessions, or good health. But the wise person does not think so.

> . . . the general run of men and people of superior refinement say that it [the highest of all goods] is happiness, and identify living well and doing well with being happy, but with regard to what happiness is they differ, and the many do not give the same account as the wise. For the former think it is some plain and obvious thing, like pleasure, wealth, or honor; they differ, however, from one another—and often even the same man identifies it with different things, with health when he is ill, with wealth when he is poor. (1095a16–25)

Like Plato, Aristotle argues that we cannot identify the Good with pleasure. The lowest sorts of human beings seem to think that pleasure is what constitutes goodness or happiness, but wise human beings do not make this equation. The Good for a human being must be uniquely human, something exclusive to human beings; that is, it must be something that human beings do not have in common with other animals. That rules out physical pleasures, because human beings and animals both enjoy physical pleasure. Aristotle argues that the ultimate good can only be found by investigating the unique function of human beings.

> To judge from the lives that men lead, most men, and men of the most vulgar type, seem (not without some ground) to identify the good, or happiness, with pleasure; which is the reason why they love the life of enjoyment. . . . A consideration of the prominent types of life shows that people of superior refinement and of active disposition identify happiness with honor; for this is, roughly speaking, the end of the political life. But it seems too superficial to be what we are looking for, since it is thought to depend upon those who bestow honor rather than on him who receives it, but the good we divine to be something proper to a man and not easily taken from him. Further, men seem to pursue honor in order that they may be assured of their goodness; at least it is by men of practical wisdom that they seek to be honoured . . . on the ground of their virtue; clearly, then, according to them, at any rate, virtue is better. And perhaps one might even suppose this to be, rather than honor, the end of the political life. But even this appears somewhat incomplete; for possession of virtue seems actually compatible with being asleep, or with lifelong inactivity, and further, with the greatest sufferings and misfortunes; but a man who was living so no one would call happy. . . . (1095b26–1096a4)

Aristotle now concludes that the Good can only be identified with happiness, because it is the only thing ultimately desirable for itself alone and not as a means to anything else.

> . . . we call final and without qualification that which is always desirable in itself and never for the sake of something else.
>   Now such a thing happiness, above all else, is held to be; for this we choose always for itself and never for the sake of something else, but honor, pleasure, reason, and every virtue we choose indeed for themselves, . . . but we choose them also for the sake of happiness, judging that by means of them we shall be happy. Happiness, on the other hand, no one chooses for the sake of these, nor, in general, for anything other than itself. . . . Happiness, then, is something final and self-sufficient, and is the end of action. (1097a33–1097b21)

What Is the Unique Function of a Human Being?

Aristotle also addresses the question of what is the unique function of human beings. As Aristotle puts it, what is "peculiar to man"? He wants to know what is the special excellence that belongs to human beings, that special talent which distinguishes human beings from other living things.

Human beings in general must have some general human function above and beyond our separate unique talents. What is the human function? Aristotle answers: the characteristic peculiar to man is *reason*. As Aristotle argued previously, happiness must be explained in terms of a human being's excellence, and reason is a human being's distinctive function or activity. Reason is only potential (not actual) unless one learns to reason, learns to use this distinctive capability. One actualizes this potentiality by living a life guided by reason.

Thus, happiness depends on the actualization (or realization) of one's rationality. Human good is the activity of soul (reason is an activity of soul) in accordance with the best and most complete virtue. Aristotle uses "virtue" in the same way that the other Greeks of his time did—not in the purely moral sense that we use today. **Virtue** is related to the function of a thing; *something that effectively performs its function is said to have virtue.* The virtue of my bread knife is its tendency to cut bread neatly and cleanly without crushing the loaf. The virtue of "Go-to-Sleep Herbal Tea" is that it helps one to relax and fall asleep easily. In the human context, virtues are tendencies, dispositions, or habits. For example, to have the virtue of courage (to be courageous) is to be disposed to do brave things. To be temperate is to have a disposition or tendency toward balance and moderation in one's pleasures. As we shall see in the following sections, virtue is an important element in the ethics of Aristotle.

Who is a virtuous person according to Aristotle? His answer: The virtuous person is the person who has a *disposition* or *habit* to live his or her life according to reason, thus realizing his or her proper function or distinctive potentiality. The opposite of a virtue is a vice. Vices work in the same way as virtues, in that a vice (a bad habit) impedes or obstructs human beings' full development instead of enhancing their situation. Thus, virtues and vices are habits.

Happiness is not possible without virtue, that is, without excellence of function. If you have a special talent, you are not happy if you perform poorly. The special talent for human beings in general is reason. Aristotle concludes that reasoning well and clearly will be the happiest life for a human being because reason is the special talent of all humans. Note that Aristotle does not exclude sensual pleasures or prosperity from happiness. He does not want someone to think that happiness is just momentary bliss—rather, it is a continuing process that takes one's full lifetime to perfect. Happiness could not consist in static virtue alone; it is activity according to virtue, and it must be manifested over a whole life and not merely brief periods.

[What is the function peculiar to human beings, unique to mankind?] Life seems to be common even to plants, but we are seeking what is peculiar to man. Let us exclude, therefore, the life of nutrition and growth. Next there would be a life of perception, but *it* also seems to be common even to the horse, the ox, and every animal. There remains, then, an active life of the element that has a rational principle. . . . Now if the function of man is an activity of soul which follows or implies a rational principle, . . . human good turns out to be activity of soul in accordance with virtue, and if there are more than one virtue, in accordance with the best and most complete.

But we must add "in a complete life." For one swallow does not make a summer, nor does one day; and so too one day, or a short time, does not make a man blessed and happy. (1097b34–1098a20)

If reason is divine, then, in comparison with man, the life according to it is divine in comparison with human life. . . . [Reason does] in power and in worth surpass everything. This would seem, too, to be each man himself, since it is the authoritative and better part of him. It would be strange, then, if he were to choose not the life of his self but that of something else. And what we said before will apply now; that which is proper to each thing is by nature best and most pleasant for each thing; for man, therefore, the life according to reason is best and pleasantest, since reason more than anything else is man. This life therefore is also the happiest. (1177b29–10)

Certain amounts of good fortune, friends, wealth, political power, and so on are necessary for human happiness. Aristotle is rather an elitist here. He thinks to be happy you ought to be a male of noble birth, you ought to have personal beauty, and you ought to be tall, because small men* cannot be called beautiful! Being personally wealthy is also very helpful for happiness.

Happiness Is the Result of an Active Life

However, these things are not enough for enduring happiness. Lasting happiness cannot be given to one; happiness is the result of an active life. Aristotle stresses *activity*.

We may define happiness as prosperity combined with virtue; or as independence of life; or as the secure enjoyment of the maximum of pleasure; or as a good condition of property and body, together with the power of guarding one's property and body and making use of them. That happiness is one or more of these things, pretty well everybody agrees.

From this definition of happiness, it follows that its constituent parts are:— good birth, plenty of friends, good friends, wealth, good children, plenty of children, a happy old age, also such bodily excellences as health, beauty, strength, large stature, athletic powers, together with fame, honor, good luck, and virtue. (*Rhetoric*, Book I, ch. 5, 1360b14–25)

. . . the happy man lives well and does well; for we have practically defined happiness as a sort of good life and good action. (*Nicomachean Ethics*, 1098b20)

Happiness is not passive; happiness does not happen to you; you don't sit and wait for happiness to alight upon your soul; you don't get happiness be-

---

*As has often been pointed out, Aristotle really is discussing males here. Aristotle does not think that females are capable of the highest human happiness because women lack the fully developed souls that men have. Adult women are more like children in Aristotle's eyes. This was a common view among the Greeks, but many Greek philosophers disagreed with Aristotle on this topic.

cause you deserve it; the happy life (= "the good life") is a life of making choices and developing habits that maximize your potential ability to reason.

Virtue, the Psyche, and the Golden Mean

To understand happiness a little better, we must understand virtue. The study of virtue (which is a disposition to perform effectively a thing's proper function) requires the study of the *psyche*, the soul, which is both rational and irrational. Among the irrational aspects of human consciousness are the passions—passions that need to be controlled by reason.

> Since happiness is an activity of soul in accordance with perfect virtue, we must consider the nature of virtue; for perhaps we shall thus see better the nature of happiness . . . one element of the soul is irrational and one has a rational principle.
>
> Of the irrational element one division seems to be widely distributed and vegetative in its nature, I mean that which causes nutrition and growth. . . . Now the excellence of this seems to be common to all species and not specifically human. . . . Let us leave the nutritive faculty alone, since it has by its nature no share in human excellence. . . .
>
> Therefore the irrational element also appears to be twofold. For the vegetative element in no way shares in a rational principle, but the appetitive, and in general the desiring element in a sense shares in it, in so far as it listens to and obeys it. (1102a5–1102b31)

This is similar to Plato's view of the soul in some ways (the rational part of the soul, and the two irrational parts, appetite and spirit). The stress on reason is similar for both Aristotle and Plato, but Aristotle divides the rational part into pure abstract reason and calculative or deliberative reason. For Aristotle the irrational part of the soul is appetite (desire and will) and nutritive (nutrition, growth, having enough of what we need). The two parts of the soul have two kinds of virtues that correspond to them: *intellectual* and *moral virtues.*

Aristotle begins Book II of the *Nicomachean Ethics* by distinguishing between intellectual virtues and moral virtues. **Intellectual virtues** are those we are taught as concepts, and they respond to reason. They also require experience and maturity. The contemplation of theoretical truths and the discovery of the rational principles that ought to control everyday actions give rise to the intellectual virtues.

On the other hand, **moral virtues** do not belong to reason. They are dispositions or habits to act rightly, and a disposition is formed by a continuous series of right actions. Moral virtues must be formed by training and by habit (note *ethos*, the root of *ethics*, in Greek is "habit"). Moral virtues are not implanted by nature nor are they against nature. Aristotle believes that human beings have a capacity for a good character, but it has to be developed by practice and habit.

> Virtue, then, being of two kinds, intellectual and moral, intellectual virtue in the main owes both its birth and its growth to teaching (for which reason it requires experience and time), while moral virtue comes about as a result of habit. . . .

From this it is also plain that none of the moral virtues arises in us by nature; for nothing that exists by nature can form a habit contrary to its nature. . . . Neither by nature, then, nor contrary to nature do the virtues arise in us; rather we are adapted by nature to receive them, and are made perfect by habit. . . . we become just by doing just acts, temperate by doing temperate acts, brave by doing brave acts. (1103a14–1103b2)

It makes no small difference, then, whether we form habits of one kind or of another from our very youth; it makes a very great difference, or rather *all* the difference (1103b25)

Clearly, Aristotle is certain that the habits we learn as we are growing up are essential to the happiness we achieve as an adult. Learning the right habits is simply the process of education, and education is essential to morality.

. . . moral excellence is concerned with pleasures and pains; it is on account of the pleasure that we do bad things, and on account of the pain that we abstain from noble ones. Hence we ought to have been brought up in a particular way from our very youth, as Plato says, so as both to delight in and to be pained by the things we ought; for this is the right education. (1104b9–14)

Moral virtue is the habitual choice of actions (the habit coming from a continuous series of right actions) in accordance with rational principles. A master of any art seeks to balance his or her skills, not to eat too much, not to eat too little, not to overdo or underdo. Thus, as mentioned earlier, virtues are habits or dispositions, and these create our character. When we respond to the world with habitual actions, we recognize that these create probabilities about how we will choose, and these probabilities create us as humans. Note that habits are not inborn; they are acquired, they are taught, they are learned, they are instilled, and they form our character.

. . . the virtue of man also will be the state of character which makes a man good and which makes him do his own work well. (1106a23)

There is a point of excess and a point of deficiency, and a point of balance between them. Aristotle argues that it is exactly at the "just-right" point that human excellence or human virtue is maximized. He calls that just-right point between extremes the **golden mean;** it is the just-right point between "not enough" and "too much."

This golden mean depends on the individual and his or her exact situation. An athlete may eat twice as much as someone not exercising; the appropriate mean depends on the level of activity. Thus, the morally virtuous person chooses to act according to the golden mean.

Virtue, then, is a state of character concerned with choice, lying in a mean, i.e., the mean relative to us, this being determined by a rational principle. . . . (1106b35–1107a1)

Moral virtue, then, is a disposition that enables the good person to perform his or her function well, and the person performs it well when he or she avoids extremes and chooses the point that is a golden mean in all actions. The golden mean is determined by a rational principle, neither excess nor deficit. In fact, for

Aristotle, this is one of the most important roles of reason: determining the golden mean in any situation.

Aristotle next examines the specific moral virtues, to provide examples of how the golden mean works. Between cowardly fear and foolhardy overconfidence, the golden mean is courage. The virtue of courage is halfway between two extremes. Between pleasure and pain, the mean is temperance, that is, aiming at the mean in pleasurable experiences. Between giving too much and sharing nothing, the mean is liberality (giving too little is stinginess or miserliness). Between honor and dishonor the mean is proper pride or dignified self-respect (not empty vanity that is too much or excessive humility). Between anger and angerlessness, the mean is found in being "good tempered" (too much is being quarrelsome, or irascibility; too little is in-irascibility or being obsequious).*

However, each of these virtues will change with the situation we are in; being brave in one situation might be a foolhardy act in a slightly different situation. And the more experiences we have had with different situations, the better we will be able to find the golden mean. And the more dispositions or good habits we have developed, the better the moral character we will have developed. This is how we become moral human beings who live a good life.

> That moral virtue is a mean, then, and in what sense it is so, and that it is a mean between two vices, the one involving excess, the other deficiency, and that it is such because its character is to aim at what is intermediate in passions and in actions, has been sufficiently stated. Hence also it is no easy task to be good. For in everything it is no easy task to find the middle; e.g. to find the middle of a circle is not for every one but for him who knows; so too, any one can get angry—that is easy—or give and spend money; but to do this to the right person, to the right extent, at the right time, with the right motive, and in the right way, *that* is not for every one, nor is it easy; wherefore goodness is both rare and laudable and noble. (1109a20–29)

For an action to be praised or blamed, Aristotle points out that the action must be voluntary. If it is not voluntary, then you are not responsible for the action.

> Those things, then, are thought involuntary, which take place under compulsion or owing to ignorance. (1109b35–1110a1)

In addition to moral virtues, there is a second kind of virtue—intellectual virtue. These are the virtues that respond to reason. Aristotle examines the intellectual virtues, which include philosophical wisdom and practical wisdom.

Intellectual virtues are those virtues that accompany the proper exercise of reason. According to Aristotle's analysis, there are two tasks of the intellect: (1) to discover truth and give us knowledge of invariable and fixed principles (like laws of nature), which Aristotle calls **philosophical wisdom;** and (2) to provide a rational guide for action in daily life, which Aristotle calls **practical wisdom.**

---

*Note that Aristotle's list of specific virtues does *not* include the typically Christian virtues such as faith, chastity, obedience, and humility—he would not regard these as independent virtues. The standard Greek virtues are courage, temperance, justice, and wisdom.

Practical wisdom allows us to discover intelligent conduct, which, as you might expect, is related to the golden mean. We become virtuous by doing virtuous actions. We *learn* to be virtuous; the various moral virtues are learned (as all habits are learned) by *practice*. This is why Aristotle calls this practical wisdom. Initially, we do things that virtuous people tell us are right, without having to analyze or determine that they are good. For example, a child is told by his parents not to lie. Without realizing the inherent goodness of truth-telling, the child obeys until it becomes a habit. These actions create a *good disposition*, which turns into a good character later on.

We learn these excellences by practicing behavior that eventually becomes habitual—we can learn habits, and we can teach habits. Practical wisdom unifies all the virtues; if you follow reason, you will not be able to develop only one virtue and not the others. Being truly virtuous is actually quite difficult. The capacity of reason to find the golden mean in a situation is not easy, but this is also what Aristotle calls practical wisdom.

Why teach virtues to our children? If our children find pleasure in the most excellent exercise of their human nature, they will be virtuous and good, for the good person is the one who takes pleasure in the right sorts of things. And, most important, this is the key to happiness.

The Good Life Is a Life of Contemplation

Aristotle considers philosophical wisdom to be superior to practical wisdom, and the life of **contemplation** comes closest to meeting the conditions for happiness.

In fact, contemplation is one of the most important elements of Aristotle's ethics. He describes contemplation as "that activity by which people may attain the highest human happiness." Aristotle's contemplation should not be confused with the focused art of meditation in Eastern philosophies. For Aristotle, contemplation is purely rational, an activity of the intellect. Contemplation is the activity of reason (that which makes us uniquely human) when the intellect focuses on the most noble things that human beings can think about, discovering and keeping in mind the first principles of things. Contemplation is the "best and most complete excellence" of a human being. The activity of contemplation is self-sufficient (it cannot be taken away from us), and it is the most pleasant life (because it exercises what is our distinctive function or excellence, our mind/reason)—therefore, it is the happiest life.

Cultivating the contemplative life produces happiness in its highest and best manifestation. Contemplation is the activity of soul that activates what is best within us (as human beings). Contemplation is the best way to live. It might be said that contemplation is self-perfection. Thus, Aristotle's ethics is often described as an ethics of self-perfection.

In support of his claim, Aristotle points out that we all agree that the gods are, above all things, blessed and happy; but what makes them happy? Happiness comes from doing things. So what sorts of actions do gods perform that bring happiness? For example, do the gods perform acts of justice?

> Will not the gods seem absurd if they make contracts and return deposits, and so on? Acts of a brave man, then confronting dangers and running risks because it is noble to do so? Or liberal acts? To whom will they give? It will be strange if they are really to have money or anything of the kind. And what would their temperate acts be? Is not such praise tasteless, since they have no bad appetites? If we were to run through them all, the circumstances of action would be found trivial and unworthy of gods. . . . Now, if you take away from a living being action, and still more production, what is left but contemplation? Therefore the activity of God, which surpasses all others in blessedness, must be contemplative; and of human activities, therefore, that which is most akin to this must be most of the nature of happiness. . . . Happiness extends, then, just so far as contemplation does, and those to whom contemplation more fully belongs are more truly happy, not as a mere concomitant but in virtue of the contemplation; for this is in itself precious. Happiness, therefore, must be some form of contemplation. (1178b10–31)

Not everyone can master this activity of discovering and keeping in mind the first principles of things. It requires an extraordinary mind and an extraordinary effort. It is "limited to the divinely gifted few." It should not be too surprising that Aristotle thought that it was only the gifted philosopher who could master this activity. However, the practical virtues (with a lesser degree of happiness) are within reach of the ordinary person.

> . . . if the gods have any care for human affairs, as they are thought to have, it would be reasonable both that they should delight in that which was best and most akin to them (i.e., reason) and that they should reward those who love and honor this most, as caring for the things that are dear to them and acting both rightly and nobly. And that all these attributes belong most of all to the philosopher is manifest. He, therefore, is the dearest to the gods. And he who is that will presumably be also the happiest; so that in this way too the philosopher will more than any other be happy. (1179a24–34)

Ordinary people live on the level of practical decisions and merely follow habitual routines—they do not contemplate, and they do not attain the highest human happiness. However, if you can teach proper habits to young people, they will grow up to be virtuous.

As we all know, these "proper habits" are not much fun, especially if you are young. They require you to be temperate (control desires and passions). They require you to be hardy (physical exercise, gymnastics). This isn't easy for anyone. Because it isn't easy, in addition to teaching proper habits to people when they are young, there will have to be laws for adults as well, because they don't respond as well to reasoned argument as they do to legal force.

> But it is difficult to get from youth up a right training for virtue if one has not been brought up under right laws; for to live temperately and hardily is not pleasant to most people, especially when they are young. For this reason their nurture and occupations should be fixed by law; for they will not be painful when they have become customary. But it is surely not enough that when they are young they should get the right nurture and attention; since they must, even when they are grown up, practice and be habituated to them, we shall need laws

for this as well, and generally speaking to cover the whole of life; for most people obey necessity rather than argument and punishments rather than the sense of what is noble. (1179b30–1180a4)

The Role of Reason in Aristotle's Ethics

The stress on reason is the heritage of the Greeks. Reason was just as important to Aristotle as it was to Plato. Recall that the use of reason produces happiness, which Aristotle defined as "the exercise of reason in accordance with virtue." In fact, Aristotle argued that happiness is not possible without the excellent functioning of a human being's unique capacity or ability, that is, reason.

Reason was also important to Aristotle because it is used to determine the golden mean, and the golden mean is required for virtue. One picks out the just-right balance point between extremes, and this is the correct thing to do in practical situations. In other words, reason is used for practical wisdom. One way to understand practical wisdom is the capacity to find the golden mean in any situation.

Finally, reason is required for contemplation, which is the highest and most pleasant life (because it exercises what is our distinctive function or excellence, our mind/reason)—therefore, it is the happiest life.

PROBLEMS TO PONDER

These are questions that any thoughtful person should think about if he or she were considering adopting Aristotle's ethical analysis. Perhaps Aristotle can answer them. How would you answer them?

1. Aristotle assumes that the Good for human beings is to be found in the life and work peculiar to human beings. Why should we think this? Why suppose that human good is to be found in what is distinctive to people? That a certain factor *is* peculiar to a species does not imply any ethical superiority in that factor. If humans were just like other animals, except that humans all had very long necks, this would not imply any ethical superiority in being long-necked. Aristotle must be assuming that humans *are* superior to other living things, and that our superiority must consist in what makes us distinct.

   Nevertheless, one could still argue that pleasure is good, and the fact that a dog or cat can feel pleasure does not detract from pleasure being a human good. Does pleasure merely *contribute* to the happy life, or might it be the very essence of happiness?

2. Aristotle claims that rationality is the distinctive mark of a human being. Is this really true? We know that chimpanzees can reason, can solve problems, can use tools, are curious, and enjoy satisfying their curiosity. Aristotle would call this practical reason, but curiosity seems to be theoretical reason. One might conclude that reason is *not* unique to human beings and is not exclusively human.

In fact, one might argue just as plausibly that culture, art, and religion, social institutions, philosophy, and science are what make humans unique.

3. Is the golden mean really a moral guide? "Avoid extremes" seems to be a counsel of prudence rather than morality, and prudence is just being careful when it comes to your own interests. Even the wicked can find the golden mean useful. A bank robber trying to blow open the bank vault seeks the golden mean in terms of the time when it is "just right" to set the dynamite charge, neither when an evening crowd might notice, nor at a time when an early passing motorist might notice.

GLOSSARY

Contemplation Contemplation refers to rationally thinking about the first principles of things, the fundamental laws of nature.

Eudaimonia The goal of Aristotle's philosophy is eudaimonia. Translated as *well-being*, or *happiness*, it is the result of fulfilling one's function well or with excellence, something like *flourishing*.

Golden mean The golden mean is the balance point between excess and deficiency, which marks the place of human excellence, which is virtue.

Happiness Aristotle defines happiness as the exercise of reason in accordance with virtue (excellence of function). The highest form of human happiness comes from exercising reason in its most abstract form, contemplation.

Intellectual virtues These are virtues that we learn and do because we intellectually understand their need. They include philosophical wisdom and practical wisdom.

Lyceum The Lyceum was the educational institution founded by Aristotle.

Moral virtues Moral virtues are those we do out of habit because we have been trained to behave this way; habitual choices of action in accord with rational principles.

Philosophical wisdom This wisdom means to discover truth and attain knowledge of fixed principles. It is achieved with contemplation.

Practical wisdom Practical wisdom is a rational guide to everyday life choices; intelligent conduct. It also refers to finding the golden mean in every practical situation.

Virtue Virtue is the quality of performing an assigned function with excellence; the virtue of exercise is that it makes you healthy. For humans, virtues are dispositions or habits to do things in a certain way, that is, using reason to find the golden mean.

A GUIDE TO FURTHER READINGS

Dover, K. J. *Greek Popular Morality in the Time of Plato and Aristotle* (Oxford: Basil Blackwell, 1974). Ethical background for Plato's and Aristotle's views.

Gutherie, W. K. C. *The Greek Philosophers: From Thales to Aristotle* (New York: Harper Torchbooks, 1960). An excellent introduction to the Greek philosophers.

Hardie, W. F. R. *Aristotle's Ethical Theory*, 2nd ed. (Oxford: Oxford University Press, 1981). A more detailed study of Aristotle's ethics.

Moravcsik, J. M. E. *Aristotle: A Collection of Critical Essays* (New York: Doubleday Anchor, 1967). Critical analyses of many of Aristotle's basic assumptions and claims.

Urmson, J. O. *Aristotle's Ethics* (Oxford: Basil Blackwell, 1988). A good study of Aristotle's ethics.

CHAPTER 3

Epicurus: Pleasure Is the Foundation of Ethical Judgments

THE BACKGROUND OF EPICUREANISM

As we saw earlier, Greece entered into a period of continuing decline after about 350 B.C.E., and irrationality and chaos began to replace the stress on the reasoned life so emphasized by Socrates, Plato, and Aristotle. The various regions in Greece continued their struggles with one another to achieve political dominance. This meant new wars, political infighting, social disorganization, and treachery. The area was filled with continually shifting political alliances and constant warfare. Around 338 B.C.E., the Macedonians (Macedonia was in northern Greece), first led by Philip and then by his son, Alexander the Great, conquered Athens. For the next hundred years, to the Athenians the world was hostile and society brutal. People had lost control over their lives and lost faith in reason as a means to control their world; instead, they grasped desperately at almost any promise to reestablish control. Ultimately, the Romans became dominant over the entire Mediterranean basin and forced peace upon the area; with it came a stability of sorts.

During this period, several "salvation philosophies" became important in the region. Previously, in the days of Socrates and Plato, there had been a decline in the superstitious belief in the traditional gods of the Greeks. However, the decline in influence and power of Greece seemed to trigger a resurgence of elements from the older Greek religions of the past: the ordinary people began a slow return to the worship of the gods of the earth and fertility; new interest was revived in ancestor worship, and many followed teachers who promised religious ecstasy. In addition, a flood of religious cults and ideas poured into Greece from Egypt and Persia. There were secret cults, often called "mystery" religions, which offered the teachings of saviors who rose from the dead and offered salvation to those who followed. Several taught that the world was filled with spirits, demons, and gods and goddesses, and they offered esoteric rituals that could help provide control over this fantastic system. Some even offered unity with the divine. All of these were two hundred years before Christianity arose in Palestine.

Astrology became important for the first time in Greek history (stars were thought to be gods, planets were living things—or controlled by living divinities). If you could understand the positions of these astral gods, this would give you information about what the gods desired, and what would happen on earth. This held out a promise of some control over existence.

Irrationality was becoming the norm for both Greece and the entire Mediterranean area. After the glories of the great philosophers and their reliance on reason, a new attitude was taking hold. The feeling was that the world could not be trusted; the gods could not be relied upon, and reason could not bring a good life. There was a decline in creative energy; no more great philosophers like Socrates, Plato, or Aristotle appeared. The great sculptors, the great tragedians, all belonged to the past, although the Greeks did not realize it yet. The philosophy of Epicurus, called **Epicureanism,** was a reaction to this environment.

THE LIFE OF EPICURUS (341–270 B.C.E.)

Epicurus was born about 341 B.C.E. (about seven years after Plato had died), and he died in 270 B.C.E. He was not born in Athens as Socrates and Plato were, but he inherited Athenian citizenship from his parents who were born in Athens. Epicurus visited Athens when he was eighteen, and then he was forced to leave Athens, joining his father in the city of Colophon. Later he wandered the Greek islands, and in his wanderings he encountered students of Plato, Aristotle, and the older philosopher Democritus (fl. c. 420 B.C.E.).* He studied the writings of Democritus and learned from all the people he encountered. But he did not agree with everything they said. Epicurus began to teach when he was about thirty years old, and he settled down in Athens a few years later.

He bought a garden and began to teach there. His institution was called the "Garden of Epicurus," and it competed with the Academy of Plato and Aristotle's Lyceum. Unlike the others, the Garden of Epicurus was open to both men and women, slaves and free persons, landowners and those who owned no

---

*Democritus argued that all matter exists as indivisible particles, all composed of the same fundamental substance and each in constant motion, colliding and connecting with one another. He called these particles "atoms." Democritus also argued that atoms need empty space in which to move. This empty space he called "the void."

property. The life was one of quiet seclusion. He, and the community of followers who formed around him, lived simple lives, living on a diet of water and barley bread most often. They did enjoy an occasional glass of wine, but it was treated as something special. Later on in Europe, the word *Epicurean* came to mean something like "a gourmet," or someone who pursues rare and delicate flavors and foods, but, as we shall see, this is a serious distortion of the values espoused by Epicurus.

EPICURUS'S PHILOSOPHY

Epicurus wrote a great deal on a range of topics, including natural science, perception and sensation, the nature of the gods, and ethics. His biographer claims that he wrote nearly three hundred rolls of text,[1] but almost all of his works were lost with the destruction of the Great Library of Alexandria. Unfortunately, only titles and fragments survive.[2]

Epicurus and his followers argued that happiness can come from studying nature scientifically, because when we don't understand nature, we believe superstitions and myths and become fearful, filled with dread and anxiety. Happiness is the key to the good life, and happiness cannot be achieved until one has eliminated irrational fears. Science is the key to happiness. Knowledge is what replaces superstition and fear.

EPICURUS'S ETHICS

The ethics of Epicurus is not as complex as Aristotle's theory. His system can be reduced to a few fundamental insights: cultivate lasting friendships; live simply, and do nothing to excess; seek to maximize peaceful and harmonious pleasures and use critical thinking to minimize superstitious fear and pain. Study philosophy and study nature, for an understanding of the nature of reality will lessen irrational fears and help one to make wise decisions in life.

Epicurus argues that the good life requires a turning away—a turning away from irrationality and superstition, and a turning away from the numerous injustices of Greek society. Instead, seeking the peaceful and serene joys that might endure beyond the fleeting shifts of political favor or popularity is the key to the good life.

The purpose of ethical philosophy is to help us understand the nature of the world, and then we can use reason to determine which pleasures we should seek and which we should avoid. Epicurus is a hedonist, but he stresses seeking the pleasures to be found with abstract thought, not sensual pleasures. His basic ideas were: the wiser you are, the sooner you realize that you do not need to own much in order to live a good life; pursue simple pleasures, aim for and find serenity and peace of mind.[3]

The main points of Epicurean philosophy are (1) a hedonism that emphasized the superiority of abstract pleasures of the mind (especially philosophy) over the more intense physical sensual pleasures of the body, (2) the material basis of reality and a reliance on rational understanding of nature, and (3) a strong commitment to the cultivation of friendship.

Like Plato and Aristotle, Epicurus asks "what is the good life for a human being?" He wants to know what a human being should seek, and what a human being should avoid, in the search for the good life. Epicurus answers that the best life is a life of peace of mind or serenity, or *ataraxia* (serenity, calm, repose, mental peace.) For Epicurus, *ataraxia* is freedom from trouble in the mind and freedom from pain in the body. As you recall, Plato argued against pleasure being equated with happiness, and Aristotle argued that pleasure is not essential, but merely *contributes* to the good life of happiness. Epicurus has a different answer: pleasure is the very essence of happiness.*

> . . . the man who does not possess the pleasant life, is not living prudently and honourably and justly, [and the man who does not possess the virtuous life] cannot possibly live pleasantly.[4]

Hedonism

Hedonism is the general name for any position that holds that pleasure is the highest good for a human being. In ethics, hedonism is a teleological (or consequentialist) theory, because if the consequences of a choice produce pleasure, then the choice is right. Hedonists argue that pleasure is an *intrinsic* good, not merely an *instrumental* good. An intrinsic good is one valued only for itself, not because it helps us to achieve something else. Epicurus is a hedonist:

> For this reason we say that pleasure is the beginning and the end of the blessed life. We recognize pleasure as the first and natural good; starting from pleasure we accept or reject; and we return to this as we judge every good thing, trusting this feeling of pleasure as our guide.[5]

Epicurus seems to hold a position sometimes called **egoistic hedonism,** that the highest good for a human being is that person's pleasure. He argues that pleasure for the individual is the supreme good, and when you experience pleasure, the pains of life are far from your mind:

> The limit of quantity in pleasures is the removal of all that is painful. Wherever pleasure is present, as long as it is there, there is neither pain of body nor of mind, nor of both at once.[6]

We must note that the pleasures which Epicurus stresses are serenity, peace of mind, friendship, and the simple pleasures that preserve physical health. Epicurus argues that single-minded pursuit of sensual pleasure would not be a good life and, in fact, would probably damage your physical health!

---

*Epicurus's philosophy derives at least in part from Aristippus (c. 435–356 B.C.E.), a student of Socrates. Aristippus argued that sensual pleasure, not reason or happiness, is the supreme good. Of course, Socrates and Plato disagreed.

As you recall, Aristotle rejected hedonism because lower animals enjoy pleasure as much as we do, and he argued that something we share with the lower animals could not be the distinctively human good. Epicurus disagrees. Pleasure is a natural good; if we carefully observe how human beings behave, we see that good and evil are simply measured by the standard of pleasure and pain—this is the way all of us operate, whether Aristotle likes it or not!

Like Plato and Aristotle, Epicurus thought that philosophy can be a means for attaining true pleasure, but Epicurus adds that philosophy must have the practical goal of bringing peace of mind. He calls "vain" any philosophical system that does not do this: "there is no profit in philosophy . . . if it does not expel the suffering of the mind. . . ."[7]

Superstitions Destroy Mental Serenity

Among the things that destroy human mental calmness are the pains and suffering caused by superstitions and irrational fears. Epicurus acknowledges that it is not possible to live a life totally free from unhappiness. Some pains cannot be avoided. For example, we cannot avoid physical pain entirely. We cannot avoid the sort of suffering we have when a friend dies, or when we are separated from a loved one, but we can avoid the sorts of pains that arise because we have foolish, superstitious, or mistaken beliefs. When we see that some of our beliefs are false (mere superstition), we can replace our mistaken beliefs with correct knowledge and thus eliminate this kind of unnecessary suffering and pain. Epicurus argues that our culture teaches us false and superstitious beliefs about the gods and offers a false mythology about death. If we do not understand the real nature of the world, we will make up myths and stories about supernatural causes of natural phenomenon, and we will hold onto superstitious beliefs that cause irrational fears. We cannot rid ourselves of fears and anxieties as long as we do not understand the way the world works; the study of natural science will eliminate the dread and fears that come from the myths and superstitions of the uncritical past.

> If we were not troubled by our suspicions of the phenomena of the sky and about death, fearing that it concerns us, and also by our failure to grasp the limits of pains and desires, we should have no need of natural science.
>
> A man cannot dispel his fear about the most important matters if he does not know what is the nature of the universe but suspects the truth of some mythical story. So that without natural science it is not possible to attain our pleasures unalloyed.
>
> There is no profit in securing protection in relation to men, if things above and things beneath the earth, and indeed all in the boundless universe remain matters of suspicion.[8]

The natural science of Epicurus is influenced by the atomism of the Greek philosopher Democritus.[9] It includes several claims. Everything that exists is either atoms or empty space. All things in the world are collections of constantly moving atoms, hooked together temporarily. The psychological center of consciousness, the "soul" (*psyche*), is also made of atoms (although exceedingly fine atoms), and thus it too is material.

Philosophy is the study of what makes for happiness: philosophical analysis can help us distinguish between those features that maximize the pleasant life, and those that interfere with peace of mind. Using philosophical analysis and reason to provide genuine understanding of the world, philosophy can free us from the irrational superstitious fears and anxieties that interfere with serenity.

Epicurus explains the existence of all things as arising due to natural causes, and causes can be understood by the methods of natural science. Supernatural causes explain nothing—only natural causes operate in the world. Epicurus argues that the study of natural phenomenon can bring about *ataraxia*, peace of mind. "The only purpose of studying these phenomena is to secure peace of mind."[10]

Epicurus begins his exploration of supernatural causes and natural causes with this claim: "Matter can be neither created nor destroyed."* Epicurus explains his reasoning:

> The first principle is that nothing can be created from the non-existent; for otherwise any thing would be formed from any thing without the need of seed. If all that disappears were destroyed into the non-existent, all matter would be destroyed, since that into which it would be dissolved has no existence.[11]

It follows then, that no thing could possibly be created out of nothingness; and no thing that exists could ever be destroyed into total nothingness. When some thing is said to be "destroyed," what has actually happened is that the atoms which make it up come apart and are rearranged.

Note that Epicurus is not just telling us what he *believes*. Epicurus is not asking us to share his belief. Like every good philosopher, Epicurus provides us with an argument (in this case, an empirical argument) for this conclusion. He gives us good reasons and if we think he is wrong, we are challenged to find flaws in his reasoning or to supply a better argument.

If something could come from nothing, then what is the point of seeds (or genetic inheritance, or DNA)? Everything could simply appear out of nothing instead of arising from seeds, and we observe that all things arise from some sort of seeds. Why could something appear from nothingness at one time and not another? What are the limits upon what can appear and what can't? If things really were destroyed into complete nonexistence when they perished, then the amount of matter in the universe would be constantly decreasing. Clearly, it is not.

Epicurus argues that what we call *Reality* is just bodies existing in time and space; and these bodies are made up of smaller parts. The smallest parts are indivisible atoms, constantly in motion, and this motion has no beginning.[12] All that exists are individual indestructible atoms that continually are in flux, continually rearranging themselves in relation to each other in an empty space.

---

*This is now known as the law of conservation of matter. As has been shown in the twentieth century, the only means of utterly destroying matter occurs in a nuclear reaction, where a small amount of matter is completely annihilated by converting it into energy. Such nuclear processes do not occur naturally anywhere on Earth, and the theoretical possibility of such destruction did not occur until Einstein's famous "$E=mc^2$."

Epicurus goes on to argue that the universe itself must be infinite. His argument is: . . . whatever is limited has an outmost edge to limit it, and such an edge is defined by something beyond. Since the universe does not have an edge, it has no limit; and since it lacks a limit, it is infinite and unbounded.[13]

Epicurus concludes, "Because atoms and space are infinite, the number of worlds, like or unlike ours, is also infinite."[14] With an infinite number of atoms there must be an infinite number of worlds, so out of an infinity of worlds, there most certainly must be other worlds very much like ours, with living things occupying them: "We may assume animal and vegetable life in the other worlds similar to that on our own";[15] and we may also assume that there are worlds very much unlike ours.

The Soul

Having established the basis for physical existence, Epicurus begins his attack on superstitious beliefs that cause needless mental anxiety. He begins by considering the nature of the *psyche,* the soul.* Like everything else in the universe, the soul (the self, the locus of awareness, consciousness or character) must also be a compound substance made up of very fine atoms: "The soul is material, composed of finely divided particles, some like breath, some like fire, and some of a third, unnamed kind."[16] The soul is the center of human feelings: "All this is made evident to us by the powers of the soul, that is, by its feelings, its rapidity of action, its rational faculties, and its possession of those things whose loss brings death to us."[17]

Using this analysis of the soul, Epicurus argues that the fear of death is a groundless fear. Superstition and religious myths tell tales of horrible things that happen to you after death, things like hells and unending tortures. Epicurus argues that pure reason tells you that none of this is true; it is mere nonsense and superstition.

Using the **atomism of Democritus,** Epicurus argues that when you die, the physical parts that make up your body disperse, the atoms that make up consciousness (soul) disperse, and there is no possibility of experiencing anything. You no longer exist; so it is irrational to fear pain and suffering after you die since you will not feel anything. When you die, "when the soul departs, the body no longer experiences sensation; for the body did not have this capacity in itself. . . . However, if the whole body is destroyed, the soul is scattered and no

---

*Just as in the chapter on Plato, we must be careful not to misinterpret the term "soul" (*psyche*) and give it connotations that were missing in the Greeks. Although Epicurus speaks of the *psyche,* or human soul, we must be careful not to read into this term the associations of later Western religion. For the Greeks, the soul is where thought and sensations arise from, and since it feels what happens throughout the structure of the body, it too must be distributed throughout the body. Epicurus argues that sensations and feelings are a genuine source of knowledge ("the most trustworthy ground of belief"). Thus, when the soul is released from the body, the body feels nothing. If the whole body structure is dissolved, then the soul-atoms disperse, so sensation of the soul stops as well. This soul cannot survive the death of the body, so there is no life after death.

longer enjoys the same powers and motions; and as a result, it no longer possesses sensation."[18]

Some Greeks had argued that the soul was eternal because it was incorporeal, or immaterial. Epicurus argues against this. The soul cannot be an immaterial substance because if it were really nonmaterial, then it is not matter, so it would be the same as mere empty space (what the translator calls "the void"), and empty space cannot act upon any body, nor can any body act upon empty space; empty space merely provides the area in which physical substances can move. How could a nonphysical soul be influenced by a physical body? How could it relate or influence a physical body, since there is no way it could *touch* or interact with any part of the physical realm? "Therefore, those who say that the soul is incorporeal are talking nonsense; for in that case the soul would be unable to act or be acted upon, and we clearly see that the soul is capable of both."[19]

The Role of God in Human Affairs

Epicurus also explores the nature of the divinities, whom the Greeks thought of as blessed and existing in perfect happiness. Some of the new popular religious beliefs and traditional Greek mythology explained the motion of the various stars and planets as moved by gods. Epicurus offers a more rational and natural explanation, opposing those who believed in astrology and the divinity of solar objects. He begins by asserting that stars and suns and moons are not under direct control of the gods; rather, natural laws of motion (astronomy) can explain their behavior. If you want to know why things are the way they are, or why they move the way they move, then study the laws of nature (science), but do not assume that gods move things, or that divinities cause things to be the way they are by prescriptive laws.

> No divinity directs the heavenly bodies, for this is inconsistent with divine happiness; nor are they themselves [stars and planets] divine. Now, as to celestial phenomena, we must believe that these motions, periods, eclipses, risings, settings and the like do not take place because there is some divinity in charge of them, who so arranges them in order and will maintain them in that order, and who at the same time enjoys both perfect happiness and immortality, for activity and anxiety, anger and kindness are not in harmony with blessedness, but are found along with weakness, fear, and dependence on one's neighbors.[20]

Popular superstition in Athens had the various divinities constantly interfering with human affairs, causing miracles, starting wars, and generally making things happen according to their whims and wishes. Many of the Mediterranean peoples believed that the gods became angry at humans unless humans offered blind worship, unless sacrifices were performed, unless donations were made to the priests, and unless the commands of the divinities (as explained by priests, priestesses, or scriptures) were obeyed.

Epicurus realized that people are frightened of their gods because no ordinary human being could ever understand the motivation of a god. So they go to astrologers, prophets, diviners, soothsayers, and priests, in a vain attempt to find out how to propitiate these irrational forces, or to predict what these forces will do next. In this way, people fall prey to charlatans who claim to be able to explain why there is chaos in the world, why there is pain and suffering, and why the influence of Athens was declining in the world. The charlatans claimed to know the mind or wishes of the gods, and they claimed to have the ultimate and true solutions for repairing the broken relationship with the divine. However, they offered solutions that disagreed with each other.

Epicurus asserts: one need not postulate divine interference in human activities to explain why things are the way they are. Fear of the gods is simple superstition, and it destroys tranquillity, peace of mind, calm, and the good life. Epicurus makes what seems a startlingly modern claim: natural laws or principles (i.e., science, in his case, the atomism of Democritus) are sufficient to explain all that occurs. Irrational superstition does not explain reality. When you learn the real true causes of why nature behaves the way it does (science), you will free yourself from the hold of superstition, which imposes fear in human minds. What causes the disturbances in the minds of people? Epicurus answers:

> First, they assume that the celestial bodies are blessed and eternal yet have impulses, actions, and purposes quite inconsistent with divinity. Next, they anticipate and foresee eternal suffering as depicted in the myths, or even fear the very lack of consciousness that comes with death as if this could be of concern to them. Finally, they suffer all of this, not as a result of reasonable conjecture, but through some sort of unreasoning imagination; and since in imagination they set no limit to suffering, they are beset by turmoil as great as if there were a reasonable basis for their dread, or even greater. . . . When we have learned the causes of celestial phenomena and of the other occasionally happenings, we shall be free from what other men dread.[21]

In other words, divinities don't interfere with events of nature. There is nothing to fear from one or more gods, not if the gods have the characteristics of blessedness and perfection that people ascribe to them. If gods exist, they too must be made of atoms and empty space, like everything else. Therefore, natural laws will apply to them as well as to the other objects in the universe.

Athenian religion held that the gods dwell in unchangeable blessedness. From this Epicurus concludes that any being who genuinely dwells in unchanging blessedness could have no concern with the world, nor with human affairs that tend to be brutish and nasty. To assume that a god who dwells in peace and blessedness focuses his attention on the sordid dealings of human beings is to make a voyeur or "peeping Tom" out of that god. Concern with human affairs would be an imperfection in a divinity, like someone we think to be profoundly religious yet we find the person morbidly fascinated with the bloody scene of an accident, or the lurid details of backyard gossip.

Thus, if divine beings exist, they would not involve themselves in the lives of human beings, and they would certainly not be concerned about judging humans, rewarding or punishing them, or controlling an afterlife or destiny. The conclusion is clear: There is no need to fear any afterlife or to fear the wrath of divinities. There is no reason to fear gods, because they have no interest in humans and would never intervene in human affairs. There cannot be anything like a miracle. The gods are blessed and immortal, and being blessed, there could be nothing like punishment sent from above, nothing like hell, and nothing like "divine wrath." Being blessed, the divine nature "knows no trouble itself nor causes trouble to any other, so that it is never constrained by anger or favor. For all such things exist only in the weak . . ."[22]

> The gods do indeed exist, for our perception of them is clear; but they are not such as the crowd imagines them to be. . . . For the opinions of the many about the gods are not perceptions but false suppositions. According to these popular [and mistaken] suppositions, the gods send great evils to the wicked, great blessings (to the righteous), for they, being always well disposed to their own virtues, approve those who are like themselves, regarding as foreign all that is different.[23]

The Fear of Death

Having concluded that only superstitious people fear calamities sent by deities, Epicurus next considers the fear of death, "the most terrifying of all ills," which gives people no rest. Epicurus argues that both good and evil consist of pleasurable sensations or painful sensations—but either way these are sensations. Death is just deprivation of sensation—you will feel nothing, neither punishment, nor pain, nor reward. Epicurus says, "Death is nothing to us; for the body, when it has been resolved into its elements, has no feeling, and that which has no feeling is nothing to us."[24]

Since "death is nothing to us," we can enjoy life and not crave immortality. "For there is no reason why the many who is thoughtfully assured that there is nothing to fear in death should find anything to fear in life."[25] Anticipating death might be painful, but if it gives no trouble when it arrives, then it is an empty pain in anticipation. As long as we exist, death is not with us and so experience life; when we do not exist, it is of no concern to us. Thus, there is nothing to fear either way!

> The wise man neither renounces life nor fears its end; for living does not offend him, nor does he suppose that not to live is in any way an evil. . . . [The wise person] does not seek the enjoyment of the longest life but of the happiest.[26]

Happiness and Pleasure

Pleasure is the only intrinsic good (everything else is instrumental); pain is the only intrinsic evil. Epicurus asserts, "No pleasure is evil in itself; but the means by which certain pleasures are gained bring pains many times greater than the pleasures."[27] In other words, if some pleasures cause pain later on, it is important to be able to distinguish those pleasures that cause more disturbance than they are worth from those pleasures that are longer lasting and less disturbing. We must choose pleasures very carefully. Abstract mental pleasures are better than physical pleasures, even though they are not as intense as the physical pleasures, because mental pleasures can last a lifetime, and intense physical pleasures are fleeting at best.

Note that when Epicurus rejects physical pleasures, he does not do so because he thinks they are evil or bad. The actual experience of the pleasure is always intrinsically good. Rather, when sensual pleasures are pursued too vigorously, they simply do not provide enduring human happiness, or they result in more pain later on.

> Neither continual drinking and dancing, nor sexual love, nor the enjoyment of fish and whatever else the luxurious table offers brings about the pleasant life; rather, it is produced by the reason which is sober, which examines the motive for every choice and rejection, and which drives away all those opinions through which the greatest tumult lays hold of the mind.[28]

Human beings seek pleasure, and the knowledge resulting from the study of philosophy can help us to distinguish lasting pleasures from those that are more trouble than they are worth. Among those pleasures that profoundly contribute to human happiness and bring about peace of mind is the enduring happiness provided by close friendships.

We cannot control a universe made up of shifting atoms moving in empty space, but if we understand the physical world, and adjust our own wants and needs so they don't conflict with the natural course of events, then we can minimize suffering and frustration.

For Epicurus, the enduring pleasures are rather passive in the sense of avoiding pain and disturbance. Actively seeking intense physical pleasures is important only to the extent that those pleasures can put an end to the pain of unfulfilled desires. Lasting happiness is gained through passive pleasures; thus, passive pleasures are the most fundamental kind of pleasures. These include things like good friends, quiet intellectual pleasures, art, thought, and music.

The Causes of Pleasure

Since Epicurus is a hedonist, and pleasure is the key insight of a hedonist, Epicurus asks: what causes pleasure? To Epicurus, the answer seems clear: we experience pleasure when we obtain what we desire. When we are prevented from getting what we desire, we feel pain. Thus, we need to understand the various sorts of desires and the different pleasures that come from the satisfaction of those desires. Not all desires can be satisfied, and not all desires need to be satisfied. We need to separate out those desires that *must* be satisfied, from those that are all right to satisfy, from those that are downright dangerous to satisfy.

Epicurus begins by dividing desires up into two groups or classes: natural desires and what he calls "idle imaginings," or desires that are neither natural nor necessary. Natural desires are provided by nature; the idle imaginings are vain desires that seem provided by society.

All Greeks knew that we are biological beings, and that we share biological needs and desires with all the other animals. Thus, natural desires can be thought of as appetites provided by nature just because we are animals: such desires include a desire for food, sleep, and sexual gratification, and to be protected from the cold. Idle imaginings are vain desires for things like luxuries, for fashionable clothing, for keeping up appearances, for impressing neighbors, or for driving a new car instead of a perfectly adequate older car. In his explanation, Epicurus writes:

> Among desires some are natural (and necessary, some natural) but not necessary, and others neither natural nor necessary, but due to idle imagination.[29]
>
> We must not violate nature, but obey her; and we shall obey her if we fulfil the necessary desires and also the physical, if they bring no harm to us, but sternly reject the harmful.[30]

Necessary desires are those that will lead to pain if they are not satisfied. If a desire does not lead to pain if unsatisfied, then it is not necessary. Some of the necessary ones are necessary for happiness (if unsatisfied, they lead to unhappiness), others necessary for the "repose of the body," and others necessary for life (if unsatisfied, they lead to death).

Things that will satisfy those desires necessary for life include food, water, and shelter from the cold. A bed and warm clothing will satisfy desires necessary for ease. One intrinsically valuable item is friendship. "All friendship is desirable in itself . . ."[31]

What about the causes of unhappiness? If you know the causes and bring them under control, you can change the result. Epicurus analyzes unhappiness and finds two distinct main causes of unhappiness: fear and uncontrolled desires. From this it follows that if you can eliminate inappropriate and unnecessary fears and bring desires under control, you can bring about what Epicurus refers to as "blessedness of understanding."

All human beings value pleasure, but not all pleasures contribute equally to a good life. We need to distinguish pleasures into two main groups: those that contribute to the good life, and those that have a greater probability of making life miserable. Thinking carefully and critically—the methods we learn from the study of philosophy—can help us to distinguish pleasures that contribute to a good life from those that are more trouble than they are worth. Thinking philosophically and carefully helps to make it clear that satisfying some of our desires will cost more than they are worth (because not all desires are on an equal level).

How do you determine whether the desires will cost more than they are worth? Epicurus says:

> All such desires as lead to no pain when they remain ungratified are unnecessary, and the longing is easily got rid of, when the thing desired is difficult to procure or when the desires seem likely to produce harm.[32]

In other words, if you have desires that do not cause pain if left unfulfilled, and if the effort required to achieve the satisfaction is intense, then they are *not worth the effort*.

A problem is that we human beings want so many different kinds of things. Our desires are unlimited, but our ability to satisfy those desires is clearly limited. Unlimited desires cannot bring about true joy or happiness; not possession of greatest wealth or honor or anything else. For example, you want money. OK, how much money? Well, you want to double your salary. OK, now are you happy? Well, it is better, but still not enough. Double your salary again. Is that enough? Better, but . . . These sorts of desires expand as you get more. How much money is enough? How much fame is enough? When do you have enough so that you are completely satisfied, so that you don't feel the need or urge for . . . more?

The desires that are unlimited are not natural; these idle imaginings are the desires shaped by the whims and fads of society. These do not need to be satisfied, and even when they are satisfied it is only temporary, for they lead to a desire to repeat the same thing endlessly.

Epicurus's analysis of desires is one of the keys to the good life. Those desires that are idle imaginings and vain do not need to be satisfied. Ignore the vain desires, satisfy the natural and necessary desires, and satisfy those desires that are natural but not necessary, when doing so will not result in pain or harm.

Epicurus provides a simple rule: If you've got just enough, you are wealthy; but if you have unlimited desires, you never have *enough* no matter how much you have. "Nothing is sufficient for him to whom what is sufficient seems little."[33] You always want *more*. And you will never be happy. If you continually seek after intense pleasures, you'll be frustrated because you will never get enough—and thus, you'll not be living a happy life.

We must reject those desires that, if fulfilled, will bring harm to us. One must not value things, nor pursue things, just because other people value and pursue them . . . one must be independent in all things. Otherwise, we become a slave to idle imaginings, which are just vain desires and can never produce the good life. Epicurus writes, "We should not spoil what we have by desiring what we have not, but remember that what we have too was the gift of fortune."[34]

Enjoy what you have; it is enough. When you know that nothing is missing, when you don't have to go wandering searching for what you imagine you need, you have the key to the good life: the enjoyment of pleasure.

Epicurus's advice is straightforward: Adopt a simple life where your wants are few and you prefer long-term pleasures of the mind over the short-term (but higher intensity) pleasures of the flesh.

> To be accustomed to simple and plain living is conducive to health and makes a man ready for the necessary tasks of life. It also makes us more ready for the enjoyment of luxury if at intervals we chance to meet with it, and it renders us fearless against fortune.[35]

For Epicurus, avoiding pain and disturbance is essential to the enduring pleasures that make up the good life, and in this sense these pleasures could be described as passive. The happiness that makes up the good life is most likely to be gained through passive pleasures; thus, passive pleasures are the most fundamental kind of pleasures. For Epicurus, the ultimate goal is serenity, "the state wherein the body is free from pain and the mind from anxiety."[36] As we have seen, this goal is described by the Greek term *ataraxia*, meaning serenity, calm, repose, mental peace.

Good bread and clear water can produce more pleasure, when living simply, than a rich and luxurious dinner. "It is not the stomach that is insatiable, as is generally said, but the false opinion that the stomach needs an unlimited amount to fill it."[37] Eat simply and you will be healthy, making you sensitive to life, and you will be fearless of fortune—no matter what happens, if you enjoy the simple life, there is not much that can happen to take it away from you. If, in your own mind, you feel luxury and excess are necessary, it is easy to lose your riches and your luxurious dinners due to the vagaries of fortune, so you will lose not only your money, but also your happiness.

Something else we need to consider is that pleasures can vary in intensity, and in duration. For Epicurus, the duration of the pleasure is more important than the intensity of the pleasure. It is usually painful to achieve these intense pleasures (such as fame or money). If you pursue drinking, merrymaking, and so on, you'll have a hangover, you'll have a headache, you'll have bags under your eyes, and you'll constantly be tired.

> The wealth demanded by nature is both limited and easily procured; that de-manded by idle imaginings stretches on to infinity. . . . The pleasure in the flesh is not increased when once the pain due to want is removed, but is only varied; and the limit as regards pleasure in the mind is begotten by the reasoned un-derstanding of these very pleasures and of the emotions akin to them, which used to cause the greatest fear to the mind. The flesh perceives the limits of plea-sure as unlimited and unlimited time is required to supply it. But, the mind, having attained a reasoned understanding of the ultimate good of the flesh and its limits and having dissipated the fears concerning the time to come, supplies us with the complete life, and we have no further need of infinite time: but nei-ther does the mind shun pleasure.[38]

There is no need to engage in competition for goods or pleasures, because the things that remove pain due to want are easy to obtain and the things that are not easy to obtain are luxuries, and luxuries do not remove the pain due to lack of necessities.

> Of desires, all that do not lead to a sense of pain, if they are not satisfied, are not necessary, but involve a craving which is easily dispelled, when the object is hard to procure or they seem likely to produce harm.[39]

The Virtue of Prudence

To live the way Epicurus recommends, one needs to cultivate the virtue of prudence—do not overindulge. Prudence is a virtue, for this brings the pleas-ant life.

> Of all this the beginning and the chief good is prudence. For this reason pru-dence is more precious than philosophy itself. All the other virtues spring from it. It teaches that it is not possible to live pleasantly without at the same time living prudently, nobly, and justly, (nor to live prudently, nobly and justly) without living pleasantly; for the virtues have grown up in close union with the pleasant life, and the pleasant life cannot be separated from the virtues.[40]

Obviously, prudence is the overall virtue that we should seek to cultivate; it is the most valuable of all the moral attributes and the source of all the other virtues that allow us to live happily. Its importance to Epicurus is clear when we see that the same point is made in another document using virtually the same language:

> It is not possible to live pleasantly without living prudently and honorably and justly, [nor again to live a life of prudence, honour, and justice] without living pleasantly. And the man who does not possess the pleasant life is not living prudently and honourably and justly, [and the man who does not possess the virtuous life] cannot possibly live pleasantly.[41]

We are not playthings of fate, or objects to be pushed around by divinities. You and I can control important areas in our lives. However, sometimes accidents occur, and our decisions do not work out as well as we hoped. But it is better to have made a wise and prudent decision, which works out badly through no fault of our own, than to merely blindly push ahead, hoping that we will be lucky. Do your best, live prudently, be honorable, and be just. These are important keys to the good life. But there is more. Remember, Epicurus did turn away from politics and the hustle of downtown Athens.

> To secure protection from men anything is a natural good, by which you may be able to attain this end. . . . The most unalloyed source of protection from men, which is secured to some extent by a certain force of expulsion, is in fact the immunity which results from a quiet life and the retirement from the world.[42]

Epicurus Values a Community of Friends

Although Epicurus rejects the big city, he does recognize that we cannot be truly safe unless we live in a community of friends whom we can depend on to help protect us from those who would harm us. We need a community where we pledge to one another to come to the assistance of anyone who needs help. This is what Epicurus calls justice.

> The justice which arises from nature is a pledge of mutual advantage to restrain men from harming one another and save them from being harmed. For all living things which have not been able to make compacts not to harm one another or be harmed, nothing ever is either just or unjust; and likewise too for all tribes of men which have been unable or unwilling to make compacts not to harm or be harmed. Justice never is anything in itself, but in the dealings of men with one another in any place whatever and at any time it is a kind of compact not to harm or be harmed.[43]

In community life, we pledge to restrain people from harming others, and to help someone being harmed. Individuals need to belong to a social organization where they pledge to help one another, and to govern their dealings by justice. Like Aristotle, Epicurus recognizes that justice cannot be a hard-and-fast rule applied in every situation, because when circumstances change, our notion of what is just will also change.

Lead a quiet life, and retire from the world of politics and intrigues. We have *almost* everything we need, but not quite. Just one thing is missing: friendship.

Friendship is also necessary for a complete life. In fact, friendship is one of the very highest of all the virtues: "Of all the things which wisdom acquires to produce the blessedness of the complete life, [by] far the greatest is the possession of friendship."[44]

Friendship starts with the small community where each one pledges to help the other, but it goes beyond this. "It is not so much our friends' help that helps us as the confidence of their help."[45]

Friendship is the key to the highest blessings that this life holds: "Friendship dances through the world bidding us all to waken to the recognition of happiness."[46]

What Is the Good Life?

With this, Epicurus has provided his answer to the Greek question "what is the good life?" His answer: avoid superstition, understand natural science, pursue those pleasures that are natural and necessary, and avoid those that are vain. Escape to a small community of friends who share the bond of justice. These are the keys. Epicurus believes that if you can follow his ideas, you can consider yourself living the good life.

> I have anticipated thee, Fortune, and entrenched myself against all thy secret attacks. And we will not give ourselves up as captives to thee or to any other circumstance; but when it is time for us to go, spitting contempt on life and on those who here vainly cling to it, we will leave life crying aloud in a glorious triumphsong that we have lived well.
>
> We must try to make the end of the journey better than the beginning, as long as we are journeying; but when we come to the end, we must be happy and content.[47]

None of us can escape the certainty and finality of death. But we do not need to fight to avoid death. According to Epicurus, you have attained the good life and you have triumphed:

> Whom then do you believe to be superior to the prudent man: he who has reverent opinions about the gods, who is wholly without fear of death, who has discovered what is the highest good in life and understands that the highest point in what is good is easy to reach and hold and that the extreme of evil is limited either in time or in suffering, and who laughs at that which some have set up as the ruler of all things. . . .
>
> Meditate on these and like precepts, by day and by night, alone or with a like-minded friend. Then never, either awake or asleep, will you be dismayed: but you will live like a god among men.[48]

PROBLEMS TO PONDER

These are questions that any thoughtful person should think about if he or she were considering adopting the Epicurean moral system. Perhaps the careful Epicurean can answer them. How would you answer them?

1. Does it seem correct that Epicurus includes the "absence of pain" as a part of his definition of pleasure? We can have a state of no pain, but this does not seem to be something we would count as pleasure. There seems to be a middle area between extremes that is neither pleasure nor pain, yet Epicurus places this area under the category of pleasure.
2. Epicurus's theory causes us to eschew pleasures such as the thrill of achievement, or the satisfaction of having overcome a great difficulty—and many humans believe that these are meaningful pleasures, not vain.
3. Epicurus teaches a philosophy of avoidance. Perhaps a better life is possible if one strives for full participation in the political life, if one takes social and political risks.
4. Where do the pleasures of others fit into this system? If we seek to maximize our own pleasures, what keeps us from treating others badly except for friendship and a pledge of justice?

GLOSSARY

Ataraxia The Greek term *ataraxia* means peace of mind, serenity, calm, repose, mental peace. For Epicurus, *ataraxia* is freedom from trouble in the mind and freedom from pain in the body.

Atomism of Democritus An atomistic view is a materialistic view. For the Greek philosopher Democritus, it meant that the only thing that is real is atoms or the empty space between atoms. All things in the world are collections of constantly moving atoms, hooking together temporarily and then coming apart.

Epicureanism Epicureanism is the hedonistic philosophy of Epicurus (341–270 B.C.E.) that stresses science, serenity, and friendship as the keys to pleasure, happiness, and the good life.

Egoistic hedonism The claim that the highest good for a human being is whatever produces the maximum amount of pleasure for that person is called egoistic hedonism.

Hedonism Hedonism is the general name for any position that holds that what is intrinsically desirable in human life is pleasure. Pleasure is the standard we use to measure how valuable other things are in our lives. Pleasure is the highest good for a human being. Clearly, an ethical hedonism is a teleological (or consequentialist) theory, because if the consequences of a choice produce pleasure, then the choice is right.

A GUIDE TO FURTHER READINGS

Bailey, Cyril. *Epicurus: The Extant Remains* (Oxford: Clarendon Press, 1926). A standard translation of Epicurus.

___. *The Greek Atomists and Epicurus* (Oxford: Clarendon Press, 1928). A study of Democritus and Epicurus, and their materialism.

Copleston, Frederick, S. J. *A History of Philosophy: Volume I—Greece & Rome, Part II*, Revised Ed. (New York: Image Books, 1962). This is the standard history of philosophy for students; chapter 37 is on Epicurus.

Geer, Russel M. *Epicurus: Letters, Principal Doctrines, and Vatican Sayings* (New York: Library of Liberal Arts, 1964). A recent translation of Epicurus.

Hicks, R. D. *Diogenes Laertius, Lives of Eminent Philosophers, with an English Translation* (Cambridge, Mass.: Loeb Classical Library, 1925), Book X: "The Life of Epicurus." The standard historical biography of Epicurus.

Zeller, Eduard. *Outlines of the History of Greek Philosophy* (New York: Meredian Books, 1957). Background of Greek philosophy.

PART TWO

The Religious Ethics of Early and Medieval Christianity (100 C.E.–1300 C.E.)

Next we will consider an ethical system that is very different from the Greek view of ethics. As we have seen, Greek philosophers sought happiness in this life and used reason and wisdom as the keys that make a good life possible. In contrast, early Christianity stressed faith in a personal God, mediated through Jesus Christ,[1] and directed individuals to follow the precepts or rules laid down by an omnipotent divinity who is the only source of morality.

Christianity is a religion, one of the many great religions that have arisen in human history. Some religions stress spirituality in the form of meditation; others place the greatest stress on sacrifice, ritual, and rites; still others stress intellectual understanding of the ultimate nature of reality. Christianity is a form of religion that stresses loving devotion to a creator deity.

In the earliest centuries, Christianity was a devotional religion, not a philosophy in the sense of the Greeks, and it took several hundred years before Christian theologians began to work out a consistent Christian ethical system. We begin with a brief discussion of the historical background for the Judeo-Christian tradition and then focus on the two major Christian theologians for the first thousand years of Christian tradition, St. Augustine and St. Thomas Aquinas.*

Because there are so many different sects and divisions in the modern Christian tradition, the chapters on the ethics of Christianity will focus on the first twelve hundred years, stressing the period before the churches divided into the

---

*A discussion of the religious teachings of the Jews regarding ethics and the afterlife (which differ from later Christianity), and which influence the Christian view, is omitted for lack of space. So too is a discussion of the historical influence of Paul of Tarsus, and the various ethical ideas implicit in the four gospels popularly ascribed to Mark, Matthew, Luke, and John. A great deal of new information on the early history of the Christian community, and its relationship with the Jewish Essenes and others, has been made available with the discovery and publication of the Dead Sea Scrolls and other scholarly studies. For more historical information, see the list of suggested works in the bibliography.

three main divisions: (1) the Roman Catholic Church (the church whose follow-ers looked to Rome for guidance and whose primary language was Latin); (2) the Eastern Orthodox Church (the church centered in Constantinople whose primary language was Greek, often called the Greek Orthodox Church) which formally divided from the Roman church around the year 1000 C.E.; and (3) the Evangelical communities that, since the Reformation beginning in the early 1500s, protested against and rejected the authority of the church of Rome and were generally designated "Protestant."

From the earliest beginnings until the twentieth century, virtually every Western philosopher who worked in ethical issues did so drawing upon both the Judeo-Christian and the Greek background. We see this with the two philosophers we discuss next: St. Augustine and St. Thomas Aquinas.

CHAPTER 4

Augustine: Ethics Is Grounded in the Love of God and the Commands of God

THE BACKGROUND OF EARLY CHRISTIAN PHILOSOPHY

For our purposes, Christianity will be defined as the religion introduced into the world by, and founded on the teachings of, Jesus Christ (who was born most probably between 6–4 B.C.E. and died around 30 C.E.). Its sacred scriptures are the Bible, consisting of the Old Testament (historical and religious texts of the Jewish people) and the New Testament. Christians believe that the New Testament contains the prophetic fulfillment of the Old Testament and is the complete and final revelation of God to human beings.

Many in the early Christian community believed that God tells us what we are required to do, and what we are allowed to do. They believed there is no basis to moral behavior other than the absolute will and commands of God, but that we must also consider the examples provided by the life of God on Earth, namely the behavior of Jesus. If we disobey the commands of God and fail to follow the examples of Jesus, sin—or guilt—and eternal punishment are the consequence. God's absolute rules are the basis for human codes of conduct, for our obligations to ourselves, to our fellow human beings, and to God. Augustine wrote that a good Christian "holds that eternal life is the supreme good and eternal death the supreme evil, and that we should live rightly in order to obtain the one and avoid the other."[2] If sometimes God's rules might seem to conflict, then we need to establish which rules have priority. We know that there are sanctions if we fail to do our duty, to fulfill our obligations, or break one of God's rules.

Greek Philosophy Encounters Judeo-Christian Religion

In the Greek classical worldview, the universe was *not* created by a loving, personal God (although Aristotle argued that an impersonal divine force was the necessary first cause to set matter into motion). The Greeks did not think that there was an ultimate goal to history and did not place any emphasis on historical linear progress.

For the Greek philosophers, human beings are rational animals, and the most important life-form, but humans are not fundamentally different from other living things. Human beings possess a life principle, often translated into English as "soul" (*psyche*, that which accounts for motion and animation, and that which is the source of the rational and feeling parts of the self). But in the Greek view animals possess souls as well, and the Greeks disagreed as to whether those souls could survive the death of the physical body.

For Socrates, Plato, Aristotle, and even Epicurus, knowledge and logic are the secret to the good life, and it is intrinsically valuable to study the universe using these tools. Knowledge obtained by observing and reasoning about the world is valuable and important.

As we saw, the goal of Greek morality is "the good life," and the happiness that makes up a good life is a product of reason. For the Greeks, reason is more valuable than faith because knowing something to be true is a product of abstract reason and gives us enduring truths; merely believing something to be true is the realm of opinion and error.

Let us compare early Christianity to the methodology springing from the heritage of Socrates (which the later Western philosophical traditions use as well). For the Greeks, the ideals are as follows: (1) propose questions that invite thoughtful critical responses; (2) an important element to determine truth is a reliance on human experience (especially important in Aristotle); (3) the appropriate response to these questions requires rationality as the only secure basis to justify one's conclusions.

None of these ideals are typical of the earliest Christian approach. In Christian thought of the early period: (1) Christianity is not a system of conclusions based on philosophical reason, but rather is taught as the fulfillment of prophecy; thus, the Christian does not expect critical discussion as a response, but rather merely proclaims the "good news"; (2) the Christian does not ask how well the claims correspond to human experience or how rational the conclusions are; if God has revealed it to humankind, it cannot be doubted; (3) the appropriate response to the "good news" is not to ask questions to see if the conclusions agree with logic and rationality, but rather to accept God's commands and follow the examples of Jesus.

The Teachings of the Early Christian Church

The great majority of Christians would agree with the following statements, which are taken to be definitive of early Christianity.[3]

Christians believe in the existence of one God (**monotheism**) in the form of Three Persons, or Trinity (Father, Son, and Holy Spirit). There are three distinct beings that are yet fully one God.*

*How one being can simultaneously be three (the concept of a Trinity) is a concept that the Christian philosophical tradition wrestled with for a long time, but generally the philosophers seem to consider the claim as lying beyond the limits of human comprehension and therefore to be a divine mystery.

Christians affirm the **Incarnation,** the belief that in the Jewish carpenter named Jesus, God assumed a human body. Jesus was "the only begotten Son of God" who was at the same time genuinely divine and genuinely human. As a result, Jesus can be identified with God and with humanity simultaneously and thus a link exists between the two. Even though Jesus was put to death, Christians believe that he was resurrected three days later, ascended into heaven, and is presently with God, the Father, awaiting the time of his return to judge every person, dead or alive, and to establish his eternal kingdom.

The justification for God to assume a human form arises from the Christian doctrine of **Reconciliation,** or **Atonement.** The *Book of Genesis* in the Old Testament tells how God created the world in seven days and tells of the first two human beings, Adam and Eve, who God created for fellowship with himself. God gave them free will and ordered them not to take a bite of the fruit from the tree of knowledge. Adam and Eve disobeyed God, and as a result, all human beings gained the divine knowledge of the difference between good and evil, but they paid a terrible price for such knowledge.

Adam and Eve estranged humanity from God by their disobedience, as a consequence of which all human beings descended from Adam and Eve are sinful and condemned to eternal death, which is often interpreted to mean eternal torment in hell. Human beings need to be redeemed. God had created all human beings with eternal souls, and after many thousands of generations, in order to give humans a second chance, he sent his son, Jesus, to redeem, to pay the ransom for human sinfulness. Jesus takes responsibility for the evil sin of Adam and Eve, to assume the burden of human guilt, thereby making possible salvation and reconciliation with God. Christians believe that Jesus assumes the burden of the original sin for those who beg for God's mercy, who acknowledge Jesus as the only begotten son of God, who submit themselves to God's will, and who have faith in Jesus. The death of Jesus is a human sacrifice to God, and a self-sacrifice that atoned for (redeemed, paid the ransom for) the original sin of the first humans, Adam and Eve. The resurrection of Jesus is interpreted as proof that God accepted this sacrifice. The ransom was accepted, which makes redemption possible. Human beings can become reconciled with God, and like Jesus, be resurrected in a heavenly realm at some time in the future where humans will be judged favorably by God on a Day of Judgment. This universal Atonement is also a triumph over eternal death.

According to medieval Christianity, after his resurrection, Jesus returned to his father in Heaven, but first he appointed his disciple Peter to be the custodian of the church that developed around the teachings of Jesus. A hierarchy of priestly authority grew up around this divine task, and after a few hundred years, the Christian Bishop of Rome was accepted in the Roman Empire as the single most important inheritor of the robe of St. Peter; ultimately this bishop became the highest spiritual leader of all those Christians who looked to Rome for spiritual authority.

Christianity is a revelatory religion. The term **revelation** refers to God *revealing* facts to humans that go beyond what our reason and our senses can tell us. Revelation is the word of an omnipotent and omniscient being, and, properly interpreted, it cannot be wrong; of course, worldly empirical knowledge obtained by senses and reason can be mistaken. To the Christian, we must accept revelation even when our senses and our reason lead us to doubt a religious claim (we will ignore the problem of the proper method of *interpreting* revelation).

This attitude toward revelation had consequences for most of the Middle Ages. There was no point in studying the world, and no point in attempting to discover truths using reason and science; neither reason nor experience were of any value for salvation. Instead, one needed to study church dogma to understand what God chose to reveal, because this was more important than worldly knowledge of things like physics, mathematics, or chemistry.

Because of the revelatory nature of Christianity, the early Church recognized that many of the things that Christians were taught to accept could not be explained or justified using sense experience or philosophical reasoning. For example, human experience does not reveal that the universe is created by a loving personal deity, and that human beings have a broken relationship with that divine being. Christians believe that is true because God tells us so in the book that discloses his revelations, the Bible. There are many additional claims that cannot be known by reason: for example, that God is simultaneously one and three; that human beings are fallen and corrupt creatures, who are incapable of avoiding sin and the never-ending punishment of hell through their own efforts; and that only the undeserved grace and sacrifice of a loving God can save human beings from eternal death or eternal torment.

If reason cannot support these most fundamental claims of the religion, it is easy to see why throughout the Christian tradition, faith has been valued more highly than reason. Christians believed that reason helps one to figure out this empirical world but can never begin to comprehend the mind of the infinite divine. Christian salvation can only be attained with faith, and salvation is more important than succeeding in a worldly life that is relatively brief compared with the afterlife (an eternity in either heaven or hell).

Since the chief concern of the Christian had to be salvation through faith, the early church was relatively uninterested in science and critical philosophy and remained indifferent to scientific investigation of the world around it. One important reason for this was that the earliest Christians believed that the risen Christ would return at any moment, so the important thing is to prepare one's own soul for judgment, not to study the patterns of the stars in the night sky.

The ethical goal of the Christian is definitely not the "good life" of the Greeks. Rather it is the moral life that has its roots in the divine order, the commands of God. The Christian tradition emphasizes how easily humans can deviate from righteousness, as well as emphasizes the yawning abyss between the divine and the human realms, and what it means to love God.

How did the Christians understand the nature of God in early Christianity? Christians reasoned that there must be a profound similarity between the divine creator and human beings, because the Bible reveals that we are made in the image of God. In the Old Testament, God is a metaphorical parent with parental love and forgiveness, but in a very human sense, God seems possessive and has a sort of human vanity that demands that we acknowledge him correctly, and that we obey him freely or else be punished. God is like a father who loves his child, but if the child disobeys his father, the father casts him out of the house and home, rejects him, and refuses to acknowledge him. God has other characteristics that resemble those he gave to his human creations. God makes plans, has expectations, and issues commands; when they are obeyed, he is pleased, and when they are disobeyed, he is angry. God rewards some and punishes others.

The actual history of early Christianity is complex, and many new discoveries have been made in the last few decades. We do know that in 57–68 C.E., the Emperor Nero was told that Christians were pacifists and would not fight to defend Rome, that they practiced infanticide, incest, cannibalism, and horrible self-mutilation. As a result of these claims, and a need to blame some group for the fire that seriously damaged Rome, Nero declared Christianity an illegal religion. Persecution was sporadic in following decades until 250 C.E. In the two centuries while Christianity was illegal in the Roman Empire, the followers were not trying to produce a logically consistent religious system. Christians expected the immediate return of the Messiah and tried to prepare themselves for the Second Coming.

Persecution of the Christians intensified under the reigns of Emperor Decius (249–251) and Emperor Diocletian (284–305), who tried hard to stamp out Christianity. Another serious persecution began in 303 and did not end until the year 313 C.E., when the newly crowned Emperor Constantine[4] declared Christianity legal and allowed Christians freedom to worship. When Christianity was legalized, it became organized, and Christian leaders sought ways of attracting a wider spectrum of society. The simple and direct message of Christian faith needed to compete with more sophisticated religions and spiritual systems. The Roman Empire was filled with citizens knowledgeable in Greek philosophy who valued rationality and logic. The spiritual center of early Christianity was a personal encounter with a Jewish peasant called Jesus, but after it was legal, Christianity had to compete in the conceptual territory already explored in the classical Greek tradition of Neoplatonism, and the competing mystery religions whose founders claimed to be gods, whose founders claimed to be born of a virgin, whose founders claimed to have died and been resurrected, and whose founders claimed to have performed numerous miracles.[5]

After Christianity was no longer an illegal religion, a council was convened in 325 C.E. to establish and define official Christian doctrines and creeds. The members of that council determined which of the dozen or so existing gospels and other texts were to be considered sacred (canonical). The group ruled that every doctrine which disagreed with the council was heretical. They settled on four gospels and ordered destroyed about ten other gospels and other early Christian texts that did not agree with their official doctrines.

In 391, Emperor Theodosius declared Christianity the single official religion of the Roman Empire; now the Christians had power and they exercised it (religious freedom and religious tolerance were not granted to non-Christian religions).

This is the background of the Roman Empire in which St. Augustine grew up.

THE LIFE OF ST. AUGUSTINE (354–430 C.E.)

St. Augustine is generally recognized as being the greatest Christian theologian of the first thousand years of Christianity in the Roman world. He was often referred to as the "Plato of the Middle Ages," partly because he utilized much of Plato's philosophy (and especially a later development called Neoplatonism) to explain Christian beliefs. Later, the influence of Neoplatonism on the religion inspired by the New Testament was clear. Note that it would not be quite correct to call Augustine a "Roman Catholic" in the modern sense of the term, because Augustine lived long before Christianity had split up into Roman Catholic, Eastern Orthodox, or Protestant. His influence on both the later Roman Catholic and Protestant sects has been profound.

The man we call St. Augustine was born Aurelius Augustinus in a small Roman town near the coast in North Africa (modern Algeria) approximately sixteen hundred years ago (354 C.E.). His mother, Monica, was a Christian, but his father was not. Augustine's father insisted that Augustine should be well educated, and so Augustine studied literature, law, philosophy, and rhetoric. He was a good student and became a teacher of rhetoric, the art of speaking and writing persuasively. Although Christianity had become legal in the Roman Empire about thirty years before he was born, at that time it was merely one among many "mystery" religions popular in the Roman Empire.

In his youth, Augustine was a hedonist (he tells about this from the perspective of a penitent Christian bishop in his autobiography, the *Confessions*, written when he was forty-four). However, he remained discontented, and his continual pursuit of wine, women, and other physical pleasures did not satisfy a deep spiritual longing. Augustine had a mistress for many years, with whom he had a son, and he earned his living as a teacher of rhetoric in Carthage, an important Roman city not too far from his home in North Africa.

Augustine was spiritually restless, dominated by a passion for lasting happiness and a desire to find a deity he could worship wholeheartedly. Under the early Roman Empire of the time, religious pluralism was tolerated, and numerous mystery cults of Egyptian and Middle Eastern origin were popular and widespread. Many of these cults (a *cult* was a group that *cultivated* devotion to a particular god or goddess) centered around a "savior god" who had died and been resurrected. Followers of these religions could become immortal by sharing in the death and resurrection of the savior god, whether he was called Mithra, or Osiris, Adonis or Attis, Orpheus or Dionysus. Some of these religions

shared a hope of a coming messiah (this was found in the ancient Babylonian religion of Zoroastrianism and later in Egyptian religion even before the idea became important in Israel).

Augustine joined one of these mystery religions, the Manichean sect, for
nine years, between ages nineteen and twenty-eight. Many of the ideas of
Manicheanism influenced his later conception of Christianity. Augustine was
particularly bothered by the problem of evil and rejected the Christianity of his
pious mother because it seemed so philosophically unsophisticated, completely
unable to deal with the following apparent contradiction: if God is all good, and
all powerful, and the creator of all, then how could evil exist? If God created
everything, then a perfectly good God created evil. How is this possible? If God
could eliminate evil and chooses not to, then God is not all good; if God cannot
eliminate evil, then God is not omnipotent; if God could not foresee the hideous
evils that would result from his creation of the universe, then God cannot be omniscient. Augustine read the Christian account of evil and felt it was crude and
naive. The religion of Manicheanism seemed to offer a satisfactory solution.

Borrowing from both Christianity and a more ancient Zoroastrian religion,
Manichean **theology** taught that there were two eternal elements, variously referred to as God and Matter, Good and Evil, Light and Darkness, and Truth and
Falsehood. Good and Evil are engaged in a battle in our world, and human souls
are entangled in the midst of the battle. We cannot help but be aware of the
struggle between Darkness and Light within us: Light within us seeks purifica-
tion and deliverance, but Darkness within us strives to hold the body with lust
and fleshly desires. The power of good is not omnipotent: rather Light and
Darkness are two matched and opposed powers in constant contention, and
their battleground is not only the earth but also our own bodies. Sexual inter-
course and children disperse the Light among more physical bodies and prevent
Light from being concentrated and escaping to the heavens above. Good and
evil desires arise from two opposed souls and wills within a single human being. The religious person identifies with the Light, but is not responsible for his
or her evil lusty desires and behavior, which is instigated by the Dark side,
which the soul of Light cannot control. The Manicheans offered the possibility
of spirituality without surrendering one's reason, and initially this appealed to
Augustine.

After nine years, Augustine left the Manichean church for many reasons.
The Manicheans believed in astrology (that the planets and stars affected human life), but the Greeks were sophisticated when it came to astronomy, and Augustine could see that the Manichean beliefs about the stars and planets were
crude and in conflict with the best scientific knowledge of his day. But more than
this, he found some of the Manichean religious doctrines quite obscure, and the
Manichean priests he knew were intellectually second-rate and could not answer his probing questions. In addition, he was disillusioned when he found
that Manicheanism did not offer any kind of personal relationship to the forces
for good, and he could never understand why the Light was so passive.

Ultimately dissatisfied with Manicheanism, Augustine studied Greek
thought and then became enthusiastic about Neoplatonism (a later

development in the ideas of Plato, especially associated with a philosopher named Plotinus).*

At age twenty-eight, Augustine left Africa and went to Rome to teach rhetoric, and ultimately he was hired at Milan. It was at this time that, for political reasons, he broke with his mistress, sending her back to Carthage in North Africa.

A proper and prestigious marriage was arranged for him; however, in Milan he heard the preaching of St. Ambrose, the Bishop of Milan, and for the first time encountered a genuine Christian intellectual. Ambrose was profoundly knowledgeable about Greek philosophy and drew upon it to explain Christian doctrines. In addition, instead of interpreting Christian teachings literally, Ambrose provided allegorical interpretations so that the passages that Augustine had thought to be silly when interpreted literally could now be understood as symbolic of deep spiritual truths.

During this period, Augustine also studied Neoplatonism, especially the work of Plotinus. Several Neoplatonic ideas influenced Augustine. One is the concept of the *Logos,* a "divine word" that mediates between the divine and the physical world; the Christians understood that the divine word could be interpreted as becoming flesh, namely Jesus.[6] Another Neoplatonic idea is that of evil as an absence of good, a "privation" of the Good itself. Here Augustine found one solution to the problem of evil that had so troubled him.

As a result, at age thirty-three he converted to Christianity (386 C.E.) and somewhat reluctantly became a priest five years later; then, after the previous bishop died, Augustine was appointed the bishop of the city of Hippo (in north Roman Africa) from 396 to 430. In his remaining years, while serving both as a judge for the court and as the spiritual guide for a small community of Christians, he produced many Christian philosophical works based on Neoplatonist metaphysics, Manichean ideas, and the Bible, which had been assembled in its final form in 325 C.E.[7]

AUGUSTINE'S PHILOSOPHY

Prior to Augustine, no comprehensive Christian philosophy had existed; no one had successfully set Christian doctrine on a rational foundation. Augustine brought together the results of nearly four hundred years of debate on Christian doctrine with what he considered to be the best in the Greek philosophers, especially Platonic thought.

As a result of Ambrose and his profound influence on Augustine, Christianity acquired a distinctly philosophical dimension. Both Ambrose and Augustine acknowledged and appreciated the force of Greek classical thought and

---

*The Neoplatonists followed Plato as interpreted by the Greek philosopher, Plotinus (ca. 205–270 C.E.). Plato argued there were two realms: the changing world and a realm of perfect unchanging Forms, or essences. Plotinus argued that the ever-changing physical realm was an imperfect copy of the perfect realm, so we can study the physical world as filled with symbols that can deepen our understanding of the perfect realm.

of the Christian message—and they attempted to bring about a synthesis of the two. It might be said that Augustine "christianized" the ethics of Plato (and the mystical Plotinus) by identifying the highest of all of Plato's Forms, the Form of the Good, with the God of Christianity, and all of the other Forms were now interpreted as the ideas in the mind of God. Evil was understood as the absence of Good.

Faith is central to Augustine's vision of Christianity, so little room is left for argument and rational demonstration in the philosophy of Augustine. He believed that reason always must be subordinate to faith. One cannot attain true knowledge without faith. One should first believe the claims of Christianity, and then one will be able to understand those doctrines. For Augustine, there is no competition between reason and faith—faith is the primary criterion of truth, and any kind of understanding depends on Christian faith first.

Thus, Augustine believed that faith in the dogmas of revealed religion *must* come first; the credibility of Christianity does not depend on experience, reason, or rational proofs. So, ultimately, faith and reason can never contradict one another because faith always overrules reason. God, by his grace, illuminates the mind—then humans can grasp the truth.

Augustine struggled to understand what his religion told him that he must believe. He began with faith and only then used his ability to reason. Augustine developed his idea of salvation: salvation is attained only by God's grace. Since God is omniscient, God must know in advance whether any individual will enjoy eternal life or eternal damnation. Every person is *predestined* for salvation or damnation. If God did not know this, God could not be omniscient.

No one can ever deserve salvation because of the severity of Adam and Eve's original sin, which all human beings inherit. Since salvation cannot be earned, salvation must be a free gift of God's grace, which is received only by the chosen few. There is no way any human being can ever be worthy of heaven, not through faith, or good works, or through loving God. We cannot even have an effective will to love God unless God first bestows the gift of grace to ignite that love.

A philosopher is one who loves wisdom, and wisdom comes from truth. But the highest truth is God. Thus, one who loves wisdom must love God. To love God is to have faith in Christ. To love God freely is the key to eternal happiness, and equally it is obeying the will of God. This is the basic worldview of St. Augustine.

AUGUSTINE'S ETHICS

Augustine argues that there is a realm of eternal unchanging truths completely independent of human beings (similar to Plato's realm of Forms). This realm includes mathematics but not just mathematical truths. Augustine believes that every human being, whether Christian or non-Christian, knows that life is preferred to death and that the soul is preferred to the body. We all value strength over weakness; we prefer beauty over ugliness; we desire happiness over unhappiness; we value eternity over time; and we all prefer good over evil. Where do these incorruptible and universal truths originate? We cannot change these truths; Augustine concludes that incorruptible truths cannot originate from a world of change and time. Some timeless and eternal rational and moral order superior to human beings must exist. Our logic and our morality depend on this superior realm. Some being must be imprinting these preferences and truths upon our souls. This is God.

This realm of eternal truth serves as a foundation for morality. God provides the ultimate basis for the moral law by supplying the eternal law. The eternal law is God's divine will, commanding us to freely obey his rules, and forbidding us to disobey.

The Goal of All Human Beings Is Perfect Happiness

All of his life, Augustine searched for happiness. He was convinced that this was the goal of all human beings. He studied the Greeks, such as Plato, who argued that perfect happiness requires us to use abstract reason to turn toward a higher more perfect and eternal Form of the Good that is capable of providing a standard for wise choices and happiness. Aristotle argued that the highest possible human happiness is founded upon the exercise of abstract human reason, contemplation. Epicurus argued that the good life is one of relatively long-lasting but nevertheless impermanent happiness associated with abstract enjoyments and some sensory pleasures.

Based on his own hedonistic life as a younger man, Augustine did not believe that he could find permanent happiness in physical pleasures, and he finally acknowledged that perfect happiness cannot exist in this world. But perfect happiness is the goal of all men, and so it must exist, if not in this realm, then somewhere else. If it does not exist in this changing world, then perfect happiness requires immortality. There is more to human existence than our life on earth. We must consider the afterlife. We must be good because the eternal rewards are perfect happiness, and because doing evil causes horrendous punishment. Human beings must struggle to turn away from evil and seek the good. The rewards of sticking with the good may not be perfect happiness on earth, but at least it will be spiritual peace followed by eternal blessedness of the vision of God, which is humanity's true happiness. The good news of Christianity is the secret of happiness as revealed by God, and God alone can satisfy the desires of the soul for eternal and perfect happiness.

Thus, for Augustine, any morality not based in the Christian religion is essentially immoral, and purely human virtues that take no account of God are devoid of God's love—such a morality may have a certain value for temporal society, but such a morality has no worth for the Kingdom of God.

The Problem of Evil

Theodicy is a technical term that describes the attempt to reconcile the traditional Western Judeo-Christian assumptions concerning God's nature with the existence of evil in the world. If the universe is the result of mindless working of purely natural forces, then it is not surprising that the world is so darn unpleasant for animals and for humans. However, if the universe was created for us by a God who is omnipotent, omniscient, and all-good, then it is surprising that there is evil in the world—because one would expect that a perfectly good supernatural being with infinite power would create a *good world*. How could a perfectly good being create a bad world? Yet it appears that a perfectly good deity created a universe in which millions of creatures live and die, eat each other, terrorize each other, and prey upon each other; terror and violent death are the rule rather than the exception in nature. How can these facts be made consistent with the God of the Christians, the infinitely good deity who created everything?

To treat the problem philosophically, Christians assert that the following statements are all true:

God is omnipotent (infinitely powerful).

God is omniscient (knows everything).

God is omnibenevolent (infinitely perfect and completely good).

God is the sole creator of everything that exists.

Evil exists.

Even as a young man, Augustine recognized that there seems to be an inconsistency in holding those propositions to be true simultaneously. It would seem that a perfectly good omnipotent being would not tolerate evil and would eliminate evil. If evil exists, then either God is not omnipotent (because he cannot eliminate evil), or God is not perfectly good (he creates everything so he created evil), or else did not foresee the evil resulting from his creation (so God is not omniscient).

This problem is often referred to as the *Theist's Dilemma*. In a slightly more modern form we might say this: If God is perfectly loving and all good, then God must wish to abolish evil. If God is omnipotent, then he must be able to abolish evil. Is God willing to prevent evil but not able? Then he is not omnipotent. Is God able but not willing? Then he is not completely good and benevolent. Is God both able and willing? Then, where does evil come from and why is there so much of it? Does God have a lack of compassion, is God impotent, is God malevolent? Then God is not all good and omnipotent. But God is all good and is omnipotent! How can a Christian solve this problem?

As mentioned at the beginning of this section the attempt to achieve a reconciliation of these apparently contradictory claims is called theodicy. One easy way to solve the problem of the existence of evil is to give up any one of the basic claims about God's nature. If God is not omnipotent, then God did his best, but that wasn't good enough to eliminate all evil. If God is not the sole creator of everything that exists, then evil can be attributable to another creator (such as an equally powerful force of Darkness, or a devil). If God is not perfectly good, then evil is a consequence of God's willing it to exist. The problem is that the Christians considered each of these claims essential. Why should any human being worship or obey a powerful being who was not good?

This problem of evil was a major obstacle for Augustine's conversion to Christianity, and he could not join the church until he thought he found several different solutions. His basic insight was that the apparent unfairness and injustices we find in this world are actually fair and just, and human beings *deserve* them. God's justice is seen in the punishment of human beings who freely choose to disobey God, or who refuse to believe in the one God of Christianity. But God does provide grace to some sinners, Christians, who could never deserve the gift of grace.

Why does evil exist? One of Augustine's solutions is to explain the existence of evil as a consequence of the "fallenness of man" due to original sin. According to this view, all **natural evils** (earthquakes, floods, diseases, drought, plagues, tidal waves, etc.) that we experience are payment for "original sin." In addition, all the **moral evils** caused by human beings (war, rape, genocide, assault, murder, etc.) are also explained because of the same original sin.

> I have said further that no member of this [human] race would ever have died had not the first two [Adam and Eve]—one created from nothing and the second from the first—merited this death by disobedience. The sin which they committed was so great that it impaired all human nature—in this sense, that the nature has been transmitted to posterity with a propensity to sin and a necessity to die. Moreover, the kingdom of death so dominated men that all would have been hurled, by a just punishment, into a second and endless death had not some been saved from this by the gratuitous grace of God.[8]

What is the original sin of Adam and Eve, the two primordial parents? God created everything that exists throughout all of time and space *for* Adam and Eve. God created a paradise for them and granted his grace to them. God's grace permitted human beings to bridge the abyss between Infinite Creator and finite created, and it permitted human beings to love God—they were made *for* God, and thus the law of their being is to love God freely and obey God freely. Adam and Eve are tempted by the serpent, who asks them, don't they want to be like God, to know the difference between Good and Evil (by tasting the fruit)? They do take a bite of the fruit; the sin they commit is the desire to be like God. They became lost in pride and falsehood.

> . . . the root of their bad will was nothing else than pride. For, "pride is the beginning of all sin." And what is pride but an appetite for inordinate exaltation?[9]

Augustine argues that God created Adam and Eve to do the will of God freely—this was their essential reason for existence—and they refused to live according to the very law of their own nature.

> . . . man has been so constituted in truth that he was meant to live not according to himself but to Him who made him—that is, he was meant to do the will of God rather than his own. It is a lie not to live as a man was created to live.[10]

Augustine's interpretation is that by taking a bite of the forbidden fruit, Adam and Eve try to rise above their proper place in the natural hierarchy. The original sin is egoism and pride; it is the desire for independence; it is a human being trying to be his or her own guide, trying to be self-sufficient.

Thus, the reason that there is moral evil is that human beings have turned their back on God.

Augustine offers another solution, which is quite straightforward. Augustine argues that (1) since God is perfectly good, and (2) since all things come from him, (3) therefore evil cannot exist. If this works, it explains why there is natural evil.

For this solution, Augustine adapts Plotinus's Neoplatonic interpretation of Plato's theory of Forms. The universe is a hierarchical ordered structure in which some things are more real and more valuable than other things. The farther away something is from the apex of the hierarchy of Forms (the Form of Goodness), the less real a thing is. Plotinus, the Neoplatonist, argued that all things emanate from God and derive their very being from God. The farther away things get from God, the less perfect they are.

For Augustine, the apex of the pyramid of Forms/Ideas is God (Goodness itself). Thus, the less things partake in God/Goodness, the less real and the less good things are. Human beings are created good, but since they are not and cannot be God himself, they are not perfectly good. God's goodness is perfect and cannot be increased or decreased. But human goodness can be increased or decreased. Goodness comes in degrees (not everything is equally good). This is the basis for the solution to the problem of evil: what we call "evil" is just a privation, a deficiency, a negative—it is where there is less good—therefore, there really isn't any evil, but just the comparative absence of good. Thus, God is not responsible for evil in the world. Augustine explains this point by comparing goodness to health, and evil to disease:

> In the bodies of animals, disease and wounds mean nothing but the absence of health; for when a cure is effected, that does not mean that the evils which were present—namely, the diseases and wounds—go away from the body and dwell elsewhere; they altogether cease to exist; for the wound or disease is not a substance, but a defect in the fleshly substance—the flesh itself being a substance, and therefore something good, of which those evils—that is, privations of the good which we call health—are accidents. Just in the same way, what are called vices in the soul are nothing but privations of natural good. And when they are cured, they are not transferred elsewhere; when they cease to exist in the healthy soul, they cannot exist anywhere else.[11]

Human beings are created good by God, but they can become diseased. However, disease does not exist independently as a substance. In the same way, evil is not a substance, so evil does not exist in reality.

> All beings were made good, but not being made perfectly good, are liable to corruption: All things that exist, therefore, seeing that the Creator of them all is supremely good, are themselves good. But because they are not like their Creator, supremely and unchangeably good, their good may be diminished and increased. But for good to be diminished is an evil, although, however much it may be diminished, it is necessary, if the being is to continue, that some good should remain to constitute the being.[12]

To the extent that a changeable being falls short of God, it is evil. Evil is the absence of the perfection of the fullness of goodness and reality (which is God).

Consider the analogy of the relationship between light and shadow: shadow is merely the absence of light, it is not a positive thing in itself at all. Similarly, evil is a "privation," or a negative thing; evil is *not* positive. Being corruption, it depends on a physical substance, which itself is corruptible—thus it does not exist independently.

> When it is corrupted, however, its corruption is an evil, because it is deprived of some sort of good. For if it be deprived of no good, it receives no injury; but it does receive injury, therefore it is deprived of good.[13]

Augustine isn't finished with theodicy yet. He offers another solution to the problem of evil. Why does God allow us to choose evil? Since God is perfectly good, and since God created everything, therefore it is good that evil exists!

> For He permits it [evil] only in the justice of His judgment. And surely all that is just is good. Although, therefore, evil, insofar as it is evil, is not a good; yet the fact that evil as well as good exists, is a good. For if it were not a good that evil should exist, its existence would not be permitted by the omnipotent God, who without doubt can as easily refuse to permit what He does not wish, as bring about what He does wish. And if we do not believe this, the very first sentence of our creed is endangered, wherein we profess to believe in God the Father Almighty. For He is not truly called Almighty if He cannot do whatsoever He pleases, or if the power of His almighty will is hindered by the will of any creature whatsoever.[14]

Since God is all good, it follows that when God permits evil to exist, this must reflect God's goodness in some way. God is infinite and omnipotent. We are finite and limited. Obviously, a human being cannot thwart God's will; so, no matter what we do, it will work out for God; God can turn evil into good no matter what we attempt to do!

> *The will of God is never defeated, though much is done that is contrary to His will:* These are the great works of the Lord, sought out according to all His pleasure, and so wisely sought out, that when the intelligent creation, both angelic and human, sinned doing not His will but their own, He used the very will of the creature which was in opposition to the Creator's will as an instrument for carrying out His will, the supremely Good thus turning to good account even what is evil, to the condemnation of those whom in His justice He has predestined to grace. For, as far as relates to their own consciousness, these creatures did what God wished not to be done: but in view of God's omnipotence, they could in no wise effect their purpose. For in the very fact that they acted in opposition to His will, His will concerning them was fulfilled.... For it would not be done did He not permit it (and of course His permission is not unwilling, but willing); nor would a Good Being permit evil to be done that in His omnipotence He can turn evil into good.[15]

Augustine believes that we cannot always perceive the wisdom of God's ways, but a good Christian will have faith, for in time, all the details will become clear. Knowing that good will come out of evils, we must accept the adversities, pains, and afflictions that life brings in order that they can be turned into a positive spiritual use.

God accomplishes some of His purposes, which of course are all good, through the evil desires of wicked men.[16]

In the long run, however, the good triumphs over the evil. It is true, of course, that the Creator permits evil, to prove to what good purpose His providence and justice can use even evil.[17]

The Free-Will Solution to the Problem of Evil

This solution, that evil reflects God's goodness, can be interpreted in a slightly different way, which leads us to yet another solution. The good that results from evil is merely God giving us a choice between good and evil. Evil is due to human free will. Evil is not God's doing at all: evil is an inevitable consequence of human free will. Evil comes from human beings exercising their independent free wills and is required if human beings are to have free will.

Augustine was well trained in rhetoric and philosophy. He recognized that there is already an obvious problem with the free-will solution. One might object that if God is omniscient, then God knows all things that are true. That means that God must know in advance what each human being will choose, *before the choice is made.* But in that case, there cannot be anything like free will, and if there is no free will, then God's punishment for what we choose is unfair and unjust.

Augustine begins his discussion of this issue by quoting an argument from the Roman Cicero,[18] who thinks that no divine being could know the future. Augustine writes:

> If there is free choice, not all is fixed by fate. If not all is fixed by fate, there is no certain order of all causes. If there is no certain order of causes, there is no certain order of events known in the mind of God, since events cannot happen without preceding and efficient causes. If the order of events is not certain in the foreknowledge of God, not all things happen as He foresaw they would happen. But if all does not happen as He foresaw it would happen, then, Cicero argues, in God there is no foreknowledge of all that is to happen.[19]

Augustine does offer a solution to the problem of divine foreknowledge. He argues that since God is omniscient, God must know what you will choose, but God does not make you choose nor cause you to choose whatever you choose. You are still responsible and have free will, even if God knows in advance what you will choose. However, from your point of view, you do not know in advance what you will choose; thus, we have free will because God does not cause our behavior.

> . . . God knows all things before they happen; yet, we act by choice in all those things where we feel and know that we cannot act otherwise than willingly. And yet, so far from saying that everything happens by fate, we say that nothing happens by fate—for the simple reason that the word "fate" means nothing. The word means nothing, since the only reality in the mind of those who use the word—namely, the arrangement of the stars at the moment of conception or birth—is, as we show, pure illusion. . . . God spoke once and for all because He knows unalterably all that is to be, all that He is to do. . . .

However, our main point is that, from the fact that to God the order of all causes is certain, there is no logical deduction that there is no power in the choice of our will. The fact is that our choices fall within the order of the causes which is known for certain to God and is contained in His foreknowledge—for, human choices are the causes of human acts. It follows that He who foreknew the causes of all things could not be unaware that our choices were among those causes which were foreknown as the causes of our acts.[20]

Augustine then arrives at the following conclusion.

The conclusion is that we are by no means under compulsion to abandon free choice in favor of divine foreknowledge, nor need we deny—God forbid!—that God knows the future, as a condition for holding free choice. We accept both.[21]

As He is the Creator of all natures, so is He the giver of all powers—though He is not the maker of all choices. Evil choices are not from Him, for they are contrary to the nature which is from Him. . . .

Our conclusion is that our wills have power to do all that God wanted them to do and foresaw they could do. Their power, such as it is, is a real power. What they are to do they themselves will most certainly do, because God foresaw both that they could do it and that they would do it and His knowledge cannot be mistaken.[22]

Augustine deals with another objection. We must use our free will to choose correctly. That is what God desires of us. If we are free to choose, and we choose evil, is this a *defect* in our will power? Did God give us defective wills? Then evil is due to God and not to human failure. Is evil once again God's responsibility and not that of humans?

Augustine argues that God did not cause a human being's evil will. In fact, the evil will itself causes an evil act or choice. Then Augustine uses the Neoplatonic idea of evil as a deficiency. The evil will is not a positive thing; rather, it is a deficiency, an absence. . . . Evil is the failure of the will to will good, and it is *not* a positive will to do evil.

No one, therefore, need seek for an efficient cause of an evil will. Since the "effect" is, in fact, a deficiency, the cause should be called "deficient." The fault of an evil will begin when one falls from Supreme Being to some being which is less than absolute. Trying to discover causes of such deficiencies—causes which, as I have said, are not efficient but deficient—is like trying to see darkness or hear silence.[23]

God did not give human beings a defective will, because a defective will is a deficiency, and that is an absence, a privation of a good will. Thus, God is not responsible. God gave human beings the freedom to choose, and the choice that God wants us to make is "a humble submission to the will of God." But when we choose evil, we have deliberately perverted our free will.

I know, further, that when a will "is made" evil, what happens would not have happened if the will had not wanted it to happen. That is why the punishment which follows is just, since the defection was not necessary but voluntary. The will does not fall "into sin"; it falls "sinfully."[24]

The good will, then, is a work of God, since man was created by God with a good will. On the contrary, the first bad will, which was present in man before

> any of his bad deeds, was rather a falling away from the work of God into man's own works than a positive work itself; . . .
>
> A bad will, however contrary as it is to nature and not according to nature, since it is a defect in nature, still belongs to the nature of which it is a defect, since it has no existence apart from this nature.[25]

We choose evil freely, and we have chosen to pervert our free will away from God's intended choice: in choosing to be evil, we deserve the punishment that we receive. It is our responsibility. If you choose evil, there is only yourself to blame.

The City of God Is at War with the City of Man

In one of Augustine's most famous treatises, *The City of God,* Augustine attempts to explain how Rome, the eternal city and the heart of the Roman Empire, could have been conquered and fallen. In August 410, Rome was attacked, defeated, and sacked by the Goths. Augustine was fifty-six years old, and living in North Africa as Bishop of Hippo. This was a shock to the entire empire. How was this possible? How could barbarians have taken Rome, the Eternal City? Augustine's solution: those who choose good (choose to live "after the spirit") live in the City of God; those who choose evil (choose to live "after the flesh") live in the City of Man.

> This is the reason why, for all the difference of the many and very great nations throughout the world in religion and morals, language, weapons, and dress, there exist no more than the two kinds of society, which, according to our Scriptures, we have rightly called the two cities. One city is that of men who live according to the flesh. The other is of men who live according to the spirit. Each of them chooses its own kind of peace and, when they attain what they desire, each lives in the peace of its own choosing.[26]

Here Augustine explains how Rome could have fallen to the barbarians. He does *not* think that the Romans were wicked pagans devoted to lust, although he does think that the Romans focused too much on earthly rewards and glory. Rather, the lesson that we should learn from the fall of Rome is that worldly empires, even the mightiest of them all, will rise and then fall. Nothing on earth is eternal. It is only the City of God that remains eternal and unshaken. The lesson we should learn from this: the most important thing in life is the individual's relationship to God, and not things like earthly success, academic investigations, or earthly empires.

Augustine does not believe that those who inhabit what he calls the City of Man are all evil. Rather, their flaw is that they seek their ultimate good here, in this world (where nothing is stable). For example, the Greek philosophers who attempted to find happiness in this world, and who sought a good life emphasizing worldly virtues such as prudence, justice, courage, and wisdom, belonged to the City of Man. They weren't evil; they simply sought goodness in this world instead of the eternal realm of God. Those who inhabit the City of Man are damned; they earn the punishment in hell as their reward for this error.

Those who inhabit the City of God realize that the only eternal good is found in God. One who inhabits the City of God "holds that eternal life is the supreme good and eternal death the supreme evil, and that we should live rightly in order to obtain the one and avoid the other."[27] These are the saved, those destined for eternal blessedness. These two cities are at war (it is possible that the influence of Manicheanism is seen here). The King of the City of God is the Son of God, the Eternal Word (*Logos*), whom Augustine interprets as the Second Person of the Trinity (Jesus Christ). Since the fall of the angels and then Adam, Jesus has been building his City of God out of all souls of good will.

There is a lesson to be learned from all this. Do not focus on this world, but instead focus on eternity. Give up reason; reason alone cannot provide guidance or cure for the evils of life; only divine guidance, in the form of revelation, can. The basis of Christian morality comes from this: Do not look for the basis of morality in this life or in this world; it can only be found in the divine commands of God and the divine City of God.

What Is the Good Life?

The influence of Plato and the Greeks is still present in the Christian philosophy of Augustine. He attempts to answer the question: What is the good life? His answer is very Greek. To begin with, the good life is a life of happiness.

Remember that the Greek philosophers thought that the highest good was obtained in this life. Aristotle and Epicurus suggested prudence and temperance as virtues leading to a good life. Augustine responds: "And what prudence preaches temperance puts into practice. Yet, neither prudence nor temperance can rid this life of the evils that are their constant concern."[28]

Augustine argues that this life cannot provide the highest happiness, because in this life, nothing lasts! Life is short and nasty.

> Those who think that the supreme good and evil are to be found in this life are mistaken. It makes no difference whether it is the body or in the soul or in both—or, specifically, in pleasure or virtue or in both—that they seek the supreme good. They seek in vain whether they look to serenity [Epicurus], to virtue [Aristotle], or to both; whether to pleasure plus serenity, or to virtue, or to all three; or to the satisfaction of our innate exigencies, or to virtue or to both. It is in vain that men look for beatitude on earth or in human nature.[29]

The Greeks sought the "good life," but Augustine feels that, at its best, the "good life" is one of temporary enjoyment and happiness associated with sensory pleasures and intellectual pleasures—it cannot last! Look around! This life is miserable and unfair, filled with pain, death, lost friendship, and unjust suffering. Augustine catalogs all the ways that people suffer in this unjust and unfair world:

> As for the primary satisfactions of our nature, when or where or how can they be so securely possessed in this life that they are not subject to the ups and downs of fortune? There is no pain of body, driving out pleasure, that may not befall the wise man; no anxiety that may not banish calm. A man's physical in-

tegrity is ended by the amputation of any of his limbs; his beauty is spoiled by deformity, his health by sickness, his vigor by weariness, his agility by torpor and sluggishness. There is not one of these that may not affect the flesh even of a philosopher. Among our elementary requirements we reckon a graceful and becoming erectness and movement; but what happens to these as soon as some sickness brings on palsy or, still worse, a spinal deformity so severe that a man's hands touch the ground as though he were a four-footed beast? What is then left of any beauty or dignity in a man's posture or gait? . . . How much sensation does a man have left if, for example, he goes deaf and blind? And where does the reason or intelligence go, into what strange sleep, when sickness unsettles the mind? . . . To witness such things, even to recall them, makes a decent man weep. Still worse is the case of those possessed by demons. Their intelligence seems driven away, not to say destroyed, when an evil spirit according to its will makes use of their body and soul.[30]

Look, now, at the great virtue called fortitude. Is not its very function—to bear patiently with misfortune—overwhelming evidence that human life is be-set with unhappiness, however wise a man may be?[31]

In addition to all of these, there are the injustices of the legal system where an innocent man may be tortured to death to determine whether he was really innocent! Augustine says that even the best of us can be tempted by Satan, the force of Darkness and evil. We mistake friends for enemies, and enemies for friends. Consider war and all the pain and death it causes. This world could never be a realm of enduring happiness, or the good life.

On the other hand, the Christian moral life has the divine God as its source, and so can generate permanent and eternal happiness. Augustine was obsessed with a search for lasting happiness. Since human happiness is not attainable in this world, Augustine shows little interest in the physical world.

It is obvious that human happiness is not obtainable in *this* world. It is equally obvious that human beings *need* eternal happiness, but it cannot be obtained in this world. What is the solution? Eternal life is the supreme good; death eternal is the supreme evil. To obtain eternal life, and eternal happiness, we must live rightly.

Neither our salvation nor our beatitude is here present, but "we wait for it" in the future, and we wait "with patience," precisely because we are surrounded by evils which patience must endure until we come to where all good things are sources of inexpressible happiness and where there will be no longer anything to endure. Such is to be our salvation in the hereafter, such the final blessedness.[32]

What makes a person happy? Augustine replies: We human beings seek eternal peace. The achievement of eternal peace is the highest human happiness.

It would be simplest for all concerned if we spoke of "peace in eternal life," or of "eternal" or of "eternal life in peace," as the end or supreme good of this City [of God]. . . . In the earthly city, then, temporal goods are to be used with a view to the enjoyment of earthly peace, whereas in the heavenly City, they are used with a view to the enjoyment of eternal peace. . . . When this peace is reached, man will be no longer haunted by death, but plainly and perpetually endowed with life, nor will his body, which now wastes away and weighs down the soul, be any longer animal, but spiritual, in need of nothing, and completely under the control of our will.[33]

In addition, Augustine argues that possession of *truth* makes a person happy. What is truth? Augustine answers: God is truth, thus contemplation of God as truth is what makes us happy! Happiness is to be found in the vision of God, and everything else is to be used in pursuit of this.

How Do the Virtues of the Greeks Differ from the Christian Virtues?

Augustine makes a rather startling claim at this point. He argues that the fundamental Christian virtues—charity, faith, hope, obedience, prayer, love—and the Greek virtues of prudence, temperance, justice, courage, and fortitude are merely prideful vices unless "used in the service of the true religion":

> Look now, at virtue herself, which comes later with education and claims for herself the topmost place among human goods. Yet, what is the life of virtue save one unending war with evil inclinations, and not with solicitations of other people alone, but with evil inclinations that arise within ourselves and are our very own.
>
> I speak especially of temperance . . . which must bridle our fleshly lusts if they are not to drag our will to consent to abominations of every sort. . . . And when we seek final rest in the supreme good, what do we seek save an end to this conflict between flesh and spirit, freedom from this propensity to evil against which the spirit is at war? Yet, will as we may, such liberty cannot be had in mortal life. . . .
>
> Take next the virtue called prudence. Is not this virtue constantly on the lookout to distinguish what is good from what is evil, so that there may be no mistake made in seeking the one and avoiding the other? . . . Yet neither prudence nor temperance can rid this life of the evils that are their constant concern.
>
> Finally, there is justice. Its task is to see that to each is given what belongs to each. And this holds for the right order within man himself, so that it is just for the soul to be subordinate to God, and the body to the soul, and thus for body and soul taken together to be subject to God. . . .
>
> Look, now, at the great virtue called fortitude. Is not its very function—to bear patiently with misfortune—overwhelming evidence that human life is beset with unhappiness, however wise a man may be.[34]

Paraphrasing Scripture, Augustine claims that the virtues of the Greeks, temperance, fortitude, justice, and so on, are not genuinely virtuous unless they are followed because one is a Christian. In other words, a non-Christian who behaves virtuously cannot be a moral human being. Virtues are vices if they don't base themselves on God.

> For, when virtues are genuine virtues—and that is possible only when men believe in God—they make no pretense of protecting their possessors from unhappiness, for that would be a false promise; but they do claim that human life, now compelled to feel the misery of so many grievous ills on earth, can, by the

hope of heaven, be made both happy and secure. If we are asked how a life can be happy before we are saved, we have the answer of St. Paul: "For in hope were we saved. But hope that is seen is not hope. For how can a man hope for what he sees? But if we hope for what we do not see, we wait for it with patience."[35]

For Augustine, a morality without religion is essentially immoral, and purely human virtues that take no account of God are devoid of God's love. God cannot reward apparently moral behavior that is not based on love of God. Secular morality may have a certain value for helping people in society to get along with one another, but such a morality has *no worth* for the Kingdom of God.

> There may seem to be some control of soul over body and of reason over passion, even when the soul and reason do not serve God as He demands. Actually, however, there is no such thing. For, what species of control can there be of the body, and its bad tendencies if the mistress mind is ignorant of the true God, insubmissive to His authority, and, as a result, a plaything to the corrupting influences of thoroughly evil demons? No, the virtues on which the mind preens itself as giving control over the body and its urges, and which aim at any purpose or possession than God, are in point of fact vices rather than virtues.
>
> Although some people claim that virtues are authentic and worthy of the name so long as their end is in themselves and they are not means to something else, even they are spoiled by the puff of pride and must, consequently, be reckoned as vices rather than virtues.[36]

Where there is no Christianity, there are no true virtues. Non-Christians cannot be moral or virtuous, for what ordinary people consider virtues are merely pride-filled vices unless the person bases his or her behavior upon the love of God. But this is not so difficult. Augustine argues that our human nature naturally tends toward God, and we are morally obliged to love God.

The Foundation of Morality Is the Love of God

Augustine believes that we must see the relative unimportance of things in this world and place greater value on the realm of God. We should use worldly goods only as tools to attain eternal lasting happiness. The supreme good is God, and God's nature is love. Augustine stresses that human love is just participation in God's divine love; we are to love one another as God loves human beings.

The foundation of morality is just the love of God. Loving God leads to God, who is the supreme source of everlasting happiness. In this world, which is unjust and unfair, we still must follow the fundamental teachings of Jesus as found in the New Testament. Everyone needs to follow Jesus' precepts: Love God; Love thy neighbor as thyself. These can produce spiritual peace.

> And, because, so long as man lives in his mortal body and is a pilgrim far from the Lord, he walks, not by vision, but by faith. Consequently, he refers all peace of body or soul, or their combination, to that higher peace which unites a mortal man with the immortal God and which I defined as "ordered obedience guided by faith, under God's eternal law."

Meanwhile, God teaches him two chief commandments, the love of God and the love of neighbor. In these precepts man finds three beings to love, namely, God, himself, and his fellow man, and knows that he is not wrong in loving himself so long as he loves God. As a result, he must help his neighbor (whom he is obliged to love as himself) to love God. Thus, he must help his wife, children, servants, and all others whom he can influence. He must wish, moreover, to be similarly helped by his fellow man, in case he himself needs such assistance. . . . Right order here means, first, that he harm no one, and, second, that he help whomever he can. His fundamental duty is to look out for his own home, for both by natural and human law he has easier and readier access to their requirements.

. . . From this care arises that peace of the home which lies in the harmonious interplay of authority and obedience among those who live there. For, those who have the care of the others give the orders—a man to his wife, parents to their children, masters to their servants. And those who are cared for must obey— wives their husbands, children their parents, servants their masters.[37]

The so-called love of God is not a more or less sensuous sympathy with nature and humanity that comes from our feelings. God is the First Truth, first Justice, first Beauty, and first Goodness (this is from Plato). To love God is to love truth, justice, beauty, and goodness—and truth, justice, beauty, and goodness are just different expressions of measure, proportion, and order. The best representation of God is to look upon God as Absolute Order. To love God is to love order.

We must love one another the way that God loves human beings, and we can learn to share the love of God and by extension, we can love our neighbors as well.

Only revelation is completely certain. Human reason is not perfect, not infallible. Unless we have a "Divine Master" whom we can obey without hesitation, our ordinary philosophical reasoning can lead us into mistakes. The Divine Master provided laws in the Garden of Paradise (Eden), then commands to Moses (Ten Commandments), and then additional commandments in the New Testament: these laws are true (coming from God) and are accompanied by sanctions (punishments if we violate them).

What does it mean to love God? In explaining this, Augustine draws upon Plato again. Plato argued that the nonrational appetite and spirit parts of the soul, the senses, must be under the control of reason. Augustine argues that to love God consists of the submission of our senses to reason. But then he departs from Plato and says that after our senses obey our reason, then our reason must submit to God. God is worth more than anything else in existence. God is worth more than the soul (reason), and the soul is worth more than the body (senses).

Thus, your senses submit to reason (Plato), and your reason submits to God—for the worship of God is the chief virtue and the foundation of all morality. What's more, your human reason cannot properly command the senses unless it is first submitted to God.

All temporal existence is moving toward the day of the final judgment of God. Augustine argues that we all deserve the most horrible punishment because we have inherited Adam's sin. Like Adam and Eve, human beings are

The Ten Commandments ("Decalogue")

The Ten Commandments appear in two somewhat different forms in the Old Testament. The Jewish and Christian traditions hold that the commandments were given by God to Moses on Mt. Sinai, and these two lists appear in Exodus 20 and in Deuteronomy 5.

Exodus 20	Deuteronomy 5
I the Lord am your God who brought you out of the land of Egypt, the place of slavery.	I the Lord am your God who brought you out of the land of Egypt, that place of slavery.
You shall not have other gods beside me.	You shall not have other gods besides me.
You shall not carve idols for yourselves in the shape of anything in the sky above or in the earth below or in the waters beneath the earth; you shall not bow down before them or worship them. For I the Lord your God am a jealous God, inflicting punishment for their fathers' wickedness on the children of those who hate me down to the third and fourth generation, but bestowing mercy down to the thousandth generation on the children of those who love me and keep my commandments.	You shall not carve idols for yourselves in the shape of anything in the sky above or on the earth below or in the waters beneath the earth; you shall not bow down before them or worship them. For I the Lord your God am a jealous God, inflicting punishment for their father's wickedness on the children of those who hate me, unto the fourth generation, but bestowing mercy down to the thousandth generation on the children of those who love me and keep my commandments.
You shall not take the name of the Lord your God in vain; for the Lord will not leave unpunished him who takes his name in vain.	You shall not take the name of the Lord your God in vain; for the Lord will not leave unpunished him who takes his name in vain.
Remember to keep holy the Sabbath day.	Take care to keep holy the Sabbath day as the Lord your God commanded you.
Six days you may labor and do all your work; but the seventh day is the Sabbath of the Lord your God. No work may be done then either by you or by your son or daughter, or your male slave or female slave or your beast or the foreigner who lives with you. In six days the Lord made the heavens and the earth, the sea and all that is in them; but on the seventh day He rested. That is why the Lord has blessed the Sabbath day and made it holy.	Six days you may labor and do all your work; but the seventh day is the Sabbath of the Lord your God. No work may be done then, whether by you, or your son or daughter, or your male slave or female slave, or your ox or your ass, or any of your beasts, or the foreigner who lives with you. Your male and female slaves rest as you do for remember that you too were once slaves in Egypt, and the Lord your God brought you from there with a strong hand and an outstretched arm. That is why the Lord your God has commanded you to observe the Sabbath day.
Honor your father and your mother that you may have a long life in the land which the Lord your God is giving you.	Honor your father and your mother as the Lord your God has commanded you that you may have a long life and prosperity in the land which the Lord your God is giving you.
You shall not kill. You shall not commit adultery. You shall not steal. You shall not bear false witness against your neighbor.	You shall not kill. You shall not commit adultery. You shall not steal. You shall not bear dishonest witness against your neighbor.
You shall not covet your neighbor's house; you shall not covet your neighbor's wife; nor his male slave and female slave, nor his ox or ass, nor anything else that belongs to him.	You shall not covet your neighbor's wife. You shall not desire your neighbor's house, nor his male slave or female slave, nor his ox or ass, nor anything that belongs to him.

proud, determined to be masters of their own destiny, turned away from the highest goods (divine) and anxiously devoted to lower (lust). Even humans who try to be good Christians have desires that are not placed in proper hierarchical order. We know that the higher things have more intrinsic value than the lower things (Plato's Forms). Furthermore, human beings continually turn away from God. We are responsible for this descent into evil because we have free will.

> The two cities, of God and of the Devil, are to reach their appointed ends when the sentences of destiny and doom are passed by our Lord Jesus Christ, the Judge of the living and the dead. . . . It is not easy to find a proof that will convince unbelievers of the possibility of human bodies remaining not merely active, alive, and uncorrupted after death, but also of continuing forever in the torments of fire.[38]

This condition is so terrible, that no human being can rescue himself or herself from it. We all deserve eternal death, we deserve the unremitting eternal agony of hell.

> . . . from its very start, the race of mortal men has been a race condemned. Think, first, of that dreadful abyss of ignorance from which all error flows and so engulfs the sons of Adam in a darksome pool that no one can escape without the toll of toils and tears and fears. Then, take our very love for all those things that prove so vain and poisonous and breed so many heartaches, troubles, griefs, and fears; such insane joys in discord, strife and war; such wrath and plots of enemies, deceivers, sycophants; such fraud and theft and robbery; such perfidy and pride, envy and ambition, homicide and murder, cruelty and savagery, lawlessness and lust; all the shameless passions of the impure—fornication and adultery, incest and unnatural sins, rape and countless other uncleanness too nasty to be mentioned; the sins against religion—sacrilege and heresy, blasphemy and perjury; the iniquities against our neighbors—calumnies and cheating, lies and false witness, violence to persons and property; the injustices of the courts and the innumerable other miseries and maladies that fill the world, yet escape attention. . . .
>
> . . . When we are not victims of the lawlessness and lust of wicked men, we have to suffer the miseries that no one in our present condition can escape. Who can be free from fear or grief in a world of mourning and bereavement, of losses and legal penalties, of liars and deceivers, of the false imputations, violences and other wickednesses of our neighbors? . . .
>
> Then there are the demons in a thousand forms that fill mankind with dread. Not even innocence is safe from their incursions. No innocence is greater than that of newly baptized children, yet, to give us a lesson in holy diffidence, even they are sometimes attacked by demons. God, who permits this tragedy, could not teach us more emphatically how much the misery of this life is to be moaned and how greatly the blessedness of eternity is to be desired.[39]

It is obvious to everyone: Life is not fair. It is equally obvious to the Christian that God certainly has not intervened to make it fair, or even to reward people who support Him, nor punish people who do not believe in Him.

> Turn, now, to the maladies that afflict our bodies. Not even medical libraries have cataloged all the diseases; in most cases, it takes pain to drive out pain, so

that medical care and cures can be as cruel as the complaints themselves. Then there is hunger and thirst. Desperate men have been driven to drink human urine, sometimes their own, and to eat human flesh, and sometimes to kill others in order to eat them—and not always their enemies. There have been mothers driven to desperation by hunger and to the unbelievable monstrosity of devouring their own children. . . .

From this all but hell of unhappiness here on earth, nothing can save us but the grace of Jesus Christ, who is our Savior, Lord and God. . . . He saves us from passing from the misery of this mortal life to a still more miserable condition, which is not so much a life as death. It is true that, even in this life on earth, through the intercession of the saints we have many holy comforts and great remedies. Nevertheless, such favors are not always given to those who ask—lest such favors be mistaken for the real purpose of religion, which is felicity in that other life in which all our ills will be no more. What grace is meant to do is to help good people, not to escape their sufferings, but to bear them with a stout heart, with a fortitude that finds its strength in faith.[40]

It was clear to Augustine, as it was to all Christians, that the justice of God is not apparent in this world; good people have evil things happening to them, and bad people sometimes get benefits and live an easy life. Augustine says that in this life we can never make sense out of God's will. At the day of judgment, then it will make sense. But, even though God is just, nevertheless, only a few will be the recipients of God's grace, a grace they can never deserve. God shows mercy to some. We do not know which ones, or why. Nevertheless, God's supernatural grace must be acknowledged. If we are a recipient of undeserving grace, if we receive the reward of faith, what we have received is the final beatific vision of God. In heaven, we enjoy a vision of the peace of God, which only God can really know.

For, it was this same God who, in the beginning, created the universe and filled it with all those things that the eye can see and all those realities which the mind can know. Of all such creations the highest were the spirits to whom He gave the gift of intelligence and the power to behold God and to be filled with His beatitude. These He has linked by a common bond of love in a single society which we call the holy and heavenly City.[41]

What is heaven like? Here Augustine has a problem. He cannot describe it:

And now, with such help as the Lord will grant us, let us try to see what is to be the activity of the saints in those spiritual and immortal bodies in which their flesh is to be alive, not merely with a carnal but with a spiritual life. I speak of activity, although, perhaps, I should rather say calm or repose. To tell the truth, I have no real notion of what eternal life will be like, for the simple reason that I know of no sensible experience to which it can be related. Nor can I say that I have any mental conception of such an activity, for, at that height, what is intelligence or what can it do? In heaven, as St. Paul assures us, "the peace of God . . . surpasses all understanding." This much is sure. If the redeemed are to live in the peace of God, they are to live in a peace "which surpasses all understanding." . . . We ought therefore, to take the text to mean that neither men nor angels can understand, as God does, the peace of God by which God Himself is at peace.[42]

Will we be able to see God the way we see trees and rivers? Or is it some other sort of spiritual seeing? Augustine tries to answer this question:

> What, therefore, is possible and highly probable is that we shall be able to see the material bodies of the new heaven, the new earth, in such a way that, by means of our own bodies and of all the others which we shall see whenever our eyes are turned, we shall see God, and we shall see Him with the utmost clarity as being everywhere present and as regulating the whole universe, including material things. We shall see Him in a way different from the way in which His "invisible attributes" are now seen, "being understood by the things that are made," for "we see now through a mirror in an obscure manner" and only "in part," and we must rely more on the eyes of faith, whereby we believe, than on the eyes of the body, whereby we see the beauty of material universe.[43]

Augustine goes on to try to describe the way he imagines the glories of heaven:

> Who can measure the happiness of heaven, where no evil at all can touch us, no good will be out of reach; where life is to be one long laud extolling God, who will be all in all; where there will be no weariness to call for rest, no need to call for toil, no place for any energy but praise. . . .
>
> These movements of our bodies will be of such unimaginable beauty that I dare not say more than this: There will be such poise, such grace, such beauty as become a place where nothing unbecoming can be found. Whenever the spirit wills, there, in a flash, will the body be. Nor will the spirit ever will anything unbecoming either to itself or to the body.
>
> In heaven, all glory will be true glory, since no one could ever err in praising too little or too much. True honor will never be denied where due, never be given where undeserved, and, since none but the worthy are permitted there, no one will unworthily ambition glory. Perfect peace will reign, since nothing in ourselves or in any others could disturb that peace.[44]

Relying on revelation and faith, which are the foundation for his rational conclusions, St. Augustine has tried to give an accurate account of what he considers the only true religion. All human beings have inherited the original sin of Adam and Eve, and consequently we all deserve hell. God is completely just when he throws human beings into hell. Nothing we can do can earn us a place in heaven.

But it is not completely bleak. God gives grace to some, but not all. We should live right, but that does not give any guarantee that we will make it to heaven. But we can *hope* to make it there.

> Meanwhile, and always, the supreme good of the City of God is everlasting and perfect peace and not merely a continuing peace which individually mortal men enter upon and leave by birth and death, but one in which individuals immortally abide, no longer subject to any species of adversity. Nor will anyone deny that such a life must be most happy, or that this life [on earth], however blessed spiritually, physically, or economically, is, by comparison, most miserable.
>
> It is true, however, that a man who makes his life here below a means to that end which he ardently loves and confidently hopes for [i.e., hopes for res-

urrection in this glorious heavenly realm] can even now be reasonably called happy—though more in hope than in present happiness. Such present felicity apart from this hope is, to tell the truth, an illusory happiness and, in fact, a great wretchedness, since it makes no use of the true goods of the soul.[45]

PROBLEMS TO PONDER

These are questions that any thoughtful person should think about if he or she were considering adopting Augustine's analysis of morality. Perhaps Augustine can answer them. How would you answer them?

1. There are a number of standard objections to Augustine's attempts at a solution to the problem of theodicy. The problem of theodicy has been discussed and debated almost incessantly from the days of Augustine until the present time. Some of the objections to Augustine's analysis are briefly outlined here.

   Consider his belief that the original sin of Adam and Eve is the cause of all evil and is inherited by the descendants of the original parents. Even if we grant that this original sin is so horrendous, we can still ask: Why do animals suffer for the fallenness of human beings—why should animals suffer as a consequence of humans' rebellion against God? It is clearly unjust that animals suffer for the sin that belongs to humans alone. A world created by God, in which most animals (innocent of any wrongdoing) live a pitifully short life characterized by suffering, terror, and violent death—is this a fair and just God, is this the behavior of a *good* deity? What definition of "good" are we using now?

   Another objection to original sin: Why do the *children* of Adam and Eve suffer for the failure of the parent? How can this be considered perfect justice? Consider the human equivalent. We would and do condemn any king or emperor who not only killed an evildoer, but then turned around and punished and tortured his newborn children for the transgression of the parent. Such a ruler is condemned as a monster. Why do we exempt God from this condemnation? If God is responsible for this injustice, is it not implausible that God should be called a just God? Clearly we are using the word *good* in some sense that no one ever heard of before.

2. Augustine borrows the Neoplatonic solution to the problem of evil. He asserts that evil is a "privation" or absence of good, and thus evil does not exist. But does this solution really work? Consider one objection: If evil is an absence, a nothing, and does not exist, then there is nothing to avoid! One cannot battle against "nothing at all" and you don't conquer "nothing," you don't overcome "nothing at all."

   A second, more philosophical, objection is that one cannot make something unreal by agreeing to label it a "privation" or "absence." Consider: Can we make war nonexistent by declaring it merely the absence of peace? Can we make peace nonexistent by declaring it merely the absence of war? Whichever way we classify it, the one (war) is as real as the other (peace). Is someone who is paralyzed by an accident helped by considering his or her paralysis merely the absence of mobility? Can I argue that being paralyzed is a negative and not real? The *facts* of reality are not changed by our method of classifying those facts; facts are not less real because we have classified them as negative or positive.

Actually, it seems that for the Christian, there are many more evils in the world than for the atheist. For the non-Christian atheist, adultery is evil, and it causes pain and suffering to one's partner and it involves breaking a promise made to another. For the Christian, it is all of this plus more: it is an offense against God and the breaking of a sacrament. There isn't less evil in the world for the Christian—there is *more* evil. Thus, evil as a privation or absence does not work.

3. The free-will argument is complex and is a difficult argument to deal with briefly. Its apparent simplicity masks a large number of difficulties. For example, is it possible, is it within God's omnipotent power to have created a world where people are free and where people freely choose the morally right thing each time they make a choice? God created a world in which the great majority of humans choose the right thing about 98 percent of the time, so that is within God's power. Can God create humans so that they choose the right thing 100 percent of the time? In such a world, no moral evil would occur. If God could have created human beings who freely choose good more often than humans do, or even every time they make a choice, then God is still responsible for evil for not creating such a world!

   For the free-will argument to solve the problem of theodicy, it must be shown that it is *impossible* for an omnipotent God to have created a world of *free* human beings in which no more evil in fact occurs. If it is merely extremely difficult, then God is still to blame because he is omnipotent and is not limited by "extreme difficulty."

4. Why be moral? According to Augustine, if we are completely moral from birth to old age and death, we still deserve hell. Even if we have engaged in evil actions all our life, God might still grant us the gift of grace.

GLOSSARY

Atonement Atonement refers to the idea of payment for sin (in this case, the original sin of Adam and Eve), and as a result of paying for that sin, rendering a favorable reconciliation of human beings with their creator, God.

Incarnation Incarnation refers to the belief that God assumed a human body, in this case, the body of the Jewish carpenter named Jesus (Greek for the Hebrew name Joshua) who lived between 6–4 B.C.E. and 30 C.E.

Monotheism Monotheism is the belief in one divine being, a God who cares about human lives, who judges, rewards, and punishes humans; who answers prayers; and who performs miracles that violate the laws of nature.

Moral evils Moral evils refer to the pain, suffering, and death caused by human beings. We humans cause pain and death to one another. For example, we humans are responsible for war, rape, genocide, assault, and murder, and so on.

Natural evils Those things that happen in nature that cause pain, injury, and death to human beings are called natural evils. For example, earthquakes, floods, diseases, drought, plagues, volcanic eruptions, tidal waves, and so on.

Reconciliation The key to Christian salvation is through reconciliation. There is a gulf between God's perfectly divine realm and the human realm. God allows for the reconciliation of humans with their Creator. Humans can be reconciled with God, and the means of reconciliation is the blood shed at the death of Jesus.

Revelation Revelation refers to God *revealing* ultimate truths that go beyond what reason and senses tell us. According to Christian belief, revelation comes from an omnipotent and omniscient being, and, properly interpreted, it cannot be wrong.

Theism Theism is the position that there is a God (monotheism) or gods (polytheism) involved in the world, who interfere and interact with human life by performing miracles, who answer prayers, and who judge, reward, and punish human beings.

Theodicy Theodicy refers literally to the "justice of God." Specifically, if the universe is the result of mindless working of purely natural forces, then it is not surprising that there is so much undeserved pain and evil in the world. However, if the universe was created especially for us by a God who is omnipotent, omniscient, and all good, then it is surprising that there is *any* evil in the world—because one would expect that a perfectly good supernatural being, who created everything and who foresaw the results of that creation, would create a perfectly *good world*. How can we reconcile all of the undeserved suffering in the world with a God who is perfectly good and perfectly just?

Theology Theology is the study of the nature of the divine, or God. A *theologian* is someone who does theology. What can be said about God? For example, is God the creator of all that exists or could there be another creator? Who created God? Is the universe created out of the body of God, or was it created out of nothingness? Does God respond to prayers? Does God want us to be baptized? If so, why?

A GUIDE TO FURTHER READINGS

Babcock, William, ed. *The Ethics of St. Augustine* (Scholar's Press, 1991). A good collection of essays that analyze Augustine's ethics.

Burns, J. Patout. "Augustine on the Origin & Progress of Evil," in *Ethics of St. Augustine,* ed. William Babcock (Scholars Press, 1991). A good discussion of the problem of theodicy.

Charlesworth, James H., ed., *Jesus and the Dead Sea Scrolls* (New York: Anchor Doubleday, 1992) An excellent and well-balanced collection of essays on the discovery of the Dead Sea Scrolls and their implications for early Christianity.

Copleston, Frederick, S. J. *A History of Philosophy*, Book I, Vol. II (New York: Doubleday, 1985). The standard history of philosophy for students with a good treatment of Augustine.

Funk, Robert L., *Honest to Jesus* (San Francisco: Harper Collins, 1996) A excellent study of historical evidence concerning the formation of early Christianity.

Kirwan, Christopher. *Augustine* (London: Routledge, 1989). An overview of Augustine and his thought.

Markus, R. A. "Augustine," in D. J. O'Connor, *A Critical History of Western Philosophy* (New York: The Free Press, 1964). A good critical overview of Augustine's philosophy.

Marrou, H. I. *Augustine and His Influence Throughout the Ages* (New York: HarperCollins, 1954). The influence of Augustine upon later theologians.

Mack, Burton L.,*The Last Gospel: The Book of Q and Christian Origins* (San Francisco: Harper Collins, 1992) This book analyzes the earliest of all the Christian Gospels, referred to as the *Book of Q,* and examines the document's implications for Christianity during the first hundred years following the death of Jesus around 30 C.E.

Miller, Robert J., ed., *The Complete Gospels* (San Francisco: Harper Collins, 1994) An excellent translation of all existent early Christian documents. including over a dozen gospels. The four gospels that Christians know in their bibles were chosen from over fourteen by a group of bishops after the year 325 C.E..

O'Connell, Robert J. *St. Augustine's Platonism* (Augustinian Institute, 1984). A detailed analysis of the influence of Neo-Platonic philosophy upon the Christianity of Augustine.

St. Augustine: His Age, Life and Thought (Meredian Books, 1951). A good overview.

Warner, Rex. *The Confessions of St. Augustine* (New York: Mentor-Omega Books/New American Library, 1963). The autobiography of Augustine, written when he was a bishop.

CHAPTER 5

Thomas Aquinas:

Ethics Is Grounded in the Natural Law Implanted by God, As Interpreted by Aristotle

THE BACKGROUND OF MEDIEVAL CHRISTIAN PHILOSOPHY

The Middle Ages (which began with the end of Late Antiquity about 400 C.E. and ended around the year 1500) produced two towering intellectual figures who laid the groundwork for our rational interpretation of the basic claims of Christianity. The first was St. Augustine, who died in 430 C.E. In this chapter we discuss the other major Christian philosopher of the medieval period, St. Thomas Aquinas. As with all the other chapters in this book, we need to try to put ourselves into the frame of mind of the era, which in this case is the culture of a medieval thinker around the year 1200 C.E.

Let's start with a brief explanation of what happened in Europe during the period between 430 C.E. (death of Augustine) and 1225 C.E. (birth of Aquinas). As you already know, we find the gradual collapse of civilized conditions in western Europe, the period we call the Dark Ages.

During St. Augustine's lifetime (410 C.E.), the imperial city of Rome was defeated in battle and sacked by the barbarians, and later, with the Roman Empire divided, the city of Rome was no longer an administrative, political, or intellectual center. Frequent rebellions occurred in various parts of the decentralized empire, which made life difficult and precarious. During this period, Christianity became the dominant religion of Europe.

St. Augustine had argued, and later Christians believed, that God wanted all human beings to be Christians, so it was a duty of a good Christian to convert non-Christians. But, the non-Christians had philosophically sophisticated doctrines and arguments to support their religious positions and claims. Thus, it became essential that there was common agreement about the creeds of Christianity. Non-Christians asked questions, and explanations of Christian doctrines were required. These non-Christian European people were not stupid or ignorant; many were sophisticated with a deep understanding of logic and Greek philosophy, and so the Christian explanations needed to be systematic and all-encompassing. The

Christians required logical demonstrations to support their theological claims. Christian theology developed as a long process of providing Christian doctrines that could appeal to sophisticated non-Christian peoples.

As Europe sank into the Dark Ages, life was very difficult for more than a thousand years, and one of the attractions of Christianity was that it provided an explanation of why life was so difficult. Stressing human sinfulness and frailty, the Church claimed that God was punishing human beings because they failed to demonstrate the proper attitudes of dependence and humility. Instead of mistakenly relying on their own inadequate powers, human beings must seek help from a supernatural power. Humans must have faith, and faith was the only thing that God rewarded.

In this way, Christianity offered a spiritual refuge as Europe sank further and further into illiteracy, and the reliance on reason receded to be replaced by reliance on faith and revelation. Knowledge of astronomy was lost; knowledge of anatomy and surgery was forgotten (but not in the Islamic world, which did *not* enter the Dark Ages). Reliance on prayer and miraculous healing was stressed.

Secular teachers and secular doctors slowly disappeared and were replaced by priests who used chants, potions, horoscopes, and amulets. It was illegal to dissect a cadaver, so those who practiced medicine were prohibited from acquiring firsthand knowledge of the human body. No medical research was stressed or developed.

For many complex reasons, Christianity finally became the dominant force in western Europe, regulating the spiritual domain, and ultimately, also exercising political authority. Slowly over the centuries, Christianity organized itself into a militant church. For almost eight hundred years, Christianity in Europe was without any serious intellectual rival. All education was Christian, all universities were Christian with only clergy allowed to teach. The stress was on faith and memorization. Christian philosophy was that of Augustine. Even the Greek philosophy that was occasionally studied was by Plato and Neoplatonic philosophers (like Plotinus) interpreted as pre-Christian theology in the manner taught by St. Augustine.

The official Christian worldview had been in place for more than eight hundred years. It could not be questioned. Every good Christian had been taught that human beings are the creation of an omnipotent, omniscient, and omnibenevolent deity, who may be good but who is also wrathful, punishing, and who demands justice. God also created everything we call "reality" and created it for the benefit of human beings. Thus, we human beings live in the center of everything. This was not a philosophical view open to discussion.

This is what the Christian of the Middle Ages believed. The church taught that nature was inferior to human beings. Nature was transient, changing, full of decay, ephemeral, and not important, not worth investigating. The Christians agreed with Plato that the truths which most mattered were not in the world around us, which changed and decomposed, but in the realm of the divine, in the sky, where the stars circled in eternally perfect circles around the earth, wheeling in eternal perfection where we can see a part of the divine plan written in the light of the moon and stars above every night of our lives.

If a human being wanted inspiration, he or she could look to the past, where the giants had figured it all out—if you wanted to know something about the world, you looked to the writings of the ancient past.[1]

Just about a thousand years ago, about 225 years before Aquinas was born, was when the Christian tradition officially divided into two. The churches in the Latin-speaking western part of the Roman Empire, referred to as Roman Catholic churches, had become a strong, centralized organization headed by a pope (originally, he was merely the Bishop of Rome), and most of western Europe looked to Rome for leadership.

The churches in the Greek-speaking eastern part of the Roman Empire, called the Eastern Orthodox churches, were completely independently administrated; most of the churches of eastern and central Europe looked to Constantinople for spiritual authority.

The popes of Rome became the equals of kings, and in the period before the birth of Thomas Aquinas, the wars of the Crusades were initiated in the name of Christianity. Later, during the Crusades, it became even more important that all believers believed the same creeds and doctrines, because Christianity was certain that God rewarded those who believed the correct creeds and doctrines, and God punished those who believed incorrect doctrines. In fact, the Crusades indirectly brought about the intellectual rebirth of Europe, because as a result of the movement of Christian armies into Islamic strongholds of Spain, Portugal, and North Africa, much of the lost classical learning of the Greeks was recovered.

THE LIFE OF THOMAS AQUINAS (1225–1274)

Eight hundred years ago was the time of Genghis Khan, Prince of the Mongols; the time when King John signed the Magna Carta; the time of the beginning of the Crusades and the Inquisition; and the time Marco Polo traveled to China. It was also the time of Thomas Aquinas.

Thomas was born near Naples in 1225, three years before the Sixth Crusade, to a noble Italian family. His father was the Count of Aquino. The Aquino family was heavily influential in politics, and Thomas Aquinas was sent to be educated at a Benedictine monastery in order to further the family's political goals. The Benedictine monks taught basic religious knowledge, academic skills, and good study habits. As was common, the teachers placed special emphasis on carefully studying and memorizing Scripture. The Benedictine monasteries became very prosperous, and their wealth was obvious for everyone to see. However, perhaps because of this very prosperity, the order had begun to decline in importance in this period.

Young Thomas Aquinas was very bright and he was accepted by the University of Naples in 1239, when he was only fourteen. Historically, this was the time of the very beginnings of the institution of the university.[2]

At the Imperial University of Naples, where only members of the clergy could teach, he made friends with some Dominican monks. Unlike the Benedictine order, Dominicans took vows of poverty, chastity, and obedience. The Dominicans were dedicated to education and to preaching to the common people (not to serving the wealthy and not to accumulating power and property). They were also renowned as great debaters and often won the great theological debates that were an important part of the university life of this period of the Middle Ages. By the end of the 1200s, the Dominicans had become the intellectual elite in Italy.

So impressed was Thomas that at age nineteen he decided to join the priesthood and become a Dominican monk, study philosophy, and take vows of chastity and poverty. His family was aghast because as a Dominican he would not become a politically powerful priest or bishop (which would be of political value to the family), but instead would be an unimportant preacher to the poor people of Naples. His family tried to convince him to change his mind, but he would not be moved, and reluctantly, the family allowed him to leave and pursue the priesthood and the vocation of philosophy.

Thomas studied philosophy at the University of Paris under Albertus Magnus (Albert the Great, c. 1200–1280). Albert was unusual because he argued that secular learning could contribute to, rather than detract from, one's religious faith. Albert the Great argued that the theological difficulties that the Christian scholars were disagreeing about could be solved by a careful reading of the Greek philosophers. Albert profoundly affected Thomas Aquinas in many ways. Albert trained Thomas Aquinas, and Aquinas spent the rest of his life studying, writing, and teaching. Thomas was exceptionally brilliant and known for his sincerity, modesty, openness, and innocence. He is the author of two great texts: the *Summa Contra Gentiles* and *Summa Theologica* (which he did not finish). It seems that he had some sort of ecstatic mystical experience in 1273, and he put down his pen declaring that nothing he had written even came close to what he had just experienced—he stopped writing. A year later he died, at age fortynine. He was declared a saint by the Roman Catholic Church in 1323.[3]

AQUINAS'S PHILOSOPHY

The influence of St. Thomas Aquinas in philosophy and theology was greater than any other medieval philosopher—the only person who came close was St. Augustine.

As was mentioned before, Christian thought had been without any serious rival for many centuries; however, that was about to change. The armies of the Crusaders went to North Africa, Portugal, and Spain. Greek philosophy had been very important to the Arabs, and the Arabs had preserved much that had been lost in the Dark Ages of the Christian Europe. Because of the Crusades, Aristotle's philosophical writings had been just recently rediscovered (via Arabic translations in Spanish libraries that were then translated into Latin), and this caused a major transformation in Christian thinking. Aristotle's metaphysics and natural philosophy had been lost for a thousand years—now it was rediscovered and as Catholic scholars studied Aristotle, it caused a crisis in the Catholic Church.

The philosophy of Aristotle was a genuinely new set of ideas, which had three remarkable properties: (1) it was created 350 years prior to the beginning of Christianity, so Aristotle's ideas showed no influence of Christian presuppositions; (2) some key arguments of Aristotle produced conclusions that were in outright contradiction with important ideas in prevailing Christian theology; (3) to those Christians who read and really understood Aristotle, Aristotle's evidence and arguments were so strong that any rational human being would have to agree that Aristotle was right!

The contrast between Aristotle and Christianity is stark and clear. Consider the Christian worldview. The Christians believe that the universe was created by a loving personal God, who created human beings in his own image (humans are unique and totally unlike all other living things; nothing else in nature has that special quality of a soul). However, human beings have a broken relationship with that divine being. Human beings are fallen and corrupt creatures, finite and ignorant. Human beings are incapable of avoiding sin and punishment of hell through their own efforts. Only the undeserved grace and sacrifice of a loving God can save a human being.

The God of Christianity rewards faith, not reason. Salvation can only be attained with faith. Christianity accepts revelation that gives us certain knowledge that goes beyond what our senses tell us, and which must overrule our sensory knowledge. The rewards of faith are eternal life and perfect happiness. God does not reward expertise in science. There is no point in studying the world, and no point in attempting to discover the truth using reason and science. God never rewarded anyone with eternal life because he or she knew mathematics, or because that person understood the laws of nature. Instead, we must study church dogma, which explains what God chooses to reveal to us, and which we need to know for salvation.

Now consider the Greek classical worldview of Aristotle. The universe was *not* created by a loving, personal God (although an impersonal force was the first cause). Aristotle thought that human beings are the most important life-form, but they are not fundamentally different from other living things. The difference is their ability to reason. Human beings do possess *psyche,* or souls (the source of the rational and feeling parts of the self), but so too did every other living thing including cockroaches and elephants. Aristotle denied that souls were immortal. The soul died when the body died.

Aristotle valued philosophical and scientific contemplation as the ultimate key to the good life. Knowledge and logic are the keys to unlock the universe, thereby improving our lives in the process. One gains knowledge by observing and reasoning about the world. Thus, the goal of life and the good life for a human being is a product of reason, not faith. Knowing something to be true is obviously a more secure foundation than merely believing something to be true (because without knowledge, belief is so often mistaken). The dialogues of Aristotle and Plato propose a position and expect a critical response. Aristotle relied on human experience (not revelation) to support his conclusions and Aristotle (and the Greeks) insisted upon rationality as the basis for evaluating conclusions.

As you can see, these are not small differences. The differences between medieval Christianity and Aristotle were profound and went to the very heart of how to understand the world and the place of human beings within the world. Intelligent and well-educated Christians (most of them in the priesthood) felt a crisis between reason and blind faith. Church authorities did not respond by undertaking a systematic analysis of Aristotle and pointing out flaws in his reasoning; the church condemned Aristotle as heretical. It tried again and again to ban the study or reading of the philosophy of Aristotle and prohibited the reading and teaching of Aristotle in schools and universities (Aristotle was banned in 1210, 1215, 1245, 1263, and 1277). The crisis between reason and faith intensified. It was Thomas Aquinas who offered a solution to this crisis, a solution that involved a compromise between Aristotle's intellectual philosophy and Christian faith.

Faith versus Reason: The Great Compromise

This was the fundamental problem of the philosophy of the Middle Ages: what is the proper relationship between faith and reason, or, the relationship between the insights revealed to humans by the grace of God, and the insights that human beings might achieve for themselves using observation and logic?

Aquinas provided a solution to the problem of faith versus reason: the **Great Compromise** between philosophy and religion made it possible for the coexistence of Christian revelation and dogma, and the rational conclusions of Aristotle and Neoplatonism. Aquinas offers a unique Christian reinterpretation of Aristotle's ethics, combining Aristotle with Plato, Augustine, and St. Paul.

Thomas Aquinas's Great Compromise was a brilliantly simple solution to the problem. Aristotle could be "properly interpreted" and when done so, the majority of his conclusions would not be contrary to faith.

What is "properly interpreted"? Just this: Accept Aristotle's reasoning and conclusions unless they come into clear conflict with the dogmas of the church. Where Aristotle and church dogma contradict one another, Aquinas either modifies Aristotle or rejects Aristotle.

Aquinas's Great Compromise came to have the effect of a turning point in medieval philosophy: faith and reason no longer needed to be seen as inevitable enemies. They could work together.

Philosophy and theology are not the same. Philosophy, the "love of wisdom," begins with observation of nature and human behavior, and questions all claims, asking whether logic and empirical evidence support the claims. Theology, the "study of the nature of God," begins with the unquestioning acceptance of the sacred principles that revelation provides and assumes all revealed religious claims are true. The compromise is to recognize that theology can and must use reason to develop these sacred revealed principles, to interpret them and turn them into a clear and comprehensible body of knowledge.

Theology begins knowing the truth. Theology begins with sacred principles that are provided by revelation, which cannot be mistaken and which cannot be doubted or questioned (although they may need interpretation). On the other hand, philosophy begins with observation and we reason about what we observe. Philosophy questions the conclusions we draw about what we observe, and it asks whether we have made errors in our reasoning to arrive at our conclusions.

But Aquinas argues that both theology and philosophy use reason to develop their different subject matter into a clear and comprehensible body of knowledge. Theology uses reason to clarify doctrine, but reason is not used to prove faith (because a faith proven would become knowledge and not faith). Philosophy would use reason to establish empirical truths about the world that are not revealed in scripture.

Aquinas thought that there were some religious claims that we could know were true using philosophical reasoning; for example, Aquinas argues that both theology and philosophy will lead us to the truth of the existence of a divine being, God. Someone thinking philosophically and rationally will conclude that there must exist a divine creator, the God of Christianity. Aquinas believes that he can prove that God exists using reason. Here, Aquinas is constructing what we could call a "natural theology," that is, thinking about God based on observing nature and thinking about it rationally. Aquinas thinks it is possible to move from nature to conclude that God exists. Aquinas as a believer is content with faith when it comes to the existence of God, but the philosopher in him is obliged to present rational and empirical evidence for that belief.

The Cosmological Argument for the Existence of God

Aquinas thought that it was essential that we can reason our way to the existence of God. That is the foundation of everything he was trying to accomplish. Aquinas believed that an earlier theologian, St. Anselm, had already proven that God must exist, based simply on a definition of God as "That Being Than Which None Greater Can Be Conceived." But Anselm's argument was based on definition and pure logic and was hard to follow. Aquinas thought the human intellect is too weak to grasp nature-transcending truths, so Anselm's argument needed to be supplemented by other truths derived from God's effects in the world. This is Aquinas's natural theology, based on observing God's effects in the world.

The argument that Aquinas provided is often called the **cosmological argument:** God is the first cause of the cosmos (all that exists) and God is the unmoved mover who starts everything moving. Aquinas begins his argument with some effect that we are all familiar with, such as movement or growth. Then he tries to show that the only possible explanation for this effect is God.

> The first and most obvious way [of proving that God exists] is based on change. For certainly some things are changing: this we plainly see. Now anything changing is being changed by something else. (This is so because what makes things changeable is unrealized potentiality, but what makes them cause change is their already realized state: causing change brings into being what was previously only able to be, and can only be done by something which already is. . .). Again, this something else, if itself changing, must be being changed by yet another thing; and this last by another. But this can't go on for ever, since then there would be no first cause of the change, and as a result, no subsequent causes. . . . So we are forced eventually to come to a first cause of change not itself being changed by anything, and this is what everyone understands by God.[4]

Aquinas reprises the same form of the argument, but this time focuses on causation:

> In the observable world causes are found ordered in series; we never observe, nor ever could, something causing itself, for this would mean it preceded itself, and this is not possible. . . . But if a series of causes goes on for ever it will have no first cause, and so no intermediate causes and no last effect, which is clearly false. So we are forced to postulate some first agent cause, to which everyone gives the name *God*.[5]

This argument was originally inspired by one found in Aristotle's writings. Just like Aristotle, Aquinas concludes that there must be an "Unmoved Mover" who sets all other things into motion, or an "Uncaused First Cause" that sets all other causal chains into being.

Aquinas believes that he has shown that a divine creator must exist. The next step is to consider what sort of properties this divinity has, and how human beings are related to the unmoved first mover, or uncaused first cause. To say that God created everything, Aquinas says God "bestows being on all that exists." When we create things, we do so to fulfill our own goals or purposes, and we are in charge because we created these objects. So, too, God must direct human beings toward a goal or purpose. Aquinas writes, "Hence it follows that He is the Lord of the things made by Him, since we are masters over those things that are subject to our will."

> We have shown in the preceding books that there is one First Being, possessing the full perfection of all being, Whom we call God, and Who, of the abundance of His Perfection, bestows being on all that exists, so that He is proved to be not only the first of beings, but also the beginning of all. Moreover He bestows being on others, not through natural necessity, but according to the decree of His will. . . . Hence it follows that He is the Lord of the things made by Him, for in making them He needs neither the help of an extrinsic agent, nor matter as the foundation of His work. For He is the universal efficient cause of all being.[6]

So Aquinas has established that God is the ruler over all. What about God's creations? Some of God's creations are intelligent (remember that intelligence is one faculty of the soul according to the Greeks), and so bear a resemblance to God and "reflect His image":

> . . . God is perfect in ruling [all that He has created]. The effect of this ruling is
> seen to differ in different things, according to the difference of natures. For some
> things are so produced by God that, being intelligent, they bear a resemblance
> to Him and reflect His image. Hence, not only are they directed, but they direct
> themselves to their appointed end by their own actions [using free will]. And if
> in this directing themselves they be subject to the divine ruling, they are admit-
> ted by that divine ruling to the attainment of their last end; but they are ex-
> cluded therefrom if they direct themselves otherwise.[7]

Unlike the Greek philosophers, Christians (and Aquinas) did not think that
all creatures possessed souls. Only human beings had been gifted with a divine
soul, and one of God's gifts to human beings is free will. Aquinas argues that if
we direct ourselves in accordance with God's divine directives, God is pleased
and pushes us toward our ultimate end. If we use our free will to direct ourselves in some other direction than the direction that God directs, then God ex-
cludes us from his divine ultimate goal.

Aquinas considers the same question that Aristotle did. Why do we do anything at all? He answers: we do things in order to accomplish goals. We must
have some purpose, some end in mind when we act. Human actions are directed
toward ends, but most of our goals are really just intermediate *means* or tools to
help us achieve higher, more important ends (as getting a good grade in a class
is really just a tool to help us achieve a college degree or attain a stimulating job).

> We must first show that every agent, by its actions, intends an end.
>   For in those things which clearly act for an end, we declare the end to be
> that towards which the movement of the agent tends; for when this is teached,
> the end is said to be reached, and to fail in this is to fail in the end intended. . . .
> It follows therefore that every agent intends an end while acting, which end is
> sometimes the action itself, sometimes a thing made by the action.[8]

Does this hierarchy of ends just continue on forever, or does it end somewhere? Aquinas agrees with Aristotle: there must be a final end toward which
all the lower ends are directed.

> But in the action of every agent, a point can be reached beyond which the agent
> does not desire to go; or else actions would tend to infinity, which is impossible,
> for since *it is impossible to pass through an infinite medium,* the agent would never
> begin to act, because nothing moves toward what it cannot reach. Therefore
> every agent acts for an end.[9]

Actions must stop somewhere; we cannot have our actions going on forever,
because Aquinas argues that no intelligent or rational creature would move toward what it cannot reach. If the final goal is infinitely far away, then we would
not pursue any goals at all. We would never move. Thus, every agent acts for an
end, and that end must be achievable. Aquinas is certain that every agent acts
for some good, and that good is happiness.

> For that every agent acts for an end clearly follows from the fact that every
> agent tends to something definite. Now that to which an agent tends definitely
> must needs be befitting to that agent, since the agent would not tend to it save

because of some fittingness thereto. But that which is benefitting to a thing is good for it. Therefore every agent acts for a good.[10]

This could have been written by Aristotle. However, Aquinas builds another layer on top of the structure left by Aristotle. Aquinas argues that Aristotle did *not* have all the information available to him when he worked out his philosophy. Aristotle's ethics is incomplete.

Humans Have Two Sources of Knowledge

Why is it incomplete? Aristotle's careful analysis of ethics describes what we can know using human reason, using careful thinking, using our "natural powers," but it ignores the truths that we can know only from revelation. This is the Great Compromise of Aquinas, mentioned earlier. He argues that Aristotle's theory needs to be enriched by Christian revelation to complete it. It was impossible for Aristotle to know any of the ultimate truths that have been revealed to Christians by God. Aristotle lived almost 350 years before Jesus began preaching, and perhaps 400 years before the earliest of the various books of the New Testament began to appear, and almost 700 years before the Christian church decided which books of the Bible were canonical and which were to be discarded as heretical (determined during the Council of Nicea in 325 C.E.).

Aquinas reasons that human beings of his era have *two* sources of knowledge, not just one. Aristotle was limited to natural sources of knowledge. Christianity has access to a supernatural source of knowledge, which will be more certain, more "absolute." This second source is God's revelation and is the heart of Aquinas's Great Compromise, which attempts to bring about a harmony between the tension of faith and reason.

> It is clear that all things are directed to one good as their last end.
>
> For, if nothing tends to something as its end, except insofar as this is good, it follows that good, as such, is an end. Consequently that which is the supreme good is supremely the end of all. Now there is but one supreme good, namely God. . . . Therefore all things are directed to the highest good, namely God, as their end.[11]

The Highest Good According to Aquinas

Aristotle concluded that the final end or goal of all action is happiness in this life, and the highest happiness in this life comes from contemplation of the first principles of things. This is wisdom, which is the key to the good life. However, Aquinas now adds something to Aristotle's structure. Every good Christian knows that there is a good even higher than the one Aristotle conceived of—a Supreme Good, and it is *God*; thus, God is that end toward which all things are directed.

Aquinas needs to show that Aristotle's concept of natural happiness is not an adequate explanation of the highest possible happiness. We cannot attain Aristotle's goal of happiness because the highest wisdom goes beyond our natural life.

> Now it is not possible that man's ultimate happiness consist in contemplation based on the understanding of first principles, for this is most imperfect, as being most universal, containing potentially the knowledge of things. Moreover, it is the beginning and not the end of human inquiry, and comes to us from nature, and not through the pursuit of the truth. Nor does it consist in contemplation based on the sciences that have the lowest things for their object, since happiness must consist in an operation of the intellect in relation to the most noble intelligible objects. It follows then that man's ultimate happiness consists in wisdom, based on the consideration of divine things.[12]

Aquinas concludes that the highest wisdom results from contemplation on divine things. Therefore, the previous arguments prove that there is an ultimate happiness, higher than Aristotle's concept of natural happiness, which results from contemplation of God. Note that Aquinas is *not* telling us what he *believes;* he has provided arguments for his conclusions using reason.

> It is therefore evident also by way of induction that man's ultimate happiness consists solely in the contemplation of God, which conclusion was proved above by arguments.[13]

Thus, Aquinas has added something to the basic structure of Aristotle: the ultimate is happiness, but not human happiness based on contemplation of this life or the first principles of nature; instead it is divine happiness, the beatific vision of God.

THOMAS AQUINAS'S ETHICS

The basic insight of Aquinas's ethical theory is simple: God created everything including laws of nature and laws of morality. This is the focus of all his ethical writings. Aquinas had no interest in writing to entertain the reader. The subject of salvation was too important for that. Instead, he wrote in a very careful, dry, and serious style using logic and analysis of arguments to support his conclusions. He wanted to produce a systematic statement and logical defense of Christian beliefs. It is important to realize that Aquinas is *not* merely sharing his beliefs with us; he is arguing for a conclusion using reason. If he has argued soundly, as rational human beings we must agree with his conclusions.

The Eternal Law

If God created everything, then God created laws of nature and laws of morality. Human beings have the ability to obey God's divine laws. Aquinas begins by quoting Augustine:

> Augustine says: *That Law which is the Supreme Reason cannot be understood to be otherwise than unchangeable and eternal.* . . . [This sort of Law] is nothing else but a dictate of practical reason eminating from the ruler who governs a perfect community.[14]

All the laws of nature (guiding all creatures, animate and inanimate) and all the laws of morality (and of society) are to be considered as particular cases of one single divine law, which Aquinas calls the **eternal law.** Because God is intelligent, God must have a plan in creating the world, and according to this plan, he directs all things to the ends or purposes he has given them. The eternal law is the divine plan of the universe, and it also directs the totality of creation. The eternal law is the fundamental law underlying the whole order of the universe. It was the plan in the mind of God, so it is prior to the universe. The eternal law is coeternal with God. The plan in the mind of God, then, carried out by the decree of God's will, we call the eternal law.

For Aquinas, the eternal law includes everything spiritual as well as physical, including the laws of physical nature and the action of physical causes, as well as human actions and human moral laws.

God is the creator, and a creator does not bring things into existence capriciously; the creative act is a rational act, deliberate and purposeful. If God has willed the universe to come into existence, then God has reasons, and God cannot be indifferent to whether his creatures carry out his plan. God must wish that creatures carry out his plan as he intends it.

Human beings have the ability to follow God's guiding principles, but they also have the ability *not* to follow God's guidance (humans have free will because God gave them a soul). Human beings are unique in this regard; nonhuman living things simply follow God's plan and they cannot deviate from it because they do not have free will; they merely have instincts.

Aquinas reasons that laws have two functions: as rules of behavior, telling you to *do* this and not to do that, and also as measures of behavior (we judge you based on how you behave, how well you follow the law).

> Law, being a rule and measure, can be in a person in two ways: in one way, as in him that rules and measures; in another way, as in that which is ruled and measured, since a thing is ruled and measured insofar as it partakes of the rule or measure. Therefore, since all things subject to divine providence are ruled and measured by the eternal law, as was stated above, it is evident that all things partake in some way in the eternal law, insofar as, namely, from its being imprinted on them, they derive their respective inclinations to their proper acts and ends.[15]

We are all subject to God's divine providence, and God both rules us and measures us according to God's eternal laws. Therefore, human beings have to be related to God's eternal laws somehow. Aquinas says we "partake" (participate, have a share in) in some way in the eternal law.

> Now, among all others, the rational creature is subject to divine providence in a more excellent way, insofar as it itself partakes of a share of providence, by being provident both for itself and for others. Therefore it has a share of the eternal reason, whereby it has a natural inclination to its proper act and end; and this participation of the eternal law in the rational creature is called the natural law.[16]

God inculcates laws within us; so we have inclinations to our proper acts and ends and this inclination is provided by God's divine law. Creatures who do not have free will are completely subject to God's eternal law, because they possess inward principles of action by which they necessarily act to attain definite ends in accord with the law, but these creatures do not recognize the law or recognize that it originated with God.

Human beings, on the other hand, are conscious of the eternal law and accept it voluntarily. Humans have natural inclinations and tendencies to act and react in certain ways. God "imprints" his guiding principle or law, the way a human ruler will "print" his laws on paper and make it known to his or her subjects. And in acknowledging this natural inclination imprinted on our souls, we are participating in God's eternal law, insofar as we can comprehend it. The eternal law is just God's plan for rationally ordered movements and actions in the created universe. As God's master plan, all other laws or rules must be derived from this law. This is revealed to us through God's grace.

Natural Law

The eternal law, as it is understandable to creatures, is natural law. **Natural law** is God's timeless eternal law, as it is seen to have an effect on creatures who are trapped in time. But natural law is also to be seen as a guide, imprinted on our souls by God, to direct us to our final end, the perfect and eternal happiness that comes from the presence of the divinity itself. We know this through our own intellects, a faculty of our souls. The part of the natural law that governs nonhumans is the natural physical law, because it physically necessitates the way things behave; it is the law of nature. The part of the natural law that governs rational creatures is the natural moral law.

No human being is born knowing anything about God's eternal law. Human beings use their powers of reason to understand patterns and laws of nature; therefore, knowledge of natural law comes before any understanding of eternal law. We must reason our way to the existence of the eternal law based on our knowledge of the natural law. First we discover natural law, which is found controlling and governing everything in nature. We realize that this must have been caused by God who has produced the natural world and human nature as well. So, although the eternal law is ontologically prior to the natural law, human beings first know and recognize natural law. No creatures can ever directly know God's eternal law, since we are created intellects, and God's plan is incommunicable because it reflects God's divine wisdom.

Thus, Aquinas has added onto Aristotle's theory of natural law; he has added eternal law and modified Aristotle's natural law by arguing that it must be grounded in God's eternal law.

Aquinas is going to use his understanding of natural laws to generate the moral rules that humans ought to use to guide our lives. Remember that natural law directs human beings to perfect happiness, so these moral rules must be God's mechanism to guide us to achieve God's purpose, perfect eternal happiness.

The Content of the Natural Law Is the Basis for Christian Morality

Having determined that God has imprinted a natural law on the souls of human beings, we can ask: what is the *content* of the natural law? To answer this question, Aquinas discusses (1) first indemonstrable principles, (2) the natural inclinations found in all things, and in all living things, and uniquely in humans, and (3) natural laws based on these natural inclinations.

Aquinas begins with "first indemonstrable principles." These are like the very first presuppositions we must start with to build the structure of geometry. All of the geometric theorems can be discovered with just five or six fundamental statements, which themselves are not provable, but using these, you can prove all of the theorems of geometry.[17]

Like geometric theorems, Aquinas argues that there are several first indemonstrable principles that will generate several precepts of the natural law. There must be some truths that cannot be proven, yet those propositions provide our starting place and allow us to get to conclusions. Aquinas claims that these indemonstrable principles are self-evident truths, evident to anyone who knows the meaning of the terms. We *apprehend* these self-evident truths.

The first thing that human beings apprehend *absolutely* and theoretically is *being* or *existence*, which simply amounts to the fact that things exist. Whatever exists cannot at the same time not exist. From that we have the first indemonstrable principle, that is, the same thing cannot be affirmed and denied at the same time. A thing cannot both *be* and *not-be* at the same time.

The first thing that human beings apprehend *practically* (or what Aquinas calls "practical reason," or our ability to get along in the universe) is that human beings all naturally act for the good, seeking the good. This rule we have already seen, as it was argued by Aristotle: *the Good is that which all things seek after.*

The First Principle of the Natural Law

From Aristotle's principle that the good is that which all desire and seek, Aquinas can generate the **first principle of the natural law:** *good is to be done and promoted, and evil is to be avoided.* The natural law found more or less expressed in all rational creatures is: Do good and avoid evil.

> Hence this is the first precept of law, that good is to be done and promoted, and evil is to be avoided. All other precepts of the natural law are based upon this; so that all the things which the practical reason naturally apprehends as man's good belong to the precepts of the natural law under the form of things to be done or avoided.[18]

Aquinas argues that this belongs to our specific nature, for all people are conscious that good must be done and evil must be avoided. The proof of this is that human beings are attracted by the good and repelled by evil. The first precept of the natural law is clear to us and obvious. This is self-evident, and the other moral principles are derived from this. This is the foundation, the origin, the fixed point that we base our reasoning upon. The human intellect accepts this as obviously true.

Human inclinations are the foundation for all natural laws; human beings have goals or ends that they want to attain. As soon as human beings become conscious of the appetites or inclinations that they possess, they know that the fulfillment of these is good.

The order of satisfaction may be a complicated problem, because we have a complex nature in which there are countless appetites seeking satisfaction. It is not always easy to determine which appetites should be satisfied and which should not. A problem for Aquinas to consider is this: Why should any natural appetite *not* be satisfied? They are all based on natural inclinations provided by God.

Aquinas's answer is that we must study human nature and its hierarchy of appetites, and such a study will result in a more detailed knowledge of the precepts of the natural law. Aquinas argues that things to which humans naturally incline are naturally called "good" [because those are what we call the ends or goals]; meanwhile, all things to which humans naturally avoid are naturally called "evil." Thus natural law as apprehended by human beings is based on natural inclinations.

> Now as *being* is the first thing that falls under the apprehension absolutely, so *good* is the first thing that falls under the apprehension of the practical reason, which is directed to action (since every agent acts for an end, which has the nature of good). Consequently, the first principle in the practical reason is one founded on the nature of good, viz. that *good is that which all things seek after.* Hence this is the first precept of law, that *good is to be done and promoted,* and evil is to be avoided. All other precepts of the natural law are based upon this; so that all the things which the practical reason naturally apprehends as man's good belong to the precepts of the natural law under the form of things to be done or avoided.[19]

What is good must conform to human nature because things we call "good" are just those things toward which we naturally incline. God must have given us an ability to know what we must do and what we must avoid to obtain perfect happiness. It only makes sense that we would do what is in harmony with our nature; but in addition, we must also avoid what is not in harmony with our natural inclinations.

Morality Is Based on Human Natural Inclinations

Aquinas finds the *first inclination:* Every substance endures, continues in its own existence (Aquinas says "seeks" to preserve its own existence, using Aristotle's teleological language), and human beings share this in common with all substances (whether alive or not). It follows that whatever tends to preserve a substance's continued existence (i.e., in our case, human life), or whatever tends to ward off the obstacles to preserving existence, belongs to natural law.

From this it follows that natural laws will be concerned with preserving human life. This natural law is one that we have in common with all things, whether living or not: everything seeks to preserve its own existence. It is pretty obvious to you that your own continued existence is a good thing; consequently, we must recognize that human beings naturally seek to preserve their own existences. Aquinas concludes that preserving human life is a natural inclination and so must belong to natural law. Hence, a principle of the natural law is: Seek the things necessary for the preservation of life; avoid those that destroy life; preserve life; do not destroy life.

> Since, however, good has the nature of an end, and evil, the nature of the contrary, hence it is that all those things to which man has a natural inclination are naturally apprehended by reason as being good, and consequently as objects of pursuit, and their contraries as evil, and objects of avoidance. Therefore, the order of the precepts of the natural law is according to the order of natural inclinations. For there is in man, first of all, an inclination to good in accordance with the nature which he has in common with all substances, inasmuch, namely, as every substance seeks the preservation of its own being, according to its nature; and by reason of this inclination, whatever is a means of preserving human life, and of warding off its obstacles, belongs to the natural law.[20]

Having established the first inclination, Aquinas moves on to the *second inclination,* which is still an inclination that humans share with living things in general. Unlike the first inclination, the second inclinations are unique to living things; we do not share them in common with nonliving things.

> Secondly, there is in man an inclination to things that pertain to him more specifically, according to that nature which he has in common with other animals; and in virtue of this inclination, those things are said to belong to the natural law *which nature has taught to all animals,* such as sexual intercourse, the education of offspring, and so forth.[21]

In other words, we all have natural appetites for food, for sexual relations, and for the care of our offspring—hence, because these are natural inclinations, it is obvious that these are also good. All animals follow these natural inclinations blindly; they cannot help it, because they cannot *choose,* they have no free will. We can see God's plan in their instinctual behavior. Natural law will of course be concerned with these things as well, in accordance with the more general rule that "good is to be promoted and evil to be avoided." Because we have a strong inclination to the procreation and education of offspring, another principle of the natural law is: Foster offspring; unite with the opposite sex in a union of love; avoid anything that would be contrary to the natural use of this power of procreation.

Next, there is an inclination that is a natural law unique to humans: an inclination to know the Good, thus an inclination to know God, and a natural inclination to live in society.

> Thirdly, there is in man an inclination to good according to the nature of his reason, which nature is proper to him. Thus man has a natural inclination to know the truth about God, and to live in society; and in this respect, whatever pertains to this inclination belongs to the natural law: e.g., to shun ignorance, to avoid offending those among whom one has to live, and other such things regarding the above inclination.[22]

Aquinas finds other natural inclinations. We have a natural inclination to communicate with God, and hence another principle of the natural law is: Reverence the Supreme Being.

We have other natural, social inclinations as well. Not only is it self-evident that good is to be promoted and evil avoided, but no person can fail to recognize that food is good, that society is good, because by nature human beings are moved toward food, and toward society. We have a natural appetite for food, and thus the fulfillment of that appetite is good. Similarly, we have a natural appetite for being in the friendly company of others, and thus the fulfillment of that appetite is good, when pursued reasonably giving each appetite the appropriate fulfillment. Thus, we have "commonsense" obligations to avoid offending those among whom one has to live. From these we can find other principles of natural law, such as seeking good for one's fellow human beings; avoiding injuring others and doing good for them; use reason appropriately and shun ignorance. Of course, we can also find: do unto others as you would have others do to you.

Aquinas finds other logical consequences that follow from natural inclinations. If preserving life is a good, then we must prohibit suicide, mercy killing, and even dueling. If God gives us a natural inclination to unite with a member of the opposite sex to produce children, then we must also prohibit divorce, polygamy, and polyandry. If God gives us sex in order to produce offspring, then we must prohibit all forms of contraception and same-sex encounters.

Using natural inclinations and reason, Thomas Aquinas has virtually constructed a rational moral system for Christianity, providing reasons for all those things that we are to do, and those things that we are to avoid.

Note carefully that Aquinas is *not* finding these moral injunctions in Scripture, in revelation, or in the commands of God—these are based on natural inclinations found in all human beings. Yet a moral system based on natural inclinations turns out to be identical with the moral system that Christians had been following for many centuries before the time of Aquinas. In the past, Christians knew that some things were moral and others immoral. Now, thanks to Aquinas's analysis, Christians know why these things are moral.

Free Will, Voluntary Actions, and Responsibility

Another area in which Aquinas built on the basic foundation laid by Aristotle is in Aquinas's analysis of what makes an action a voluntary action. This is relevant for law, and also relevant for free will, because it helps us to understand when we are responsible for our choices, and when we are not responsible. Aristotle analyzed voluntary actions, and Aquinas pursues and builds on the distinction.

Aquinas analyzes the nature of a voluntary action, and then asks under what conditions is one responsible for his or her voluntary actions. When I am overcome with desire or anger or fear, am I responsible? When I am ignorant of important facts, am I responsible?

Thus, Aquinas begins by asking, what makes an action voluntary? He replies: A voluntary action is one that is chosen by the will. This is a necessary condition, but it is not sufficient to make the action voluntary.

In Aquinas's time, the courts recognized as a defense that defendants did what they did because they were overcome by fear (thus not responsible), or overcome by desire (and thus even rape could be excused).

Clearly, some actions originate from outside ourselves (we are coerced or forced to do something), and other actions originate from within (one's own desires, wishes, etc.). Aquinas deals with the question: If we are overcome by our own lust/desire, doesn't that mean that our act was *not* voluntary, and thus we are *not* responsible for our action? Aquinas says that a voluntary action is not merely chosen by the will. To be genuinely voluntary, the action must also include a knowledge of the goal, purpose, or end for the obtaining of which the will acts. If we choose to do something, it seems as though we must have an end or "good" in mind, and thus "some knowledge of the end is necessary" in order that the act be voluntary.

> Now, in order that a thing be done for an end, some knowledge of the end is necessary. Therefore, whatever so acts or is so moved by an intrinsic principle that it has some knowledge of the end, has within itself the principle of its act, so that it not only acts, but acts for an end. On the other hand, if a thing has no knowledge of the end, even though it have an intrinsic principle of action or movement, nevertheless, the principle of acting or being moved for an end is not in that thing, but in something else, by which the principle of its action towards an end is imprinted on it. Therefore such things are not said to move themselves, but to be moved by others. But those things which have a knowledge of the end are said to move themselves because there is in them a principle by which they not only act but also act for an end. And, consequently, since both are from an intrinsic principle, i.e., that they act and that they act for an end, the movements and acts of such things are said to be voluntary; for the term *voluntary* signifies that their movements and acts are from their own inclination.
>
> Things done through fear and compulsion differ . . . in this, that the will does not consent, but is moved entirely counter to that which is done through compulsion; whereas what is done through fear becomes voluntary because the will is moved towards it, although not for its own sake, but because of something else, that is, in order to avoid an evil which is feared. For the conditions of a voluntary act are satisfied, if it be done because of something else voluntary; since the voluntary is not only what we will for its own sake as an end, but also what we will for the sake of something else as an end. It is clear therefore that in what is done from compulsion, the will does nothing inwardly, whereas in what is done through fear, the will does something.[23]

Although courts had ruled that someone "mad with desire," or acting from concupiscence (lust), could be excused for their behavior, Aquinas disagrees. Even if one is overcome with lust, the actions are still voluntary.

> Concupiscence does not cause involuntariness, but, on the contrary, makes something to be voluntary. For a thing is said to be voluntary from the fact that the will is moved to it. Now concupiscence inclines the will to desire the object of concupiscence. Therefore the effect of concupiscence is to make something to be voluntary rather than involuntary.
>
> Fear has reference to evil, but concupiscence has reference to good. Now evil of itself is counter to the will, whereas good harmonies with the will. Therefore fear has a greater tendency than concupiscence to cause involuntariness.

> He who acts from fear retains the repugnance of the will to that which he
> does, considered in itself. But he that acts from concupiscence, e.g., an inconti-
> nent man, does not retain his former will whereby he repudiated the object of
> his concupiscence; rather his will is changed so that he desires that which pre-
> viously he repudiated. Accordingly, that which is done out of fear is involun-
> tary, to a certain extent, but that which is done from concupiscence is in no way
> involuntary. For the man who yields to concupiscence acts counter to that which
> he purposed at first, but not counter to that which he desires now; whereas the
> timid man acts counter to that which in itself he desires now.[24]

Aquinas next considers this argument: A person who has been genuinely
driven "mad from desire," and raped a woman as a consequence of his mad desire, is not responsible, because at least for a time, the person is *mad*, or insane,
and so the person's behavior should be considered involuntary, thus he should
be excused by the courts.

> If concupiscence were to destroy knowledge altogether, as happens with those
> whom concupiscence has rendered mad, it would follow that concupiscence
> would take away voluntariness. And yet, properly speaking, it would not make
> the act involuntary, because in beings bereft of reason there is neither voluntary
> nor involuntary.[25]

In other words, if you have gone genuinely "mad from desire," and if you
are really insane, then your act is neither voluntary nor involuntary. If you are
really "bereft of reason," then the distinction does not apply to you. Nevertheless, if you are not insane, then knowledge is still present, and you still have the
power to will the act, or not will the act—for the will can resist passion.

Another issue is relevant to voluntary, or free, actions. To what extent can individuals avoid responsibility for their behavior if they are ignorant? Is ignorance
of the law (whether human law or God's law) a legitimate excusing condition?

Aquinas finds this way of wording the question too simplistic, making a
complex issue into an overly simplified one, and overlooking several different
cases that might fall under the heading of "ignorance"; that is, **concomitant,
consequent,** and **antecedent ignorance.**

> Accordingly, we must take note that ignorance has a three-fold relationship to
> the act of the will: in one way, *concomitantly;* in another, *consequently;* in a third
> way, *antecedently.*[26]

According to Aquinas, if your ignorance is "concomitant with the act of
will," this means that your ignorance occurs simultaneously with the act of will.
If your ignorance is "consequent to the act of will," this means that your ignorance is after the act of will. Finally, if your ignorance is "antecedent to the act of
will," this means that it occurs before you willed your behavior. Aquinas goes
on to explain these distinctions:

> *Concomitantly,* when there is ignorance of what is done, but so that even if it
> were known, it would be done. For then ignorance does not induce one to will
> this to be done, but it just happens that a thing is at the same time done and not
> known. Thus, . . . a man did indeed will to kill his foe, but killed him in ignorance,

thinking to kill a stag. And ignorance of this kind, as the philosopher [Aristotle] states, does not cause involuntariness, since it is not the cause of anything that is repugnant to the will; but it causes *nonvoluntariness*, since that which is unknown cannot be actually willed.[27]

In other words, ignorance is "concomitant with the act of will" when you might be ignorant but wouldn't change your behavior even if you knew the facts (thus what happens is something that you would have wanted to happen if you'd known). Aquinas's analysis is that this is neither voluntary nor involuntary (coerced) but just nonvoluntary. Your ignorance accompanies the performance of a moral action, but the ignorance is *not* the cause of the action. You would have chosen to perform that action if your ignorance were replaced by knowledge. Consider Aquinas's example: you want to kill someone you call an enemy, and while out hunting you see what appears to be a stag in the bushes. You shoot at it, kill it, and then ride into the forest only to discover the body of your enemy lying dead. Did you intend to kill your enemy? No. You didn't even know your enemy was anywhere nearby. Based on this, Aquinas concludes that you are *not* responsible, because "that which is unknown cannot be actually willed."

> Ignorance is *consequent* to the act of the will, insofar as ignorance itself is voluntary; and this happens in two ways in accordance with the two aforesaid modes of the voluntary. First, because the act of the will is brought to bear on the ignorance, as when a man wills not to know, that he may have an excuse for sin, or that he may not be withheld from sin. . . . And this is called *affected* ignorance.—Secondly, ignorance is said to be voluntary when it regards that which one can and ought to know, for in this sense *not to act* and *not to will* are said to be voluntary, as was stated above. And ignorance of this kind happens either when one does not actually consider what one can and ought to consider (this is called *ignorance of evil choice,* and arises from some passion or habit), or when one does not take the trouble to acquire the knowledge which one ought to have; in which sense, ignorance of the general principles of law, which one ought to know, is voluntary, as being due to negligence.[28]

Here Aquinas is considering a situation where one is ignorant of what one ought to know, in an attempt to avoid responsibility. For example, suppose I see a speed limit sign ahead, and I turn to look out the window in the other direction so that I won't know what the speed limit is. Can't I tell the police officer that, in all honesty, I did not know what the speed limit was? Aquinas says this won't work. The reason is that you have chosen not to know, chosen to be ignorant. And this is something you *ought* to know. Of course, you are still responsible (and the act is considered voluntary). Ignorance of the law is no excuse, as long as you have ignored what you *ought* to consider, or you purposely avoid knowing so that you have an excuse for your action, or possibly you simply do not bother to take the trouble to find out what you *ought* to consider. This ignorance is consciously and voluntarily procured and fostered by the agent.

Ignorance of the law (but a law that you ought to know) is voluntary and you are responsible (because you were negligent). Because the ignorance was willed, the acts that the ignorance causes are also willed and you can be held responsible. Of course, from Aquinas's perspective, each human being *ought* to know God's moral laws, and no human being can successfully plead ignorance of God's laws and escape responsibility for his or her actions.

> Ignorance is antecedent to the act of will when it is not voluntary, and yet is the cause of man's willing what he would not will otherwise. Thus a man may be ignorant of some circumstance of his act, which he was not bound to know, with the result that he does which he would not do if he knew of that circumstance. For instance, a man, after taking proper precaution, may not know that someone is coming along the road, so that he shoots an arrow and slays a passer-by. Such ignorance causes what is involuntary absolutely.[29]

This third case is an absolutely excusing condition. Put simply, ignorance is "antecedent to the act of will" when you are ignorant, and are not responsible for that ignorance, and would have behaved differently if you knew—this does excuse responsibility and is involuntary. You are shooting arrows at a target a long distance away; you look and see no one about and then you loose the arrow. Just then you see a man on a horse galloping from behind some trees straight into the path of the arrow. You yell "Look out," but before he hears you, the arrow strikes him and kills him.

A modern equivalent would be someone driving carefully down a city street, obeying the traffic laws and paying attention. Suddenly someone on a bicycle darts out from between two cars directly into the path of your automobile. You slam on the brakes and twist the steering wheel in an attempt to avoid hitting the person, but there is not enough time.

You are *not* responsible; "such ignorance causes what is involuntary absolutely." You did not do the act voluntarily, so you have lost the voluntariness, but you have also lost free will in this case as well; your will was not inclined at all to do this.

Aquinas has been analyzing when one is responsible for his or her voluntary actions. When I am overcome with desire or anger or fear, am I responsible? When I am ignorant, am I responsible? A related issue remains to be considered, and this one is directly relevant to Aquinas's analysis of Christian morality. He asks: What makes my act of will a good act of will? What makes my act of will a bad act of will? The influence of Aristotle's theory of virtues will be evident in Aquinas's treatment of this important issue.

> Virtue is a habit through which men wish for good things. But a good will is one which is in accordance with virtue. Therefore the goodness of the will is from the fact that a man wills that which is good.
>
> Good and evil are essential differences of the act of the will. For good and evil pertain essentially to the will; just as truth and falsehood pertain to the reason, the act of which is distinguished essentially by the difference of truth and falsehood. . . . The specific difference in acts is according to objects, as was stated above. Therefore good and evil in the acts of the will is derived properly from the objects.
>
> The will is not always directed to what is truly good, but sometimes to the apparent good; and this has indeed some measure of good, but not of a good

that is suitable absolutely to be desired. Hence it is the act of the will is not always good, but sometimes evil.[30]

Stated simply, if you direct your will toward something good, it is a good act of will. If you fix your will on a good object, it can never be evil. And it is reason that tells the will what object it ought to direct its attention toward. It is what you intended to happen that tells us whether your act of will was a good act of will or a bad act of will.

> Given that the act of the will is fixed on some good, no circumstance can make that act evil. Consequently, when it is said that a man wills a good when he ought not, or where he ought not, this can be understood in two ways. First, so that this circumstance is referred to the thing willed. According to this, the act of the will is not fixed on something good, since to will to do something when it ought not to be done is not to will something good. Secondly, so that the circumstance is referred to the act of willing. According to this, it is impossible to will good when one ought not to, because one ought always to will what is good; except, perhaps, accidentally, insofar as a man, by willing some particular good, is prevented from willing at the same time another good which he ought to will at that time. And then evil results, not from his willing that particular good, but from his not willing the other. The same applies to the other circumstances.
>
> The will's object is proposed to it by the reason. For the understood good is the proportioned object of the will, while the sensible or imaginary good is proportioned, not to the will, but to the sensitive appetite; for the will can tend to the universal good, which reason apprehends, whereas the sensitive appetite tends only to the particular good, apprehended by a sensitive power. Therefore the goodness of the will depends on the reason in the same way as it depends on its object.[31]

Conscience and Morality

Next, Aquinas explores the role that one's conscience plays in morality and acts of will. Is conscience a reliable guide to moral behavior? If one follows one's conscience, doesn't this guarantee that the resulting act of will is good? If one goes against one's conscience, doesn't this mean that the act of will which follows is evil? Put another way, if you follow your conscience (even if it is wrong), doesn't that mean that your action is still good? Aquinas says no. Aquinas does not understand the conscience to be some sort of additional source of knowledge, and he does not consider the conscience to be a reliable guide to moral behavior. For Aquinas, conscience is basically just a form of reason, and people can reason incorrectly or poorly.

> Since conscience is a kind of dictate of the reason (for it is an application of knowledge to action . . .) to inquire whether the will is evil when it is at variance with erring reason is the same as to inquire whether an erring conscience binds. . . .
> . . . Ignorance sometimes causes an act to be involuntary, and sometimes not. And since moral good and evil consist in an act insofar as it is voluntary, as was stated above, it is evident that when ignorance causes an act to be in-

voluntary, it takes away the character of moral good and evil; but not, when it does not cause the act to be involuntary. Again, it has been stated above that when ignorance is in any way willed, either directly or indirectly, it does not cause the act to be involuntary. And I call that ignorance *directly* voluntary to which the act of the will tends, and that, *indirectly* voluntary, which is due to negligence, since a man does not wish to know what he ought to know, as we have stated above.

If, therefore, reason or conscience err with an error that is voluntary, either directly or through negligence, so that one errs about what one ought to know, then such an error of reason or conscience does not excuse the will, which abides by that erring reason or conscience, from being evil. But if the error arise from the ignorance of some circumstance, and without any negligence, so that it cause the act to be involuntary, then that error of reason or conscience excuses the will, which abides by that erring reason, from being evil. For instance, if erring reason tell a man that he should go to another man's wife, the will that abides by that erring reason is evil, since this error arises from ignorance of the divine law, which he is bound to know. But if a man's reason errs in mistaking another for his wife, and if he wish to give her her right when she asks for it, his will is excused from being evil; for this error arises from ignorance of a circumstance, which ignorance excuses, and causes the act to be involuntary.[32]

In Aquinas's analysis, human conscience is fundamentally a dictate of reason, based on rational principle, and not some separate and distinct source of moral knowledge. Thus, the conscience is no more reliable in moral matters than is one's ability to reason. If your action is based on your conscience, but your conscience is mistaken about the proper application of a moral principle, then your act is morally incorrect. It is not automatically good just because it is in accord with your conscience. In addition, if your conscience is mistaken about specific facts, and you will something based on the approval of conscience, the action is evil, even if the ignorance may excuse you from moral responsibility for the action.

Deontological Ethics

Next, Aquinas considers one of the fundamental questions of Western ethics. Is an action morally correct because it produces good consequences, or can an action be morally correct even if it produces evil consequences? The first position is called a **teleological,** or *consequentialist*, position in ethics, and the second is referred to as **deontological,** or *nonconsequentialist*. Which does Aquinas think correct? Aquinas writes, "The consequences do not make an act that was evil, to be good; nor one that was good, to be evil."[33] From this, Aquinas's position seems to be basically a deontological position, but he goes on to argue that consequences can be appropriately considered under some circumstances.

> For instance, if a man give an alms to a poor man who makes bad use of the alms by committing a sin, this does not undo the good done by the giver; and, in a like manner, if a man bear patiently a wrong done to him, the wrongdoer is not thereby excused. Therefore the consequences of an act do not increase its goodness or malice.

The consequences of an act are either foreseen or not. If they are foreseen, it is evident that they increase the goodness or malice. For when a man foresees that many evils may follow from his act, and yet does not therefore desist from it, this shows his will to be all the more inordinate.

But if the consequences are not foreseen, we must make a distinction. For if they follow from the nature of the action, and in the majority of cases, in this respect the consequences increase the goodness or malice of that action; for it is evident that an action is of its nature better, if better results can follow from it, and of its nature worse, if it is of a nature to produce worse results. On the other hand, if the consequences follow by accident and seldom, then they do not increase the goodness or malice of the act; for we do not judge of a thing according to that which belongs to it by accident, but only according to that which belongs to it essentially.[34]

Aquinas argues that an act which produces good consequences is not a better act because of the consequences. Suppose I see someone on the street who looks hungry, and I feel especially generous, so I give the person $25 so that she can feed herself for several days. However, suppose the person buys a gun with my money, holds up a bank, and shoots someone. Aquinas says that these obviously evil consequences do not make my original act of generosity less good.

However, consequences are appropriate to consider if you could foresee the consequences of your action. Suppose I know that the person is addicted to a drug such as alcohol, and I could reasonably foresee that the money which I gave the person would most likely go to support the addiction. Then, the consequences are relevant and I should have taken them into consideration. Even if the consequences are not foreseen but follow "from the nature of the action," and a reasonable person might expect such consequences, then they are relevant. If the consequences are not foreseen (such as the person robbing a bank), and follow by accident, then they do not contribute to the goodness or evilness of the action. Thus, Aquinas seems primarily deontological in his orientation, and not as much teleological.

AN OVERVIEW: THE RELATIONSHIP BETWEEN ARISTOTLE AND AQUINAS

Aquinas felt that the ethical theory of Aristotle provided "the proper philosophical foundation for the study of morality." So what does Aquinas add to Aristotle's foundation? We have noticed several things. First, Aquinas points out that Aristotle didn't know about the possibility of an eternal supernatural happiness, so he only spoke about ordinary human happiness. That final supernatural happiness is the ultimate goal that all human action aims towards, it is the "beatific vision of God." The term *beatific* means something like spiritual bliss, or saintly.

Second, Aquinas asserts that there is natural law, agreeing with Aristotle, but Aquinas says that this natural law reflects the eternal law of the divine order. Third, Aquinas points out that Christians have two sources of knowledge, one of which was unavailable to Aristotle, and God intended that we utilize *both* fully. This is another instance where Aquinas adds Christian theology onto the structure provided by the careful analysis of Aristotle.

Next, Aristotle's goal was happiness in this life, but Aquinas argues that there are two kinds of happiness, natural happiness and supernatural happiness, and we cannot attain both forms of happiness completely in this life. It requires the intellectual ability of the philosopher for natural happiness, and the spiritual intensity of a Christian saint for supernatural happiness. In addition, all human beings are still living in the state of Original Sin, and as a consequence, even a wonderful philosopher like Aristotle cannot attain even natural happiness, much less supernatural happiness.

Next, consider virtue. The most important Aristotelian virtues were courage, temperance, justice, wisdom, and prudence (natural virtues, according to Aquinas). Aquinas adds several "higher" virtues: faith, love, and hope.

Also, Aquinas modifies Aristotle's theory of voluntariness by adding free will (choice becomes a subset under free will). Finally, Aquinas attributes the source and authority for these moral principles to the divine being, to the natural laws God makes available to human beings. Moral judgments ultimately are based on "our intuitive knowledge of the natural law." We are rational creatures. Rational creatures experience the eternal law. The eternal law is God's plan, the ultimate norm of all morality.

AFTER AQUINAS: AN EPILOGUE

Let's briefly discuss what happened in Christian Europe for the next three hundred years after the death of Aquinas in 1274.

Around 1350 the pneumonic and bubonic plagues struck Europe (carried by fleas on rats on trading ships), and this had major theological consequences. With approximately 30 percent of the population dying, including true believers, children too young to have committed any sins, and even priests, it seemed that the ultimate and final punishment of God was near. Loyal Christians had been told to expect the end of the world for thirteen hundred years, and perhaps now it was coming.

The people prayed to God and relied on the intercession of the Catholic Church to stop the plague, to help protect innocent children and good priests. But children and priests continued to die daily, just like everyone else. Not everyone died. Some very evil people survived while their innocent neighbors died. It was clear to the medieval mind that God was punishing human beings. Some Christians concluded that the wealthy and powerful Catholic Church was being punished for not following God's commandments properly. Other conclusions even more radical were sometimes proffered: perhaps God didn't care, or perhaps God wasn't good (since good people died as well as not-so-good); even more seriously, perhaps God didn't exist at all.

The theological movement called the Reformation arose partly out of this crisis of Catholic authority. On October 31, 1517,[35] the German monk Martin

Luther challenged the Catholic Church, rejecting the religious authority of the papacy, emphasizing the individual's responsibility for his or her own salvation through faith and denying that only a Catholic priest could provide salvation. He also attacked the privileges and wealth of the Catholic Church and even argued that the state should supervise the church. This movement is often treated as the beginning of Protestant Christianity.

PROBLEMS TO PONDER

These are questions that any thoughtful person should think about if he or she were considering adopting Thomas Aquinas's moral system. Perhaps Aquinas can answer them. How would you answer them?

1. Aquinas argues that actions must stop somewhere; we cannot have our actions going on into infinity with no final or ultimate goal, because no intelligent or rational creature would move toward what it cannot reach. If the final goal is infinitely far away, then we would not pursue any goals at all. We would never move. Is it true that no one moves toward a goal that cannot be attained? Is it true that we would do nothing if we knew that our ultimate goal was unattainable?

2. There are numerous serious objections to the first cause arguments for the existence of God, which has been recognized by the various Christian churches. In fact, for more than a hundred years the position of most Christian theologians was that the existence of God cannot be proven; however, that can be explained by saying that if we could prove that God existed, then there would be no need for faith. Therefore, we should expect that all arguments that try to prove the existence of God will be fallacious and fail to prove that God exists. The cosmological argument is so seriously flawed that it was nearly unanimously rejected by Christian theologians by the eighteenth century.

   Aquinas's proof of the existence of God fails, and if that fails, then there is no justification for everything else in his ethical system. If we cannot know for certain that God does exist, then we cannot know that there are any eternal laws, so we cannot know that natural laws are based on eternal laws.

3. Aquinas confuses (1) prescriptive laws and (2) descriptive laws. Prescriptive laws are laws passed by a legislature or ruler, and they have penalties attached if they are not followed. Descriptive laws are not at all like prescriptive laws; descriptive laws are merely descriptions of patterns in nature, based on observation; if the descriptive laws are not followed, we say that they are not accurate and we junk those so-called laws and start with more observations to try to make them more accurate (no punishments attached). Laws of nature are descriptive. God's divine commands are prescriptive. Aquinas confuses the two.

4. Aquinas seems to be stretching matters in the way he works out specific moral laws from "natural inclinations." Given our many natural

inclinations, we might possibly argue that by following natural inclinations, we can justify polygamy and polyandry and even adultery.

GLOSSARY

Antecedent ignorance Ignorance is antecedent if the ignorance was there before you chose to act, and the ignorance was at least partly responsible for your actions. Ignorance is "antecedent to the act of will" when you are ignorant, you are not responsible for that ignorance, and would have behaved differently if you knew—this does excuse responsibility and is involuntary.

Concomitant ignorance Ignorance is "concomitant with the act of will" when your ignorance arises simultaneously with and accompanies your act. Aquinas says that this is when you might be ignorant but wouldn't change your behavior even if you knew the facts. Your ignorance accompanies the performance of a moral action, but the ignorance is *not* the cause of the action. You would have chosen to perform that action if your ignorance were replaced by knowledge.

Consequent ignorance Ignorance is "consequent to the act of will" if the ignorance is consciously chosen after you've decided to act. Here Aquinas is considering a situation where one is ignorant of what one ought to know, in an attempt to avoid responsibility. You have chosen not to know, chosen to be ignorant of something you *ought* to know. You have ignored what you ought to consider, or you purposely avoid knowing so that you have an excuse for your action, or possibly you simply do not bother to take the trouble to find out what you ought to take into consideration.

Cosmological argument This is one of the famous arguments that attempts to prove that God exists. It was started by Aristotle, who argued that reality must have started at some point, that there must have been something that started the universe. Aquinas argues that the God of Christianity is the first uncaused cause and God is the unmoved mover.

Deontological A deontological ethical system is nonconsequentialist, that is, an ethical system that argues that the rightness or wrongness of an act is not determined by the consequences. When Aquinas argues that the purpose of the act determines its rightness, and not the consequences of the act, he is taking a deontological position.

Eternal law This is the plan in the mind of God for all of creation. It is just God's plan for rationally ordered movements and actions in the created universe; that is, God's master plan. All other laws or rules must be derived from this law.

First principle of the natural law From Aristotle's principle that "the good is that which all desire and seek," Aquinas generates the *first principle of the natural law: good is to be done and promoted, and evil is to be avoided.* Do good and avoid evil.

Great Compromise of Aquinas Aquinas brings about a compromise between what reason tells us about nature, and what revelation is interpreted to tell us about nature. The two do not always agree. For example, faith tells us that the earth is the center of God's attention and the center of the universe, but telescopes tell us that the earth is only a minor planet nowhere near the center of our galaxy (the Milky Way), and our galaxy is only one of trillions of galaxies. Aristotle is the example of what reason tells us about the world. The Christian dogmas are examples of what we must believe because we have faith. Aquinas argues that the two need not conflict. What we need to do is "properly interpret" Aristotle (and reason). Accept Aristotle's reasoning and conclusions unless they come into clear conflict with the dogmas of the church. Where Aristotle and church dogma contradict one another, Aquinas either modifies Aristotle's conclusions to bring them into accord with church teachings, or else rejects Aristotle.

Natural law Natural law refers to a rational creature's participation in the eternal law or the plan in the mind of God. These are the laws that human beings can figure out by observing the world, and humans can feel within themselves as natural inclinations.

Teleological A teleological ethics system is a consequentialist ethical system; that is, any ethical system that says that we determine the moral rightness or wrongness of an act by the consequences of that act. For example, a common teleological ethical system would be one that asserts that if an act produces happiness, then it is morally correct.

A GUIDE TO FURTHER READINGS

Copleston, F. C. *Aquinas* (Baltimore, Md.: Penguin Books, 1955). An excellent introduction to the full range of Aquinas's ideas.

Kretzmann, Norman, and Eleonore Stump, eds. *The Cambridge Companion to Aquinas* (Cambridge University Press, 1993). Good scholarly articles on aspects of Aquinas's philosophy.

McDermott, Timothy. *Thomas Aquinas: Selected Philosophical Writings* (Oxford: Oxford University Press, 1993). Anthology of Aquinas's writings.

Pegis, A. C. *Thomas Aquinas: Basic Writings of St. Thomas Aquinas*, Vol. II (New York: Random House, 1945). Another good anthology of the writings of Aquinas.

PART THREE

Buddhist Ethics in India (5th Century B.C.E.)

W e are now going to discuss an ancient civilization that was not influenced by either Greek thought or the Judeo-Christian tradition: the Buddhist religious tradition of India. Although some people refer to any Indian religion as "Hinduism," this is not accurate. Western scholars usually use the term *Hinduism* to refer to the many varied religious traditions that acknowledge the sacred authority of a group of ancient holy writings called the *Vedas*. The **Vedas** were the sacred books of a group who called themselves the **Aryans,** the "Noble Ones," who invaded and conquered the indigenous people of India around 1500 B.C.E., and brought their own deities and religious practices to India with them. Basic Hindu religious beliefs were drawn from the *Vedas*, and from a later group of books, the **Upanishads.** One key concept was the immaterial soul, the *atman*, which was thought to be reincarnated again and again. This continuing cycle of birth and death was thought to be fueled by ego-centered actions. The goal of many Hindus was to escape this cycle, to achieve **liberation.**

The term *Hinduism* actually names a number of profoundly different religious approaches; some stress meditation, some stress elaborate religious rituals, some stress devotion to gods and goddesses, and some stress intellectual understanding. Some Hindu groups are **polytheistic,** some are **monotheistic,** some are **monist** (they hold that "all is one and all differences are illusory"), and some are atheistic. There are even Hindu materialists.

Buddhism begins around 500 B.C.E. In India during this period, like Greece during the same time period, there was considerable ferment. The dominant religious tradition at the time of the Buddha was that of the warrior Aryan conquerors. In addition to these **orthodox** traditions, which accept the authority of the *Vedas*, there were contemplative traditions (most probably derived from the pre-Aryan religious culture), which argued that the highest liberating knowledge is personal, gained by meditative intuition and direct insight into reality. Some of these incorporated their ideas within the Vedic framework, and others did not.

The **heterodox** traditions in India are those that did not accept the authority of the *Vedas* as ultimate revelation. Buddhism was one of these. It is a rejection of Hindu Vedic religion.

Hindu religion divided people into different groups: the **Brahmin** priests, the protectors and warriors, the farmers and landowners, and the workers. The person called "the Buddha" taught in the Ganges Valley, the middle region of India, and in this area especially the religious authority of the traditional Brahmanic priesthood was being challenged. Groups of wandering ascetics* who had left society and who were no longer householders, claimed religious authority, propounded philosophical and religious ideas, and advocated many different religious practices. One of these heterodox groups was called Buddhism, and Buddhism was the most successful of these new religions.

*Ascetics are individuals who deny themselves bodily pleasures in order to achieve spiritual freedom or liberation. Their practices might include prolonged fasting, sleeping on the ground under trees all year long, standing or sitting in one fixed position for hours, or even piercing their skin with metal objects. These are called austerities. The purpose of austerities was to free the follower from the strong physical demands that our bodies make, so that our spiritual essence could become liberated from our temporary physical bodies.

CHAPTER 6

Early Buddhism:

To Be Moral Is to Lessen Suffering

Westerners are often confused by early Buddhism, a world religion that seems to share almost none of the characteristics that Western cultures often think of as essential to religion. In early Buddhism, there is no deity to worship or pray to, and no spiritual benefits resulting from worship.[1] There is no original sin, no eternal damnation for any sinful deeds; human beings are fundamentally good.[2] There is no all-powerful God, no first cause, no prime mover, no creator. The Buddha is not a divinity, he does not reward the faithful or punish the unfaithful, does not reward virtue or punish vice, neither does he "save" anyone. A very early collection of Buddhist verses makes the point: "You yourself must make the effort. The Buddhas only point the way."[3]

Buddhists never thought that humans have a broken relationship with a divine order of being, and thus Buddhists do not think that humans require the grace of an external divine power, or a priesthood, in order to attain liberation or salvation. In fact, no one else but individuals themselves can accomplish that liberation. Students must follow a path grounded in their own efforts. The Buddha says,

> By oneself alone is evil done, by oneself alone is evil avoided and by oneself alone is one saved. Salvation and damnation depend on oneself—no one can save another.[4]

However, although Buddhism seems to have more in common with Greek philosophers than Christian religion, certainly it includes many central ideas that are clearly spiritual, such as Nirvana, Liberation, Enlightenment, karma, and meditation.

Throughout its long history, Buddhism has had a stronger appeal to a wider range of people than the other philosophies originating in India.

Buddhist teachings became dominant in China, Tibet, Sri Lanka, Southeast Asia, Japan, and Korea, and recently it has developed strong roots in Europe and in both North and South America. Buddhism has skillfully adapted to many different cultures. The philosophical ideas and the practices have shifted in interesting ways from country to country, but a core of concepts and practices have survived. In what follows, we discuss the early ideas offered by the Buddha, which have formed the common core of Buddhism, whether it be in ancient India or contemporary Buddhism as practiced in San Francisco or New York.

THE BACKGROUND OF BUDDHISM

Scholars usually try to begin with what might be called "original" or "early" or "primitive" Buddhism, that is, as close as we can come to what the Buddha taught. As in all the world religions, in Buddhism there are developments and changes over time; in this chapter, I separate early Buddhism from the numerous later groups that make up the Buddhist tradition.

The earliest Buddhist discourses, called *sutras,* contain quotations of the Buddha. Scholars have labored hard to disentangle the earliest words in the sutras from the later additions and elaborations. The process is aided by reading what the earliest critics of Buddhism said about the teachings. Before we analyze early Buddhist teachings, we'll start with a brief biography of the founder of Buddhism.

THE LIFE OF THE BUDDHA (563–483 B.C.E.)

Among Western scholars, there is general agreement that the man whom we know as "the Buddha"[5] lived for eighty years, approximately between 563 and 483 B.C.E.[6] He was born on the border of what is now Nepal and India, to the Gautama family, and was a member of the extended Shakya clan. He was given the name Siddhartha ("the one who accomplishes his goals"). Thus, the founder of Buddhism was named Siddhartha Gautama; he is also referred to as Shakyamuni, the "sage" or wise teacher of the Shakya clan. Siddhartha's family were not Brahmins (priests), but rather belonged to the group of warriors and protectors of Indian society.

A fortune-teller carefully examined the newborn child and made several predictions. The wealthy father, the ruler of a small tribal kingdom of the Shakya clan, was told that his son would become either a great monarch of India or an enlightened religious leader. You must understand that in that area of India, a religious leader was a homeless ascetic who isolated himself from society, living in the forest practicing austerities. Of course, Siddhartha's father would rather have his son become a king than a religious leader, and so he attempted to shield his son from experiences that might lead the child to embrace a religious life. He seems to have reasoned that if life posed no problems for Siddhartha, then he would have no interest in religious matters.

Siddhartha grew up in hedonistic luxury, isolated from the everyday world and the frustration, pain, and suffering we naturally experience as human beings, caused by things like grief, sickness, old age, and death. Yet in spite of all the luxury and pleasure, Siddhartha did not feel satisfied. There must be more to life than the pleasures that come from games, sex, food, and power. But what?

Siddhartha was about twenty-nine years of age when, on several consecutive trips into the nearby town, he encountered an old man, a sick man, and a dead man. Siddhartha was stunned—he was already feeling spiritually dissatisfied, but now, for the first time, he began to realize the true depths of pain and suffering in the world. The idea of anguish, frustration, dissatisfaction, and suffering becomes a key concept in Buddhism and is called *duhkha.*[7]

On a subsequent trip into the village he saw a wandering yellow-robed mendicant who stood silently, calmly, peacefully, holding a begging bowl. Learning that the ascetic had renounced the world in an effort to achieve liberation from suffering, Siddhartha decided that he too would renounce the world. Thus, at age twenty-nine, Siddhartha gave up his hedonistic life in the castle of his father. He said good-bye to his sleeping wife and infant son and slipped away later that night. He cut his hair and beard and put on the rags of a beggar, or mendicant, and entered the forest to begin his spiritual quest.

The Period of Study

For the next six years, Siddhartha roamed southward in India studying with various spiritual teachers. Although Siddhartha learned much, he was independent of mind and not content to merely accept what he was told on faith— he needed to verify the truth of the teachings for himself. And, after a period of study with each teacher, Siddhartha concluded that, although he had learned much, the teacher himself had not yet attained ultimate liberation. How could the teacher show the way to liberation to his students if he had not gotten there himself?

After six years of ardent study and intensive practice mastering the existing teachings, Siddhartha and several other students decided to go off on their own, to push themselves even harder than they had before in an extraordinary effort to attain what their teachers had not accomplished—complete enlightenment. After brutal self-punishment and starvation, and near death, Siddhartha realized that the path of extreme self-mortification was a dead end. He had practiced asceticism for six years, but it did not lead to enlightenment; it only led to death. He had to find another way.

Siddhartha accepted nourishment from a kind woman who was passing by. No longer torturing himself with extreme fasting, he ate sufficient food, found a pleasant spot near a river, and then he sat down beneath a large fig tree (the *Bodhi* tree), resolving to meditate until he broke through the tangle of desire, attachment, frustration, and rebirth, and attained the complete end of all *duhkha*. Studying the nature and causes of suffering and evil, Siddhartha was prepared to eliminate them. He was thirty-five years of age at this point.

As the night progressed, he became more mindful, more aware. He began by recognizing the cause-effect patterns that were active in his own life. He began to understand the pattern of death and rebirth in other living beings. He comprehended the causes of dissatisfaction and suffering, and their connection to rebirth. Using the meditation techniques he had learned from his teachers, he put an end to the last traces of self-centered grasping by developing insight into the nature of the world. He recognized the things that cause suffering and eliminated them: sensual desire, desire for continued existence, self-centered craving, false views, and primeval ignorance. With these fetters removed, Siddhartha Gautama saw things as they really are: he directly experienced the causal nature of the world—that all things are interdependent and interconnected. This means that there isn't some mysterious unchanging substance that underlies changing reality. All phenomena that we experience are changing, and they are caused. All things depend on prior causes and conditions.*

This causal understanding of the world allowed him to recognize that suffering is caused, and then eliminate the causes of suffering within himself. In doing so, Siddhartha woke up; it is from this point on that he is called the Buddha ("One Who Woke Up"). With life-changing insight into the causally interdependent coarising nature of reality, Siddhartha attained **Enlightenment;** with an end to *duhkha*, dissatisfaction, Siddhartha attained Nirvana.

Note that in early Buddhism, Nirvana is not a heavenly reward attained after death. Rather, **Nirvana** is eliminating ignorance, self-centered attachment, and anger. It is a "blowing out" or "cooling off" of the violent and egocentric passions that dominate the ordinary person's personality.[8]

> The elimination of lust, hatred, and confusion . . . constituted his enlightenment and freedom. . . . It represents a transformation of his whole personality, cognitive, conative, and emotive. With that transformation, Siddhartha was able to perceive the world paying attention to the human predicament and the way out of it, which he summarized in the four noble truths.[9]

Following the awakening of Siddhartha, he recognizes how long and hard he had to strive to achieve liberation from suffering. Was it possible for him to explain to others what he had experienced and understood? Yes. Buddhism as a religion and as a pathway to liberation begins with the need to explain to others the inner realization achieved under the Bodhi tree.

Explaining these practices and insights to everyone, to women as well as men, ignoring traditional caste distinctions, the Buddha wandered on foot throughout northern India for the rest of his life, holding his begging bowl in a peaceful yet mute appeal for food every morning, and explaining his insights in the afternoons to anyone who cared to ask. Many of those who followed him put an end to *duhkha* and attained enlightenment as deep and as profound as that of the Buddha. Such people were called *arhats.* The main difference between the Buddha and an *arhat* is that the Buddha discovered the initial path and pointed

---

*This is the concept of *pratityasamutpada,* which is discussed in more detail in the section "Buddhist Philosophy."

out the way, and the *arhats* followed it, but both arrived at the same destination—Enlightenment and Nirvana.

The Buddha died at age eighty, refusing to leave anyone in complete authority over the disciples and followers.* He continued to stress the individual's ability to liberate himself or herself. His dying words to his cousin Ananda were:

> And whoever . . . shall not seek refuge in anyone but themselves—it is they, Ananda, among my disciples, who shall reach the Further Shore [of Nirvana]! But they must make the effort themselves!
>
> Then the Buddha addressed the monks and said: "This I tell you, monks. Decay is inherent in all conditioned things. Work out your own salvation with diligence."[10]

BUDDHIST PHILOSOPHY

After the awakening experience under the Bodhi tree, the Buddha explained to his friends what he had achieved and how he had achieved it. He described this as a pathway that runs between the extreme of asceticism (or self-mortification), and the other extreme of **hedonism** (or pleasurable self-indulgence). He called it the "Middle Way" between extremes.

His explanation of the path to Nirvana began with the key liberating insight: causality (which Buddhists call **pratityasamutpada,** translated as causality, or dependent coarising).[11] Under the Bodhi tree, Siddhartha awakened to the nature of reality. Reality is not composed of separate and independent and unchanging substances. Reality is not something eternal and unchanging that underlies all the changing appearances of phenomena. Reality is just ever-changing processes, interdependent and interacting. Everything is impermanent and changing.

Some immediate implications flow from *pratityasamutpada:* nothing lasts forever, not a person, not a city, not a mountain, not a planet, not a universe. Nothing in the world is independent, nothing is self-existent. All things arise from causes and conditions, change as the causes and conditions vary, and finally cease. Everything depends on prior causes and conditions.

If nothing is eternal and unchanging, then there is no eternal and unchanging *atman*, or soul.[12] Although human beings project the illusion of unchanging permanence onto the ever-changing process we call "the self," there is no evidence whatsoever that there exists an eternal and unchanging inner essence. In fact, what experience teaches us is just the opposite—everything is changing

---

*One consequence of his refusal to put someone in charge was that over the centuries, various interpretations of his words could, and did, develop. But, because there was no one with the authority to declare one interpretation correct and another interpretation inconsistent with the original teachings, the seeds for different schools and traditions of Buddhism start here. Within the following two hundred years, Buddhism broke into numerous subdivisions, and within about four hundred years, several more socially inclusive forms of Buddhism developed, which called themselves "Mahayana." This is the dominant form of Buddhism in China, Japan, Tibet, and Korea.

and nothing is permanent. In addition, there is no element of human experience which the soul is needed to explain. It is an empty concept.

This has implications for Buddhist morality. It is not going to be concerned with a permanent self acting as an independent moral agent. Rather, Buddhist ethics will stress understanding the ever-changing nature of the self, and reorienting one's way of looking at things to bring that worldview into accord with the way things really are. Moral behavior will derive from a transformation of one's understanding and a concomitant transformation of one's character.

Another immediate implication of *pratityasamutpada* is as follows: there is no eternal unchanging essence underlying reality. All is just process. By the same understanding, there is no eternal and unchanging deity. Consequently, Buddhist ethics does not rest upon the commands of an all-powerful deity. Just interdependent processes exist, which are impermanent. All things depend on causes and conditions.

The causal framework for the Buddha's insight provided a simple understanding: frustration, dissatisfaction, suffering, and evil arise or are caused; much of your dissatisfaction arises from your own mind, and you have the power to liberate yourself. You are the only one who can work out your liberation. No one else can do it for you.

According to the Buddha, what is truly good is what contributes to one's own freedom and happiness and the freedom and happiness of others.[13] The practice of the Buddhist Middle Way is a behavioral pathway that can help you eliminate the causes of evil and dissatisfaction. The human mind is capable of liberating itself. Put your energies into your own liberation![14]

The Four Noble Truths

The core of the practice of the Middle Way of Buddhism constitutes a three-pronged approach composed of wisdom, morality, and meditation.[15] These are explained in what the Buddhists call the **Four Noble Truths:**

1. The existence of *duhkha*.
2. The arising of *duhkha*.
3. The cessation of *duhkha*.
4. The Noble Eightfold Path to eliminate *duhkha*.

The First Noble Truth   All existence is suffering and frustration (*duhkha*) for one who does not understand the flowing ever-changing nature of reality. Everything we do is impermanent, and nothing is solid or substantial enough to sustain us in our search for meaning, happiness, contentment, bliss, peace, or serenity. Every success ends in failure. Every gain ends in a loss. Every meeting ends in a parting. Every birth ends in death. People try to get happiness or serenity from their lives by tightly holding onto things or persons, but life can only provide change. The result is grief, frustration, sickness, dissatisfaction, unhappiness.

The Second Noble Truth   This dissatisfaction, frustration, or suffering (*duhkha*) arises from several causes. Among those causes are a self-centered possessive attitude toward things; self-centered attachment to and desire for sense pleasures; a desire for power, for wealth, for beliefs and opinions that everyone around you regards as correct; and even a desire to find some absolute "truth" to which one can hold. Self-centered desires rage in the mind, on both the conscious and the subconscious levels, generating conflict within and negative consequences without. Even if you get what you desire, it is not enough to bring about mental serenity, and certainly is incapable of bringing lasting spiritual bliss.

Another cause of *duhkha* is found in human dispositional tendencies to behave in ways toward the world that ultimately produce pain and suffering, such as anger, hatred, and greediness. Being ignorant and destructive, sometimes we cause harm to others in the pursuit of our own happiness and pleasures. However, hurting any living thing can only result in further suffering. In verse 270 of the *Dhammapada* we find:

> Whereby one hurts living beings, one does not become a noble person. Through non-injury to all beings, one comes to be called a noble one.[16]

Having an unrealistic appraisal of life is an additional cause of *duhkha*. We expect our self to continue unchanging through life, from childhood to old age, and then we want that same self to continue on into another realm—but reason and experience both tell us that nothing is permanent and unchanging anywhere in the universe, and certainly nothing is permanent and unchanging about you as an individual. Think back to how you were at age twelve or age fifteen. You have changed in fundamental ways, and you will continue to change as long as you are alive. Your identity gradually changes and is dependent on all of the experiences that occur to you as you live.

We remain ignorant of the true dependent nature of life and this makes us poorly prepared to deal with or eliminate this sense of unsatisfactoriness in our life. Being ignorant, we continue to crave things that cannot provide happiness in the mistaken belief that they will ultimately make us happy if we just keep on acquiring enough of them, and this leads to an unending cycle of desire, activity, grasping, craving, activity, self-centered thirst, and again, activity.[17] The triad of (a) self-centered craving or attachment, (b) envy, anger, or hatred, and (c) confusion or ignorance of the nature of reality, are often referred to as the **Three Poisons.** These are the primary causes of misery, and they can be brought under your control.

The Third Noble Truth   The profoundly disturbing experience of dissatisfaction can be ended, and the end of *duhkha* is Nirvana. Knowing the causes of *duhkha* allows one to eliminate the causes and thus eliminate the *duhkha*. The insight or understanding of the nature of reality is called Enlightenment, and the condition of one who has eliminated *duhkha* is called Nirvana. If we can eliminate the Three Poisons from our personalities, and deal with the world in ways that are not self-centered, not seeking to satisfy egoistic cravings and desires, and can see things the way they really are, without ignorance of confusion, then life is Nirvana.

The Fourth Noble Truth   This truth describes what we can do to eliminate the Three Poisons. It is a series of eight practices called the Noble Eightfold Path, often broken into groups of morality, wisdom, and meditation. These are things that you can do to get rid of the causes of *duhkha*. The process is one of discarding false understanding, abandoning unrealistic expectations, rejecting harmful behavior grounded in confusion, and eliminating habitual unaware kinds of consciousness. The Noble Eightfold Path is (1) Right Understanding, (2) Right Thought (these two constitute wisdom), (3) Right Speech, (4) Right Action or Conduct, (5) Right Livelihood (these three constitute morality), (6) Right Effort, (7) Right Mindfulness, and (8) Right Concentration (these three constitute mental discipline). These eight are the prescription for ending suffering. In verse 191 of the *Dhammapada*, we find a brief summary of the Four Noble Truths:

> . . . suffering, the arising of suffering, the surpassing of suffering and the noble eightfold path leading to the appeasement of suffering.
>   This indeed is a safe refuge; this is the highest refuge. Taking upon this refuge, one is released from all suffering.[18]

Thus, the goal of early Buddhist philosophy is realistic insight into the nature of things and using that insight to end frustration and dissatisfaction. The fundamental teachings that, when understood and practiced, will end *duhkha* are insight into the impermanence of reality, recognition of the lack of a permanent unchanging soul, and the understanding of the frustration that results when we try to live as though things were permanent and unchanging.[19]

BUDDHIST ETHICS

Like almost all the other central Buddhist concepts, the ethical theory of Buddhism is grounded in *pratityasamutpada* (causality, "dependent coarising"). *Pratityasamutpada* was the liberating insight of Siddhartha under the Bodhi tree.

The Greeks asked "What is the good life for a human being?" and answered the question in terms of reason, individual virtues, social values, and politics. The Buddha asked "Why do we experience so much dissatisfaction and suffering, and how is it possible to eliminate it?"

The awakening insight of the Buddha led him to answer that the good life, a life free from *duhkha*, is possible if you can understand the causes of *duhkha*. The good life is achieved with a combination of wisdom, meditation, and morality, which result in Enlightenment.[20] In addition, the moral person will try to perfect the *Buddhist virtues*, the most important of which include: generosity, loving kindness (compassion), morality, meditation, nonattachment, wisdom, zealousness in pursuit of awakening, patience, peacefulness, and honesty or truthfulness.[21] Many of these are obviously social virtues, but, in addition, these are qualities that if cultivated, lead to the cessation of *duhkha*.

Living a Moral Life Leads to the Elimination of Suffering

Living a moral life is a necessary precondition for the ultimate liberation from suffering and the attainment of Nirvana. This is the justification for morality.[22] Why be moral? If you do not live a moral life, you cannot lessen the *duhkha* in your life. What if you choose to be immoral? Then you will continue to suffer frustration, dissatisfaction, and anguish and will generate additional amounts of these same pains because of your behavior. In short: you harm yourself. The justification for following moral rules arises here.[23] Morality is the heart of early Buddhism. In verse 183 of the *Dhammapada* we find:

> Not to do any evil, to cultivate the good and to purify one's mind
> —this is the teaching of the Buddhas.[24]

As we have seen, the concern with morality is tied tightly to the question of how to eliminate suffering. Essential to the elimination of suffering is following a moral path leading to liberation from the unsatisfactoriness of life. Thus, moral behavior plays a key role in Buddhism.

As we have seen, Buddhist ethics is grounded in the causes of *duhkha,* and the elimination of those causes. This is causality, or *pratityasamutpada* ("dependent coarising"), the liberating insight of the Buddha under the Bodhi tree. If everything arises in dependence on a great number of causes and conditions,[25] then it follows that nothing is independent and unchanging. When the causes change, the effects that are dependent on those causes will also change. *Duhkha* is an effect that depends upon self-centered craving, anger, and ignorance.

If everything is impermanent and changing, and we live as though things were permanent, then our life will be one of frustration and dissatisfaction. The roots of a moral lifestyle are found here. If we live in the world as though we could hold onto unchanging things that could provide permanent happiness, we are operating on the world with a faulty guide, a faulty road map, and many of our decisions and choices will result in frustration and unhappiness.

What is an accurate road map? We must not be trapped into seeing things the way we wish they were, or the way we want them to be, or the way our culture and religion have taught us that they must be. How are things, really? According to the philosophy of Buddhism, what you and I call "reality" is just a flowing continuous process of change. Even the term "self" simply refers to a continuous stream of dependent processes, both physical and mental, and not to an eternal unchanging metaphysical substance called "soul." The impermanent continuous changing aspect of reality provides the foundation upon which ethics are grounded.

Recall the Fourth Noble Truth: the way to end suffering is by practicing the Noble Eightfold Path. The Noble Eightfold Path is traditionally broken into three larger areas: wisdom, morality, meditation. These three are then broken into eight interrelated techniques (or practices) to produce personal insight into the way things really are, and to develop the mental ability to practice techniques that will reduce and ultimately eliminate ignorance and self-centered grasping and craving.

The moral system of early Buddhism reflects this dimension of gradual deepening of insight and morally improving oneself; although the ultimate theoretical principles of morality are the same for everyone, their appeal, their application, and the way they are explained change depending on the depth of one's understanding. There are stages of moral development, and the kind of claims made in the tradition depend on the level of the listener. For this reason, the kind of answer to "why be moral?" that will appeal to the beginner will be a different explanation of "why be moral?" offered by the enlightened *arhat* who is no longer self-centered and who sees things clearly. The rules for the monk or nun are not identical with those for the layperson, and the justification for morality for the mendicant is not identical with that of the *arhat*, either. We will need to consider this in our understanding of Buddhist ethics.

The Three Parts to Buddhist Morality

Buddhist morality begins with the ordinary person living an ordinary life in society. He or she is a householder whose primary source of knowledge is the authority of tradition. This person has little or no insight into his or her own character or motivation, and little time to work on understanding the ultimate nature of reality. The householder in society is primarily concerned with the satisfaction of his or her own needs.[26] The householder is most likely an **egoistic hedonist.** This position says that we seek our own pleasure and try to avoid pain; thus, we will tend to do whatever is to our own best advantage. Because self-centeredness dominates the ordinary person's activities and attitudes, to this person, you say "Be virtuous because this will provide good consequences to you."

This conclusion is justified by the Indian theory of **karma,** that certain actions are reflexive in the sense that the consequences of these actions return back to the agent like a boomerang. In other words, if you act with evil intent, you will suffer evil consequences in this life and in the next one. The evil you do will come back to hurt you. If you do good, the natural law of karma[27] asserts that good consequences will follow such action. Act with good intent and you will be happy; both here and in the hereafter. The point is clearly made in the words of the Buddha:

> If one were to speak or act with a polluted mind, as a result, suffering follows him, like a wheel that follows the foot of the beast of draught . . .
>   If one were to speak or act with a serene mind, as a result, happiness follows him like a shadow that does not depart.[28]

The appeal of this is clear; it is in your own best interests to be moral; good things will happen to you if you live morally. So the ordinary Buddhist householder is told to do what is right because it is in his or her own best interests to do so. The householder can lead a morally good life by being virtuous and following rules, whose ultimate effect is to reduce his or her self-centered cravings, anger and hatred, and confusion. These three, the Three Poisons, are the foundation of an immoral life. Thus, the Buddhist at this stage follows moral rules for self-centered reasons. Of course, the Buddhist householder also has social obligations to others, duties to parents, husbands, wives, and others.

At a higher level of understanding, this self-centered motive becomes less important as one makes progress along the Buddhist path, because the grasp of the ego-centered way of dealing with the world is lessened by insight gained through meditation and the practice of various virtues. To the person who is less self-centered, the promise of personal rewards holds less attraction. The Buddhist who has left the life of a householder, who has abandoned society, is called a mendicant monk or nun, one who depends on alms for a living during the quest for liberation. As a result of moral and meditative practices, the mendicant slowly becomes less self-centered than the householder and has a much easier time considering the welfare of others. The Buddha says, "Little by little, from moment to moment, let a prudent man gradually purge [himself of] his blemishes, even as a smith [removes the impurities] in silver."[29] Such a person will move from the self-centered egocentric hedonistic ethic to one stressing compassion, one that takes into consideration the needs and desires of others. But the appeal of personal advantage is not entirely gone yet. The mendicant is still attracted by the morality of: Do what is right because it will lead to your freedom and a permanent end to your *duhkha*. The guide is moral rules and virtues. Other people play a role here because as the ego is weakened, the happiness of others and the pains of others are felt almost as if they were one's own.*

In early Buddhism, the highest attainment is the *arhat*, one who has eliminated the habitual tendency to deal with the world from a standpoint of (1) self-centeredness, craving, greed, possessiveness; (2) envy, hatred, anger; and (3) confusion and ignorance of the true nature of the world.[30] With these habits no longer dominating the personality, the *arhat* no longer is attached to philosophical theories, religious dogma, or any such things—the result will be a "letting go." Responding to the world with an altered character, the accomplished Buddhist is not behaving morally because he or she ought to be compassionate; rather, that person simply *is* compassionate and behaves in accord with their character. When enlightened, one's harmful tendencies are pacified, and whatever you do, you will never act from a motive that is harmful or will increase *duhkha*. In verse 225 of the *Dhammapada*, the Buddha says, "Those sages who are forever restrained in body are harmless." The *arhat* does not follow rules at all. When an *arhat* does something good, such acts flow spontaneously because the *arhat* has eliminated craving, hatred, and delusion and is now compassionate, wise, and no longer ego-centered. The social virtues flow freely from such a person. In one of the early discourses of the Buddha, the *Middle Length Savings*, we find this description of the person who has eliminated the negative states.

---

*At this stage, Buddhist morality is not primarily a social morality, because there is no personal stake in the maintenance of the structure of society, no sense of a social contract.

He dwells, having suffused the whole world everywhere, in every way with a
mind of friendliness that is far-reaching, wide-spread, immeasurable, without
enmity, without malevolence. He abides, having suffused . . . the whole world
. . . with a mind of compassion. . . . He abides, having suffused . . . the whole
world with a mind of sympathetic joy. . . . He abides, having suffused . . . the
whole world with a mind of equanimity. . . .[31]

In other words, the *arhat* is free from all self-centeredness, free from anger
and envy, and someone with this sort of personality will act spontaneously,
compassionately, and with deep understanding. They do not behave morally
because of an expectation of karmic rewards, or heavenly rewards. They do not
even act from some sense of duty, and they do not follow moral rules. They simply respond to the world.

For all three parts of Buddhist morality, an action is good if it produces good
consequences, that is, a tendency to eliminate *duhkha*, and evil if it produces an
increase in *duhkha*, that is, bad consequences. However, consequences are not
the sole determiner of the rightness or wrongness of an action. Early Buddhism
also stresses the agent's motives and intentions. If a person's motive was to
cause harm or injure another, then the action is wrong.

Thus, the ultimate determination of rightness or wrongness of an act is
neither intentions alone, nor consequences alone. Mere good intentions are
not sufficient, although they are necessary to make a good action. The consequences are also essential: will this action bring about a lessening of suffering
for oneself as well as for the community? Does the action bring freedom
closer, or farther away? The deeper one's understanding of cause and effect
(*pratityasamutpada*), the easier it is to understand what sorts of actions result
in *duhkha*.

If you are in doubt as to what sorts of behavior cause pain and suffering, the
Buddhists provide a list of actions that increase *duhkha*. That was determined by
observing patterns and connections between actions of certain types (e.g., self-
centered behavior) and consequences that follow those actions (an increase in
suffering). Note that the expectations of society may have a profound effect on
the consequences of one's actions. An action that in one society might cause profound pain and suffering for others (e.g., a pregnancy to an unmarried woman)
might be a cause for joy and celebration in a different culture. The Buddha recognized this aspect as well, asserting that "what is reckoned immoral at one
time may be reckoned to be moral at another time."[32]

The Moral Rules of Buddhism

Buddhism is not deontological. In Buddhism there is no fixed invariable moral
law or principle. Moral principles derive from human experience of the interdependent causal flow that we call "reality." However, there are regularities, obvious patterns of behavior and personality that we see produce happiness or unhappiness. We can generalize on the basis of such patterns. That such patterns
are uniform is what allows us to generalize to moral rules.[33]

We must remember that the Buddha had a large following, and those follow-ers were forced to stop their wanderings during the rainy season and wound up forming monastic communities for three months of the year. When such groups get large, they need rules to guide members in communal living. Thus, a basic list of rules was generated for householders, and a more strin-gent list of rules and regulations was created for those who were mendicant monks and nuns.[34]

It is important to notice that the Buddhist rules are not telling what you must do, they are not commands to do this or do that. Rather, they tend to be formulated negatively; they are telling you to avoid certain kinds of behavior because those sorts of actions will increase human suffering, your own and the suffering of others. These actions cause disharmony and interfere with the abil-ity of others to achieve Nirvana. They are forbidden for these reasons. Thus, Buddhist morality is teleological.

Buddhism provides moral rules in several ways. Two of the most important are the Noble Eightfold Path and the Five Precepts (which can be interpreted as falling under several of the eight practices of the Noble Eightfold Path). These rules are not commands of an omnipotent deity. Instead, rules are provided so that the Buddhist can have a guide for modifying his or her behavior to conform to things as they truly are ("reality"). If you understand the nature of reality, but do not behave according to your insight, then you have made no progress in eliminating *duhkha*. You cannot *be* less self-centered unless you *behave* in a less self-centered manner.

The rules for modifying behavior are provided by moral portions of the Noble Eightfold Path. For example, consider Right Speech, the third of the eight. The rule is: Do not allow your language to falsify your experience. Your use of language must be changed so that it does not mislabel, mislead, or misrepresent. Obviously, this means that only the truth should be spo-ken. Negatively, it means that to live according to reality, abstain from telling lies, from slander, and from idle or useless gossip. Even if you know something negative about someone else, and it is true, don't repeat it. The *Dhammapada* says:

> Not the [verbal] transgressions of others, nor their deeds of commission and omission, but one's own deeds of commission and omission should one examine.[35]

The fourth of the Noble Eightfold Path, Right Conduct, is central for moral guidance. All behavior that flows out of craving and ignorance must be avoided, because actions that arise from craving and ignorance perpetuate suffering. All acts of aggression and self-indulgence must be avoided. In terms of moral rules, the core values of Buddhist rules are contained in the idea of Right Conduct (also translated as Right Action). The Five Precepts fall under this heading, and these five guide the conduct of the Buddhist layper-son[36] as follows:

1. Refrain from killing or hurting living creatures.
2. Refrain from taking anything not given.

3. Refrain from misuse of sensual pleasures.
4. Refrain from speaking untruths.
5. Refrain from self-intoxication with drinks or drugs.

These precepts are fundamental for living a good life, but they also lead to the establishment of a healthy community. In addition, the Buddhist lifestyle rejects harmful pleasures, such as alcoholism and drug addiction, because when one's mind is not clear, one engages in behavior that harms others and one's self. If the individuals follow the Five Precepts, the society composed of such people will itself minimize much *duhkha*.

The fifth of the Noble Eightfold Path, Right Livelihood, provides rules for your choice of occupation. To see the world clearly and accurately, the way you earn your living must not be based on aggression, taking advantage of, or misleading others, or catering to the self-indulgent desires of others (which perpetuate suffering). Buddhists were not to work selling poisons, drugs, or weapons. Buddhists were not to earn their living in the military life.

Mental Effort and Morality

The mental effort of meditation is helpful because it can help us to recognize and break the self-centered patterns of thoughts that keep us from recognizing the true nature of the world and the ways in which our own actions cause the pain and suffering we experience. As a result, the experienced meditator can begin to understand things as they truly are, and ultimately attain liberation.

> The sagacious ones, contemplative, with ever present effort and uninterrupted firm endeavor, experience freedom, the incomparable release from bondage.[37]

The sixth of the Noble Eightfold Path is Right Effort. It is a process in which the individual strives to maintain increasingly wholesome states of mind, such as being at peace. It also includes avoiding unwholesome states of mind, such as fear, anxiety, and pride.

> Beneficial is the restraining of thought that is difficult to restrain, which is fleeting and wandering at will; restrained thought is a bringer of happiness.[38]

The seventh of the Noble Eightfold Path is Right Mindfulness, and this step is very important. You must be attentive to what is going on. Pay attention to the activities of your own body, to sensations or feelings, to mental activities and ideas, thoughts, and conceptions. Don't be distracted; be aware. Nothing is to be done absentmindedly or out of mere habit.

Wisdom and Morality

Wisdom is also relevant to morality. Under the heading of wisdom, we find Right Thought and Right Understanding. Right Thought means developing a consciousness that is free from hatred, ill will, or aversion. It includes selfless compassion, which is a nonegocentric love for others. Selfless detachment, love, and nonviolence are to characterize our way of dealing with others.[39]

Right Understanding encourages us to see things clearly, as they have come to be as a result of cause and effect. We do not see permanent and eternal entities such as unchanging realities, essences, or souls. We see change, processes, each arising from causes and dependent on conditions. Right Understanding means seeing things as they really are, not as you wish they were, hope they will be, or demand that they must be. See things without ignorance, confusion, anger, or self-centered egocentric perceptions. Right Understanding is ultimately the highest wisdom, which permits us to comprehend reality, "things as they truly are."

AN OVERVIEW OF BUDDHIST ETHICS

Buddhist ethics is primarily teleological, which means that the consequences of actions determine their morality. Acts that increase *duhkha* are wrong; acts that decrease suffering and increase happiness are morally right. A good action is one whose consequences include neither harm to oneself or to others and produces happy results; an immoral action is one that produces harm to another or to oneself, and its results are *duhkha*.

> If you, Rahula, are desirious of doing a deed with the body, you should reflect . . . thus: "That deed which I am desirious of doing . . . is a deed . . . that might conduce to the harm of myself and that might conduce to the harm of others, and that might conduce to the harm of both; this deed of body is unskilled, its yield is anguish [duhkha], its result is anguish." . . . a deed of body like this, Rahula, is certainly not to be done by you. But if you, Rahula, . . . should find, "That deed which I am desirious of doing with the body is a deed of my body that would conduce neither to the harm of myself nor to the harm of others nor to the harm of both; this deed of body is skilled, its yield is happy, its result is happy"—a deed of body like this, Rahula, may be done by you.[40]

The fundamental question in Buddhist morality is "What sort of a person do I want to be?" and the answer is—a person who is free from *duhkha* and free from the continuous cycle of birth and death. The highest good, and the ultimate goal of Buddhism, is a state of freedom and self-realization. The means for attaining this are found in the Four Noble Truths, which have wisdom, meditation, and morality as components. Meditation is used to develop moral attitudes of nonattachment and compassion, and to clear the mind from craving. Meditation is also needed to calm the mind, allowing one to gain insight into *pratityasamutpada*, the causally interdependent coarising nature of reality. Thus, the elimination of *duhkha* and the attainment of Nirvana have two components: (1) the moral component: refraining from actions that cause harm; and (2) the wisdom component: developing liberative insight into the nature of reality. Both of these components are supported by the practice of meditation.

The moral component is necessary (but not sufficient; wisdom is also required) to eliminate suffering and the feeling of dissatisfaction we experience.[41] A person who chooses to do wrong things is a person who is karmically increasing his or her own burden of suffering; a person who chooses to do morally right things is a person who is alleviating his or her own suffering and helping to alleviate the suffering of others. The feeling of unsatisfactoriness can be eliminated, and when it is, the person is said to have attained Nirvana, a blowing out of the causes of *duhkha*, that is, anger, hatred, confusion, ignorance, craving, and self-centeredness.

Buddhist morality has three tiers. The householder follows moral rules because guiding one's behavior by these rules produces happiness for the person in this or in a future life, combined with a diminution of *duhkha*. The mendicant monk or nun follows moral rules because they are necessary to produce liberation from all frustration and Nirvana. The monk or nun is also more sensitive to the pains of others because of the lessening of ego-centeredness. These two groups follow rules and try to perfect virtues such as compassion, generosity, wisdom, nonattachment, zealousness in pursuit of the truth, patience, and truthfulness.[42]

The *arhat* does not follow rules. Having reduced the harmful components of the personality, *arhats* can respond openly and freely to all of life's situations. Responding spontaneously, the motives for their behavior and actions will be selfless, and their wisdom and insight into the causally dependent nature of human beings will prevent them from making choices from self-centered motives that will increase the total amount of human suffering.

If I am in a moral situation, how can I tell what is the right thing to do? The answer is, I ask whether the consequences of my choice will bring about an increase in *duhkha* or a decrease. If I am well along the Buddhist path, I have a deep understanding of the causal interconnections around me, and those provide profound insight into the probable consequences of my choices. If I am not sure, if I am not clear whether telling a lie or stealing will increase *duhkha*, then I can use the general moral rules provided by the Noble Eightfold Path and the Five Precepts. I can also ask someone with greater moral maturity, greater wisdom, and greater insight into the interdependent, interconnected nature of human experience.

PROBLEMS TO PONDER

These are questions that any thoughtful person should think about if he or she were considering adopting the Buddhist moral system. Perhaps the careful Buddhist can answer them. How would you answer them?

1. Although the Buddhist path is elegantly simple, there are some problems. One of them is what to do when the various precepts produce conflicts. How can I determine the right action when telling a lie may save a life but cause suffering for other people? What standard tells me whether it is right to kill an animal and eat it, if doing so will allow someone to live? What if my choice could lead to my own enlightenment, yet cause suffering for others?

    The Buddhist answer seems to be to simply consider the consequences. The best action is the one that produces the least amount of *duhkha* and the greatest amount of happiness over any other choice. But we do not have any method for doing the calculations.

2. Question: Buddhism treats the end of *duhkha* as equivalent to happiness. Is the end of suffering really identical with happiness? Is "no-pain" the same as happiness, or is it a state of neither happiness nor suffering, a neutral state? When I have put an end to *duhkha*, it certainly could be equanimity or balance, but it is not a positive emotion (which is clearly implied by the term "happiness"). Why equate the ending of suffering with *happiness?*

3. *Duhkha* is the key for early Buddhism, but where does it come from? What is the ultimate origin of *duhkha?* Any individual experiences suffering because of the Three Poisons, but why is there suffering in the world?

The ultimate *cause* of *duhkha* is not explained in Buddhist philosophy. However, early Buddhism specifically rejects the claim that a complete philosophical explanation must be provided for every possible question. Buddhist practice is aimed at eliminating your *duhkha*, and there is little concern with answers to ultimate questions. The Buddha described the doctrines of Buddhism as a raft, as instruments or tools that you use to escape from this shore of *duhkha* and use to get to the other shore of freedom. But, once you have crossed the river, you are not to remain attached to the raft, you do not carry it with you on your journey on the other shore. It was like medicine; once cured from the disease of *duhkha* using the medicine of the teaching, you do not continue to take the medicine (Buddhist doctrines). You put the medicine aside; you do not regard Buddhist doctrines as absolute truths to be held to at all costs.

The Buddha regarded the conceptual search for the metaphysical origins of suffering and evil to be of no help in eliminating your own dissatisfaction. Instead, the truth of "Life is *duhkha*" is justified on the basis of your own personal experience. Is this your experience? If so, then, like the physician offering medicine, Buddhism offers to you a series of steps that you can take to alleviate that frustration. If your experience is not that life is *duhkha*, then there is no particular reason why you should follow the Buddhist Middle Way.

The question on the ultimate origins of *duhkha* is philosophically interesting, but is not directly relevant to the goal of the Buddhist path—the elimination of your suffering.

GLOSSARY

Arhat Arhat refers to one of the followers of the Buddhist path who has put an end to *duhkha* and attained Nirvana.

Aryans Lit. "Nobles," the invading armies from central Europe who conquered the indigenous peoples of northern India about 1500 B.C.E., a thousand years before the birth of the Buddha.

Brahmins This hereditary group is the priests of Indian society, who occupy the highest level of status in Indian civilization.

Dhammapada The *Dhammapada* is a collection of the sayings of the Buddha primarily dealing with questions of morality.

Duhkha *Duhkha* means suffering, frustration, grief, dissatisfaction, unsatisfactoriness.

Egoistic hedonism Egoistic hedonism is the ethical position that the only rational course of action is for each person to try to maximize his or her own pleasure, or own advantage, when making moral choices.

Enlightenment The experience of realizing the causally interdependent nature of reality, and putting an end to *duhkha*, is referred to as Enlightenment.

Four Noble Truths The truths are (1) the existence of *duhkha*; (2) *duhkha* has causes; (3) the end of *duhkha* is possible and is called Nirvana; and (4) the Noble Eightfold Path is a means to put an end to *duhkha*.

Hedonism Hedonism refers to the view that the good is equivalent to pleasure.

Heterodox Those Indian religious traditions that reject the absolute authority of the *Vedas* are defined as heterodox. This includes Buddhism, as well as Jainism and Sikhism.

Karma Karma is understood as a natural law (like gravity) that returns consequences to the actor which are similar to the actor's original actions; that is, good acts generate good consequences for the person who performs the acts and evil acts return undesirable consequences.

Liberation Liberation refers to being free from suffering, free from the continuing painful cycle of birth and death.

Monist A religious position is monist if it holds that all that exists is fundamentally one. All the apparent differences we experience daily involve some sort of error or illusion. The majority of Hindu schools are not monist, and early Buddhism is not monist.

Monotheistic The religious position that is monotheistic believes there is just one divine being, or god.

Nirvana Nirvana is the state of any human being who has put an end to self-centered grasping, ignorance, anger, and hatred in their dealings with the world. It is blowing out the violent self-centered passions that dominate ordinary lives. This state describes the life of someone who has attained Enlightenment. Nirvana is attained here and now while one is living.

Orthodox Those schools that accept the sacred books of the Aryans, the *Vedas*, as revelation or as absolute truth are considered orthodox; the orthodox traditions are the ones called "Hinduism." There are many, and they differ considerably in their basic religious orientations from polytheism to monotheism to monism to atheism.

Polytheistic The religious position that there is more than one divinity, or god, is defined as polytheistic.

Pratityasamutpada This is dependent coarising, the causally interdependent nature of all of reality, the interdependent processes which make up all of reality.

Three Poisons The Three Poisons refer to the three things that obstruct Nirvana and are the causes of *duhkha*, i.e., self-centered craving, anger/hatred, confusion/ignorance. The elimination of these three from the personality results in Nirvana.

Upanishads The last group of the Hindu holy books, the *Upanishads*, were composed around the period of 500–100 B.C.E. These are a wide range of philosophical treatises on the ultimate nature of reality (which was thought to be eternal and unchanging) and the relationship of the human soul, or *atman*, to that ultimate reality.

Vedas The *Vedas* are the holy books of the non-Buddhist Aryans. The earliest is the *Rig Veda*, a collection of hymns to the Aryan gods composed prior to 1500 B.C.E.

A GUIDE TO FURTHER READINGS

Dharmasiri, G. *Fundamentals of Buddhist Ethics* (Antioch, Calif.: *Golden Leaves Publishing Co.,* 1989). Basic discussion of the Buddhist precepts and rules.

Dumoulin, Heinrich, and John C. Maraldo. *Buddhism in the Modern World* (New York: Collier Books, 1976); "Buddhist Ethics (pp. 25–30)" in "Background" by Hajime Nakamura. Good discussion of the background for Buddhist ethics.

Herman, A. L. *An Introduction to Buddhist Thought* (Lanham, Md.: University Press of America, 1983). The major concepts of Buddhism are discussed from a Western philosophical perspective.

Humphreys, C. *The Wisdom of Buddhism* (New York: Random House, 1960). A good anthology of Buddhist writings from many eras.

Jayatilleke, K. N. *Ethics in Buddhist Perspective,* The Wheel Publication No. 175–176 (Kandy, Ceylon [Sri Lanka]: Buddhist Publication Society, 1972). A brief discussion of the rules and precepts of Indian Buddhism.

Kalupahana, David J. *Buddhist Philosophy: A Historical Analysis* (Honolulu, Hawaii: The University Press of Hawaii, 1976). An excellent discussion of the most fundamental Buddhist philosophical concepts.

Kalupahana, David J. *A History of Buddhist Philosophy: Continuities and Discontinuities* (Honolulu, Hawaii: University of Hawaii Press, 1992). Basic Buddhist philosophy explained clearly and accurately.

Kalupahana, David J. *A Path of Righteousness: Dhammapada* (Lanham, Md.: University Press of America, 1986). A translation and analysis of one of the early Buddhist texts dealing with morality and ethics.

Rahula. *What the Buddha Taught* (New York: Grove Press, numerous reprintings). One of the very best introductions to early Buddhism.

Saddhatissa, H. *Buddhist Ethics: Essence of Buddhism* (London: George Allen & Unwin, 1970). A book-length study of the role of morality and precepts in Indian Buddhism.

Tachibana, S. *The Ethics of Buddhism* (Oxford: Oxford University Press, 1926). A brief discussion of rules for monks, nuns, and laypersons.

PART FOUR

Ethics in China During the Classical Period (5th–2nd Century B.C.E.):

Confucianism and Taoism

In this section we discuss ethical thought in China, in particular, two of the most important Chinese philosophical traditions, Confucianism and Taoism (pronounced "Daoism"). Sometimes people assume that all "Oriental philosophies" are pretty much the same, and so they lump together philosophies of India, China, and the other countries of the East. Nothing could be farther from the truth. As we shall see, Chinese philosophy is profoundly different from the various Indian philosophies. In addition, the Chinese philosophical traditions have as long, as rigorous, and as important a history as the Greek, Buddhist, and Christian traditions.

The two indigenous Chinese traditions, Confucianism and Taoism, are genuinely alternative ethical traditions to the West, and neither of them fit neatly into the categories that Western philosophers have devised for Greek and Judeo-Christian thought.

The Chinese philosophical and religious writings are carefully thought out, sometimes wise, and occasionally even sublime. These traditions sustained one of the world's great civilizations for well over two thousand years. The importance of these non-Western Chinese ways of conceptualizing ethical principles is that they challenge our own presuppositions, they contradict our own traditions of wisdom, and thus they offer us an opportunity to examine our own values that seem so obvious and so unchallengeable. In other words, we can learn from them.

THE BACKGROUND OF CHINESE PHILOSOPHY

Any discussion of Chinese philosophy requires a brief discussion of the Chinese written language. The Chinese language is pictorial, not phonetic, and one cannot tell the pronunciation of a Chinese character by its visual form. The problem

151

is how to take a Chinese ideogram, or character, and express it using roman letters like *a, b,* and *c;* this process is called romanization of Chinese. There are two systems of doing this: the Wade-Giles system (developed by linguists in the 1800s) and the Pinyin system (developed in mainland China in the 1950s). The Wade-Giles system has been in use in the West for well over a hundred years. The Pinyin system has been used in the West since 1979. Both systems are in use in academic publications. In this chapter, I use primarily the Wade-Giles romanization, followed by the Pinyin in parentheses (if it is different), and I provide an informal guide to pronunciation if there is any doubt.

According to archaeological findings, Chinese civilization has its roots in the Yellow River Basin around 2500 B.C.E. The Chinese consider the Hsia (written "Xia" in Pinyin and pronounced something like "Sha") dynasty to be the first dynasty and traditionally date it about 2200–1700 B.C.E., although the evidence for its existence is scanty. It is the succeeding dynasty, the Shang, that laid the ground for many of the fundamental Chinese beliefs about the world, and the religious and courtly rituals used by later dynasties. The dates for the Shang are approximately 1700–1122 B.C.E. The Shang dynasty was overthrown in 1122 B.C.E. by the Chou (written "Zhou" in Pinyin and pronounced something like "Joe").

The culture of the previous Shang dynasty had such immense prestige and was so highly valued that the new Chou rulers preserved the Shang written language as well as Shang rituals, literature, and laws. The Shang language also was used for Chou poetry, ritual, law, and for writing down the deepest sayings of the wisest among them. This is the language of ideograms that evolved into the written Chinese language that is still used today.

The new Chou emperor claimed that he ruled by the grace of Heaven (*t'ien* [*tian* in Pinyin], pronounced "tee-en"). According to the Chou emperors, *t'ien* graced them with a "Mandate of Heaven," which gave them the moral authority and spiritual connections to justify their rule. In the beginning, the Chou ruler claimed that he received the Mandate of Heaven as a reward for his virtue, not because he was born into a certain family. Thus, the ruler was called the *Son of Heaven,* but this was symbolic of a relationship of reward, not an ancestral relationship. Thus, it was the Chou who stressed the idea of the ruler who had the authority to rule because of his virtue, and whose chief duty was the welfare of his subjects and maintaining the harmony between heaven and earth. Of course, the European political (and religious) rulers made a similar claim; kings claimed to rule by the grace of God, and their authority came from the Divine. This was the divine right of kings to rule.

Confucianism, Taoism, and a dozen other religious and philosophical movements originated during the chaos that followed the collapse of the Chou dynasty. As the centuries passed, the Chou dynasty lost power as succeeding emperors became more corrupt, weaker, less competent, and finally, powerless. Historically, the sixth century B.C.E. is the beginning of a lengthy period of chaos; virtually independent feudal lords each attempted to establish themselves as the new emperor of China. The majority of feudal leaders were completely corrupt. They did not honor agreements and treaties, and the result was social chaos and economic deterioration. Traditional order and authority crumbled. Assassination and even patricide was common among feudal lords. Loyalty and trust no longer existed. Political boundaries were constantly shifting. Armies were on the move, and when armies move, farmers lose their seed, their stock, everything. Famine haunted the area for years later.

During this period we find the beginnings of the most important of the many philosophical traditions, including Confucianism and Taoism. However, neither of them became dominant during this period. China would not experiment with a Confucian form of government for another three to four hundred years after the death of Confucius.

The political decay and destruction continued on unabated to create what the Chinese refer to as the "Period of the Warring States" (403–221 B.C.E.). It was not to end until the founder of the Ch'in dynasty (*Chin* in Pinyin) defeated all the rival states and established himself as first emperor of the Ch'in dynasty (221–206 B.C.E.). He reestablished a central government with strict controls and adopted a successful political philosophy called Legalism as the official philosophy of the Ch'in government. Legalist techniques resulted in a "Law and Order" society of unprecedented strength. Strict rewards and punishments were used to control the people. The government ordered the burning of all the classical literature of China that suggested ideas other than Legalist ideas. This action resulted in the near total destruction of almost all the great Chinese classics, many of which were reconstructed later, with varying success.

The spectacular collapse of the Ch'in dynasty was followed by the Han dynasty (206 B.C.E.–220 C.E.), and it was in the period of approximately 100 B.C.E. that the ideas of Confucius became the official philosophical foundation for the Chinese government. The Han era reflected a belief that using force to control the people is uncivilized. Government should rule by providing moral examples.

Confucianism and Taoism initially took shape in this period of social chaos, between 600 and 200 B.C.E.

THE PRESUPPOSITIONS AND CHARACTERISTICS OF ANCIENT CHINESE PHILOSOPHY

The Chinese philosophies shared the same common roots and presuppositions. They did disagree, but their arguments were more often about details. Customs and traditions were held in common. The dominance of Confucianism and Taoism was virtually uncontested by any non-Chinese system for nearly 800 years. Buddhism did not even enter China until between 50 B.C.E. and 50 C.E., and it did not become of central importance in China for another three hundred years. After the fifth century C.E., we find different systems generated by the mixture of Confucianism, Taoism, and Buddhism.

We should begin by noting that classical Chinese philosophy tends not to be systematic in the way we have seen in previous chapters. In the major Chinese philosophical writings, the authors do not proceed using clearly defined premises, conclusions, and logical structures. Rather, Chinese thinkers tended to use aphorisms and metaphors to express profound insights.

In general, Chinese philosophy has two central concerns: relationships between human beings, and the relationship of humanity to nature. In China, nature was never seen as something intrinsically different from human beings. There is a clear sense of continuity and harmony between human beings and nature. The Chinese would say that human beings share a relationship with heaven and earth. Heaven and humans are parts of a single reality. Human beings and human societies participate in the works of nature; we grow out of nature as a flower or plant grows out of nature; we flower as naturally as a rose flowers. Humans may be the center of the universe, but the universe is somehow very much like us and we are very much like it. We belong here; this world is our home.[1]

Absolutely essential to all Chinese thought is the idea that cultivating one's own mind is the means for understanding the ultimate, for attaining liberating wisdom. The highest goal of all Chinese philosophy and religion is to become a sage, and although difficult and rare, this is attainable by each individual and results from cultivating what is within you.[2] There is no need for any intermediary, be it a priesthood or a savior divinity.

The Chinese did not think of causation the way the West did. Western thinkers tended to think of things influencing one another by acts of mechanical causation, in which the prior impact of one thing is the cause of the motion of the other. For much of Western philosophy, the universe is very much like a machine, like an immensely complicated clockwork mechanism. From this understanding, it follows that physics and biology can explain anything in the physical world.

In contrast, the Chinese view was to think of the universe of things and events as patterns. In this kind of thinking things influence one another, not by acts of mechanical causation, but rather by mutual influences, similar to the way that one person's mood can affect another person's mood. The universe is one vast interdependent system. One component takes the lead for a while, spontaneously, and then another component takes the lead—and all parts cooperate together in perfect freedom, the larger and the smaller playing their parts. All things react to one another by a kind of mysterious resonance. In the early Chinese worldview, nothing was uncaused, but nothing was caused mechanically either.

The ancient Chinese noticed alternations of aspects. If two things happened to be connected, as noon is connected to midnight, it was not because of sequential cause and effect, but rather because they were somehow paired. Paired things are related like concave and convex, like the figure and the shadow, like the echo and the sound, like the shadow and the light. These things go together naturally, not because they are mechanically joined.

Thus, all things exist together in harmony, interrelated, functioning like an organism, in a dynamic unity—and humanity has a special responsibility. Human beings can disrupt the harmony, or they can support and maintain this harmony.

The Tao

This dynamic interactive pattern and the resultant harmony, eventually came to be called the **Tao** (*Dao* in Pinyin, pronounced "Dow"), which means "road," "path," or "Way." The Chinese systems have differing ideas about how the Tao is conceived, known, and followed. To the Confucians, Tao was relatively clear and knowable and had a profound moral content consisting of patterns in social and ritual behavior. With Tao understood this way, it follows that human beings are fundamentally moral beings whose activities should result in moral good. Scholarship and education were indispensable means of knowing the Tao. On the other hand, Taoists used the term Tao for a metaphysical reality that was prior to the distinction between good and evil, treating Tao as essentially mysterious, best approached in simplicity and "naturalness."

Principles of Yin and Yang

Tao was the ultimate ordering principle of the world, and although it meant "road," or "path," it came to mean the paths of the stars in the sky, the patterns of celestial change, and finally the path of all nature. These patterns correspond to seasons, to cold and hot, to wet and dry, to patterns of growth, to flourishing, followed by a period of dormancy. Tao is the continuous field in which all multiplicities are harmonized.

Things are naturally paired, and those pairs are primordial. The universe cycled between poles, one of which was called *yin* and the other called *yang*. These are symbolic. *Yin* included things covered by clouds; dark, hidden, secret, cool. *Yin* is fall and winter; it is the dark of night. *Yang* included things bright and shiny; light, open, warm. *Yang* is spring and summer; it is high noon.

Yin might be ascendant for a while, but then it will go into decline and be replaced by its *yang* counterpart. Nothing is completely *yin* or completely *yang*. Reversal is inevitable to the pattern. We see this in nature. Summer (*yang* is bright, warm, and the time of active growth of plants; winter (*yin*) is dark and cold, and the time of dormant plants. This pairing applies to human beings as well as everything else. Consider human sexuality: the male as *yang* (overt, active, aggressive) and the female as *yin* (hidden, passive, and yielding). If you live on a farm and pay attention, you see the cycling of the seasons, the cycles of the farm animals, and even the cycles of human existence. You live with an extended family and see the birth of brothers and sisters, the passing away of great-grandparents and grandparents. We cannot help but notice that we are born soft and weak (*yin*) and we grow to strength (*yang*), and then we return again to weakness and death.

The primordial *yin-yang* pair cannot exist independently of each other, unlike the way absolute goodness is completely independent of and at war with evil in Christianity. In China, each element of the pair is essential to the other, each is necessary; they are mutually dependent. *Yin* and *yang* are modalities of Tao, equal and opposite forces, one active and one quiescent. The two act together in complete harmony—not strife.

Attitudes Toward the Past

In an important sense, Chinese thought tends to look back to the past as the perfect time. History is not a progressive movement where things will get better; rather, history begins with the moral perfection of the Golden Age of the Chou dynasty of the past, followed by a falling away from the virtues of the Golden Age. The Chinese thought that in the Golden Age the rulers had been sages, wise men who embodied perfect wisdom. Current emperors were clearly not perfect. Among those who were idealized were the legendary sage-kings Yao and Shun, and the Duke of Chou (the perfect administrator and scholar).

CHAPTER 7

K'ung Fu-tzu (Confucius):

Rules Combined with Benevolence and Insight

THE LIFE OF CONFUCIUS (551–479 B.C.E.)

The man we know as Confucius,* K'ung Fu-tzu (written as *Kong fu-ze* in Pinyin romanization) was born in 551 B.C.E. and died at age seventy-two in 479 B.C.E. Thus, he was born about the same time as the Buddha, and died shortly before Socrates was born in Greece. As with most of the people from this period, we have very few uncontested facts about his life. However, many claims were made within the later Confucian tradition about the life of Confucius.

He was born in an impoverished family of lower nobility in what is today Shantung Province in eastern China. His ancestors may have been related to ancient Shang nobility. We know that he studied ceremonial rites and became a learned expert in ancient rituals. He was an unimportant bureaucrat (later tradition says that he was a clerk in the Memorial Temple for the Duke of Chou, and after that led ceremonies for a local community village temple).

He held several minor political positions and attracted a number of students as his reputation for wisdom spread. According to legends and tradition, at age fifty, Confucius was appointed to the position of chief magistrate of a city near the Lu capital—but becoming disillusioned when his advice was mostly ignored,

*The name "Confucius" is not a Chinese term at all. In fact, the Christians who were in China attempting to convert the Chinese to Christianity wrote letters in Latin and mailed them back to their superiors in Rome, and "Confucius" is their Latinized form of the Chinese name K'ung Fu-tzu.

he resigned. Since none of the leaders would pay heed to his advice, he retired from politics and earned his living as a private teacher, accepting tuition from his students. Like Socrates, Confucius was a wandering teacher (perhaps the first private teacher in Chinese history). As a private teacher, he and his students traveled throughout northern China trying to convince various rulers to change their ways and follow his insights. However, no ruler would pay serious attention to his ideas. Confucius is quoted as follows:

> At fifteen, I set my heart on learning; at thirty, I took my stand; at forty I came to be free from doubts; at fifty I understood the Decree of Heaven; at sixty my ear was attuned [to the truth]; at seventy I followed by heart's desire without overstepping the line.[3]

When he was fifteen, Confucius began to study the classics of Chinese philosophy. With this understanding of the classics, he began to understand the Tao of the sages of the past and the *li*. When he was thirty, he could apply the *li* appropriately. After twenty more years, he understood that morality and virtue are built into the fabric of reality, and he understood that Heaven rewards virtuous behavior. When he was sixty, his behavior was in effortless accord with the Decree of Heaven. At age seventy, no matter what he wanted to do, he could follow his desires and at the same time, he could act with perfect benevolence.

During his own lifetime, Confucius was not particularly important, and even his followers who established the tradition we call "Confucianism" did not become dominant until almost three hundred years after his death.

CONFUCIAN PHILOSOPHY

As you recall, the essential question for the Greek philosophers was "What is the good life for man?" The Confucians had two fundamental questions. The first reflected the central problem for all the Chinese philosophical systems during this historical period of chaos: "How can we bring about order and harmony among individual humans and a well-ordered society?"

The second is related to the first. Confucianism asked, "What is the right thing to do?" Ultimately, Confucius answers this question: Understand yourself to know what is right, and then do it because this will bring about a well-ordered society; it will affect the quality of your life. There were no supernatural or divine sanctions to the moral laws, and there were no rewards beyond simply knowing that you had done the right thing.

In his discussions, Confucius did not indulge in theological speculation. He ignored most popular religious rituals and ceremonies as superstition. He advised his students to work with honesty and be upright in their personal conduct, but not worry about the spirits or other divinities. The concern was with what we would call ethical issues rather than religious issues.

Confucianism refers to both the original teachings of Confucius and the later tradition of additions and modifications by later generations of followers. In Confucianism, human beings are fundamentally social and moral creatures, who are capable of living on a very lofty moral plane, but usually do not do so. Confucianism teaches rules of good order and right behavior for everyday living, including the social, personal, and political realms. If these rules are followed, human affairs will be in accord with the **Way of Heaven,** and this will bring human development to its highest point by bringing it into accord with all things. Thus, Confucianism can be described as promulgating a set of ethical, social, and political guidelines. As such, original Confucianism seems more a system of philosophy rather than a religion. Confucius did not support his claims using religious sanctions; in fact, there is no religious structure discernible in his sayings.

On the other hand, the tradition of Confucianism does include elements that we would ordinarily classify as religious. For example, Confucianism stresses ancestral rites and includes reverence toward Heaven. In later popular forms of Confucianism, we see a stress on ceremony, sacrifices, and temples. Actually, Confucian temples are an outgrowth of later folk religion; in early Confucianism, the temples were places for memorial monuments and not religious institutions in the sense that Buddhist temples were.

Ultimately, Confucianism came to dominate all of Chinese life—in politics, in social and moral areas, and in some aspects of religious life.

CONFUCIAN ETHICS

The basic book of Confucianism is known as the Confucian *Analects*[4] and is a record of numerous moral maxims, anecdotes, sayings of Confucius, and conversations between Confucius, his immediate students, and his grandson, as remembered and passed on by the later generations of students. The *Analects* (**Lun-yü**) has twenty short chapters, and about 12,700 Chinese characters. The words of K'ung Fu-tzu were not written down until after his death, and the version we have is from about the first century C.E. The *Analects* stress ethics, but these ethical teachings apply to both the personal and the social and political ideology. In the *Analects* we find no discussion of the preferences of the gods, no mention of life after death, and no belief in the physical immortality of a unitary soul. There are no metaphysical speculations about the ultimate nature of the universe.

The tradition of Confucianism relies on the *Analects* and other books written by later Confucian philosophers, especially the *Meng-tzu** ("Meng zi" in Pinyin, pronounced something like "Mung zu" or "Mencius" as Latinized by the West) and the *Hsün-tzu* ("Xinzi" in Pinyin).† These also had a profound influence on the later development of Confucianism in China.

---

*Mencius (Meng-tzu) lived from about 372 to 289 B.C.E., supported Confucius's ideas, arguing for benevolence in government, the doctrine that people are born with the seeds of goodness and the claim that everyone has the potentiality of becoming a sage.

†Hsün-tzu lived from about 300–235 B.C.E., and he disagreed with Mencius as much as he agreed with Confucius. Hsün-tzu's key idea is that human beings are born self-centered and greedy (not good as Mencius argued), and thus human beings needed to be taught Confucian ideas to make them good.

The Glorification of the Past

Confucius did not see himself as the creator of his teachings; rather, they come from studying the ancient past of five hundred years before. In the *Analects,* Confucius says, "I transmit but do not innovate; I am truthful in what I say and devoted to antiquity."[5] Confucius pointed out that the sage-kings who ruled during the Golden Age of the Chou dynasty had ruled with virtue, not with power and armies. By extension, then, modern rulers must set a moral standard by exemplifying the moral perfections of the past. This allows them to rule by moral persuasion and personal example, and not by laws and punishment.

The ruler and his subjects were intimately related, and the society needed to consider both in order to develop harmoniously. The people serve the rulers, but the rulers also serve the people, principally by being an example that people can model themselves upon. People will follow when the ruler is virtuous:

> In administering your government, what need is there for you to kill? Just de-sire the good yourself and the common people will be good. The virtue of the gentlemen is like wind; the virtue of the small man is like grass. Let the wind blow over the grass and it is sure to bend.[6]

Thus, we can recall the central problem for all the Chinese philosophical sys-tems during the period of chaos was: "How can we install order and harmony among human beings? How can we bring about a well-ordered society?" Con-fucius believed he had found the answer to this problem. To instill order and har-mony among men, Confucius stresses the necessity of returning to the principles of the past. One of the most important components to his solution was *li.*

Li and Social Order

One of the most important concepts essential to Confucius's thinking is *li,* which is also a central component of his solution to the problem of instilling order and harmony. Before Confucius, the term probably referred to the "ritualistic eti-quette" prescribed by the court as proper aristocratic conduct. However, as used by Confucius, the term *li* has no exact English equivalent. *Li* describes how hu-man beings interact when they are genuine and sincere with each other. Hu-mans interact with one another following some rules. We say "thank you" and we say "please." Strangers introduce themselves following a standard greeting, and then shake hands. These bring out the inherent dignity in the ceremony of human interaction. Friends speak to friends differently than they do to strangers. Husbands greet their wives differently than they greet friends, or their children. In church we behave differently than if we are at a sporting event. We behave differently if we are speaking to a priest than if we are speaking to a child, and even these responses shift depending on whether we are in a church or at a picnic. Unmarried couples going out for a date have some unspoken rules by which both parties are expected to abide.

We know that human interaction is guided by rules. Proper conduct is guided by social rituals, moral rules, private manners and etiquette, religious rituals, and even courtly rituals. *Li* has been translated by many different words that carry a sense of the wide-ranging meaning: *rite, ritual, custom, decorum, propriety, manners, moral norms, moral laws, proper conduct, religious practices, social rules, good manners,* and *etiquette.*[7]

For Confucius, *li* are the patterns by which we ought to live, and they supply the guides that a human being should use to regulate his or her life. *Li* are all-encompassing and can be used to direct all aspects of one's life. If you regulate your life with *li*, you will avoid conflict with others, provide for harmony, and preserve harmony.

> The Master said, "Unless a man has the spirit of the rites [*li*], in being respectful he will wear himself out, in being careful he will become timid, in having courage he will become unruly, and in being forthright he will become intolerant."[8]

Confucius thought that *li* depended on two things: (1) the relationship between the people involved, and (2) the situations that the human beings were in. The relationships were rather straightforward. The proper behavior varied depending on whether we have the relationship of ruler to his subjects, of father to son, of husband to wife, of elder brother to younger brother, or of elder friend to younger friend. Note that each of these are reciprocal and hierarchical; the relationship is that of superior to subordinate, except for the last, friend to friend. A hierarchy is built into the Confucian view of the world. Inasmuch as three of the five have to do with immediate family, we can see how central family relationships are in the Confucian value system.

Li also depends on the situation in which the human beings find themselves. For example, is it an occasion for mourning, like a funeral? Is it an occasion for joy (perhaps a wedding, celebrating a birth, etc.)? Is it an occasion that calls for giving a gift, or are you going to request a favor?

It is clear that one is not born knowing the proper greetings to strangers, neighbors, siblings, or parents. The social rules are learned. They are taught. Education is essential to becoming a gentleman. But, some things are innate. What human beings have that separates them from the animals is innate, and Confucius called that property *jen*.

The Central Virtue: *Jen*

The central Confucian virtue is *jen* (*ren* in Pinyin, pronounced something like "wren"). It is what separates humans from animals, and it is essential for a human relationship.

> The Master said, "Of neighbourhoods benevolence [*jen*] is the most beautiful. How can the man be considered wise who, when he has the choice, does not settle in benevolence?"[9]

The Chinese ideograph for *jen* is a combination of the graph for human being and the number 2. Thus, *jen* is what humans have in common and what joins them together; it is the ideal relationship between two human beings. Scholars have attempted to capture this sense by translating *jen* as benevolence, humaneness, humanity, love, human-heartedness, goodness, human-goodness, human fellowship, and brotherly love. When asked to explain *jen*, Confucius replied, "*Jen* consists in loving others" (*Analects*, 12.22).

Jen is what is within you that makes you a human being instead of an animal.[10] *Jen* is the potential moral character that humans need to cultivate, and when cultivated, humans can perfect themselves as human beings. Thus Confucius can describe *jen* as the Way of Heaven. *Jen* is completely natural; it is the essential nature of being human. In Confucianism, there is no original sin, no inherited bias toward evil or sin. Human beings can fail to do the correct thing, but they are not sinful.

> The Master said, "Benevolence [*jen*] is more vital to the common people than even fire and water. In the case of fire and water, I have seen men die by stepping on them, but I have never seen any man die by stepping on benevolence."[11]

Jen is the foundation of all particular virtues: the Master said, "If a man sets his heart on benevolence, he will be free from evil."[12]

Jen is the measure of individual character, to be a person who perfected *jen* was the goal of Confucian self-cultivation. Confucius concluded that the person of *jen* will be conscientious toward himself and altruistic toward others. It is a potentiality that manifests itself differently in different social situations.

> Fan Ch'ih asked about benevolence [*jen*]. The Master said, "While at home hold yourself in a respectful attitude; when serving in an official capacity be reverent; when dealing with others do your best. These are qualities that cannot be put aside, even if you go and live among the barbarians."[13]

In fact, Confucius supplied a number of rough guides to fill out the idea of being conscientious toward oneself and altruistic toward others. For example, a variation on the Golden Rule (Do unto others what you would have them do unto you) is found in the following oft-quoted passage from the *Analects* (this negative form is sometimes referred to as the "Silver Rule"):

> Chung-kung asked about benevolence [*jen*]. The Master said, "When abroad behave as though you were receiving an important guest. When employing the services of the common people behave as though you were officiating at an important sacrifice. Do not impose on others what you yourself do not desire. In this way you will be free from ill will whether in a state or in a noble family."[14]

Confucius urges: Perfect yourself, and then you can extend yourself to others so they can perfect themselves.

> The person of *jen*, wishing to establish his own character, also seeks to establish the character of others. Wishing to succeed, he also seeks to help others to succeed. To be able to judge of others by which is near in ourselves, this may be the method of achieving *jen*. (*Analects* 6:28)

Thus, *jen* is not simply an individual virtue; it is also a social virtue. *Jen* is natural to a human being, but it is cultivated and developed within oneself and one's relationships with others. In fact, in one place Confucius said "*Jen* consists in loving others" (*Analects* 12.22).

There seem to be three interrelated meanings for *jen:* (1) the virtue of loving one's fellows; (2) the virtue of respecting oneself and doing what is proper; and (3) establishing oneself in order to establish others, perfect oneself, and then help others to perfect themselves.

Although Confucius explained *jen* as "*Jen* consists in loving others," we cannot simply start out loving everyone. Where should we begin? The answer given by Confucians is to begin with the most fundamental human relationship, that between child and parent. The virtue corresponding to this connection is called *filial piety,* the primary unit of mutual connection between persons. It is the love, respect, and honor due to one's parents. But filial piety is only the starting point of *jen.*

The Relationship between *Jen* and *Li*

It is instructive to see how these two key ideas are related. According to Confucians, the public rites of *li* are the external expression of the internal virtue of *jen.* *Jen* is a state of being; it is your essence. *Li* is the unique human activity that expresses this *jen.* The *li* spell out the proper way of expressing *jen.* Until the *li* are mastered, one's *jen* cannot be fully realized. Thus, to lead a life according to the traditional and conventional codes of *li* is to live a life that allows for the full flowering of one's moral nature (*jen*).[15]

The Cultivation of *Yi,* Righteousness

Another essential concept of Confucianism is *yi* (pronounced as the letter *e* in English). It has two components. The first refers to an objective quality in a situation we can perceive that tells us the "rightness" or "oughtness" of a situation. The second component is in the person; it is the moral sense we use to apply our *jen* to a specific situation. Thus, *yi* is a property of situations, and an internal sense that tells us what is fitting and proper. *Yi* is the moral sense that enables us to relate universal moral principles to particular situations. We can recognize which action is the right one to do, and then we do it. *Yi* is recognizing the most appropriate way to express our *jen,* which means picking out the appropriate *li* in a particular situation. Considerations of self-advantage, profit, or benefit are not relevant. Confucius says, "The gentleman understands what is moral [*yi*]. The small person understands what is profitable."[16]

This area reveals that, for Confucius, one's motives are more important than the consequences of one's actions. If people have good intentions, but circumstances prevent them from carrying out the behavior they wish to, nevertheless we still consider them praiseworthy. Their character is what counts. This accounts for Confucius's dogged persistence in seeking public office:

> The reason why the ideal man tries to go into politics is because he holds this to be right, even though he is well aware that his principles cannot prevail. (*Analects* 18.7)

The content of righteousness [*yi*] is not quite the same as the Western translation suggests. For example, Confucius did not think that one should love one's neighbors as much as one's own family, and Confucius certainly did not think that one should love one's enemies.

> Should one love one's enemy, those who do us harm?
>   By no means. Answer hatred with justice and love with benevolence. Otherwise you would waste your benevolence (*jen*). (*Analects* 14.36)

In another dialogue, someone asked Confucius what he thought of the moral maxim, "Repay an injury with a good turn," and the Master disagreed with this, saying "What, then, do you repay a good turn with? You repay an injury with *straightness*, but you repay a good turn with a good turn."[17]

Other Confucian Virtues

The Chinese term *te*, translated as "virtue" (*de* in Pinyin, pronounced "duh"), is related to how effectively a thing performs its function. The meaning of *te* varies from Taoism to Confucianism, but in Confucianism it has a very strong moral slant that is absent in Taoism. It can be suggested by translating it as "moral force" or "good conduct."

Confucius regarded *jen* as the root of the other virtues. Among the key virtues of a Confucian gentleman we find justice, propriety, courage, wisdom, sincerity, conscientiousness, and filial piety (*hsiao, xiao* in Pinyin, meaning reverence and honor for one's parents). Sometimes later Confucians regarded it as the most desirable of all moral qualities. It included not only honoring one's parents, but also never disobeying their wishes, being sincerely concerned with their health and welfare, being concerned about the family name and fortunes, and bringing sons into the world to ensure the continuation of the family line. Many of the rites (*li*) concerned ceremonies to be continued after the death of the ancestors for seven generations in the past.

> The Master said, "When your parents are alive, comply with the rites in serving them; when they die, comply with the rites in burying them; comply with the rites in sacrificing to them."[18]

One other important Confucian virtue is altruism (*shu*, also translated as reciprocity).

> Tzu-kung asked, "Is there a single word which can be a guide to conduct throughout one's life?" The Master said, "It is perhaps the word '*shu*' [reciprocity]. Do not impose on others what you yourself do not desire."[19]

The sage was the person who manifested these virtues in perfect harmony, and then expressed these in his daily conduct (*li*).

The Ideal Gentleman

The highest achievement and ultimate goal for the Confucian tradition was the sage. The sage had perfected all virtues, was perfect in *li* and *jen*, and could not make any mistakes. Becoming a sage was extraordinarily rare and difficult. However, there was a goal one step below that of the sage, which any conscientious male could achieve. This is what we might translate as an "ideal gentleman" (written *chun-tzu*, or *zhun-zi* in Pinyin, pronounced something like "jun-zu").

Originally, the Chinese characters *chun-tzu* referred to the son of a wealthy ruler, someone who belonged to the old hereditary elite classes, a young man of good birth and high social status. Confucius gave a new moral meaning to the phrase, using the same combination of characters but redefining them to refer to someone of true moral worth regardless of social class, in other words, an "ideal man" or a "true gentleman." Such a person sincerely cultivates inner qualities and is a member of the elite because he *deserved* to be.

According to Confucius, the ideal gentleman is someone who is striving for moral excellence. He consciously strives to cultivate the virtues within himself. He states the truth without consideration of profit. He tries to become refined, cultured, and virtuous. He is a man of *jen*. He is altruistic, but not yet a sage. The ideal gentleman can make mistakes, but he learns from his mistakes. He is not egocentric and is not dominated by selfish desires. Rather, he values those desires that contribute to the well-being of the group. He is concerned about the common good, and therefore, he seeks public office to serve others.

The ideal gentleman would not be a narrow specialist in some technical art or craft, but would be competent in all those areas essential for self-development. The ideal gentleman is concerned with self-perfection, but such self-development is not just a self-centered activity; there is another dimension to self-development. The ideal gentleman actually brings about the transformation of others because of his character. He will serve as a positive role model for others, and others will naturally admire and respect him, and pattern themselves after him.

The superior ideal man is not a sage ("a person of perfect *jen*") and is not completely above selfish desires. However, he is not dominated by selfish desires; he strikes a balance between selfish desires and selfless altruism. He knows *li*, he knows how to treat others according to their station in life and their relationship to him.

The ideal gentleman is also part of Confucius's solution to the problem of social chaos. Order and harmony could be restored if government officials would emulate the virtues of the true gentleman. If they had the inner sincerity typical of a person of *jen*, then the people would follow and emulate them. The highest moral exemplar is provided by the emperor, and if the emperor is not a person of *jen*, then laws and punishments will not be enough to cause the populace to obey.

> The Master said, "Guide them by edicts, keep them in line with punishments, and the common people will stay out of trouble but will have no sense of shame. Guide them by virtue, keep them in line with the rites [*li*], and they will, besides having a sense of shame, reform themselves."[20]

From this we can see that in Confucianism, politics is the extension of personal moral virtues into the political and social realm.

AN OVERVIEW OF CONFUCIAN ETHICS

Confucius was not concerned with creating or justifying particular moral laws, nor did he ground morality in anything supernatural. The Master said, "In his dealings with the world the gentleman is not invariably for or against anything. He is on the side of what is moral."[21] Morality is grounded in Tao and in human nature. We already know what is right and what is wrong and have known since the ancient days of the Golden Age. Confucius claimed that he merely wrote down the guidelines that help us to do what we know is right. We need to ask ourselves, "What is the right thing to do?" *Jen* and *li* provide the answers. We realize order and harmony among people on the basis of the moral nature of humans, brought about by what we know about ourselves. If you can get your own self in order, behave with sincerity toward yourself and with *li* toward others, everything else follows. If your own will is sincere, you will have a mind that is in balance. When your mind is harmonized, your personal life will serve as a proper example to your wife and children. Following your example, your family members will serve as exemplars for friends and neighbors. The community becomes harmonious and well regulated. One by one, communities become peaceful and orderly, and the nation is in order.

The model of the individual cultivation of virtue and family perfection starts the process in an upward direction; the model provided by the emperor starts the process downward. Order and harmony reign in the world, and there is peace everywhere.

If you can cultivate those natural virtues within yourself, happiness will follow the development of *jen*. Knowing *li*, you will act morally toward all human beings; following *li*, there will be no social problems.

The original expression of *jen* is found in filial piety (the proper attitude of respect and reverence for one's parents and ancestors), which then extends outwardly toward the other members of one's own family. From there, *jen* develops toward neighbors, expands to members of the community, and then it flows out as altruistic behavior toward all human beings.

Confucius's answer to the problem of instilling order and harmony among human beings can be summarized easily: we realize order and harmony on the basis of what we know about ourselves. Thus, conformity to the past, plus reason, can solve human problems. By cultivating *jen*, human beings can perfect themselves, perfect their society, and achieve peace, harmony, and happiness.

PROBLEMS TO PONDER

These are questions that any thoughtful person should think about if he or she were considering adopting the Confucian moral system. Perhaps the careful follower of Confucius can answer them. How would you answer them?

1. Confucianism urges that people should simply do what they know to be right, and if they do, social harmony will result because the virtuous examples provided by the rulers will ensure that people follow it. But

what should we do when our values conflict? What should we do when being a loyal subject conflicts with one's filial obligation to one's parents?

2. It could be argued that Confucianism is an unrealistic idealization of a past that never existed, a past in which rulers successfully portrayed themselves as ruling by virtue, but never did so in actuality. This objection is primarily historical and cannot be settled because we do not have the sort of historical information to either support or criticize Confucius's interpretation.

GLOSSARY

Analects These are the collected sayings of Confucius, and is one of the most important books in Chinese philosophy. In Chinese this is the *Lun-yü*.

Chun-tzu (zhun-zi) Chun-tzu is usually translated as "Superior Man" or "ideal gentleman." This person is farther along the spiritual path than an ordinary man but is not yet a sage—thus, someone who is striving for moral excellence, someone who consciously strives to cultivate the virtues within himself. The ideal gentleman learns from his mistakes. He is not egocentric and is not dominated by selfish desires. Rather, he values those desires that contribute to the well-being of the group. He is concerned about the common good, and therefore, he seeks public office to serve others.

Hsün-tzu (*Xinzi*) Hsün-tzu is the name of a Confucian philosopher who argued that human nature is basically evil; it is also the name of the book of his collected sayings.

Jen (*ren*) Jen is the inner essence of a human being, that which makes one truly human and the foundation of all virtues. It has been translated as benevolence, humaneness, humanity, love, human-heartedness, goodness, human-goodness, human fellowship, and brotherly love.

Li Li is a Chinese term with a broad range of interrelated meanings, all connected to proper conduct; thus, social rituals, moral rules, private manners and etiquette, religious rituals, and courtly rituals. Li has been translated by rite, ritual, custom, decorum, propriety, manners, moral norms, moral laws, proper conduct, religious practices, social rules, good manners, and etiquette. For Confucius, li are the patterns by which we ought to live, and they supply the guides that a human being should use to regulate his or her life. According to Confucius, following li helps us to avoid conflict with others, provides for harmony, and preserves harmony.

Lun-yü (*Analects*) This is a collection of the sayings of Confucius (K'ung Fu-tzu), which formed the basis for Confucian philosophy.

Meng-tzu (*Meng-zi*) Meng-tzu is the name of a Confucian philosopher and also the name of the book of his collected sayings.

Tao (*Dao*) Tao refers to the pattern of ceaseless change that we call "reality," or "nature," an unending circular flowing from one pole (*yin*) to its opposite (*yang*), and then the process of transformation returning back to *yin* once again; the pattern of nature, always in perfect harmony and balance. Each individual thing is a part of the pattern, oscillating between opposite poles while responding to the movement of the Tao. Tao is the pattern with which human beings ought to be in accord.

Te (*de*) Te means "virtue," the effectiveness of a thing to carry out its function. In Confucianism it has a very strong moral slant that is absent in Taoism. It can be suggested by translating it as "moral force" or "good conduct." Among the Confuciuan virtues are justice, propriety, courage, wisdom, sincerity, conscientiousness, and filial piety (*hsiao* reverence and honor for one's parents). Later Confucians regarded it as the most desirable of all moral qualities.

Way of Heaven Heaven is an impersonal force and it responds to the virtue, or lack of virtue, in the emperor and people. Heaven responds favorably to the virtue of the emperor and people, and it responds with disasters when the emperor or the people are not acting in the way that Heaven decrees.

Yang One of the two poles in Chinese thought, *yang* refers to the brightness, the active, the warm, the logical, the aggressive; summer, male.

Yi *Yi* is translated as righteousness. It has two components. The first refers to an objective quality in a situation we can perceive that tells us the "rightness" or "oughtness" of a situation. The second component is in the person; it is the moral sense we use to apply our *jen* to a specific situation. *Yi* is a property of situations, and an internal sense that tells us what is fitting and proper. To cultivate *yi* is the moral sense that enables us to learn how to relate universal moral principles to particular situations. We can recognize which action is the right one to do, and then we do it.

Yin The complement to *yang*, *yin* refers to the negative pole, the darkness, the passive, the hidden, the mysterious, the cool, the intuitive, the receptive; winter, female.

A GUIDE TO FURTHER READINGS

Ames, Roger, and David L. Hall. *Thinking Through Confucius* (Albany: State University of New York Press, 1987). An excellent Western philosophical analysis of the basic ideas of Confucius.

Creel, Herlee G. *Confucius and the Chinese Way* (New York: Harper and Row, 1960). A very good introduction to Confucianism and Chinese civilization.

Fung Yu-lan. *A History of Chinese Philosophy,*. Derk Bodde, 2 vol. (Princeton: Princeton University Press, 1952, 1953). The basic source for Chinese philosophy.

———. *A Short History of Chinese Philosophy* (New York: Macmillan, 1968). A good historical introduction to Chinese philosophy.

———. *The Spirit of Chinese Philosophy*, tr. E. R. Hughes (Boston: Beacon Press, 1962). A careful analysis of Chinese philosophy for students.

Graham, Angus C. *Disputers of the Tao: Philosophical Argument in Ancient China* (La Salle, Ill.: Open Court, 1989). A scholarly analysis of the use of logic and philosophy in ancient China.

Lau, D. C. *Confucius: The Analects* (New York, Penguin Books, 1979). The basic scholarly translation of the *Analects* of Confucius.

CHAPTER 8

Taoism:

Just Let Go!

As we discussed in the chapter on Confucianism, the Chinese thought of nature as a succession of constantly reoccurring patterns. In the fifth century B.C.E., most Chinese (and most people anywhere in the world) were farmers. When you live on a farm, growing your own food and raising animals, it is obvious that nature operates according to cyclical processes: night follows day followed by night again, the seasons of the year flow back and forth—spring, summer, autumn, winter, and then a return to spring again. Things are born, grow to fullness, and then decline, whether it be the life cycle of the moon (full, new, full), the life cycles of the farm animals, or the life cycles of all living things, including human beings. The obvious explanation is that nature itself is bipolar: everything has its opposite, and the pattern nature follows is one of swinging back and forth between these opposite poles. The paradigms of these poles are **yin** and **yang.** The *yin* is the dark, *yang* the bright; *yin* the soft, *yang* the hard; *yin* the winter cold, *yang* the summer heat.

Neither Confucians nor Taoists thought of nature like a machine, or like a giant clock wound up by the hand of God. Nature is not even the intentional creation of a rational supreme being. Especially for the Taoists, nature continually arises of itself in a spontaneous, mutually resonating process wherein each individual thing simultaneously creates the pattern and has a place in the pattern, as each separate dancer creates the pattern of the dance and has a unique place in that dance. All things exist together, interrelated, functioning like an organism in a dynamic unity—a grand pattern flowing back and forth.

The Chinese gave the name **Tao** to this ceaseless pattern.* It is not a thing, it is not an entity of some sort. According to the Taoists, the term *Tao* functions to draw our attention to the ultimate, the totality, that which is prior to all categories, prior to differentiation; that out of which all opposites arise; that which cannot be categorized, differentiated, summarized, or described (for it is the ultimate pattern behind all thought, and thus thinking cannot get back to its preconceptual source out of which thinking itself arises).

---

*The original Chinese character means "road," "path," "crossroads" and thus by association, Tao becomes "pathway," and then "The Way."

LAO-TZU AND THE *TAO TE CHING* (6TH CENTURY B.C.E.)

The founder of Taoism (pronounced "Daoism") and the author of the Taoist classic entitled *Tao Te Ching* (*Dao de jing* in Pinyin, pronounced "Dow Duh Jing" and translated "The Classic of the Way and Its Virtue") is a man named Lao-tzu (*Lao zi* in Pinyin). Lao-tzu is thought to have been an older contemporary of Confucius, so his dates are given as sixth century B.C.E.[1] Since Confucius was born in 551 B.C.E., some scholars assign a birth date of 571 B.C.E. to Lao-tzu.

We know nothing for certain about the life of Lao-tzu, and there is genuine doubt that the biographical bits which we have apply to the same person who created the *Tao Te Ching*. The traditional biography describes Lao-tzu as a librarian. The biographer may have confused Lao-tzu with a librarian who lived in about the same time period. However, for our purposes, we will use the name "Lao-tzu" to apply to the author of the classic, *Tao Te Ching*, whomever it might be.

The *Tao Te Ching* is a short book of approximately five thousand Chinese characters, composed of "philosophical poetry." It is filled with concrete poetic images with profoundly wise overtones. One insight is followed by another, without arguments to connect the intermediate "conclusions."

The *Tao Te Ching* stresses the patterns and rhythms of nature and sets these up as models for human beings. The stress is placed on living one's life in accord with the grand pattern of Tao, living as the rest of nature's creations live.

THE CHINESE WORLDVIEW OF TAOISM

There are two forms of Taoism. The one discussed in this chapter is often called "philosophical Taoism." It is associated with the ideas found in the writings of the two preeminent Taoist philosophers, Lao-tzu (sixth century B.C.E.) and **Chuang-tzu** (Zhuang zi in Pinyin, pronounced something like "Jwang-zu"), who flourished between 369 and 286 B.C.E. Philosophical Taoism is another of the numerous movements centered around a search for wisdom that developed during that remarkably creative period in the history of humanity, the fifth century B.C.E. The philosophical Taoists tended to be the intellectuals of Chinese society; they were scholars, artists, poets, and retired politicians. They were a minority even among educated Chinese people. As such, the philosophical ideas of the Taoists were primarily an upper-class phenomenon. The writings of the Taoists reflect this origin and include some of the great literature of China, universally recognized as masterpieces of wisdom, wit, and imagination.

The Taoist approach to ethics (and to life) is very different from anything we've seen so far. The approach of the philosophical Taoist to morality and ethical questions seems to be simple: You don't need any moral rules at all; just trust yourself! Be spontaneous! Although this does seem extreme, it does make sense once we understand the way the Chinese Taoists thought of the world.

The other form of Taoism is a popular religious approach, and many of its aspects are associated with traditional Chinese folk religion. Scholars distinguish several kinds of nonphilosophical Taoism, and the goals of the nonphilosophical Taoists were extraordinarily varied, including making money and acquiring power; curing illness; achieving immortality; performing rites for seasonal renewal of the village; bringing blessings on the village, or groups, or individuals; obtaining salvation for souls of dead punished in hells; obtaining control over spirits in supernatural realms who will do one's bidding including hurting others with magic spells, calling upon demons, spirits.

The Greeks and Buddhists emphasize rationality as a tool to understand moral principles. Even the later Christian philosophers thought that moral rules would not be incompatible with reason. But the philosophical Taoists do not think that reason alone will help us to arrive at the answers to questions about moral behavior. Most philosophers tend to stress being logical, precise, exact, specific, and consistent; these are the sorts of virtues advocated by the Confucians. On the other hand, Taoist thinking tends to be metaphorical, analogical, approximate, diffuse, humorous, even playful.

For the Taoist, human beings are neither captains of their fate nor masters of their destiny. The Taoist would claim that in real life, when faced with dilemmas, the use of cool reason to choose the most rational alternative will not necessarily produce the best solution. This is a fantasy of philosophers. Neither rationality nor irrationality are keys to living a moral life. We are affected by forces that are difficult to understand and more powerful than we. Attempting to understand them will not put us in command of them. We are not in command of ourselves or our world. Nothing is in command. But there is a pattern.

Lao-tzu and Chuang-tzu, and those who were inspired by their writings, understood existence as ever-changing swirling processes, and they thought that underlying these processes there is a principle of spiritual unity so deep that it can never be satisfactorily comprehended by the limited human intellect. However, this spiritual unity is not a god in the Christian sense; it is not conscious, not aware, and does not have any special feelings of warmth for human beings. It is Tao. It is described as the nameless source of all things, something so fundamental that it is prior to the distinction between Existence and Nonexistence. Putting oneself into harmony with this pattern is the goal of the philosophical Taoist.

The Tao, or "The Way"

For the philosophical Taoist, Tao is so vast that it far exceeds the limitations of the human intellect. Tao is the unity of all creation, the state of oneness prior to all separation, prior to all duality (even prior to God, says Lao-tzu). Tao itself is not so much a thing as it is a *sound* that human beings can make, which is intended to draw our attention to whatever underlies what we call reality.[2]

This is a description of the Way in the book entitled the *Chuang-tzu:*

> The Way has its reality and its signs but is without action or form. You can hand it down but you cannot receive it; you can get it but you cannot see it. It is its own source, its own root. Before Heaven and earth existed it was there, firm from ancient times. It gave spirituality to the spirits and to God; it gave birth to Heaven and to earth. It exists beyond the highest point, and yet you cannot call it lofty; it exists beneath the limit of the six directions and yet you cannot call it deep. It was born before Heaven and earth, and yet you cannot say it has been there for long; it is earlier than the earliest time, and yet you cannot call it old."[3]

The opening verse of the *Tao Te Ching,* the classic attributed to Lao-tzu, makes a similar point:

> The Tao that can be named is not the Tao itself;
> The name that can be named is not the real name.
> The origin of heaven and earth is nameless;
> The named is the mother of all things.[4]

If we must try to conceptualize Tao, Lao-tzu offers some suggestions. We can think of Tao as the One, the source, and as a "mother" out of which all things are born. Tao is supremely natural, spontaneous, and nameless because no concept is adequate. The term "Tao" serves like a pointing finger; don't try to understand Tao; instead, look in the direction that the finger points.

> There was a thing, undifferentiated yet complete,
> Which existed before heaven and earth.
> Soundless and fathomless,
> Depending on nothing, unchanging,
> Pervading everywhere yet it is never exhausted.
> It might be called the mother of the world.
> I do not know its name.
> I simply *call it* Tao.[5]

Thus, Tao is the sound we use to draw attention to the great matrix out of which all things emerge, grow, and develop, and Tao is the great receptacle back into which all things return at death. Tao is the pattern that is the harmony of nature, wherein all opposites exist in unity.

> The True Man of ancient times knew nothing of loving life, knew nothing of hating death. He emerged without delight; he went back in without a fuss. He came briskly, he went briskly, and that was all. He didn't forget where he began; he didn't try to find out where he would end. He received something and took pleasure in it; he forgot about it and handed it back again. This is what I call not

using the mind to repel the Way, not using man to help out Heaven. This is what I call the True Man.[6]

In chapter 34, Lao-tzu describes Tao as:

> The Great Tao flows everywhere, to the left and to the right.
> All things are born from it, and none are excluded.
> It completes its activity, yet it makes no claims.
> It nourishes all things, but it doesn't control or rule them.[7]

The world of nature is in continual flowing harmony and balance between the extremes of *yin* and *yang*. The Taoists thought that everything in the universe has a time when it is beginning, soft, and weak, and then a time when it is vigorous, strong, bright, and finally, a time when it reverts to weakness (death) again. As each element in the pattern that is Tao flows according to the natural cyclical process, the total pattern remains in perfect balance. It is like a small musical ensemble, where each instrument may be silent, may be loud, may play accompaniment, or may take the lead. Each individual considered in isolation may be sometimes soft, sometimes blaring, but the overall harmony of the composition is preserved at each step. There is balance, a pulsation, an ebb and flow.

We can describe the operation of Tao as acting through spontaneity, tranquillity, gentleness, and an unplanned simplicity so profound and effortless that it seems to be in nonaction; nature certainly shows no signs of carefully planned action. To achieve fulfillment as a human being, one must be in tune with the sweeping flow, which is nothing less than to be in accord with nature. The Chinese Taoists did not think that nature was "good" but they did think of the world as nurturing.

Lao-tzu Criticized Confucius and Confucianism

In Confucianism, the rules (*li*) tell us what is proper and appropriate in each and every situation. These rules of etiquette and rules of behavior guide moral decisions about what is appropriate in this situation, and what is appropriate in dealing with that person who stands in a certain social relationship with me.

Lao-tzu argues against this approach using an analogy. Human beings are like all the other living things in this world, and because we are as much a product of nature as anything else, thus we should be guided by nature's ways. The rest of nature does not follow rules, regulations, and etiquette. None of the other animals make these kinds of distinctions. In fact, Lao-tzu concludes that it is precisely because humans make up rules and regulations; divide the world into good and bad, right and wrong; and make these kinds of separations, categories, and decisions that they are frustrated, unhappy, and behave destructively and immorally. We are out of touch with our own nature and that of the world.

The solution is to listen again to nature and attune ourselves to the patterns of nature, to simplify, to give up trying to be too clever, too calculating, to give up the futile attempt to make the world fit into the abstract human-constructed categories we use for evaluating, judging, and preferring. Do not try to make things right; they are all right just as they are if we will stop meddling. In chapter 8, Chuang-tzu advises us to leave things be:

> He who holds to True Rightness does not lose the original form of his inborn nature. . . . The duck's legs are short, but to stretch them out would worry him; the crane's legs are long, but to cut them down would make him sad. What is long by nature needs no cutting off; what is short by nature needs no stretching. That would be no way to get rid of worry.[8]

So what is the secret? Let things happen without interference. Our categories distort what is really happening. In chapter 45 of the *Tao Te Ching* we find:

> The greatest perfection appears imperfect,
> yet its usefulness is not hampered.
> True fullness seems empty,
> yet its use is not exhaustible.
> True straightness seems crooked.
> The highest skill seems awkward.
> The highest eloquence seems so simple.
> Quiescence overcomes activity.
> Tranquility puts everything right in the world.[9]

Deliberate action, rational choices, and desires all are generated by the labels, categories, and distinctions we learn—and they are all conventional. The world could be divided up differently. The terms we use are evaluative, like beauty and ugliness, and if we can abandon the distinctions, the language of discriminations, we can achieve a state prior to discrimination that is in accord with Tao. For Lao-tzu, discriminations get us out of the flow of Tao, so drop them.

The Goal of the Taoist

As you recall, the central problem for all the Chinese philosophical systems during this historical period of chaos was: how can we install order and harmony among human beings? How can we bring about a well-ordered society? The Taoist solution: get back in harmony with the natural pulse and flow of the universe. When you do this, you become a sage. The means to accomplish this is to participate in the pattern effortlessly by absorbing and responding to the Tao. Do not try to make reality operate according to your partial and incomplete viewpoint. Leave things to themselves, without interference and artificial efforts; leave things in their natural state. Human beings have a useful skill, the ability to reason. It has been very useful for making, building, and surviving. But we human beings have misapplied that reason to separate ourselves from the rest of nature, to elevate ourselves out of natural patterns. Using reason inappropriately will diminish our spontaneous awareness of and response to all the rest of nature. For example, when applying reason to a problem leaves us in a quandary between choices, and we fall asleep wrestling with a moral dilemma, sometimes we awake the next morning with an answer, knowing what must be done. But it is not that we reasoned it through carefully while we slept. Rather, we relaxed and allowed the situation to sort itself out, to become clear and in becoming clear, our response to the situation also becomes clear; the spontaneous path became clear. We respond to the Way just as a dancer responds to the beat in the music.

The philosophical Taoists wanted to be left alone to enjoy life in freedom. Those who could afford it tended to retreat to the countryside, spending their days in contemplation of the wondrous interacting patterns that make up nature (Tao), writing poetry, painting, discussing, and drinking wine.

To become unified with the pattern that is Tao is to achieve oneness with Tao; to experience Tao is to experience inner tranquillity. All becomes clarity. The Taoist sage frees his mind and roams the world, reflecting reality, responding to things according to their own nature. He is not attached to things when they appear, and he does not try to hold onto things when they leave. Things leave no trace of clinging in the mind of the sage. The sage is free from all attachments.

Wu-wei, No Unnatural Action

Lao-tzu urges us to return to a state of unity with our origins, to regain the state of mind before the power of our intellect divided the world up into good and evil. How does one become in accord with the Tao? There is a method for accomplishing this: *wu-wei.*

Wu-wei is usually translated as "nonaction" or "inaction," but you misunderstand it if you think it means inactivity. For a human being, *wu-wei* means not acting contrary to the *pattern*, and you do this by not forcing things to fit into your molds, not forcing things against their nature to be what you want, by not meddling, by not "going against the grain." You do this by refraining from exerting force in dealing with people; simply let things alone to take their own natural course. Through nonaction, one simply "goes along" as nature does; the world gets created, things grow and pass away, all without a sign of effort. In a famous passage from chapter 48, Lao-tzu stresses noninterference with the Way using nonaction (*wu-wei*):

> To pursue learning is to accumulate knowledge day by day,
> To pursue Tao is to let things go day by day.
> Less and less do you need to make things happen,
> until finally you arrive at non-action (*wu-wei*).
> When nothing is done, nothing is left undone.
> You can master everything by letting things go their own way.
> By interfering you cannot master anything.[10]

In human terms, this is taking no hostile or aggressive action, not going against the grain of things; it is flowing with the patterns of nature, not trying to swim upstream against the river.

> The Virtue of emperors and kings takes Heaven and earth as its ancestor, the Way and its Virtue as its master, inaction [*wu-wei*] as its constant rule. With inaction, you may make the world work for you and have leisure to spare; with action, you will find yourself working for the world and never will it be enough. Therefore the men of old prized inaction.[11]

If you have a strong sense of ego-self and ego-separation, then you will stress differences between your "self" and everything else. You see yourself as different from everything. According to the Taoist, this sense of difference is a problem. You can no longer sense your own unity with the grand flow of reality. The only way to identify yourself with the flowing pattern of Tao is to lose the grasp of the self-centered ego that separates you from the world. When one has identified the self with nature itself, the grip of ego is relaxed. If one is to act as nature does, one's actions must become selfless actions and must become genuinely spontaneous. To be egocentrically aware of self is to make genuine spontaneity impossible.

Becoming selfless, your actions are precisely those of nature, completely and charmingly natural as any genuinely spontaneous actions will be. Thus, the method of *wu-wei*, or nonaction, might be called the method of taking "no artificial action."

Wu-wei implies spontaneity, and this spontaneity has profound consequences for the philosophic analysis of morality. The Taoist gradually learns to apply concepts and conceptualization less and less to all those matters where they are inappropriate. Neither Lao-tzu nor Chuang-tzu think that the analysis of concepts can solve life's riddles, but that does not mean that we give up thinking. Creative intelligence and analysis is very useful for building a house or fixing an automobile. Spontaneity won't repair a broken carburetor, but it will produce a life in accord with nature. So, use reason to repair a carburetor, but don't assume that the same reason will produce a free and spontaneous life. Reason is like a tool; use it for the appropriate task, and don't use a hammer when you want to saw a board. It is the wrong tool. Creative spontaneity is the tool to use to live life naturally in accord with the Tao. This method of "nondoing" can be achieved by obtaining a mental stillness and identifying oneself with nature (Tao).

Tzu-Jan, Naturalness, Spontaneity

If one is in accord with nature, and one is selfless, one becomes completely natural. The term for "naturalness" is ***tzu-jan*** (*ziran* in Pinyin, pronounced something like "zu-ran"). This is another key term for Lao-tzu. It can be literally translated as "of-itself-so," or "naturally so." In human terms, this means being naturally spontaneous. The opposite of *tzu-jan* would be all actions that interfere with free-flowing creativity and spontaneity; that is, self-centered scheming, calculating ahead, cleverness, judging, and so on.

In some sense, the spontaneous choice is the inevitable choice, it is the choice that nature itself would have made. The *wu-wei* choice is the best one, but one must wait until it is the right time to act. You do not intellectually figure out the right time. Rather, it is like playing a twelve-bar blues pattern—when four measures of the E chord have sounded, the music itself requires a change to the A chord. The key of the music itself moves the player to the next chord. The change is appropriate; it is felt, but not calculated. The musician responds with a change of chord that can be heard, but the change occurs spontaneously, the instrumentalist simply responds with awareness, even "thoughtlessly."

Te, Virtue

Lao-tzu's book, the *Tao Te Ching*, has the term "virtue" in its title. We have already seen that *te* (*de* in Pinyin) is a strong moral sense in Confucianism. However, *te*, translated as "virtue" (pronounced "duh"), is not moral virtue in Taoism. Like Aristotle and the Greeks, the Chinese *te*, or virtue, has to do with function, with how effectively a human performs his or her function. For the Taoist, *te* is a kind of charismatic power or spontaneous skill that a person manifests when he or she has become in accord with Tao. A person of *te* has attained a mind that is free from self-centeredness, and as a result has an inner quality of character that is powerfully effective for getting things done, for molding events without conscious effort. *Te* is the natural force we manifest when we are in accord with the Tao; it is the vital force of Tao itself. We get a charismatic energy that allows us to float gracefully through life with the least possible stress and pain. This power is acquired by practicing the method of *wu-wei*, by becoming naturally spontaneous (*tzu-jan*) and also by fasting and attaining a stillness of mind. We become able to do things, to accomplish things that seem almost supernatural—but it is a kind of skill, a force of character that influences without taking action; it is *not* a divine power.

Five Models That Humans Should Emulate to Attain Virtue

If I want to attain *te*, to become creatively spontaneous, how do I do it? The *Tao Te Ching* provides us with several models that human beings should pattern themselves after in order to comply with nature, or attain resonance with the flow of Tao.

The first model is water. Water takes the shape of its container, because it is essentially indeterminate, or formless. Water is apparently the weakest and humblest of all things, always seeking the lowest position. Yet the power of water comes precisely from this fact; it wears away mountains, carves mile-deep canyons. Human beings too should be humble, not pushing themselves forward; that is a genuine source of strength.

> The highest form of goodness is like water.
> Water is beneficial to all things, yet it does not contend with them.
> It occupies places which people do not like,
> But this is what makes it near Tao.[12]

The second is to become more childlike. The young child is a classic model of innocence. This innocence is the source of a great strength, which cannot be resisted. This does not refer to sexual innocence. It is the innocence of spontaneity, the willingness to see everything as new and wonderful. It is the ability to be fascinated by a leaf, by a butterfly, by an empty box. It is also a relaxed source of tremendous power and strength. The infant can scream all day long without getting hoarse. The utter helplessness of the infant is also a source of its strength; people do not scheme against a defenseless child, but only against the strong and powerful.[13]

The person of ample *te* may be compared to a child.
No venomous insects will sting him,
No wild beasts will claw him,
No birds of prey will attack him.
His bones are still supple, his muscles still weak,
But his grip is strong. . . .
He may cry all day long yet not grow hoarse—
this is because his inner harmony is perfect.[14]

The third model is the uncarved block, an image of simplicity. Think of this as a block of wood sitting on the floor of a sculptor's studio. Being uncarved, the sculptor's block can be shaped into almost anything; it can be used for innumerable things. Being not yet determined, it can be carved into an infinite number of forms. It still has the bark on it, so it is untooled, not artificial; it is raw material, and hence, it symbolizes the natural state of things. The uncarved block is plain, simple, sincere nature.

In the days of old, those who were masters of Tao were subtle, exquisite, mysterious, and penetrating.
Their depth was unfathomable . . . I shall attempt to describe them.
Cautious, like one crossing a frozen river in winter;
Watchful, like one aware of what is happening on all sides;
. . . Yielding, as ice on the point of melting;
Simple as the uncarved block.[15]

For the Taoist, the uncarved block is a metaphor for the original and primordial state of your mind, before rules, regulations, and human cultural brainwashing turned you into a terribly conditioned, unnatural, unfree, uncreative, nonspontaneous person. We have learned to be afraid to let others see us without our masks. But, in the depths of your mind, your original nature, you are quite wonderful. You are uncarved potentiality. Once carved, the block has lost its potentiality; it becomes rigid and fixed.

The fourth model is to emulate the virtue of *yin*, the female. Feminine images abound in the *Tao Te Ching*. For example, in chapter 6, Lao-tzu refers to the feminine indirectly in the phrase "spirit of the valley"[16] and explicitly as well:

The spirit of the valley never dies.
It is called entrance to the profoundly mysterious feminine,
And it is the source of both heaven and earth.
It is endless, and has only a hint of existence,
When you draw upon it, it can never be used up.[17]

Tao itself is often described like a mother. "Mother Nature" is our nearest Western equivalent. In China, as in the West, the stereotype of the female has been someone physically weak and submissive; yet the Taoist uses this same stereotype paradoxically, to symbolize someone simultaneously strong without resorting to brute physical strength, powerful without being aggressive, and creative without forcing things to happen. The female is the creative source of life, of fertility, of art, while not using strength, while refraining from aggression. The virtues associated with the feminine include tranquillity, nonaggression, nonhaste, gentleness, creativity, subtlety, and profound mystery. Even though a woman is not aggressive, and does not take the initiative to force things to happen, she is still able to accomplish her goal; she can "act without [aggressive] action," that is, *wu-wei*.

The idea is to recognize the power (*te*) of the feminine, beyond the obvious and apparent female characteristics; all human beings, both men and women, should incorporate these feminine qualities into their own lifestyles in order to become more at one with the flow of the Tao.

> Know the masculine,
> Keep to the feminine.[18]

Cultivate the feminine aspects of yourself, that is, be nonaggressive yet creative and powerful; be tolerant, yielding, receptive, and intuitive.

> Herein is the subtle illumination of life:
> The soft and weak overcomes the hard and strong.[19]

The fifth model is the positive potentiality of *emptiness* (*hsu*, pronounced something like "shoe"). To be full is to have no room left for change or growth; nothing can be added. It is the emptiness in the wall that allows the light to shine through the window; it is the emptiness in the wall that provides the doorway. The empty container can be filled with many different things; the full container cannot be used for anything else because there is no room. A mind filled with certainty has no room for growth or development; an empty mind is without self-centered desires, it is humble and has no preconceived ideas of how things must be, and thus it can perceive things just as they are. To be empty is to allow the possibility of being filled with Tao; to be full is to have no possibilities left.

> Bend and you will be straight.
> Be empty and you will be filled.
> Grow old and you will be renewed.
> Have little and you will have all you need.
> Have much and you will be confused.[20]

The Taoist Virtues According to Lao-tzu

Based on our previous discussion, we are now in a position to summarize the positive values that Lao-tzu believes humans should strive to incorporate into themselves. As you recall from our discussion of the ethics of the Greeks, the Greek virtues included courage, temperance, justice, and wisdom. The list of virtues of the Christians included faith, chastity, poverty, obedience, and prayer.

Although the Taoists did not make any sort of formal list the way the Greeks and Christians did, a number of central themes can serve the same function. The virtues (*te*) of the Taoists that we should strive to attain would include:

wu-wei (inactivity, no-action, no unnatural action)

tzu-jan (spontaneity, naturalness)

ming (illumination, insight, clarity, awakening)

p'o (the indeterminate potentiality of the uncarved block)

hsu (to see the positive potentiality in emptiness, in vacuity, in making oneself empty so that Tao can fill up the vacuum)

The Moral Life

By now you should be asking, "What kind of morality can be created by someone who is behaving totally spontaneously? Doesn't that mean that *anything goes*? Are there no limits? How can this be moral?" The answer is that Lao-tzu trusts human nature. Human beings are natural. We arise out of Tao and return to Tao—we are not innately evil or sinful. The Taoist who is in accord with the Tao may not follow conventional rules of morality, but neither will she or he do things that are harmful. If you are truly spontaneous and the self-centeredness has diminished, you will have no motive to do harm to others; if you are genuinely selfless, what could impel you to steal, lie, or hurt anyone?

The Taoist sage has no need for moral rules such as those prescribed by the Confucians; according to Lao-tzu, the sage will simply *live* spontaneously, with simplicity. A profound sense of belonging and unity with the world cannot result from unnatural moral principles and rules with no analogues in natural patterns; nor can we change nature to work the way we want it to. Instead, return to your original harmony with the patterns of nature (losing the ego along the way). The closer you get to working the way nature works, the stronger your *te* (virtue, power), and the clearer your insight (*ming*). This means seeing things clearly and responding to the world from your deepest self. Such a person is now a sage and will not be evil. She or he will respond the way nature responds. Unlike the Confucians, the Taoists did not think that morality is built into nature; Tao is neither benevolent (*jen*) nor immoral. Similarly, the awakened sage is neither moral nor immoral by human standards. Morality takes its origins in human preferences and is not based in nature. Lao-tzu writes:

> Heaven and earth are not benevolent (*jen*);
> They treat all things as straw dogs.
> The Sage is not benevolent;
> He treats human beings as straw dogs.[21]

A straw dog is a figure of a dog woven out of straw, used in ancient Chinese religious ceremonies. The straw dogs were treated with extravagant respect during the rituals, but once the ceremonies were over, they were discarded with indifference. Similarly, the sage treats human beings appropriate to the situation, depending on the circumstances, on a par with all things. But humans are not more valuable than anything else in nature.

Moral philosophers ask a lot of questions. How can I tell what is the right thing to do? How can I tell what sorts of things are good and what sorts of things are evil? What rules should I use to guide my life? These are not the kinds of questions that interest Lao-tzu. In fact, for Lao-tzu, if you have to ask these questions, something is profoundly wrong with you. You have lost touch with the source of all decisions, you have lost touch with Mother Nature.

The more prohibitions and restrictions there are in the world, the less virtuous
people will be. . . .
The more complications which arise,
The more laws and orders are promulgated,
The more thieves and robbers there will be.
Therefore the Sage says:
I do not act [*wu-wei*] yet of themselves people become honest. . . .
I love quietude and tranquility, yet of themselves people become correct.
I do nothing, yet of themselves people become prosperous.
I have no desires, and of themselves people return to a state of primordial
simplicity.[22]

In conclusion, Lao Tzu urges us to give up calculating rational choices because all the options are generated by the conventional categories and distinctions we have learned. Abandon the distinctions and the language of discriminations. Achieve *te*, a state prior to discrimination that is in accord with nature.
Drop distinctions.

Give evil nothing to oppose,
And it will disappear by itself.[23]

This attitude is nicely summarized in the following by Chen Ku-ying:

The Sage of the Taoists follows spontaneity, entrusts himself to the inner life,
considers the ideal life to be attainable only through preserving tranquility and
an attitude of non-contention, contemptuously disregards the teachings of Confucianism, and wholly rejects the fetters which impede the free functioning of
the heart and mind. Among these fetters he would include moral regulations,
considering them to be nothing more than subjective, arbitrarily imposed standards. The Taoist Sage and the Confucian Sage are obviously dissimilar in their
attitudes towards government and towards man in the cosmos, and should not
be inadvertently confused.[24]

CHUANG-TZU (fl. 369–286 B.C.E.)
AND THE *CHUANG-TZU*

The other great philosophical Taoist is Chuang-tzu. We know a little more about
the life of Chuang-tzu than we do about Lao-tzu, although the majority of the
information comes from the book that bears his name, the *Chuang-tzu*, and since
so much of the book is clearly fable and fantasy, it is not regarded as completely
reliable.[25]

Chuang-tzu flourished between 369 and 286 B.C.E., during the fourth century B.C.E. This makes him roughly contemporary with Plato, Aristotle, and Epicurus. He lived in what is known as Honan Province today. He was the author
of a number of brilliant and original essays (entitled simply the *Chuang-tzu*). Traditionally, these are regarded as carrying on the insights of Lao-tzu, though he
did not share Lao-tzu's concern for good government and a utopian society.
There are thirty-three chapters in the *Chuang-tzu*, but not all are by Chuang-tzu
himself. Scholars generally agree that the majority of the first seven chapters are

by Chuang-tzu; these seven chapters are called the "Inner Chapters."[26] In addition, much of the content of later chapters may be the work of Chuang-tzu himself.

The picture of Chuang-tzu that we get from reading the seven "Inner Chapters" is of someone enjoying a profound sense of unity with nature, an experience that allows him not to take society's artificial customs very seriously. He doesn't even take Tao too seriously; he refers to it as the "Great Clod" and other less-than-reverent terms. He is a free-and-easy wanderer, too deeply in accord with the interdependent flow of the Tao to accept too seriously the discriminations and dualities that are stressed by others around him.

Idly they [sages] roam beyond the dust and dirt; they wander free and easy in the service of inaction [*wu-wei*]. Why should they fret and fuss about the ceremonies of the vulgar world and make a display for the ears and eyes of the common herd?[27]

Chuang-tzu is a poet, just like Lao-tzu, but Chuang-tzu is also a philosopher, willing and able to use logic to find flaws in the logical positions of the competing philosophical schools (often referred to as the **Hundred Schools**). But logic is not his only tool. The inner chapters of the *Chuang-tzu* are rife with humor and satire; he continually uses images that are absurd and fantastic. He relies on analogies, aphorisms, stories, and anecdotes to make his points. In the process, Chuang-tzu makes fun of the rational conceptual framework of the Confucians and the other schools. He is a philosophical jester with genuine insight into the Tao.

Harmony with the Tao

Chuang-tzu provides us with a clear understanding of the practical consequences of living the Taoist life. Chuang-tzu stresses the idea of becoming one with the flow of the Tao as a release for creativity, and creativity requires both freedom and spiritual integrity. Be free, be unfettered—the only freedom worth having is a freedom that results from perfect harmony with that power which we call Tao.

To live, attune yourself to the rhythm, to the pattern. To be identified with that flowing pattern is to lose anxieties, to lose worries, and eliminate conscious striving for the goals that others consider important. Follow the Way, respond with awareness, live spontaneously. The result is peace and contentment.

The essence of the Perfect Way is deep and darkly shrouded; the extreme of the Perfect Way is mysterious and hushed in silence. Let there be no seeing, no hearing; enfold the spirit in quietude and the body will right itself. Be still, be pure, do not labor your body, do not churn up your essence, and then you can live a long life.[28]

Unlike the *Tao Te Ching*, in the *Chuang-tzu* the pattern of Tao isn't simply flowing back and forth between *yin* and *yang*. It is portrayed as something in constant flux, it is throbbing and pulsing, in continuous motion. Reality is just a natural and spontaneous process of transition and change. Tao is *change*.

Lao-tzu urged us to give up the labels, categories, and distinctions of morality. He thought that if we can stop using artificial discriminations, we can achieve a state prior to discrimination that is in accord with nature. Lao-tzu says that discriminations are unnatural—drop them. Chuang-tzu is a little different. He advocates being free to use the discriminations without believing that there is any ultimacy to them. Do not make the mistaken assumption that reality corresponds to your distinctions. Recognize them as relative to a situation, to a viewpoint. They are not absolute.

> The Sage embraces things. Ordinary men discriminate among them and parade their discriminations before others. So I say, those who discriminate fail to see.[29]

No distinction could ever reflect reality perfectly; whatever we say will fail to completely describe the Tao. We are filled with wonder, with amazement, with awe at the Tao, but we cannot conceptualize it accurately. All distinctions are part of a system of arbitrary and conventional judgments accepted by those around us; but they are conventional. These ways of discriminating will always reflect a particular standpoint, and no particular standpoint is privileged or absolutely correct. We could divide and distinguish things differently if we wished. Our categories depend on our perspective.

Chuang-tzu's View of Death

Chuang-tzu's attitude toward death is profoundly different from the Christian perspective. Look around at nature. Death is as natural as life, and to fear one and cling to the other is to misunderstand profoundly the world and our place in it. After all, all things arise out of Tao and return to Tao. There is neither reward nor judgment after death. The process of life and death simply continues to cycle along. If you are going to enjoy your life, you must also enjoy your death, for the two are equally important. Several passages in chapter 6 of the *Chuang-tzu* make this clear:

> The Great Clod [nature, Tao] burdens me with form, labors me with life, eases me in old age, and rests me in death. So if I think well of my life, for the same reason I must think well of my death.[30]

and in this passage:

> . . . the human form has ten thousand changes that never come to an end. Your joys, then, must be uncountable. Therefore, the sage wanders in the realm where things cannot get away from him, and all are preserved. He delights in

early death; he delights in old age; he delights in the beginning; he delights in the end.[31]

In chapter 3, Chuang-tzu recounts the death of the great Lao-tzu, and even here, he chides those students of Lao-tzu who respond to his death with sadness and tears:

> Your master [Lao Tzu] happened to come because it was his time, and he happened to leave because things follow along. If you are content with the time and willing to follow along, then grief and joy have no way to enter in. In the old days, this was called being freed from the bonds of God.[32]

The Tao continues to pulse between *yin* and *yang*, between birth and death, and wisdom is simply riding the pendulum between the two poles; to prefer one and reject the other is a waste of energy, and a falsification of the nature of reality.

> I received life because the time had come; I will lose it because the order of things passes on. Be content with this time and dwell in this order and then neither sorrow nor joy can touch you.[33]

The Moral Life According to Chuang-tzu

For the Taoist, the universe is an amazing place that we cannot completely predict or control. It is like a wave thunderously rolling along; we can be overrun by its power, but we can also surf the top of the wave and exult in the continuous process of constant transformation swirling around us at every moment.

What kind of morality is possible in such an ever-changing world? Both Chuang-tzu and Lao-tzu are what Western philosophers would call **epistemological relativists.** In other words, nothing can be known with absolute certainty. All truth claims are relative. That includes the claims of morality. Chuang-tzu does not think there is anything objective or absolute about moral judgments. They are relative to one's position, to one's situation, to one's point of view. There are no absolute rules, norms, or standards of virtue, justice, or happiness that apply at all times and in all places.

Chuang-tzu discusses the lack of any independent standpoint that could be used to determine the Ultimate Truth in much greater detail than Lao-tzu did. For example, in the following passage from chapter 2 of the *Chuang-tzu*, the student, Nieh Ch'ueh, asks the enlightened Taoist sage, Wang Ni, whether he knows the distinction between right and wrong.

> Nieh Ch'ueh asked Wang Ni, "Do you know what all things agree in calling right?"
> "How would I know that?" said Wang Ni.
> "Do you know that you don't know it?"
> "How would I know that?"
> "Then do things know nothing?"
> "How would I know that? However, suppose I try saying something. What way do I have of knowing that if I say I know something I don't really not know

it? Or what way do I have of knowing that if I say I don't know something I don't really in fact know it? Now let me ask YOU some questions. If a man sleeps in a damp place, his back aches and he ends up half paralyzed, but is this true of a loach?[34] If he lives in a tree, he is terrified and shakes with fright, but is this true of a monkey? Of these three creatures, then, which one knows the [absolutely] proper place to live? . . . Men claim that Mao-ch'iang and Lady Li were beautiful, but if fish saw them they would dive to the bottom of the stream, if birds saw them they would fly away, and if deer saw them they would break into a run. Of these four, which knows how to fix the standard of beauty for the world? The way I see it, the rules of benevolence and righteousness and the paths of right and wrong are all hopelessly snarled and jumbled. How could I know anything about such discriminations?"[35]

In chapter 2 of the *Chuang-tzu*, we find a classic statement concerning right and wrong.

What does the Way rely upon, that we have true and false? What do words rely upon, that we have right and wrong? . . . When the Way relies upon little accomplishments and words rely on vain show, then we have the rights and wrongs of the Confucians and Mo-ists. What one calls right the other calls wrong; what one calls wrong the other calls right. But if we want to right their wrongs and wrong their rights, then the best thing to use is clarity [*ming*].

Everything has its "that," everything has its "this." From the point of view of "that" you cannot see it, but through understanding you can know it. So I say, "that" comes out of "this" and "this" depends on "that"—which is to say that "this" and "that" give birth to each other. But where there is birth there must be death; where there is death there must be birth. Where there is acceptability there must be unacceptability; where there is unacceptability there must be acceptability. Where there is recognition of right there must be recognition of wrong; where there is recognition of wrong there must be recognition of right. Therefore the Sage does not proceed in such a way, but illuminates all in the light of Heaven. He too recognizes a "this," but a "this" which is also "that," a "that" which is also "this." His "that" has both a right and a wrong in it; his "this" too has both a right and a wrong in it.[36] So, in fact, does he still have a "this" and "that"? Or does he in fact no longer have a "this" and "that"? A state in which "this" and "that" no longer find their opposites is called the hinge of the Way. When the hinge is fitted into the socket, it can respond endlessly. *It's right* then is a single endlessness and *its wrong* too is a single endlessness. So, I say, the best thing to use is clarity [*ming*].[37]

Chapter 2 of the *Chuang-tzu* recounts the relativism of Chuang-tzu clearly. We may feel strongly that most of our choices are objectively right, but in truth they are relative to our likes and dislikes. In the big picture, the flowing Tao, each choice is good from some perspective.

Suppose you and I have had an argument. If you have beaten me instead of my beating you, then are you necessarily right and am I necessarily wrong? Is one of us right and the other wrong? Are both of us right or are both of us wrong? If you and I don't know the answer, then other people are bound to be even more in the dark. Whom shall we get to decide what is right? Shall we get someone who agrees with you to decide? But if he already agrees with you, how can he decide fairly? Shall we get someone who agrees with me? But if he already agrees with me, how can he decide? Shall we get someone who disagrees with both of us? But if he already disagrees with both of us, how can he decide? Shall we get someone who agrees with both of us? But if he already agrees with both of us, how can he decide? Obviously, then, neither you nor I nor anyone else can decide for each other. Shall we wait for still another person?

But waiting for one shifting voice [to pass judgment on] another is the same as waiting for none of them. Harmonize them all with the Heavenly Equality, leave them to their endless changes, and so live out your years. What do I mean by harmonizing them with the Heavenly Equality? Right is not right; so is not so. If *right* were really *right*, it would differ so clearly from *not right* that there would be no need for argument. If *so* were really *so*, it would differ so clearly from *not so*, that there would be no need for argument. Forget the years; forget distinctions. Leap into the boundless and make it your home![38]

Clearly, Chuang-tzu does think that one lifestyle is preferable to another, that living in accord with the Tao is to be preferred. To accomplish this, he recommends "nourishing one's nature"; he advocates "mental fasting," and "concentrating one's attention." Chuang-tzu prefers wisdom, the wisdom that lies in the quietude underneath or behind one's conceptual mind, conceptual thought, and logical reasoning. Wisdom is to be sought inside, by "fasting the mind." Chuang-tzu does suggest that it is better to live in reality than illusion, and he recommends responding spontaneously rather than with calculation.

The Taoist Sage

The goal of the Taoist is to become a sage, but the Taoist sage is very different from the Confucian sage. The Taoist sage will respond with awareness of all points of view and without any feeling of absolute correctness toward his or her own standpoint. When you have made the "boundless" your home, you are at home everywhere. Everything is in balance. Chuang-tzu wants us to reduce our limited individual and personal viewpoint and replace it with the view from the center of the circle. All partial standpoints are on the periphery of the circle, but from the center, my personal viewpoint is reduced to equal importance with the importance of other possible viewpoints. I become independent of my self-centered view. I remain centered by not adopting any particular personal standpoint as privileged, as ultimately more correct or proper than any other. Self-centeredness gradually disappears, and with it the motivation that impels people to take what is not theirs. The motives of greed and possessiveness simply diminish to the point where they no longer control our behavior. The Taoist sage does not do evil. Why? Because he or she is not self-centered any more. In chapter 17 of the *Chuang-tzu*, we find:

Therefore the Great Man in his actions will not harm others, but he makes no show of benevolence or charity. He will not move for the sake of profit, but he does not despise the porter at the gate. He will not wrangle for goods or wealth, but he makes no show of refusing or relinquishing them. He will not enlist the help of others in his work, but he makes no show of being self-supporting, and he does not despise the greedy and base. His actions differ from those of the mob, but he makes no show of uniqueness or eccentricity. He is content to stay behind with the crowd, but he does not despise those who run forward to flatter and fawn. All the titles and stipends of the age are not enough to stir him to exertion; all its penalties and censures are not enough to make him feel shame. He knows that no line can be drawn between right and wrong, no border can be found between great and small.[39]

And again:

Such a man will leave the gold hidden in the mountains, the pearls hidden in the depths. He will see no profit in money and goods, no enticement in eminence and wealth, no joy in long life, no grief in early death, no honor in affluence, no shame in poverty. He will not snatch the profits of a whole generation and make them his private hoard; he will not lord it over the world and think that he dwells in glory. His glory is enlightenment, [for he knows that] the ten thousand things belong to one storehouse, that life and death share the same body.[40]

This person is the sage, the ultimate attainment for the Taoist, and in the following passage from chapter 2, Chuang-tzu waxes poetic about the sage:

The sage leans on the sun and moon, tucks the universe under his arm, merges himself with things, leaves the confusion and muddle as it is, and looks on slaves as exalted. Ordinary men strain and struggle; the sage is stupid and blockish. He takes part in ten thousand ages and achieves simplicity in oneness. For him, all the ten thousand things are what they are, and thus they enfold each other.[41]

As mentioned before, Chuang-tzu did not think that human beings are fundamentally rational agents pursuing their goals and purposes using reason. A much more fruitful life would be to freely pursue awareness of the Way, and respond to alternatives by waiting for the moment when the appropriate response is clear. When most aware, when least egocentric, when most *wu-wei*, you have achieved clarity (*ming*) and your response is spontaneous. Do not try to be moral; just reflect reality the way a perfect mirror reflects whatever passes before it. A poor mirror will distort what is reflected; in a similar manner, a rational person will distort what is filtered through rational categories. On the other hand, the sage reflects clearly without anything added or subtracted:

Do not be an embodier of fame; do not be a storehouse of schemes; do not be an undertaker of projects; do not be a proprietor of wisdom. Embody to the fullest what has no end and wander where there is no trail. Hold on to all that you have received from Heaven but do not think you have gotten anything. Be empty, that is all. The Perfect Man uses his mind like a mirror—going after nothing, welcoming nothing, responding but not storing. Therefore he can win out over things and not hurt himself.[42]

and:

. . . Therefore I say, cut off sageness, cast away wisdom, and the world will be in perfect order.[43]

AN OVERVIEW OF THE ETHICS
OF PHILOSOPHICAL TAOISM

For the Taoist, human beings behave immorally because they have gotten out of touch with their own source, nature. Human beings grow out of nature and are as much a part of nature as everything else on the planet. Human beings are not special in any positive sense; the Taoists do not think that nature has some special affection for human beings, above and beyond other living things. Our unique capacity is the ability to reason, but when misused, this ability causes problems, we have war and other conflicts, and no one can be at peace with himself or herself. We harm ourselves and we harm other things when we have lost touch with Tao.

Tao is nature, and nature is patterns that occur independently of our preferences, our pleas, and our prayers. Tao is selfless and impersonal; it is the realm of balmy days and hurricanes, gentle showers and floods that wipe out cities and coastlines.

To understand Taoist ethics, one must understand that both Lao-tzu and Chuang-tzu stress the futility of working hard to achieve goodness and eliminate evil, the futility of trying to conquer wrong and replace it with the right. These pairs are mutually dependent. They are related like concave and convex, like uphill and downhill; if you eliminate one, the other one is gone as well.

> Now do you say that you are going to make Right your master and do away with Wrong, or make Order your master and do away with Disorder? If you do, then you have not understood [*ming*] the principle of heaven and earth or the nature of the ten thousand things. This is like saying that you are going to make Heaven [what is above the earth] your master and do away with Earth [what is below heaven], or make Yin your master and do away with Yang. Obviously this is impossible. If men persist in talking this way without stop, they must be either fools or deceivers! . . . From the point of view of the Way, what is noble or what is mean? These are merely what are called endless changes. Do not hobble your will, or you will be departing far from the Way![44]

The Taoist sage is a person of virtue (*te*), but he or she is not virtuous in the way a moralist might be described as virtuous. The sage never plans, calculates, or ponders moral dilemmas. The sage never follows rules. The sage just lets go.

> Only when there is no pondering and no cogitation will you get to know the Way. Only when you have no surroundings and follow no practices will you find rest in the Way. Only when there is no path and no procedure can you get to the Way.[45]

So how shall we live? Chuang-tzu invites us to roam freely with him:

> Why not join me in inaction, in tranquil quietude, in hushed purity, in harmony and leisure? Already my will is vacant and blank. I go nowhere and don't know how far I've gotten. I go and come and don't know where to stop. I've already been there and back, and I don't know when the journey is done. I ramble and relax in unbordered vastness; Great Knowledge enters in, and I don't know where it will ever end.[46]

and again:

> Who can climb up to heaven and wander in the mists, roam the infinite, and forget life forever and forever?[47]

There is something of a quietistic withdrawal in the ethics of the Taoist; the Taoist does not engage the world. Instead, the Taoist sage seeks to return to his or her own roots, return to a primal nonbeing in Tao. Nature is a rhythmic pulsation, change and transformation, birth, growth, decay, and dying. The wise hears the universal rhythm, and "claps along with it" (so to speak). The Taoist saint is not sour, not dour, not strict. The face of the sage will have lines in it from laughing so much:

> . . . Running around accusing others [logically challenging them] is not as good as laughing, and enjoying a good laugh is not as good as going along with things. Be content to go along and forget about change and then you can enter into the mysterious oneness of Heaven.[48]

And, as Lao-tzu says in chapter 41 of the *Tao Te Ching:*

> When a superior person hears of the Tao,
> He practices it diligently.
> When a middling person hears the Tao,
> Sometimes he keeps it and sometimes loses it.
> When the inferior person hears the Tao,
> He laughs loudly at it.[49]

PROBLEMS TO PONDER

These are questions that any thoughtful person should think about if he or she were considering adopting the Taoist analysis of ethics. Perhaps the careful Taoist philosopher can answer them. How would you answer them?

1. Is the claim that Tao exists empirical? What observation would be relevant to it? If no one can know Tao and no experience corresponds to it, then how do we know it exists? Why believe it exists?
2. What can we do when faced with any sort of ethical disagreement? If morality is relative, then two people could contradict each other and nevertheless both could be correct (or both could be wrong). Chuang-tzu and Lao-tzu do not offer any solutions; rather they seem to prefer not getting too upset about it.
3. Is Taoism practical in the twentieth century? Can it be used to deal with racism, sexism, serial killers, rapists, child molesters, or those who try to practice genocide upon their neighbors?
4. If someone were to use a gun to kill a Taoist, he/she could not consistently say that this was immoral, wrong, or deserving of punishment. Morality is just relative to a particular person's perspective.
5. There is a clear tendency in people who read Taoism to misunderstand it to be license, to be unrestrained with no moral limits. Is it? The Taoists

would reply that Taoism stresses overcoming the ego-self, and the danger is to use Taoist ideas to encourage feeding the ego, indulging the ego. The ego-self can be mistaken for the deepest self, and then one justifies doing whatever feels good. This is an error.

GLOSSARY

Chuang-tzu The Taoist philosopher named Chuang-tzu (fl. 369–286 B.C.E.) is also the author of a book entitled the *Chuang-tzu.*

Epistemological relativists Epistemology is the study of knowledge. The epistemological relativist argues that nothing can be known with absolute certainty. All truth claims are relative, including the claims of morality. No one can know anything for certain. Truth is relative to one's perspective, one's likes and dislikes.

Hundred Schools The Hundred Schools is a Chinese term used to refer to the numerous different philosophical schools that arose during the period from roughly 600 B.C.E. to 200 B.C.E. It includes Taoism, Confucianism, and others such as Moism, Legalism, and the Logicians.

Tao Tao refers to the pattern of ceaseless change that we call "reality," or "nature," an unending circular flowing from one pole (*yin*) to its opposite (*yang*), and then the process of transformation returning back to *yin* once again. Tao is the pattern of nature, always in perfect harmony and balance. Each individual thing is a part of the pattern, oscillating between opposite poles while responding to the movement of the Tao. Tao is the pattern with which human beings ought to be in accord.

Tao Te Ching This is the Classic of the Way and Its Power/Virtue; a book of eighty-one very short chapters attributed to Lao-tzu (sixth century B.C.E.).

Te Translated as "virtue," *te* refers to the powerful grace and ability to do things effortlessly demonstrated by those who have put themselves into accord with the Tao.

Tzu-jan Translated as "of-itself-so," *tzu-jan* means spontaneousness, naturalness.

Wu-wei Translated as "nonaction," *wu-wei* means taking no unnatural actions, responding spontaneously, leaving things in their natural states instead of forcing things to fit into your categories and desires.

Yang *Yang* is the positive pole, the brightness, the active, the masculine.

Yin *Yin* is the negative pole, the darkness, the passive, the feminine.

A GUIDE TO FURTHER READINGS

There are thousands of books and articles on aspects of Taoism, and many dozens of English translations of the *Tao Te Ching*. The following brief list comprises a few of the works of which the author is inordinately fond, or works that are of exceptional usefulness in the area of philosophical Taoism and the *Tao Te Ching*. A older but still useful bibliography on Taoism can be found in David Chappell and Michael Saso, eds., *Buddhist and Taoist Studies I* (Honolulu: The University Press of Hawaii), Asian Studies at Hawaii 18, 1977.

Chan, Wing-tsit. *The Way of Lao-tzu* (Indianapolis: Bobbs-Merrill, 1963). An excellent translation and analysis of this Taoist classic.

Chang, Chung-yuan. *Creativity and Taoism* (New York: Harper Colophon Books, 1970). One of the very best books on Taoism. Now out of print, but worth finding.

————. *Tao: A New Way of Thinking* (New York: Harper Colophon Books, 1975). A translation and study of the *Tao Te Ching* using major concepts of European philosophy, especially Heidegger.

Cheng, Chung-ying. "On *yi* as a Universal Principle of Specific Application in Confucian Morality." *Philosophy East and West,* Vol. 22, #3 (July 1972), pp. 269–280. A good study of the Confucian virtue of righteousness.

Feng, Gia-fu, and Jane English. *Lao Tsu: Tao Te Ching* (New York: Vintage Books 833, 1972). A poetic translation of this text, embedded in atmospheric photographs.

Graham, A. C. *The Book of Lieh-tzu: A Classic of Tao* (New York: Columbia University Press, Morningside Edition, 1990). A translation of one of the early Taoist texts.

————. *Disputers of the Tao: Philosophical Argument in Ancient China* (La Salle, Ill.: Open Court, 1989). Excellent scholarly discussion of the assumptions and approaches of ancient Chinese philosophy.

————. "Spontaneity and the Dichotomy of "Is" and "Ought," in Victor Mair, *Experimental Essays on Chuang-tzu* (Honolulu: University of Hawaii Press, 1983). A scholarly study of the ethical relativism of Chuang-tzu.

Henricks, Robert G. *Lao-tzu: Te-Tao Ching, A New Translation Based on the Recently Discovered Ma-wang-tui Texts* (New York: Ballantine Books, 1989). A translation and study of the earliest version of this Taoist classic.

Lau, D. C. *Lao Tzu: Tao Te Ching* (Baltimore: Penguin Books, 1963). One of the standard translations that has set a very high standard.

Mitchell, Stephen. *Tao Te Ching* (New York: Harper & Row, 1988). A very modern yet sympathetically accurate translation.

Needham, Joseph. "The Tao Chia (Taoists) and Taoism," in *Science and Civilization in China*, Vol. 2, pp. 33–164. (Cambridge: Cambridge University Press, 1954). A scholarly analysis of both philosophical and religious Taoism.

Waley, Arthur. *The Way and Its Power* (London: George Allen and Unwin, Ltd., 1934). A classic study and translation.

Watts, Alan. *Tao: The Watercourse Way* (New York: Pantheon Books, 1975). An excellent analysis of Tao, *yin-yang*, *wu-wei*, and other key concepts in philosophical Taoism.

CHINESE EDITIONS USED BY THE AUTHOR

Chiang Hsi-ch'ang. *Lao-tzu chiao ku* ("Collation and Explanation of the *Lao-tzu*"). (Taipei, Taiwan: Ming Lun, 1937; reprinted 1973).

Chu Ch'ien-chih. *Lao-tzu chiao shih* ("Annotations on and Explanations of the *Lao-tzu*"). (Taipei, Taiwan: Chung-hua shu-chu, 1963).

Fukunaga, Mitsuji. *Rōshi* ("Lao-tzu"). (Kyoto, 1968).

Han-shan Te-ching (1546–1620). *Lao-tzu Tao-te-ching Han-shan chieh* ("Han-shan's Explanation of the *Lao-tzu Tao-te-ching*"). (Taipei, Taiwan: Shin Wen Hua Yin Shu Kuan, 1973).

Wang Huai (1127–1190). *Lao-tzu t'an-i* ("The Meaning of Lao-tzu"). (Taipei, Taiwan: Taiwan Commercial Press, 1969).

Wang Pi (226–249). *Tao Te Chen ching chu* ("Commentary on the True Classic of Tao and Te"), edited by Yen Ling-feng, in *Wu-ch'iu pei-chai Lao-tzu Chi-ch'eng: Chu Pien* ("Collected works on the *Lao-tzu* as compiled by Wu-ch'iu Pei Studio, first series"), 1965. (Taipei, Taiwan: Yee Wen Publishing Co., 1965).

PART FIVE

Western Ethics from the Renaissance to the Nineteenth Century: The Beginnings of Modern Ethics

We are now going to move from the medieval period of Thomas Aquinas to the beginnings of modern philosophy in the West. The world had changed a lot in the five hundred years between Aquinas and the philosopher we'll discuss next, Joseph Butler (1692–1752), who lived as the Renaissance period was coming to an end.

Following the Great Compromise of Thomas Aquinas, it was the theories of Aristotle, combined with the Christian Bible, that provided a complete explanation of the entire universe, and that explanation was the ultimate and final truth for the medieval world. It could not be questioned, and Aristotle's ideas became identified with Christianity until the late 1600s, when scientists such as Galileo began to find flaws in Aristotle's explanation of the universe.

THE COSMOS ACCORDING TO ARISTOTLE

Aristotle argued that the Prime Mover (which Christians identified with the Christian God) set the heavens in perfect and eternal circular movement. Everything that happened in the cosmos was initiated by the Divine First Prime Mover. Christians argued that God's direct intervention was necessary to maintain the system—you could see that God existed by seeing the moon rise and set, the sun rise and set, the stars circle around the earth every night. The stars and planets rolled on crystal spheres, all of which revolved around the earth. There were eight crystalline spheres on which the sun, moon, planets, and stars were fixed, and the spheres rolled eternally around the earth, which was fixed and unmoving at the center. The spheres were made of ether. Ether is a substance that can neither be destroyed nor changed into anything else. The friction caused by the various spheres influences the earth; thus, the study of the spheres can tell us about human life, and signs in the heavens (things like comets and an eclipse) need to be interpreted. Thus, astronomers are astrologers. Everything that exists in the heavens is significant, because it exists for the sake of human

193

beings! Everything in the heavens above was perfect and unchanging, so there was no point in studying the stars and planets. The heavenly spheres were perfect and incorruptible, in contrast to the earth, where things died.

The Greeks argued that the earth was a sphere, because that was the perfect shape, and because the earth's shadow could sometimes be seen on the moon, and the earth stood motionless in the center. That the earth was the center of the universe must be true because we can see that all things fall in a straight line toward the center.

CHRISTIANITY ADOPTED ARISTOTLE'S VIEW OF THE UNIVERSE

Thomas Aquinas modified Aristotle's vision: God created everything for us. The universe was viewed as a harmonious and coherent whole, created by an infinite and good God as an appropriate home for human beings, for whose sake it was made. The earth was physically at the center of the universe, and it was also the religious center because human beings inhabit the earth, and human beings were created in the image of God. For the Christian, the cosmos, and everything in it, was a manifestation of God's plan, and thus belief in Aristotle was the bedrock of social stability.[1] God placed every object in the heavens above, and the earth below, in its proper place. Everything in existence had its preferred position in an immense, complex, and unchanging hierarchy that ranged from inanimate rocks up through planets and animals to man, heavenly beings, and finally God, the Prime Mover.[2] Every member of society had a designated place. It was against God's plan for any person to try to escape their social situation. Everything was created for man. Everything revolved around man, literally and symbolically.

As the Middle Ages came to an end and the Renaissance was beginning, the world was understood as harmonious, ordered, finite, and daily displaying the glories of its creator. To understand the world at that time was to understand the purpose set by God. Every scientist knew that absolutely everything depends on God and everything leads to God.

During this entire period, the great majority of people were illiterate; knowledge of the past was dependent on the ability of the old to remember past events and customs. Elders were the source of authority. Memory was the source of information. All experience was personal; what existed in the world outside was a matter of hearsay. People had little interest in the future because it would be exactly like the present. Everyone relied on common knowledge for their day-to-day information. Their lives were regular, repetitive, and unchanging.

The church authority was initially weakened with the arrival of the plague in Europe in the middle of the fourteenth century. Then, in the fifteenth century, Gutenberg developed the printing press, and the printed page became the carrier of memory, now available to those who could read, and expanded the horizons of everyone.

This led to the rediscovery of classical learning, three hundred years after Aquinas. There was a new appreciation for classical poetry, histories, essays, and philosophy. For many, it was a shock to discover that the Greeks and Romans had a very high level of society before the perpetual Dark Ages. People who had the ability to cultivate arts, literature, poetry, painting, and writing began to flourish. These individuals were often referred to as "Humanists," although they were not against the church or opposed to Christianity. These events mark the end of the medieval period and the beginning of the Renaissance.

For the illiterate villager, the church was the main source of information, and the church stressed the inerrant revelation of the Bible and the worldview of Aristotle. The church saw itself as the keeper and protector of divine truths, the harbor of salvation. However, historically, it had become a means for securing worldly power, prestige, and wealth for those who were clever and ruthless. The Roman Catholic Church was directed by the papacy in Rome, which had succeeded in bringing under their control a great variety of incomes, privileges, and powers. Popes were continually engaged in political intrigues to establish and extend their powers. Often the pope would have more influence, wealth, and power than any ruler, king, or emperor: his court was more splendid, his staff more extensive, his will more feared. The pope had the power to cast a soul into hell; if displeased with a monarch, the pope could put the entire land under "interdict," which meant no church services or sacraments. If your child or your parent died while the land was under interdict, they could not receive the sacraments. This meant that they were damned to hell; eternal salvation was lost for those who lived there and died there!

In the wake of criticisms, some attempts were made to institute reform, but the church responded with the Inquisition in 1231, which continued unabated for the next five hundred years. The role of the Inquisition was to put an end to heresy, which was any questioning of church dogma, any dissent, or even rebellion (all Protestants were guilty of rebellion against church authority). Heresy was considered as the greatest of all sins because it was a personal affront to God, because God rewarded faith in church dogma, and God abhorred doubt. Heresy was worse than pride, worse than homosexual or adulterous behavior, worse than treason, worse than thievery, and even worse than murder. If church inquisitioners could force a heretic to recant under torture, then the heretic's soul would be saved, and he would be granted the mercy of being strangled before being burned at the stake. The church burned people clamoring for church reform and went from corruption to corruption holding tightly to its privileges and wealth. Ultimately, in the early 1500s, the reform movement gained so much strength that Protestant churches began to be formed. For example, Lutheranism in Germany was founded by Martin Luther in 1517; the Church of England (the Anglican church) was founded by King Henry VIII in 1534; and the Presbyterians and Calvinists began in 1560. The Congregationalist branch of Puritanism branched off in the early 1600s in England; the Baptists, founded by John Smith, began in Amsterdam in 1607; Methodism was founded by John and Charles Wesley in England, 1744; the Episcopalian church was brought from England to the American colonies and made a separate religion by Samuel Seabury in 1789.

THE CHRISTIAN UNDERSTANDING
IS CHALLENGED BY SCIENCE

The Aristotelian universe began to crumble after 1500. In 1543 Copernicus questioned the entire Aristotelian system and argued instead that there was a sun-centered system. He thought that the center of the universe was a spot somewhere near the sun.

The evidence seemed clear—the earth was not the center of the universe and had never been. This had profound implications. If the earth is not the center of the universe, then perhaps the earth is not the focus of God's purpose. If the earth is not the center of the universe, then perhaps human beings are not the creatures for whose use and elucidation the cosmos had been created. If the earth is not the center, and if the earth moves through space, then the earth is in the heavens. This was shattering to Aristotle's worldview, for it meant that there was no barrier between the corruptible and the divinely incorruptible. If the earth were heavenly, then it must be incorruptible. But it wasn't. Things died and decayed on earth. If one accepted the claim that the earth was not the center of the universe, then other major theological doctrines must be false! The heavens above would have to be imperfect, corruptible, and capable of change! The church worked hard to stamp out such heresy.

Then an exploding star, a supernova, lit up the heavens in 1572 and burned brightly for two years before fading. Aristotle was wrong. The church was wrong! They had both argued that the heavens were perfect and unchanging—and yet that distant supernova changed in the sky overhead.

In 1577, a comet flashed across the heavens, and it was obvious that the tail of the comet was always streaming out away from the sun—this meant that the sun must be affecting the comet, but according to Aristotle, there was only *one* heavenly object in each sphere. Even worse, the comet was passing *through* the planetary spheres. The crystal spheres should be shattering, and they weren't. But, if the planets were not held up by being embedded in crystalline spheres, why didn't they fall? In what medium were they moving if not in an ether-crystalline sphere?

In 1591, the astronomer Galileo proposed that we should give up Aristotle's crystalline spheres. In 1610 Galileo used a telescope and saw the moon. It seemed to have mountains and flat areas he called "seas"—but according to Aristotle, it was a heavenly body and therefore perfect and without irregularities! Galileo looked at the stars and discovered that there was vastly more of them than Aristotle had thought. Then he turned his telescope on Jupiter and found that it had moons. In 1611, Galileo studied sunspots on the surface of the sun, and he found that the sun rotated. Two more blows at Aristotle's model. The church could no longer ignore this challenge to its authority.

If the church were wrong about the heavens, then it might be wrong about other things as well—and this was heresy and could not be tolerated! The Catholic Church put Galileo under house arrest in 1633, where he remained until he died in 1642. The church put his book on the list of prohibited books for the next two hundred years until 1835.

The Roman Catholic Church demanded that all scientists must produce theories that did not contradict Holy Scriptures. This ended all scientific work in Italy, and in all countries under the control of Rome. Science continued in those areas in the north of Europe where the Roman Catholic Church was not in total control, places like Austria and Germany, Holland, Amsterdam, and Prague.

The explosion of scientific discoveries created a crisis for intelligent Christians, not just the authority of the Roman Catholic Church. All of the Christian churches had a history of disagreeing with scientific discoveries (i.e., Galileo) and in every single case, without exception, the church had proven to be wrong and science correct. This situation created a fertile ground for people who were skeptical of the Scriptures and teachings of the Christian churches. These people were called Deists and freethinkers.

In the middle 1600s, a group of freethinkers met in Paris to discuss philosophy and science. They questioned the authority of Christianity. As scholars continued to make new discoveries in astronomy, geography, and history, there was a decline in faith. For a hundred years, the Protestants had criticized the Catholic understanding of the Bible and history, and then the numerous Protestant sects fought with one another, exposed each other's doctrinal weaknesses, and as they studied the Bible, it led to doubts in the meaning and infallibility of the Christian Bible.

Scholars were no longer simply discussing and doubting the authority of the pope; some of them were now debating the very existence of miracles, questioning the divinity of Jesus, and doubting the very existence of God. Religion itself had been undermined by the wars of religion going on in Europe. Some of the best educated in Europe began to assert that religion is composed of unprovable mysteries and absurdities, and that all forms of Christianity have been guilty of barbaric behavior and intolerant cruelties.

Some of these freethinkers were atheists, who laughed at the idea that the Bible was anything other than a collection of Christian myths, and they denied the very existence of divinity. Others were Deists, people who thought that a divine being must have created the world, but they argued that a divine being did not answer prayers, did not care about humans personally, did not reward or punish, and would never intervene in human history with a miracle.

This is the background for the modern ethical philosophies of Joseph Butler, David Hume, Immanuel Kant, and John Stuart Mill.

CHAPTER 9

Joseph Butler:

Conscience Is the Basis for Christian Morality

THE LIFE OF JOSEPH BUTLER (1692–1752)

Joseph Butler was born in England in 1692. Henry the VIII had died a hundred and fifty years before (1547) and had changed England from a Catholic country to a country governed by the Church of England with the king as the head of the church. The 1700s was a very exciting time in Europe. In 1703, one of greatest

scientists of all time, Isaac Newton, was elected President of the Royal Society, and J. S. Bach was writing his early music. This was also the time of Francis Bacon, William Harvey (who discovered that blood circulated), Descartes (creator of analytic geometry), Pascal, Edmund Halley (discoverer of "Halley's Comet"), Gabriel Fahrenheit, the physicist Bernoulli, and Joseph Priestley.

Young Joseph Butler was raised as a Protestant Dissenter (it was only a few years before Butler's birth when English law allowed *most* non-Anglican Christian groups to worship freely). He was attracted to religious topics and trained for the ministry, but he finally decided that the relatively liberal doctrines of the Protestant Dissenters were not as much to his liking as the much more formal and conservative theology of the Church of England (Anglican) and so converted to the Church of England.

He attended Oxford and became a priest after graduation in 1718. In 1736 he was court chaplain and served Queen Caroline and then George II. He became Bishop Butler. This gave him prestige and a pulpit from which to provide his own Christian explanation of the foundation of moral behavior. His influence is certainly due in part to his role as chaplain to the King and Queen of England as much as it is to his philosophical acuity. It is important to remember that almost all of his philosophical writings originally were delivered as sermons, addressed to a well-educated upper-class London congregation of the eighteenth century.

BUTLER'S PHILOSOPHY OF THEISM

Joseph Butler was living during the explosion of scientific discoveries, when people began to be skeptical of the scriptures and teachings of the Christian churches. Butler felt that he had a mission: to defend the faith of traditional Christianity over religious skepticism and freethinking. Butler was defending **theism** (the religious position that a God exists who transcends the natural world, is personally interested in human affairs, who answers prayers and performs miracles). Butler was arguing against **deism** (the religious position that God exists, is transcendent, and created everything perfectly at the moment of creation, but has no concern with human affairs and exerts no influence over humans; God does not answer prayers or perform miracles). The Theist and the Deist agree that a divine creator exists and transcends nature, but they disagree as to whether that creator has any interest in creation and pays attention to human beings.

Butler was not arguing against **atheism** (the claim that a divine being does not exist). Butler's Deist opponents agreed with traditional Christianity that the universe is the work of a benevolent designer, but they rejected all miracles and understood the stories of Noah's ark, and even the resurrection of Jesus Christ, to be pure mythology. Thus, Butler wanted to convince the Deist that the main theistic claims of Christianity concerning a personal God were not unreasonable.

Joseph Butler was very bright and well educated; he had read the ethical philosophers of the Greek and Christian traditions. He was very partial to Aristotle, and much of Aristotle's theory of human virtue found its way into Butler's writings. Like Augustine, Butler believed that human reason would support the various dogmas of Christianity. He thought that any reasonably intelligent person should be able to see that Christianity was correct because of human experience combined with the logical reasons that support the claims of Christianity.

BUTLER'S ETHICS

What is the basis of morality? Bishop Butler recognizes that there are some problems with the claim that morality is based on the commands of God (the position of St. Augustine). Butler feels that moral demands are felt so strongly in humans that morality could not be explained as moral laws imposed on us from some outside force, even the force of God's commands to obey or else be punished. Instead of basing morality on the divine commands of an omnipotent deity, Bishop Butler argues that the ground of morality can be found within human nature. Morality is what is in accord with that human nature, and immorality is a violation of the unity and order of that human nature. Human nature is complex, but it can be analyzed into a hierarchy, and the most fundamental aspect of our human nature is the human conscience, which Butler defines as "the reflective or rational faculty which discerns the moral characteristics of actions." For Butler, conscience is not some sort of "sixth sense," or independent source of knowledge. Neither is conscience merely another name for subjective feelings of approval or disapproval. Conscience is a type of moral reason, but Butler does imply that sentiment or feelings are also involved.* Conscience distinguishes what is right from what is wrong, and conscience makes that perfectly clear to us.

Butler's sermons reflect his disagreement with several different ethical systems, including that of Thomas Hobbes (1588–1679), the Earl of Shaftesbury (1671–1713), and the Deists. Thomas Hobbes argued that a scientific understanding of human nature left no room for ethics except in terms of self-centered desires. Hobbes held that people always must choose whatever will maximize their own advantage or pleasure. They cannot help it. Whatever we choose, we choose it to get the pleasure that comes from attaining that thing. The reason I do something is to attain pleasure and not to obtain some goal or thing. Butler argues that there is some truth in this, but **egoistic hedonism** has overlooked our nonegoistic concern for others. The Earl of Shaftesbury argued that the entire foundation of morality is found in feelings of benevolence, that benevolence is the totality of virtue.

In addition to disagreeing with Hobbes and Shaftesbury, Butler is disagreeing with the Deist position. If you are arguing with a Deist, it is of no use to quote Scripture to prove your point, because the Deist rejects the authority of the Bible. Butler wants to show that revealed truths are rational, and you can't do that by quoting Christian **revelation** to prove that Christian revelation is correct (Butler was too smart to argue in a circle). In general, for the Deist the Creator never performed a miracle after the miracle of creation; thus, for a Deist none of the miracles recorded in the Jewish Old Testament are correct, and Jesus could not have been the son of God sent to pay the price for original sin. Deists think of the Christian Scriptures as just the myths of credulous people. This is one reason why Butler avoided basing his arguments and conclusions on supernatural authority, even though he was a devout Christian (remember that he died a bishop in the Church of England). Some notable Deists of the period include Voltaire and the American Benjamin Franklin. Butler wrote *An Analogy of Religion* (1736) as a Christian defense against the Deist positions, attempting to show that the Christian understanding of God and God's interaction with humanity is not unreasonable. Butler's *Sermons* are genuine sermons upon scriptural verses, and so each begins with a quotation from Scripture, but his arguments are based on reason, not authority.

Butler and the Deists agree on one important point: nature is a product of divine design. Butler is certain that by studying nature, one can find support

---

*We see here the influence of Thomas Aquinas; in Aquinas, conscience is "practical wisdom" and is tied to reason; conscience is applying general intellectual principles to concrete situations. This issue will divide later generations of ethical philosophers. Some, like Hume, will argue that conscience is nothing but moral sentiments or feelings. Others, like Kant, will argue that moral conscience has nothing to do with feelings but is pure reason.

and confirmation for the revealed doctrines of Christianity, and that support can be used to convince the Deist that traditional Christianity is correct. For Butler, revelation and nature complement each other, and thus he thought he could find a support for morality in natural phenomenon. Butler's basic position is consistent with **empiricism.**

An important implication follows from Butler's ethics: Everyone may find *within himself or herself* the knowledge of what is right, as well as the obligation to follow what is right. Your human conscience is the supreme authority.

Ethics Is Based in Human Nature

Butler begins by arguing that to understand ethics, one must understand human nature, because it is within human nature that each person can find the knowledge of what is right ("virtue") and what is wrong ("vice"); and within our own natures we can find the inner sense that we have an obligation to do what we know to be right. Therefore, the first step is to try to figure out how human nature was designed and determine what God's intent was in creating human beings. But we must be careful not to oversimplify our analysis of human nature.

The Deists and Theists both agree that a divine being created human beings and the world, and thus human beings were made with some purpose, plan, or goal provided by the creator, God.[3] This allows Butler to begin his exploration with the assumption that there is some plan or purpose to human nature, and therefore an empirical study of human beings should reveal the broad structure of that purpose.

> There are two ways in which the subject of morals may be treated. One begins from inquiring into the abstract relations of things; the other from a matter of fact, namely, what the particular nature of man is, its several parts, their economy or constitution; from whence it proceeds to determine what course of life it is, which is correspondent to this whole nature. In the former method the conclusion is expressed thus—that vice is contrary to the nature and reason of things; in the latter, that it is a violation or breaking in upon our own nature.[4]

Butler begins by arguing that when you know what the basic human nature is, then you will see that virtue is determined by that which is in accord with human nature. Vice is whatever deviates from human nature. So we need to analyze the nature of a human being to figure out what sort of moral life is appropriate for the nature of man.

> Whoever thinks it worth while to consider this matter thoroughly, should begin with stating to himself exactly the idea of a system, economy, or constitution of any particular nature, or particular anything; and he will, I suppose, find that it is an one or a whole made up of several parts; but yet that the several parts even considered as a whole do not complete the idea, unless in the notion of a whole you include the relations and respects which those parts have to each other. Every work both of nature and of art is a system; and as every particular thing both natural and artificial, is for some use or purpose out of and beyond itself, one may add, to what has already brought into the idea of a system, its conduciveness to this one or more ends. . . . Appetites, passions, affections, and the

principle of reflection, considered merely as the several parts of our inward nature, do not at all give us an idea of the system or constitution of this nature, because the constitution is formed by somewhat not yet taken into consideration,
namely, by the relations which these several parts have to each other; the chief
of which is the authority of reflection or conscience. It is from considering the
relations which the several appetites and passions in the inward frame have to
each other, and, above all, the supremacy of reflection or conscience, that we
have the idea of the system or constitution of human nature. And from the idea
itself it will as fully appear that this our nature, that is, constitution, is adapted
to virtue, as from the idea of a watch it appears that its nature, that is, constitution or system, is adapted to measure time. . . . Every work of art is apt to be out
of order, but this is so far from being according to its system that let the disorder increase, and it will totally destroy it.[5]

Human nature is seen to be a system composed of several different parts
that interact in a complex manner. We must know each part separately, and then
see how all the parts function together as a system. To understand human nature, we must analyze the parts, but not the parts in separation or isolation.

Butler also urges us to not come to conclusions based on knowing only ourselves and our own nature, and do not give too much weight to the unusual
cases, the exceptions from the general lot of human beings. Rather, we should
observe the bulk of humankind, in general, and not pay too much attention to
the exceptions.

So now that we have decided that human beings were designed for some
purpose, the next question is: what was human nature, with reason, appetites,
passions, designed for?

The Purpose of Human Nature

To begin with, we know that human beings are concerned about their own welfare, their own health, their own private good; indeed, sometimes human beings
are profoundly self-centered, selfish, and egoistic. But it makes sense that we
must be concerned about what preserves our own lives, and what promotes our
own happiness. However, Butler argues that we cannot find the totality of human nature in this self-benefit aspect of human nature. There is one more aspect
to human nature that we must not overlook. Humans are also concerned with
the happiness of others. We care about others! Human beings are interested in
what promotes the public good for all.

> From this review and comparison of the nature of man as respecting self and as
> respecting society, it will plainly appear that there are as real and the same kind
> of indications in human nature that we were made for society and to do good
> to our fellow creatures, as that we were intended to take care of our own life and
> health and private good.[6]

Butler refers to concern about social welfare as *benevolence*. We want to help
others, to do things that actually benefit our fellow humans and human society.
We are naturally altruistic. Butler feels that this is common to all of us, just as
self-love is, and therefore must have been designed into us by our creator and

so it must also be a part of the purpose of human nature. He says, "we were made for both":

> First, there is a natural principle of *benevolence* in man, which is in some degree to *society* what *self-love* is to the *individual*. And if there be in mankind any disposition to friendship; if there be any such thing as compassion, for compassion is momentary love; if there be any such thing as the paternal or filial affections; if there be any affection in human nature the object and end of which is the good of another—this is itself benevolence or the love of another. . . . I must however remind you that though benevolence and self-love are different, though the former tends most directly to public good, and the latter to private, yet they are so perfectly coincident that the greatest satisfaction to ourselves depend upon our having benevolence in a due degree, and that self-love is one chief security of our right behavior toward society. It may be added that their mutual coinciding, so that we can scarce promote one without the other, is equally a proof that we were made for both.[7]

There is an important insight here. Self-love and benevolence are equally natural. Butler concludes that self-love and benevolence complement each other so well ("their mutual coinciding") that we must conclude that "we were made for both": we were created by God to take care of our own life, health, and private good, and also created by God to do good for our fellow creatures, to serve human society.

Now, self-love and benevolence are not the only natural instincts that human beings have. Butler acknowledges that humans have lots of other passions and affections, but he feels that if we analyze them, we will see that a great many of these other instincts are ultimately kinds of self-love and benevolence: they promote both public and private good.

> Secondly, this will further appear, from observing that the *several passions and affections*, which are distinct both from benevolence and self-love, do in general contribute and lead us to *public* good as really as to *private*.[8]

For example, we find that we desire the esteem of others and want to avoid the contempt of others; we feel a natural sense of indignation against people who do evil/vice and get away with it. Ultimately, these natural reactions lead us to regulate our behavior for the good of our fellow citizens.

In Sermon IV,[9] Butler deals with the objection that self-love and benevolence must be in conflict. Isn't it obvious that what is best for me will not be good for others, and what is best for others will go against my own personal interests? Butler disagrees vehemently: just because something is good for us does not mean that it cannot be good for others as well.

> And since, further, there is generally thought to be some peculiar kind of contrariety between self-love and the love of our neighbor, between the pursuit of public and of private good, . . . it will be necessary to inquire what respect benevolence hath to self-love, and the pursuit of private interest to the pursuit of public . . .[10]

With this, Butler goes on to establish that there is no natural and innate conflict between self-love and benevolence. In fact, he argues that the two work together in harmony most of the time. Doesn't this indicate that we were designed to carry out the preservation of ourselves and of society? All of this proves that "our Maker" intends that we should do good to each other as well as do good to ourselves.

Is Self-Love Merely the Unrestrained Gratification of Our Impulses?

At this point, Butler deals with an objection. If we love ourselves (self-love), doesn't that mean we are self-centered as well? If we are self-centered, doesn't this mean that we just want our impulses fulfilled? I see something, I have an impulse to get it. Isn't this what we mean by self-love? Isn't it just gratifying our impulses? I like this, I want this!

If this is what Butler means by self-love, how could any decent Christian believe that we were created to selfishly lurch after one pleasurable object after another? How could this be the basis for Christian morality? Butler must respond to this criticism, because otherwise his ethical theory turns into something like "If it feels good, do it! Gratify your impulses."

Butler's response is that self-love cannot be just wanting stuff and getting stuff that we want. Clearly, every person wants his or her own happiness, and we also want other external things, but self-love is not merely "unrestrained gratification of our impulses."

It is important to note that Joseph Butler isn't just telling us what he believes. His own personal beliefs are only of interest to his family and his psychotherapist. Butler is providing an *argument* for his claim. He will attempt to prove to you that self-love is not just unrestrained gratification of impulses.

To do this, he creates an argument in four steps. In step 1 Butler asks, what is the object of self-love? The object of self-love is internal to ourselves; we want to achieve a lifetime of happiness. The object of self-love is a lifetime of happiness, an internal goal.

In step 2 Butler asks, what is the object of gratifying a particular impulse or desire? Well, I see something and I want it for myself. The object of my impulses is some specific particular external object. The object we desire is food, a car, a dress, a painting, a CD (compact disc), and so on—we seek the external thing.

In step 3, having shown that the objects of self-love and unrestrained gratification of impulses are different, Butler asks us to see the implications of that fact. If self-love and unrestrained gratification of the senses were the same, then their objects would be the same. But consider this: the long-term object of self-love is general and internal to ourselves; the long-term object of an impulse is something specific and external to ourselves. The object of self-love is never an external thing; instead it is an internal state.

From these, at the fourth step Butler arrives at his conclusion. Since their objects are different, self-love and gratification of impulses must also be different.

> Every man hath a general desire of his own happiness, and likewise a variety of particular affections, passions and appetites to particular external objects. The former proceeds from or is self-love, and seems inseparable from all sensible

creatures, who can reflect upon themselves and their own interest or happiness, so as to have that interest an object to their minds; what is to be said of the latter is that they proceed from, or together make up, that particular nature according to which man is made. The object the former pursues is somewhat internal—our own happiness, enjoyment, satisfaction; whether we have or have not a distinct particular perception what it is or wherein it consists, the objects of the latter are this or that particular external thing which the affections tend towards, and of which it hath always a particular idea or perception. The principle we call "self-love" never seeks anything external for the sake of the thing, but only as a means of happiness or good; particular affections rest in the external things themselves. One belongs to man as a reasonable creature [reflecting upon his own interest of happiness]. The other, though quite distinct from reason, are as much a part of human nature. . . .

Every particular affection, even the love of our neighbor, is as real our own affection as self-love; and the pleasure arising from its gratification is as much my own pleasure as the pleasure self-love would have from knowing I myself should be happy some time hence, would be my own pleasure.[11]

Conscience: The Supreme Governing Principle

Having shown that his ethical theory is not just "If it feels good, do it!," it is time to explore further human nature and the various kinds of desires and instincts we have. Are human beings simply a collection of instincts, such as self-love and benevolence? No, because we've overlooked something. We human beings possess a faculty that is capable of judging our impulses and our choices. If you see something you want, and you recognize that in obtaining it, your life will be destroyed, it is still natural to want to get the thing; but human beings are capable of recognizing that the action is rash and unnatural. We can deny a present impulse or desire (appetite), because we can see that the consequences will be a disaster. Note what is happening here: your particular impulse or desire is overridden by some other part of your nature as a human being. Butler calls the part that judges and overrides particular impulses a *governing principle*. A governing principle can override particular impulses, and Butler argues that therefore it is superior to particular impulses. The governing principle can stop certain kinds of behavior; if it can stop it, it must be superior to the particular behavior or impulse. First, let's ask: Is there some supreme governing principle?

> . . . there is a principle of reflection in men by which they distinguish between, approve and disapprove, their own actions. We are plainly constituted such sort of creatures as to reflect upon our own nature. The mind can take a view of what passes within itself, its propensions, aversions, passions, affections, as respecting such objects and in such degrees, and of the several actions consequent thereupon. In this survey it approves of one, disapproves of another, and toward a third is affected in neither of these ways, but is quite indifferent. . . . And that this faculty tends to restrain men from doing mischief to each other, and leads them to do good, is too manifest to need being insisted upon.[12]

Thus, Butler has argued that we all have the ability to judge our own actions. We are all familiar with it. What is it? It is conscience.

This principle in man by which he approves or disapproves his heart, temper, and actions, is conscience [for this is the strict sense of the word, though sometimes it is used so as to take in more]. . . . It cannot possibly be denied that there is this principle of reflection or conscience in human nature. Suppose a man to relieve an innocent person in great distress, suppose the same man afterwards, in the fury of anger, to do the greatest mischief to a person who had given no just cause of offense; to aggravate the injury, add the circumstances of former friendship and obligation from the injured person, let the man who is supposed to have done these two different actions coolly reflect upon them afterwards, without regard to their consequences to himself; to assert that any common man would be affected in the same way toward these different actions, that he would make no distinction between them, but approve or disapprove them equally, is too glaring a falsity to need being confuted. There is therefore this principle of reflection or conscience in mankind.[13]

Conscience is a reflective or rational faculty that discerns the moral characteristics of actions. This reflective principle is what we use when we pronounce some actions to be right, good, or just, and other actions to be wrong, evil, or unjust. This is the principle that restrains us from doing evil to each other, and leads us to do good to our neighbor. Butler says that conscience approves of whatever contributes to the good life of the whole person and condemns whatever disproportionately favors some part of the whole. This is how conscience regulates our lives: by approving or disapproving/condemning our own actions or intended actions.

Next, we'll explore the relationship between the natural impulses of benevolence and self-love, and the role of conscience. Self-love is a regulating principle. Benevolence is a regulating principle. Conscience is a regulating principle. How are they related? When desire and conscience conflict, which has a natural authority over the other? Butler's conclusion is that the principle of conscience or reflection is the superior one, the highest one, and should have authority over the others.*

... there is a superior principle of reflection or conscience in every man which distinguishes between the internal principles of his heart as well as his external actions, which passes judgment upon himself and them, pronounces determinately some actions to be in themselves just, right, good; others to be in themselves evil, wrong, unjust, which, without being consulted, without being advised with, magisterially exerts itself, and approves or condemns him the doer of them accordingly; and which, if not forcibly stopped, naturally and always of course goes on to anticipate a higher and more effectual sentence which shall hereafter second and affirm its own. . . .

Passion or appetite implies a simple tendency towards such and such objects, without distinction of the means by which they are to be obtained. Consequently, it will often happen there will be a desire of particular objects in cases

---

*If you remember Plato, there is a certain obvious similarity here. Butler says that conscience is a rational principle that should exert control over self-love and benevolence; Plato argued that reason should exert control over passion and appetites.

where they cannot be obtained without manifest injury to others. Reflection or conscience comes in, and disapproves the pursuit of them in these circumstances; but the desire remains. Which is to be obeyed, appetite or reflection?[14]

We all know that our conscience does not always win in this conflict. If conscience were really a superior principle, then it ought to have authority over desires. But sometimes we do what we want, and sometimes we follow our conscience. Does our conscience always control our passions and desires? Clearly, the answer is "no, not always." There is an obvious problem with Butler's claim that conscience has a natural authority. If conscience has natural authority over self-love and benevolence, why don't we do what our conscience tells us to do all the time? Sometimes human desires and impulses override our feelings of benevolence; sometimes we even do things that are self-destructive (thus conflict with self-love). We know we should obey our conscience, but sometimes we obey our whims, our desires. How can Butler explain this apparent contradiction?

To deal with this, Butler makes a distinction between *authority* and *power*. He acknowledges that desires can be more powerful than conscience, which is a reflective principle and thus is equivalent to reason, but Butler insists that reason (in the form of conscience) still has the authority.

> All this is no more than the distinction which everybody is acquainted with, between *mere power* and *authority*; only instead of being intended to express the difference between what is possible and what is lawful in civil government, here it has been shown applicable to the several principles in the mind of man. Thus that principle by which we survey and either approve or disapprove of our own heart, temper, and actions, is not only to be considered as what is in its turn to have some influence, which may be said of every passion, of the lowest appetites, but likewise as being superior; as from its very nature manifestly claiming superiority over all others, insomuch that you cannot form a notion of this faculty, conscience, without taking in judgment, direction, superintendency. This is a constituent part of the idea, that is, of the faculty itself; and to preside and govern from the very economy and constitution of man, belongs to it. Had it strength as it his [sic] right; had it power, as it has manifest authority, it would absolutely govern the world.[15]

If conscience had as much power or strength as it has authority, then conscience would "absolutely govern the world." To make sense out of this, imagine an authority figure, say a military officer like a general, who is not as physically strong as the new recruit. The new recruit has more physical strength, more power, but the new recruit still obeys the officer because the officer has the authority. This is Butler's idea of the relationship between conscience, with natural *authority*, and self-love and benevolence, which have the *power* to overcome conscience. But conscience still possesses the authority.

Self-love regulates individual desires in order to promote an individual's own best interests. Benevolence refers to controlling desires and appetites in order to further the public good. Often these two complement and reinforce each other, but not always. Sometimes there are conflicts between these two, between personal interests and benefits, and public interests and benefits.

Butler argues that conscience is the *highest regulative principle,* the arbiter of conflicting interests of self-love and public benevolence. Conscience arbitrates between the two conflicting demands of public good and private good.

Conscience and Human Nature

Butler has argued that we should follow our conscience. Any good philosophy student should ask, "why"? Why should we follow what our conscience (principle of reflection) says? *Where does conscience get its authority from?*

> It is by this faculty [conscience], natural to man, that he is a moral agent, that *he is a law to himself;* by this faculty, I say, not to be considered merely as a principle in his heart, which is to have some influence as well as others, but considered as a faculty in kind and in nature supreme over all others, and *which bears its own authority of being so.*
>
> This prerogative, this natural supremacy of the faculty which surveys, approves, or disapproves, the several affections of our mind and actions of our lives, being that by which men "are a law to themselves"—their conformity or disobedience to which law of our nature renders their actions, in the highest and most proper sense, natural or unnatural—it is fit it be further explained to you, and I hope it will be so if you will attend to the following reflections.[16]

Butler's point is that conscience is (a) the author of our moral obligations, and (b) the authority for our moral obligations. Where does conscience get its authority from? Butler answers: Conscience gets its authority from human nature.

> . . . Now as brutes have various instincts by which they are carried on to the end the Author of their nature intended them for, is not man in the same condition, with this difference only that to his instincts (that is, appetites and passions) is added the principle of reflection or conscience? And as brutes act agreeably to their nature, in following that principle or particular instinct which for the present is strongest in them, does not make likewise act agreeably to his nature or obey the law of his creation by following that principle, be it passion or conscience, which for the present happens to be strongest in him?[17]

Conscience tells us what is right and what is wrong. But that is not all. Conscience also carries an obligation to follow one's conscience, to act upon conscience.

> But allowing that mankind hath the rule of right within himself, yet it may be asked, "What obligations are we under to attend to and follow it [conscience]?" I answer, It has been proved that man by his nature is a law to himself, without the particular distinct consideration of the positive sanctions of that law; the rewards and punishments which we feel, and those which from the light of reason we have ground to believe are annexed to it. The question then carries its own answer along with it. Your obligation to obey this law is its being the law of your nature.[18]

Butler's conclusion is interesting: it is human nature for conscience to have the ultimate authority. It is the way we are built. Why obey conscience? *Because it is the law of your own human nature.* Butler claims that this is self-evident.

Conscience itself is the highest human principle; nothing else can override it. Because you are a human being, conscience has its authority. There is no higher principle that justifies it.

> . . . That your conscience approves of and attests to such a course of action is it-self alone an obligation. Conscience does not only offer itself to show us the way we should walk in, but it likewise carries its own authority with it; that it is our natural guide, the guide assigned us by the Author of our nature; it therefore belongs to our condition of being, it is our duty to walk in that path and follow this guide, without looking about to see whether we may not possibly forsake them with impunity.[19]

Conscience keeps us from being a slave to whatever passion is dominant for the moment, the way the animals respond. In fact, according to Butler, conscience is what separates us from the other animals. Conscience is what makes us a moral agent, enabling us to become a law unto ourselves, but it is a law that we must obey because it is the law of our own human nature.

When the various parts are "in proportion to each other," and when that "proportion is just and perfect," and under the absolute control of conscience, we have a perfectly moral human being. No ordinary human was ever perfectly moral; but, if when we find disorder within ourselves, we try to control it, this is the best that can be attained.

A person is good, worthy, virtuous, insofar as conscience maintains superiority over all the appetites and passions, superiority over the pull of self-love and the attraction of benevolence.

PROBLEMS TO PONDER

These are questions that any thoughtful person should think about if he or she were considering adopting Butler's analysis of morality. Perhaps Butler can answer them. How would you answer them?

  1. Is Butler's "law of conscience" really "self-evident"? To say that a statement is self-evident does not mean that the proposition is unquestionably true. Certainly, a proposition is called self-evident when its truth seems obvious to some people without the need for additional argumentation, inference, or evidence. Self-evident means: If you think about it, you will see that it must be true.

     The problem is this. False propositions may seem (and have often seemed) self-evident. Whether a proposition is self-evident to a person may depend on numerous psychological factors apart from and independent of the truth of the proposition itself. Mostly, self-evident only means that the statement is in agreement with what the majority of one's society believes.

     If the proposition is self-evident to A but not to B, there is no way of testing whether it is *really* true except by using other tests independent of whether it is considered self-evident. Thus, to say that a proposition is self-evident to person A tells us something about person A, but not much about the proposition.

2. How can Butler's theory settle a genuine ethical disagreement between highly moral people? One very moral person's conscience says "capital punishment is wrong!" while the other very moral person's conscience says "capital punishment is perfectly OK."

   Sometimes we have an ethical disagreement that survives even after all the nonethical facts are agreed upon, and after the logic of the situation is agreed upon. Such a disagreement is called an ultimate ethical disagreement. Within Butler's ethical system, how are ultimate ethical disagreements to be settled? Ultimate ethical disagreements must be puzzling for Butler. Can we say that one of the two people have not listened to his or her own conscience enough? But what does this mean, except "you disagree with me"? How will I know which one of us has not listened carefully enough? How can I know that I have listened enough and you have not? When you finally come to agree with me? Or is it when I finally come to agree with you?

3. How is the very existence of ultimate ethical disagreements to be explained? Given two people who are equally good in ability to reason, equal in mental capacities, and who still hold ultimately conflicting moral views, how would we know that one is right and the other wrong? With an ethical disagreement, we believe that agreement must be possible because we all share the same God-given conscience, but we can't say how to settle an ultimate disagreement; we can't say who is wrong, who isn't listening, who needs to grow up; there are no objective tests (and none are even possible).

4. Butler did not recognize that the judgments of human consciences seem to vary from one culture to another. If this is true, then there are two possible ways to explain this cultural variation. Perhaps conscience simply is not an adequate guide to a uniform moral truth that transcends cultures. The other possibility is that there are moral truths, but those moral truths are diverse, and they work only within the customary practices and attitudes of the cultures where they dominate (i.e., they are culturally relative). Neither is compatible with Butler's moral system.

5. What about a sociopath, a person born without a conscience? What does that do to (a) human nature, or to (b) the claim that God is the maker or author of our human nature? Did God leave conscience out of some people? And if so, are they not human (more like an animal)? Butler seems compelled to say so.

6. Butler's theory is tightly tied to the elementary psychology of the sixteenth and seventeenth centuries. Our more modern understanding of the mind does not support Butler's understanding of how conscience works. In other words, Butler's ethical philosophy rests on a faulty understanding of psychology, and if his psychological analysis of human nature and its drives and appetites is mistaken, then his entire ethical philosophy is also resting upon a mistake at its very foundation.

7. Butler is never very clear on precisely how the conscience determines what to approve and what to disapprove. What are the standards in accordance with which conscience makes its judgments? Butler says that conscience approves of whatever contributes to the good life of the whole person and condemns whatever disproportionately favors some part of the whole. But how does conscience decide what to approve? Where do the standards of conscience come from? Butler answers: They are innate to human nature, they are a law of our own being.

GLOSSARY

Atheism   The position of disbelief in the existence of a theistic deity, or God, is referred to as atheism.

Deism   Deism refers to the religious position that an omnipotent, omniscient, and omnibenevolent God exists who created everything perfectly at the moment of creation. Because the world must be exactly as God wanted it to be, God would never interact with this world (answer prayers or perform miracles), because that would imply that a perfect God made a mistake when he created the universe (any changes to a perfect universe would change it from perfection to an inferior status). For the Deist, God is transcendent and has no concern with human affairs and exerts no influence over humans; God does not answer prayers or perform miracles. The Theist and the Deist agree that a divine creator exists, but they disagree as to whether that creator has any interest in creation and responds to human beings. Deists tend to rely on unaided human reason to understand the world and human morality.

Egoistic hedonism   Egoistic hedonism is the view that, under all circumstances, human beings must choose whatever will maximize their own advantage or pleasure. They cannot help it. We are born egoistic, and we seek to maximize our own advantage, always. The British philosopher Thomas Hobbes held such a position.

Empiricism   The basic claim of empiricism is that all human knowledge of the external world is gained through sense experience, through seeing, hearing, touching, tasting, or smelling. Pure reason can tell us how one idea or concept is related to another concept, but pure reason is never a source of knowledge of the external world.

In his *Sermons*, Butler argues that ethics can only be understood by studying actual human nature, not by reasoning about human nature alone. You cannot derive virtue from the abstract relations among concepts or ideas. You must study human nature. Thus, Butler is taking an empiricist approach (although his conclusion differs profoundly from the most famous empiricist philosopher, David Hume).

Revelation   Revelation refers to the facts revealed to human beings by the deity that humans could never have figured out by human experience; for example, that God created the universe in six days, that God created two original human beings who disobeyed God, that God is three separate and distinct persons and yet one God, and so on.

Theism   Theism is a general religious position that asserts that one or more gods exist (Christian theism asserts that only one God exists), that God is transcendent, is personally interested in human affairs, and answers prayers and performs miracles.

A GUIDE TO FURTHER READINGS

Broad, C. D. *Five Types of Ethical Theories* (Patterson, N.J.: Littlefield, Adams & Co., 1959). One chapter discusses Joseph Butler's ethical philosophy.

Butler, Joseph, ed. by Stephen L. Darwall. *Five Sermons* (Indianapolis, Ind.: Hackett Publishing Co., 1983).

————. *The Works of Joseph Butler,* Introduction and Notes by J. H. Bernard (London: The English Theological Library, 1900), 2 vols. Basic editions of Butler's ideas.

Copleston, Frederick. *A History of Philosophy: Volume 5, Part I* (New York: Image Books, 1964). This volume includes a lengthy discussion of English philosophy from Hobbes to Butler.

Duncan-Jones, Austin E. *Butler's Moral Philosophy* (Harmondsworth, England: Penguin Books, 1952). A valuable treatment of Butler's ethics.

Mackinnon, D. M. *A Study in Ethical Theory* (New York: Collier Books, 1962). Chapter 5 discusses Butler's ethics.

CHAPTER 10

David Hume:

Morality Is Based on Feelings

THE LIFE OF DAVID HUME (1711–1776)

What was going on in the world around the time of David Hume? Well, Joseph Butler was born a few decades before Hume (who was born in 1711). Johann Sebastian Bach wrote his Brandenburg Concertos when Hume was ten years old. Daniel Defoe's *Robinson Crusoe* was published in 1719. The greatest German philosopher, Immanuel Kant, was born in 1724, when Hume was about thirteen years old. One of the greatest physicists who ever lived, Isaac Newton, died in 1727, when Hume was sixteen years old. The time of David Hume is also the time

of Galileo, Kepler, Francis Bacon, William Harvey, Descartes, Pascal, Edmund Halley (discoverer of "Halley's Comet"), Gabriel Fahrenheit, Bernoulli, and Joseph Priestley.

Ben Franklin began publishing a newspaper in Pennsylvania in 1729, and George Washington was born in 1732 when Hume was twenty-one. The same year there was a giant earthquake in Lisbon that killed an estimated 30,000 people. The musical prodigy and genius composer, Wolfgang Amadeus Mozart, was born in 1756 and died in 1791.

David Hume died in 1776. As you remember, in the 1770s England was having trouble with the American colonies; the first Continental Congress was called in 1774, and Paul Revere made a famous ride in 1775.

Hume was born in 1711 of an aristocratic family in Edinburgh, Scotland. His father died when Hume was only two years old, leaving Hume's mother to raise him. A very intelligent child, David Hume was admitted to Edinburgh University when he was twelve years old. After only a few years there, he left and began to study at home—and he put all of his energy into the study of philosophy, reading the great philosophers of the past.

215

The Christian church that dominated Scotland was the extremely harsh Calvinist church. Church services lasted at least three hours on Sundays. Church sermons tended to emphasize the fall of Adam and Eve, the human condition of sin and degradation, the helplessness of humanity, and the terrible wrath and punishment of God. According to Calvinism, human beings, their activities, and their choices continue to offend God, and God will respond with wrath and condemnation; God is an implacable despot, swift to anger, slow to forgive.

Hume grew up surrounded by Calvinism, but he rejected it (and Christianity) as irrational. He thought that religion arises out of human beings' ignorance of natural causes, combined with anxiety and fantasy. He argued that the consequences of religion are destructive of inner psychological harmony (especially because of the guilt that Calvinism fostered), and it was true that Christianity of that period severely limited individual freedoms of behavior as well as thought.

Hume thought Calvinism inhibited religious and intellectual freedom, created unnecessary personal conflicts within people, and fostered cultural repression. Needless to say, the Calvinist church (and the other Christian sects) were very unhappy with all of Hume's writings, and good Christians were forbidden to read anything that Hume wrote.

Hume is the first **atheist** in the Western tradition whom we have discussed. Although he was notorious for his critical approach to religion, he was respected. There is a story about Hume's funeral procession. At the time of David Hume's burial, as the coffin passed by, a bystander commented "Ah, he was an atheist." "No matter," his companion replied, "he was an honest man."[1]

Even for those who disagreed with him, it was obvious that Hume was a fiercely honest man, whose quest was for truth but not blind belief. For the sake of this honesty, Hume cultivated doubt just as seriously as people in earlier times had cultivated belief. Hume felt that people who believe things too easily wind up believing a lot of nonsense. Hume proposed critical thinking as essential for intellectual honesty. Thus, his attitude toward all claims was to analyze the claim to see what evidence supported the claim. Hume applied this same technique to the claims of religion. His attitude toward religion was an attitude of inquiry, analysis, and criticism; he had no use for blind faith or blind belief. Blind belief had been the cornerstone of Christianity for well over fifteen hundred years.

When he was twenty-three, Hume published *A Treatise on Human Nature*, revised into *Philosophical Essays Concerning Human Understanding*. In 1751, he published *An Enquiry Concerning the Principles of Morals* (an amplification of Book 3 of the *Treatise*). His *Dialogues Concerning Natural Religion* annoyed his contemporaries, but it is now recognized as a classic text in the philosophy of religion.

HUME'S PHILOSOPHY OF EMPIRICISM

In Europe during Hume's lifetime, there was a philosophical controversy concerning the sources of human knowledge. One group, called **Empiricists**, argued that all human knowledge of the external world has its ultimate origins in sense experience, in seeing, hearing, touching, tasting, and smelling. The other group, the **Rationalists,** argued that although sense experience may provide us with most of our knowledge of the external world, at least one thing can be known about the world purely by reason alone, independently of any experience. This is called **a priori** ("prior to experience") knowledge.

Empiricists denied that there was any a priori knowledge of the external world. Hume was an Empiricist; he argued very persuasively that everything we know about the external world is based on some experience, or reasoning based on some experience. Hume skillfully used empiricism to evaluate the claims of philosophy and religion.

As mentioned before, the time of David Hume is also the time of scientific and mathematical geniuses like Galileo, Kepler, Descartes, and Newton. Great scientific discoveries were being made, often in the face of the opposition of the Christian churches. But, every time the church opposed a claim of science, the church ultimately was shown to be wrong.

Hume was impressed by the advances that "natural philosophy" (science) had made. But what about science accounted for the ability of scientists to make such discoveries and what was the secret that accounted for the fact that scientific discoveries were correct? Hume attributed the success of science to the *methods* that it used.

Science is *empirical* (based on what you can see, hear, touch, taste, and smell), and science is *experimental* (ideally, the scientist will propose a hypothesis to explain a problem, draw out implications, and then test for the presence of the predicted implications; if found, the evidence supports the hypothesis and if more implications are discovered to be as predicted, the hypothesis is tentatively confirmed).

Hume wanted to apply these same empirical methods to the more abstract questions of philosophy. Hume's plan was to apply the experimental method to investigate the powers and principles of the human mind. He wanted a truly experimental science of human nature.

No one had ever been able to test the claims that the ancient philosophers had made about the Forms, about the soul, about the mind, about free will, or about morality. Hume sought a method whereby the hypotheses and claims of the philosophers could be tested, by asking which experience provided the source of such knowledge. Hume wasn't interested just in challenging religion. The speculations of all of the philosophers had to be tested, the jungle of claims needed to be cleared, because philosophical superstitions could grow there as well as folk myths.

Knowledge of Reality Comes from Sense Experience

He begins by asking about the human mind. When we look inside, introspect, what do we find? Hume concludes that the only things present to the mind are its own perceptions, or memories of previous perceptions ("sense impressions"). In our mind are perceptions, things we have touched, tasted, smelled, heard, or seen. We also have memories of previous sense impressions. In addition, we reason about our experiences, we have ideas based on our sense experiences, where we draw inferences from what we've seen, heard, touched, tasted, or smelled. We have emotions as well, but emotions are feelings, they are not knowledge grounded in our experiences.*

That leads Hume to conclude that all human knowledge consists in either judgments about matters of fact (what you have experienced) or else reasoning about the relationships between ideas (inferences based on what you have experienced). Emotions, feelings, dreams, fantasies, and stories are not factual and are not knowledge. All factual (and useful) knowledge is sense knowledge; it is arrived at from data supplied by the senses, or inferences based on our knowledge of cause and effect when applied to that sense data. David Hume's empiricism can be summed up in two propositions:

1. All our ideas are derived from impressions of sense or inner feeling. ["Every simple idea is derived from a corresponding impression."]
2. A matter of fact can never be proved by reasoning a priori. It must be discovered in our experience, or inferred from experience.

These two propositions are pretty clear. The first one claims that every thought in our head ultimately derives from some experiences or some feeling. A flying horse is clearly derived from experiences of horses combined with things that fly. A dragon is derived from experiences of reptiles, flying things, and our experience of fire, perhaps combined with fear.

The second one says that if you tell me something is true about the external world, the only way you could know that (or prove it) is by seeing, hearing, touching, tasting, or smelling (combined with reason). You cannot simply sit at your desk and reason abstractly and arrive at some truth that applies to the external world.

These two propositions may seem pretty obviously true, but they have some very severe consequences. Hume concludes that philosophical systems which claim to tell us about any matter that transcends all possible human experience are nonsense. Such claims have no meaning, and even if they had, they could not be shown to be true (or false). Statements purportedly telling us about the existence of God, about the existence of an immaterial soul, or about matters of faith transcend all possible human experience. Such claims are not based on anyone's experience. Thus they could never be known to be true (or false). They are nonsense.

Hume argued that human beings have a tendency to move from things in our empirical experience, such as tables and chairs (which are based on human sensory experience), to things that go far beyond experience, such as souls, life after death, divine creators, and so on. Moreover, Hume noted how dogmatically absolutely certain people feel about their own views on these matters where those claims are not grounded in any human experience; they have no evidence whatsoever and no experience that could provide such knowledge.

---

*Anger or love are neither true nor false; they simply are present. If I reason about my emotion and draw a conclusion, that might be true or false. But emotions in themselves are neither true nor false.

Hume considered this superstition (so did Epicurus), and Hume's analysis was an attempt to eliminate these sorts of claims as an error, as ultimately meaningless since they were not grounded in any experience whatsoever. We can know our own experiences, but we cannot know that there are metaphysical entities such as souls and God "out there."

Hume on Empirical Causality

Hume's ethical theory is profoundly affected by his interest in science, and especially his interest in the nature of causal connections. Concerning causation, we say event "A" causes event "B." The relationship between A and B is called a *causal connection*. Reasoning from cause to effect is crucial in daily life, in science, in the study of history, in law and morality (to be responsible for an action, you must have caused it).

Hume's problem: How does experience enable us to discover causes and make inferences? We have the idea of cause and effect; if it is knowledge of the external world (which it clearly is), this must be reducible to simple ideas and impressions. Our entire notion of causation must be based on sense impressions, but when we examine our experiences, we don't ever find an experience of one event *causing* or *making* or *forcing* a second event to occur.

Consider a simple causal relationship between two billiard balls on a pool table. We watch ball A roll, bump into the stationary ball B, and we see A *make* B move. But is this really what we see? Where exactly do we see A *force* B to move? Where do we see A *make* B roll? We don't.

All we have is an impression of billiard ball A rolling toward motionless billiard ball B. Then we have an impression of ball A stopping, followed by ball B rolling. We have an association of ideas, but that is all. Hume says that what we observe is **constant conjunction**. We see A roll, we expect to see B roll as soon as A touches B, and this is what we see. But this is all that we see. The idea of ball A moving, touching B, followed by the motion of B are constantly conjoined in our minds.

Hume concludes that causality is merely a belief, an association of ideas and impressions. We associate events like A and B in our minds. Causality is a mental habit, a mental tendency to associate one event with the other.

According to Hume's analysis, morality will work the same way. Ultimately, our moral judgments are based on the constant conjunction of events and feelings.

A moral proposition (e.g., "murder is immoral") tells us about a relationship between an external event (someone murdered) and an internal mental event (outrage, disapproval). Events like murder are constantly conjoined with strong feelings of disapproval. Just as human beings observe constant conjunction of two events and attribute causal necessity to that constant conjunction (mistakenly believing that causal necessity is *out there* when two billiard balls strike together), in a similar manner we are psychologically constituted to attribute a moral quality or moral property to an external action constantly conjoined with our internal feelings of approval or disapproval. Morality is *not* out there in the world, but it seems to be because of the way human minds work.

HUME'S ETHICS

We have already discussed Hume's attitude toward religion. Even with those people who agreed with Hume that religion did not have any strong evidence to support any of its claims, that it was repressive of human freedom and of science, still it was standard to regard religion as a positive social good, which restrained evil by fostering moral virtue. In other words, even if religion was probably false and had so many negative features, it was commonly believed that religion was the only possible foundation for morality. We cannot get rid of religion because then we would be getting rid of the only possible basis for morality, people would no longer behave morally, and the world would become an evil chaotic immoral world.

Hume did not agree with the claim that religion was the only possible explanation for human morality and moral virtues. Hume argued religion often is an enemy of natural virtues, because religion has a history of encouraging intolerance and inculcating dogmatic attitudes about truth; religion even imposed the torturous Inquisition to enforce a common religious vision.

Hume did not think that religion made a good basis for morality. In fact, Hume is quoted as follows: "While mistakes in philosophy are merely ridiculous, mistakes in religion are genuinely dangerous." People are willing to kill or be killed because of their religious beliefs, but being willing to die (or kill) for one's beliefs tells us nothing about whether one's beliefs are true—it only tells us something about the believer's mind, his or her psychology.

Think back to the ethics of the Greeks. Reason is the foundation of morality. In the Christian tradition, Thomas Aquinas argued that reason is the basis for morality. Bishop Butler argued that one's rational faculty (conscience) is the basis for morality. Hume begins his exploration of ethics by asking, is reason the general foundation of morals?

> There has been a controversy started of late, much better worth examination, concerning the general foundation of Morals; whether they be derived from Reason, or from Sentiment; whether we attain the knowledge of them by a chain of argument and induction, or by an immediate feeling and finer internal sense; whether, like all sound judgement of truth and falsehood, they should be the same to every rational intelligent being; or whether, like the perception of beauty and deformity, they be founded entirely on the particular fabric and constitution of the human species.[2]

If the general foundation of morals is derived from abstract reason, it will follow that we obtain knowledge of morals by chains of argument and induction. But there is another possibility: is the general foundation of morals derived from our sentiment or feeling? Can we know what is right and wrong by merely examining how we feel about the issue? Another way to think about the issue: Are moral judgments the same for every intelligent human being, like the truths of mathematics, or are they more like judgments of beauty, dependent on the individual (and thus a matter of taste)? Is morality about objective truth or subjective preferences?

> Truth is disputable; not taste; what exists in the nature of things is the standard
> of our judgement; what each man feels within himself is the standard of senti-
> ment. . . . No man reasons concerning another's beauty . . .[3]

We can start out by noticing that in Western civilization, there has been a
tendency to see the world in terms of opposites—things are either black or
white, either good or bad. We see this in the way that the question has been
asked: Is morality either derived from reason and objective, or is it derived
from sentiment, and thus subjective? Hume offers an alternative: Morality derives from both reason and passions.

Some things are so easy to judge that we can just look and declare the sun-
set beautiful or not beautiful, and then further reasoning doesn't help. Beauty is
clearly subjective and depends only on your own feelings of like, or approval,
or disapproval, right?

Hume answers, "not quite." Appreciation of natural beauty is one thing.
Some of the finer arts are different; your initial judgment can be changed by the
application of reasoning and understanding, and one can come to appreciate the
beauty that was overlooked. Many students have had the experience of first listening to a piece of classical music, not liking it, and then hearing a very good
teacher lecture on it, explain the parts, show how the themes develop. Upon a
rehearing of the music, the student likes it. Consider a fine modern painting. The
student looks at it, and says, "Ugh, my dog could do better than that." Again, a
gifted teacher explains the components, the colors, the shapes, the philosophical vision, the social commentary, all of which is relevant to the work of art.
Now, upon viewing the painting, the student brings a new and deeper appreciation to it and finds herself enjoying what she did not enjoy previously.

> Some species of beauty, especially the natural kinds, on their first appearance,
> command our affection and approbation; and where they fail of this effect, it is
> impossible for any reasoning to redress their influence, or adapt them better to
> our taste and sentiment. But in many orders of beauty, particularly those of the
> finer arts, it is requisite to employ much reasoning, in order to feel the proper
> sentiment; and a false relish may frequently be corrected by argument and re-
> flection. There are just grounds to conclude that moral beauty partakes much of
> this latter species, and demands the assistance of our intellectual faculties, in or-
> der to give it a suitable influence on the human mind.[4]

Hume is suggesting that morality might be like these finer arts, and moral
judgments involve personal taste (or sentiment), which demands the assistance
of our intellectual faculties (reason).

Even if Hume has convinced us that both sentiment and reason could play a role
in moral judgments, we can still wonder whether one of the two is more basic, more
fundamental than the other. Is morality primarily reason or is it primarily feelings?

Morality Is Primarily Feelings

Hume offers an argument to show us that it is basically feelings, sentiment, and
likes and dislikes that are the basis for moral judgments. He begins by asking,
what is the end of all moral speculation?

> The end of all moral speculations is to teach us our duty; and, by proper representations of the deformity of vice and the beauty of virtue, beget correspondent habits, and engage us to avoid the one, and embrace the other.[5]

Hume agrees that morality should affect our behavior. The result of morality is that we should choose virtue and avoid vice. Then he asks which motivates us to take action, our feelings or our reason? Are you more likely to engage in some sort of physical activity if you are angry or blissful, or if you have understood some abstract relationship between ideas?

Hume concludes that abstract reason does not motivate us to take action; inferences, reasoning, conclusions do not affect conduct and behavior.

> Abstract reason does help us to . . . discover truths: but where the truths which they discover are indifferent, and beget no desire or aversion, they can have no influence on conduct and behavior.[6]

Reason alone is a matter of understanding the relations between ideas or matters of fact. Abstract ideas do not motivate me to do anything. Even knowing the matter of fact that exercise produces better health, by itself, does not motivate me to act unless I *care emotionally* about my health, unless I care about the end to which my choices lead.

Discovering abstract truths does not affect our conduct, our behavior. But moral judgments do motivate us, do affect our choices, our behavior: what is honorable, what is fair, what is noble, what is generous—all of these "animate us to embrace and maintain it."

So, what do we know? Morality influences our behavior, it motivates us to take action. But what is "intelligible, what is evident, what is probable, what is true, procures only the cool assent of the understanding; and gratifying a speculative curiosity, puts an end to our researches."[7] But reason alone can never motivate any action. Therefore, morality cannot be a matter of reason alone. It must also involve feelings, one's sentiment.

If morality is primarily abstract reason, then it could be objective (**objective morality**) and the same for everyone, as the conclusions of mathematics are the same for everyone. If morality is primarily sentiment, then we would expect it to be more subjective (**subjective morality**), and varying from person to person. If the basis for moral judgments is found in the external world, independent of the observer, then it must be objective, and not in the feelings of sentiment of the beholder.

Hume considers this in the appendix to his classic work on morality. Consider: when we make moral judgments, we judge things to be good or bad, we judge behavior to be moral or immoral. Suppose I observe a crime, and I conclude "that was wrong!" Was the *wrongness* in the crime that I observed and in the world and external to myself? Is the *wrong* an objective feature found in the facts of the case?

Suppose that at the end of the previous class period, your professor asked to borrow $20 until the next class meeting. You loan the professor $20 until the next class meeting. The next class meeting occurs, and your professor says that the money won't be given back to you. She has decided to keep your money. Your reaction? You say "a philosophy professor ought to know the difference between right and wrong! And what you did was wrong!"

Your professor asks you to make up a thorough and complete list of the objective facts; write it *all* down. You list the time of day, the location of the classroom. You write down every word you heard the professor say, you describe opening your wallet and handing the teacher a $20 bill, and you know the professor promised to return it. You also include the conversation the next day when the teacher refuses to return your money.

Here is the problem: Wrongness is not on your list anywhere. Nowhere on your list do we have you experiencing the "wrongness" of the crime. Here is Hume's point: "Wrongness" or the "crime" is not found in any experience whatsoever. If the "wrong" is not found in the external world, where else could the "wrong" be?

> The hypothesis which we embrace is plain. It maintains that morality is determined by sentiment. It defines virtue to be *whatever mental action or quality gives to a spectator the pleasing sentiment of approbation;* and vice the contrary.[8]

Hume's answer: The "wrong" is found in the *mind* of the person who loaned the money, or in the mind of the person who hears the story; we listen to the story and we *feel* how wrong the action was, we feel anger, we may feel ill will or outrage toward the professor.

The Basis of Morality Is the Sentiment in the Mind of the Observer

From this, Hume concludes that the basis of morality is in the sentiment (or feelings) in the mind of the observer, not in abstract reason and not in the external facts. Certainly, reason can tell you what the facts are, but it cannot tell you how to value the facts—only your emotions, your sentiment, your passions can do that. Thus, the wrongness is not inherent in a particular fact; rather it is in the *sentiment* in the mind of the spectator.

With this, David Hume has provided a completely nontheistic foundation for morality, and his conclusion was startling: Sentiment is the source of morality. Morality is determined by feeling, by sentiment, by the passions. Morality is not found objectively in the things we see, hear, touch, taste, or smell. And morality is not determined solely by reason.

At its heart, things we call "good" are things that give us a feeling of approval or approbation. Things we call "evil" or "wrong" are things of which we disapprove. Hume says that virtue is "whatever mental action or quality gives to a spectator the pleasing sentiment of approbation."

There is a wide range of things of which we approve, which we call "moral" or "good." We can wonder what sorts of actions give rise to feelings of approbation, and then we can ask: what do they all have in common? After a lengthy analysis, Hume says that what they have in common is ". . . some sentiment of blame or approbation; whence we pronounce the action criminal or virtuous."[9] When someone commits a crime or behaves in an immoral fashion, ". . . the crime or immorality is no particular fact or relation, which can be the object of the understanding, but arises entirely from the sentiment of disapprobation, which, by the structure of human nature, we unavoidably feel on the apprehension of barbarity or treachery."[10]

Thus, Hume answers the question of what it is that things we approve of have in common. He answers that we tend to approve of those things that are either personally *agreeable* or *useful*, or *agreeable* or *useful* to others.

Is morality purely a matter of feelings of approbation or disapprobation? What role does reason play in all of this? Hume argues that reason plays an important role in moral decisions, but reason is not the source of moral decision making.

> But in moral deliberations we must be acquainted beforehand with all the objects, and all their relations to each other and from a comparison of the whole, fix our choice or approbation. No new facts to be ascertained; no new relation to be discovered. All the circumstances of the case are supposed to be laid before us, ere we can fix any sentence of blame or approbation. If any material circumstance be yet unknown or doubtful, we must first employ our inquiry or intellectual faculties to assure us of it; and must suspend for a time all moral decision or sentiment. While we are ignorant, whether a man were aggressor or not, how can we determine whether the person who killed him be criminal or innocent. But after every circumstance, every relation is known, the understanding has no further room to operate, nor any object on which it could employ itself. The approbation or blame which then ensues, cannot be the work of the judgement, but of the heart.[11]

When judging some action right or wrong, we cannot rely purely on our emotions. We need to know all the facts, and we need to think about the facts. If a person is accused of murder, we must know whether the dead person attacked the accused; whether the killing was in self-defense or unprovoked attack.

However, once we have all the facts, circumstances, relations—then we can react with our feeling of approbation (approval) or blame or disapproval, and judge the act "moral" or "immoral." Thus the role of reason is to provide the facts, and then our emotional reaction to those facts determines whether we feel the action was morally right or morally wrong. Sentiment or feeling is still the foundation of the moral judgment.

The Two Great Social Virtues of Benevolence and Justice

If we want to criticize Hume's theory, there are many places to start. Aren't there moral features of human society that cannot be explained by whether we personally find the act *agreeable* or *useful*, as Hume claimed? For example, some virtues are really social virtues, which affect others. There are many social virtues, two of the most important being benevolence and justice. Hume has to be able to explain these in terms of what is agreeable or useful, or else his theory is not able to account for an important feature of ethics.

Hume starts out considering benevolence. Can we explain the social virtue of benevolence using simply the sentiments of agreeable or useful? There is no doubt that we all value benevolent behavior, humane behavior, friendly and merciful actions. Don't we think that generosity is a virtue, and it is a virtue to be grateful for good things that others do for us?

Hume points out that people who develop these virtues are highly esteemed; and if they have these combined with other qualities and are expressed in good government, or expressed with useful instruction of mankind (i.e., religious teachings), "they seem even to raise the possessors of them above the rank of human nature, and make them approach in some measure to the divine."[12]

So why is it that we so value and approve of benevolence? Hume answers: because it is both agreeable or useful to ourselves, and to others. A kind and benevolent person creates happiness and satisfaction for others whenever they are around such a person, and interacting with him or her. You approve of benevolence because it makes you happier to be around someone who is kind and benevolent. But happiness for you is not the only thing to recommend benevolent behavior.

> . . . may it not thence be concluded, that the utility, resulting from the social virtues, forms, at least a *part* of their merit, and is one source of that approbation and regard so universally paid to them?[13]

It is socially useful if we behave benevolently, and we receive the approval of others when we are benevolent. Benevolence results in happiness and satisfaction to members of such a person's society, and to the individual who is esteemed by his or her fellow citizens.

Hence, benevolent behavior is considered virtuous for two reasons: partly because it is agreeable to be around someone who behaves benevolently, and partly because it is useful to society to have its members behave benevolently. It is in the interests of humankind that we behave benevolently.

> Upon the whole, then, it seems undeniable, *that* nothing can bestow more merit on any human creature than the sentiment of benevolence in an eminent degree; and *that* a *part*, at least of its merit arises from its tendency to promote the interests of our species, and bestow happiness on human society.[14]

The second great social virtue is a little more difficult to account for. Justice may not be at all agreeable to the individual. It may be just for the police officer to give you a citation for exceeding the speed limit, or failing to come to a complete stop at a stop sign, but it certainly is not personally agreeable. It may not even be agreeable to your friends and neighbors, who commiserate with you because of your citation.

So, if justice cannot be accounted for with agreeableness, that only leaves social utility. Can Hume show that social utility is the only basis for considering justice a social virtue?

> That Justice is useful to society, and consequently that part of its merit, at least, must arise from that consideration, it would be a superfluous undertaking to prove. That public utility is the sole foundation of its merit; this proposition, being more curious and important, will better deserve our examination and enquiry.[15]

It is obvious that at least a part of the merit of justice must lie in the fact that justice is useful to society, but it is more difficult to show that the only foundation for its merit lies in social utility or usefulness—Hume attempts to show this with some thought experiments.

If justice is intrinsically valuable, then it will be considered a virtue in every society, no matter whether it were wealthy or extremely poor. Hume wonders if it is true that justice would be considered a virtue no matter what sort of society we encounter. For example, would justice be considered especially valuable in a society that was so wealthy that everything you needed was supplied and we all had everything we wanted? Would justice be important if you never had to work or worry about anything? Would it be valuable if there was too much of everything?

> It seems evident that, in such a happy state, every other social virtue would flourish, and receive tenfold increase; but the cautious, jealous virtue of justice would never once have been dreamed of. For what purpose make a partition of goods, where every one has already more than enough? . . . Why call this object *mine*, when upon the seizing of it by another, I need but stretch out my hand to possess myself to what is equally valuable? Justice, in that case, being totally useless, would be an idle ceremonial, and could never possibly have place in the catalogue of virtues.[16]

When there are a thousand cookies on the stack and only three people nibbling, you don't worry about receiving your fair and just share. When there are only three cookies, and three people, then you want your fair share. In our present civilization, we do not consider it just to divide up the air we breathe or the water we drink, unless there isn't quite enough to go around. You cannot be unjust by using water or air, unless there is a danger of running out. Thus, justice is not considered a virtue until we arrive at a situation where there isn't quite enough to go around.

Now consider a society that is just the opposite—a society where there is never enough, and the majority of the population will die from lack. Hume argues that here too justice will be ignored—it will be every person for himself and all will do their best to preserve their own lives (and the lives of their loved ones); one will not likely sacrifice the life of one's wife or child simply because justice requires you to share your food equally with another person and his or her family. You will all be dead in the morning if you share it with too many people. So, you won't be just. You can't afford to be just.

> . . . it will readily, I believe, be admitted, that the strict laws of justice are suspended, in such a pressing emergence, and give place to the stronger motives of necessity and self-preservation.[17]

In a society of extreme poverty, justice will be useless and no one will share what they need to live based on an argument appealing to the virtue of justice. We value justice as a virtue only in those societies that are between excess and extreme poverty, because justice will be useful in such a society. Justice is useful to the public in any society that is not one of those extreme situations. The majority of civilizations fall somewhere between these two extremes. Thus, the majority of civilizations will consider justice to be a virtue.

If justice were intrinsically valuable, then justice should be valuable in every society no matter what its condition. Hume concludes that the merits of justice and moral obligations of justice both arise from the fact that justice is socially useful. Hume's thought experiment has shown us that justice is not intrinsically valuable but rather of instrumental value. Thus, social utility is the sole foundation of the virtue of justice.

Is Morality Radically Subjective?

In the conclusion to his work on morality, Hume considers the problem of relativism. If morality depends on what you personally approve of, and find socially useful, then morality is subjective. Hume agrees with this. However, is morality **radically subjective,** that is, is every single individual the basis for his or her own moral system? If there are forty students in the ethics class, do we actually have forty different moral systems? It is fairly obvious that the students agree about almost all the major moral issues. They agree that killing is wrong, they agree that it is wrong to abuse a child, and they agree that one should not lie.

How in the world can Hume account for the fact that, in general, the majority of human beings agree about moral virtues and moral behavior? The great majority of us approve of truth-telling, approve of generosity, approve of keeping promises, and disapprove of inflicting unnecessary pain and suffering on our fellow humans. Why do we almost universally disapprove of those who would harm children, or force unwanted sexual attention on another person? How can Hume account for the near universality of morality if morality is subjective, if it is just the sentiment in the mind of the observer?

Hume agrees that the majority of our moral judgments are commonly agreed upon. He replies that even though morality has as its source individual human feelings of approbation or disapprobation, it also involves social utility, and these considerations tend to be universally shared. In addition, we care for others. For example, Hume says that:

> ... when he bestows on any man the epithets of *vicious* or *odious* or *depraved*, he then speaks another language, and expresses sentiments, in which he expects all his audience are to concur with him. He must here, therefore, depart from his private and particular situations and must choose a point of view, common to him with others; he must move some universal principle of the human frame, and touch a string to which all mankind have an accord and symphony. . . . While the human heart is compounded of the same elements as at present, it will never be wholly indifferent to public good, nor entirely unaffected with the tendency of characters and manners. . . . The humanity of one man is the humanity of every one, and the same object touches this passion in all human creatures.[18]

All people have some benevolence, some spark of friendship for fellow human beings, some feelings of peace toward others—no matter how weak. We might imagine that this comes from being born into a family, having parents and siblings who care for you and for whom you care.

Even slight feelings will produce a slight intellectual inclination to behave in these ways, a "cool preference of what is useful and serviceable to mankind, above what is pernicious [hurtful] and dangerous. A *moral distinction* therefore, immediately arises; a general sentiment of blame and approbation; a tendency, however faint, to the objects of the one, and a proportionable aversion to those of the other."[19]

Hume might have pointed out many observations that would strengthen his position. First, human beings share a common biology and physiology. The sorts of things that make me say "ouch" tend to be the same sorts of things that cause you pain. The sorts of sensations that I find pleasurable tend to be the same sorts of things that others find pleasurable. Wouldn't we all prefer a back rub to a poke in the eye with a sharp stick?

In addition, almost all of us grow up in a family environment; we have family members who love us and whom we love. We may have siblings with whom we can fight, but they also care for us. Most humans learn sharing and caring in their family, and we value these in others.

Almost every human has grown up in a society. A system of values that permits and sanctions features essential for the maintenance of life is inevitable in all societies. Every society must provide for mating and rearing of offspring. Every society must provide for educating offspring in those tasks necessary for survival. There must be differentiation of jobs, assignment of individuals to those jobs, means of training, and motivation. Sufficient security must be provided to prevent serious disruption of activity, such as security against violent attack.

Some values, and some institutions, are so inevitable, given human nature and the human situation in society, that we can hardly anticipate serious questioning of them by anybody.

Hume argues that we humans have a natural feeling of sympathy, humanity, or fellow feeling; we therefore feel approval for things agreeable to others as well as to ourselves. This means that these sentiments are common to all human beings; we all prefer the same sorts of actions; we tend to agree in the same opinions or decisions.

Thus, although morality is based on taste, sentiment, and feelings, it is not as radically subjective as it sounds. These sentiments are universally shared.

We are all human beings, we all tend to have very similar psychological make-ups, so we will tend to have similar or comparable moral responses. We won't agree about every action, or every detail, but we will tend to respond similarly.

> Whatever conduct gains my approbation, by touching my humanity, procures also the applause of all mankind, by affecting the same principle in them. . . . There is no circumstance of conduct in any man, provided it have a beneficial tendency, that is not agreeable to my humanity, however remote the person. . . . Virtue and Vice become then known; morals are recognized; certain general ideas are framed of human conduct and behavior; such measures are expected from men in such situations.[20]

Because of all these commonalities, if people are provided the same facts and understand the consequences, people will tend to make the same moral judgments. This accounts for the broad agreement in ethical matters and also accounts for the fact that human beings disagree about ethical matters.

Hume claims that society tends to approve acts that it finds socially useful and to condemn actions that it finds disruptive or detrimental. This has a beneficial consequence: social utility is a more objective quality than just a person's idiosyncracies, their immediate personal preferences. Moral judgments will be more alike, and even more impartial, because the standard is "conforming to social utility." A society that does not provide security for its members will not last long. A society that allows one person to take another person's home or family will be a society that will ultimately become an anarchy, and it will collapse. In general, what is "socially useful" is somewhat objective and invariant between societies.

Therefore, although morality is based on your personal approval or disapproval, the great majority of us will tend to approve of similar sorts of things, and disapprove of similar sorts of things. We have much more in common than we have differences. We have a common root of humanity, but it can be explained by natural phenomena and does not require a belief in a supernatural force to account for the common human moral judgments.

AN OVERVIEW OF HUME'S ETHICS

All those ethical philosophers who believe that pure reason alone is the basis for morality, or who argue that morality is objective and independent of individual selves, have trouble explaining why we have so much disagreement within a particular society on moral issues (very moral and very good human beings disagree about important moral problems in society), and those philosophers have trouble explaining the wide variety of moral behavior between different societies.

Hume has provided an explanation. Both as individuals and as societies, we have so very much in common that we seem to have some objective or universal basis for our moral judgments. However, when we examine them closely, we see that many of these judgments differ, that one individual concludes that abortion is profoundly immoral and is a danger to society, and another individual concludes that it is regrettable but morally permitted. One individual argues that same-sex marriages are profoundly immoral, while another individual concludes that it is neither a danger to society nor is it immoral.

Hume's ethical system accounts for this: Because of upbringing, environment, or society, some feel disapproval or disapprobation where others approve or are neutral. The action itself is not wrong; rather, it is our personal reaction to the facts that determines whether an act is right or wrong, combined with the social utility of the behavior.

Hume has also shown that religion is not the only possible foundation that can account for morality in human beings. Having learned from science to trust the orderliness of the external world of nature, Hume saw no reason not to trust natural human inclinations, sentiments, and instincts.

Hume concludes that moral value judgments are based primarily on emotion, and only secondarily on reason. It is human nature, not religion, that is the real foundation of morality. Judgments of moral approval are expressions of the pleasure that we experience when presented with behavior that we find agreeable or useful. It is human nature to associate our negative or positive feelings about some events with the event itself. We project our inner feelings onto the external event, of which we approve or disapprove. Just as we are psychologically constituted to attribute causal necessity to the constant conjunction of two kinds of empirical events, similarly we are psychologically constituted to attribute a moral quality or moral property to an external action constantly conjoined with our feelings of approval or disapproval.

PROBLEMS TO PONDER

These are questions that any thoughtful person should think about if he or she were considering adopting Hume's analysis of morality. Perhaps David Hume could answer them. How would you answer them?

1. Hume's ultimate position is a sort of moral relativism and subjectivism. This means that there is no ultimate moral order independent of human beings. Is social utility enough to account for the strong feeling we have about moral rules?

2. If morality is ultimately based on feelings of approval or disapproval, then morality is effortless: when in doubt whether something is right, merely check to see if you approve of it. In fact, you can make any choice morally right! To make an action right, merely work yourself into the psychological state of approval toward it. If you don't approve, then it isn't right—that's all there is to it! How can Hume respond to this?

3. If morality is ultimately subjective, then we can never really disagree with another person about morality. To say "X is right" means "I, Smith, approve of X." To say "X is wrong" means "I, Jones, disapprove of X." There is no ethical disagreement here. Each person is merely describing their own psychological states. It is like two people arguing about ice cream flavors: "I love vanilla." "But I love strawberry!" There is not a genuine disagreement here. They are merely telling each other what they approve of.

   But, when people disagree about ethical matters, they do not seem to be disagreeing about whether the other person approves of the matter. When Smith tries to convince Jones that X is right, is Smith really trying to convince Jones that *Smith* approves of X?

GLOSSARY

A priori   A priori means "prior to experience." This term is used to describe knowledge we have that we can know even before experience of the world. I can know a priori that all bachelors are unmarried, but I cannot know a priori if the adult male living nearby is a bachelor without checking, that is, without experience.

Atheist   An atheist holds the view that there is no deity, no God. "The "a-" is a prefix that means "not," and "theism" refers to a divine being who interacts with the world, answers prayers, and performs miracles. The atheist does not believe that such a being exists.

Constant conjunction   Two events occur one immediately after the other; we see the first event and then it is immediately followed by the second event. We find this same pattern repeated over and over. Hume argues that causality is merely a belief, an association of ideas and impressions. We associate one event with another. Causality is a mental habit, a mental tendency to associate one event with the other. However, the first event does not force the second event to occur; rather, the two events are merely constantly conjoined.

Empiricists   Empiricists hold the view that all human knowledge of the external world has its ultimate origins in sense experience, in seeing, hearing, touching, tasting, and smelling. If we know anything that is true about the external world, either we experienced it, or else we reasoned about our experiences.

Objective morality   This is the view that moral truths are like facts, true or false independent of the observer. Thus, if two people disagree on a moral matter, and one says the choice is moral and the other says it is not moral, the objectivist would argue that they cannot both be correct.

Radically subjective   The radically subjective view holds that morality depends entirely on the individual. If there are ten people in the room, then there must be ten different moral systems.

Rationalists   Rationalists hold the view that although sense experience may provide us with most of our knowledge of the external world, at least one thing can be known about the world purely by reason alone, independently of any experience. This is called a priori ("prior to experience") knowledge.

Subjective morality   This is the view that moral truths depend on the person and/or the situation. For the subjectivist, if two people disagree on a moral matter, and one person says the choice is moral and the other says it is immoral, both can be correct. The choice is moral from the perspective of one person, and nevertheless immoral from the perspective of the other person.

A GUIDE TO FURTHER READINGS

Flew, Anthony. "Hume," in O'Connor, *A Critical History of Western Philosophy*, p. 271ff; A critical examination of Hume's philosophy.

Hume, David. *An Enquiry Concerning the Principles of Morals*, Reprinted from the edition of 1777, 2nd ed. (LaSalle, Ill.: Open Court, 1966). David Hume's basic writings on morality.

Merrill, Kenneth R., and Robert W. Shahan, eds. *David Hume: Many-sided Genius* (Norman, Okla.: University of Oklahoma Press, 1976). Several essays on Hume's philosophy, including his ethics.

O'Connor, D. J., ed. *A Critical History of Western Philosophy* (New York: The Free Press, 1964).

CHAPTER 11

Immanuel Kant:

Duty Is the Foundation of Morality

THE LIFE OF IMMANUEL KANT (1724–1804)

The lifetime of Immanuel Kant overlaps with the life of Ben Franklin, George Washington, and philosophers Joseph Butler and David Hume. In fact, David Hume's empirical philosophy had a profound effect on Kant's thinking.

The year Kant was born, J. S. Bach was writing his "Notebook for Anna Magdalena Bach," and Handel was writing operas. In 1727, when Kant was just three years old, Isaac Newton died. The Methodist sect of Christianity was founded in 1730 by John Wesley when Kant was six years old; when Kant was

twelve years old, Joseph Butler copied down many of his sermons on ethics, and a year later Stradivarius (maker of fine stringed instruments) died; David Hume wrote on human nature when Kant was fifteen. Benjamin Franklin was working in Philadelphia in the 1740s and invented the lightning conductor in 1752. In 1789, when Kant was sixty-five years old, George Washington was inaugurated as the first president of the United States with John Adams as vice president and Thomas Jefferson as Secretary of State.

Kant was born in 1724 in the town of Konigsberg, East Prussia (the area is near present-day Poland and Lithuania), and his parents were of the middle class (his father made saddles). Immanuel was their fourth child. Kant's parents were Lutheran Pietists* and were devoutly religious; his early education was strictly religious. As a university professor, he never lost his

*The Pietists were a devout German Lutheran revivalist sect, founded around 1700, stressing personal piety and not strict doctrinal orthodoxy.

deep respect for religion, but he was uncomfortable with the mechanical discipline and narrow range of ideas allowed in the Pietist school he attended. He had a stern, uncompromising sense of morality, and there is no doubt that this helped to shape his moral system, which bases morality upon duty.

Young Immanuel initially studied to be a minister, but science and philosophy were the areas in which he excelled. He entered the university at sixteen and paid for it by tutoring wealthier students. After graduation he earned his living as a private tutor. At age thirty-one he was hired by the university as an instructor of philosophy and logic. He taught philosophy, geography, and mathematics.

Kant lived a remarkably uneventful life of polite academic poverty. He had a schedule and routine for everything, and never married (although he had a busy social life with many friends). He was very highly regarded as a teacher; his popular lectures were famous for his eloquence, brilliance, and wit. Immanuel Kant reshaped European philosophy in the areas of **aesthetics, metaphysics,** and theory of knowledge. He never traveled more than forty miles from his place of birth, was very careful of his health, and lived until age eighty.

Just like Hume and the other well-educated Europeans of the era, it was clear to Kant that the methods and techniques of science were producing a deep and correct understanding of the world, a Newtonian world that was a mechanical system of bodies operating in accordance with mathematically formulated laws. In his major scientific work, *General Natural History and Theory of the Heavens,* Kant accounts for the origin of the solar system by a hypothesis of matter as a great nebula that was slowly drawn together to form stars and planets.

Immanuel Kant loved science, and he loved Christianity. However, it was clear to him that the truths of religion were *not* as certain as science. Religious disagreements were severe, and there was no possible evidence to settle conflicting claims of theologians. This tension was reflected in the later philosophy of Kant, where he tries to reconcile empirical science based on observing nature, and supernatural religion. This is seen in Kant's ethical theory as well. In fact, one could say that Kant was attempting to expound a Christian view of morality, using reason alone. As we shall see, Kant's profoundly rational ethical system ultimately produces a variation on the Golden Rule found in the Jewish holy books and in the Christian Gospels: "Do unto others as you would have them do unto you." As we noted in a previous chapter, the Chinese Confucian philosophers also stressed this insight.

The influence of Kant upon all later philosophers has been immense. Virtually all of German and European philosophy was profoundly influenced by Kant; indeed, nineteenth-century philosophy is built on the philosophy of Kant.

KANT'S PHILOSOPHY OF RATIONALISM

Kant was a German professor, and he wrote like a professor. Although both Hume and Descartes are read today for their literary brilliance, Kant's writings are not a contribution to literature. Kant's aim was *thoroughness* rather than elegance or literary style. His books are difficult to read and difficult to understand. Even professional philosophers have trouble getting through Kant's elaborate schematic structure, filled with technical terms, many of those terms made up by Kant when he could not find ordinary words to satisfy his needs.

The Fundamental Principles of the Metaphysics of Morals (1785) is Kant's primary treatise on morality. He also wrote the *Critique of Practical Reason* to explore the implications of morality for religion. In a way, Kant can be understood as attempting to find some middle ground between the rationalist claim that pure reason alone could be a source of some information about the external world, and the empiricism of David Hume, which persuasively argued that all our knowledge of the external world comes from sense experience alone. Also, Kant attempted to reconcile the science of Isaac Newton with the claims of religion and morality. We can see this tension within himself between science and morality especially clearly in an autobiographical remark he made about himself: "two things fill the mind with ever new and increasing admiration and awe . . . the starry heavens above and the moral law within." The two poles of Kant's thought were at one extreme, astronomy, nature, science, and at the other extreme, inner moral law and one's moral duty.

Kant was certain that the truths of science are certain knowledge and not mere opinion, not personal belief, not tentative. However, Hume and other empiricists had shown fairly conclusively that the content of one's experiences cannot generate certainty.

Hume's Empiricism Creates a Problem for Kant

David Hume had argued that human thought moves too easily from things in our empirical experience, such as tables and chairs (which are based on human sensory experience), to things that go far beyond experience, such as souls, life after death, divine creators, and so on. Moreover, Hume noted how dogmatically absolutely certain people feel about their own views on these religious matters where those claims are not grounded in any human experience; humans have no evidence whatsoever and no experience that could provide such knowledge. Hume considered religion to be superstition. We can know our own experiences, but we cannot know that there are metaphysical entities such as souls and God "out there."

Kant neatly sidesteps the problems created by the Empiricists. He does not attempt to show empiricism is mistaken. Rather, he tries to find some way of reconceptualizing the world that can make room for human knowledge of the external world based on experience, and still make room for the possibility of abstract reason to know things about the external world. He does this by shifting the entire ground of discussion. Instead of asking Hume's question, *is all knowledge of the external world based upon sensory experience?* Kant asks another fundamental question, *what makes knowledge claims possible?* How is it possible to know anything for certain? How do our minds go about representing the reality of the things that make up the external world?

To answer the question "What makes knowledge claims possible?" Kant attempts to analyze thought itself, asking if there is some sort of inborn natural structure to the mind itself that makes knowledge possible.

The Structure of the Mind Makes Knowledge Possible

Kant attempts to map the structure of reason, its relationship to its objects, and then precisely clarify the limits within which reason can work with confidence. In doing this, Kant comes to some genuinely surprising conclusions.

We Can Never Know the External World

The first surprising conclusion is that Kant provides powerful arguments that show that we could never know the external world the way it really is. Never. In other words, he denies that objects exist "out there" in the external world just the way we perceive them. He denies that our mental images correspond accurately to things in the external world. He denies that we have the truth about objects when our mental images of them *correspond accurately* to the objects. We are wrong when we think that our thoughts mirror or conform to reality precisely the way it is in itself, when no human is experiencing it. We are mistaken if we think that our mental images resemble the physical world outside of ourselves.

Kant argues that truth is *not* when our beliefs correspond to the way objects are out there. Truth is *not* getting our beliefs to correspond accurately to the way things are *really*, to reality.

If objects out there in the external world do not exist independently of our apprehension of them, just the way we perceive them, what is happening? Here is another surprising conclusion: *The objects of our experience are constructed by our minds*, using innate categories that our minds use to sort out the raw stuff of existence.

Our Minds Construct the Way the External World Appears to Us

Kant uses two technical terms to distinguish between (a) the way the world appears to us, the world of our own inner experiences, and (b) the way things are in themselves, apart from human experience. The first he calls **phenomena,** which consist of appearances or sensations caused by particular objects. Kant uses the term **noumena** to refer to **things-in-themselves,** the way they are independent of any observer or any sense perception. Using Kant's distinction, the way we experience the world, the appearance of things (phenomenon) is due to our subjective mental apparatus (reason), which imposes structure upon external objects (noumena).

With this way of thinking about the world, Kant brings empiricism and rationalism together. Kant agrees with Hume, that all we know about the external world is our own sensations and experiences. Hume was right—we can never know with certainty the way things are in themselves (noumena). But Kant claims that the Rationalists are correct, too: pure reason alone allows us to know something for sure—we can be certain about the way things-in-themselves (noumena) must *appear* to us (phenomena), because we can know something about the general structure human reason will impose upon noumena.

To summarize: for Kant, the world has two aspects. The first aspect is the world as it is in itself; what exists, simply exists. It is noumena, and we can *never* know this things-as-they-truly-are (because all we can know is how things appear to us). The concrete sensory world of human experience is a sensory manifold, which exists external to ourselves and from which all of our knowledge begins.

But this sensory world of noumena cannot be perceived directly; first there are the raw sensations that come from our sense organs, but this is not the same as phenomena. The raw sensory manifold must pass through our innate categories, our ideas, and our perceptual apparatus. Having been restructured by our categories, it becomes what we call phenomena. The world of things in themselves, noumena, is forever unknowable.

Phenomena are the ways the world appears to us. Phenomena are knowable. Things appear to us in certain ways, and human beings then classify these appearances, interpret, categorize, and describe them in our own particular ways. We can never have knowledge of objects themselves, noumena; we cannot have direct access to things-in-themselves. We only know how things appear to human beings.

The objects of our experience are constructed by our minds, using categories that our minds use to sort out the raw stuff of existence. The objects of experience are (at least in part) the result of a construction by a rational mind, using several built-in innate categories.

We understand the world using our minds; our mind is the only source we have to turn the raw stuff into colors, sounds, shapes, and then into knowledge. Kant explores what the mind is, the mind that makes knowledge possible. The rational mind has an innate structure. *The only things possibly knowable are things that correspond to the structure of the rational mind.*

Human Categories Create the Structure of the External World

The structure you and I seem to perceive *in* the world is actually *imposed upon* the world by the categories of the rational mind. It is as though we are wearing glasses that are sensitive to only a part of the light spectrum—if I am wearing yellow sunglasses, I know for a fact that *everything* I look at will be tinted yellow . . . why? Because every possible color will get tinted yellow as it goes through my sunglasses! It seems as if I know something about the external world (everything will have a yellow cast to it), but in fact, I don't know something about the world at all. All I know is how the world will appear to me when I'm wearing yellow-tinted sunglasses.

Kant argues that any thing which does not correspond to the categories of reason will simply not be a possible experience for a rational human being. Human minds use several fundamental categories (concepts or mental structures) to create what we call "reality." These fundamental categories describe how humans must think; they describe the possibility of all human knowledge. We *must* experience the world in certain ways because those ways make human experience possible.

The Fundamental Categories of Thought

What are these fundamental categories of thought? Kant, following Aristotle's ideas, says these categories include basic structures like *space* (every event experienced by our senses will be perceived as though it occurs in space), *time* (events occur sequentially), and *causality* (every event is caused). We must see things in space and in time; we have no choice—this is the structure that human reason imposes on all of our experiences.

It seems to us that time and space and causality exist out there, in the external world. Kant says we are wrong. These categories are not derived from our human experience of the external world; rather, these categories are *prior* to our experiences; they are imposed on our experiences at such a fundamental level that we have never noticed it. Being prior to all possibility of experience, these mental categories are called **a priori** because they are independent of all experience, and will shape our potential experiences before we can become aware of the experiences themselves. These categories must apply to everything we think because they are the tools we use to think, the fundamental categories. These categories are like colored sunglasses we wear; everything we see will be colored by these—and we cannot take them off. These are what Kant calls the "conditions for the possibility of experience."

If Kant is correct, it follows that we can know a priori that everything which humans know about the world will fit into the category of causality, because the human mind imposes causality upon the raw perceptions. We cannot help but perceive things causing one another because that is a structure we impose on noumena. For example, "every event must have a cause" is not a statement about reality at all—rather, it is a description of the categories and concepts that human beings must use to categorize their experiences; cause and effect is a fundamental category (concept) of human reasoning, and we all apply it naturally and unthinkingly, even though there is no evidence whatsoever that this principle is a true and accurate description of reality. Human minds impose causality on nature, but we can never know for sure whether causality is in nature, in things-in-themselves (noumena).

We can be certain about the causal nature of our experience but not because the universe itself follows the law of causality; rather, the universe itself will *appear* to follow the law of causality because human minds *must* think using this as one of our fundamental categories by which we must interpret our experiences (like colored glasses). Causality is a product of the mind, not innate in nature. We use many other fundamental categories to make sense out of the raw noumena.*

---

*For example, Kant argues that we have a fundamental category of quantity, which means we will impose number upon what we experience (i.e., unity, plurality, totality). We have a fundamental category of quality, which means we will experience reality in terms of degrees, in intensity (i.e., reality, negation, and limitation). We have a fundamental category of relation, substance and accident, and reciprocity. We have a fundamental category of modality (possibility, existence, and necessity).

Some Things Can Be Known with Complete Certainty

Now Kant can deal with the problem of certainty that David Hume wrestled with. If we are talking about the way *things* are *in themselves*, we have no way of saying that things must be one way or another way. Hume is right. We have no certainty about the external world the way it is in itself.

However, if we are talking about the world as a possible object of human experience, the case is different. Human beings are equipped with peculiar faculties, capacities, and modes of thought, and thus only a particular kind of world could present itself as an object of experience for human beings. What we experience must exist in space, must occur in time, must be orderly and predictable. Humans cannot directly perceive noumena. Without these categories, there would be no world at all and no experience of anything!

KANT'S ETHICS

In general, Kant wants to know how any knowledge is possible. However, that question can be narrowed to "How is morality possible?"

If you recall, David Hume, the Empiricist, analyzed ethics and argued that moral judgments are subjective, and vary from person to person, because we never can perceive moral rightness or wrongness in the world. Hume concluded that therefore moral rightness and wrongness did not exist independently of the self. Hume argues that ethics has to do with human beings' practical needs as social human beings, and with our relations with one another; thus, morality is subjective and tied to feelings or sentiment. For Hume, morality is *not* absolute, and moral judgments are not binding upon every person. We are naturally inclined to do things that are pleasurable, or socially useful. Morality is tied to our inclinations, our likes and dislikes, the things we approve of and disapprove of. And these are all subjective.

Kant was heavily influenced by David Hume but in a negative way; Kant strongly objected to Hume's conclusion that ethics is sentiment, but he respected the strength and rigor of Hume's arguments and knew that he would have to come up with something extraordinarily strong to justify his disagreeing with Hume's arguments.

Morality Is Objective, Not Subjective

Kant was certain that morality is absolute and objective, not subjective. That is, he was certain that what is morally right for one person will be morally right for all persons at all times in all places. Morality must be independent of all human feelings, because otherwise it will not be absolute and binding upon every person. Kant felt certain that morality cannot be based on inclinations toward what feels good, or what is pleasant, or what is useful, because these can vary from person to person.

Of course, his position reflects his Christian beliefs in this area. But he is not asking us to believe what he believes just because he believes it. Kant is a philosopher.

His conclusion that morality is absolute is based on rigorous analysis and thorough arguments. Kant is sure that all human beings are certain that valid moral principles apply without exception to all human beings—they are objective and universally binding, not merely empirical. But how is this possible?

To answer this question, Kant asks, "What is the purpose of morality?" He agrees with Hume that the purpose of morality is to affect our behavior. We want to know how to act correctly, to do the right thing. In addition, Kant agreed with Hume that empirical knowledge of facts cannot tell us how we *ought* to behave. But Kant believes that pure reason can give us knowledge of what ought to be.

Kant is a Rationalist, not an Empiricist like Hume. Kant argues that it is human reason, not feelings, sentiment, utility, or preferences, that makes human beings moral beings. Agreeing with Plato, Kant argues that the principles of morality are objective like mathematics, that both are rationally demonstrable.

So Kant agrees with Hume that morality is not out there in the world. But Kant argues that Hume was mistaken when he thought that there were only two possibilities: (1) morality is either objectively in the external world and independent of human perceptions; or (2) morality is subjective, totally dependent on human perceptions. Hume concluded that since morality was not found in the external world, it must be subjective, dependent on our inclinations and preferences, varying from one person to another. Kant provides a third possibility in between the other two: morality is a property of human minds that all humans will impose on their raw experience and project on the world. Morality is not out there in the world, but neither is it subjective. It is a fundamental category of human experience. Morality is something that every human mind will impose on noumena; morality is a complete abstraction, detached from the actual empirical world.

In Kant's system, the problems of ethics* are not empirical questions about usefulness or approbation; ethical problems are essentially intellectual problems, in need of philosophical answers. Moral behavior is purely rational and nonempirical (divorced from psychology, anthropology, etc.). Kant wants to know about the a priori foundations of morality. Ultimately, Kant will conclude that the foundation of morality is found in *legislation by pure reason*, with nothing empirical whatsoever about moral judgments.

The Demands of Morality Are Categorical

Kant argues that morality is not a property belonging to the world of noumena, and it is not attached to social utility or interactions between human beings. But Kant was certain that the demands of morality are peculiarly and characteristically unconditional and absolute. He calls them *categorical*.

Kant attempted to build a moral system where moral principles would be objective and invariant. Feelings change from person to person, and some humans may not even have these feelings, but all humans have reason, and the principles behind reasoning remain unchanging—they are the same for everyone.

*Recall that we defined ethics as the study of moral actions, moral behavior, and moral rules.

For Kant, just like Aristotle, reason is a key to the moral system. Each one of us is rational. For Kant, that meant that we can use our reason to determine what acts are right and which acts are wrong. We are able to will ourselves to do what is right (and avoid what is wrong). We use our will in the rational control of desires and appetites for the purpose of right action. This is what a person of moral worth will do.

Is Anything Intrinsically Good?

Kant begins his exploration of morality by asking what sorts of things are good, and under what circumstances. Is there anything at all that could be called intrinsically good, good without any qualification?

> It is impossible to conceive anything at all in the world, or even out of it, which can be taken as good without qualification, except a *good will*. Intelligence, wit, judgment, and any other *talents* of the mind we care to name, or courage, resolution, and constancy of purpose, as qualities of *temperament,* are without doubt good and desirable in many respects; but they can also be extremely bad and hurtful when the will is not good which has to make use of these gifts of nature, and which for this reason has the term "character" applied to its particular quality.[1]

Money may be good, but not without qualification; money is only a tool. If used badly, it may become a source of disaster, a force for destruction. You can pay to have someone assassinated! If you have courage, but a bad will (bad character), then that courage can be used to rob banks—and so courage cannot be called good in itself, good without qualification.

Next Kant argues that even happiness, Aristotle's candidate for that which is good in itself, is not good without qualification:

> . . . even . . . that complete well-being and contentment with one's state which goes by the name "happiness," produces boldness, and as a consequence often over-boldness as well, unless a good will is present by which their influence on the mind—and so too the whole principle of action—may be corrected and adjusted to universal ends; not to mention that a rational and impartial spectator can never feel approval in contemplating the uninterrupted prosperity of a being graced by no touch of a pure and good will, and that consequently a good will seems to constitute the indispensable condition of our very worthiness to be happy.[2]

Here Kant seems to be arguing that happiness is not good without qualification, because we believe that those people who are happy, but who do not have a pure and good will, are not worthy of happiness and do not deserve it.

What about Aristotle's virtues based on the golden mean? Kant argues that moderation, self-control, and calm deliberation are not good in themselves, because without the principles of a good will, they may become bad (moderation, self-control, and calm deliberation in an evil person make that person more dangerous, not good!).

Is anything at all good in itself, without any qualification? Kant answers yes. But, if it isn't happiness, then what is good in itself, without qualification? Kant answers: the only thing that is good without qualification is the good will. The good will is good in itself; it is not considered good because of the results of one's choices (the consequences of one's action).

> A good will is not good because of what it effects or accomplishes—because of its fitness for attaining some proposed end: it is good through its willing alone—that is, good in itself. Considered in itself it is to be esteemed beyond comparison as far higher than anything it could ever bring about merely in order to favour some inclination or, if you like, the sum total of inclinations.[3]

We need to analyze what Kant means by a "good will." There are two questions here. What is the *will*, and what property makes that will *good* instead of evil or neutral?

We will start with the will. An "act of will" is something like an internal command, something like "I've thought it over and decided to raise my hand . . . OK, hand, now go up! Let me now raise my hand!" It is something I do because I've thought rationally about it, decided, and then issued a command to my own body.

On the other hand, when the motive for my internal command is not rational, but rather because I want something, because I like something, or believe it will be good for me, or on a whim, or for no reason at all, then Kant says that I am acting from *inclination* and not from will.

An act of will is an internal command that comes at the end of a process of rational deliberation. You cannot separate out the rational aspect from will; will is just the practical application of reason.

Since an act of will requires a process of rational deliberation, animals cannot act out of will. Animals act out of instinct or inclination; only rational human beings can act out of will. When reason deliberates about a practical matter, reason issues a command, "I've thought it over and decided to assist this person . . . let me help this suffering person," and this is an act of will.

Every act of will has some sort of content: "Let me now do 'A'!" where A means "raise my arm" or "open this door," and so on. If our will is going to be concerned with moral issues, then the content, A, will have to be something about "keeping my promise" or "not telling a lie," and so on. When the content concerns moral behavior, Kant calls the content a **maxim.**

Now that we have a rough idea of what an act of will is, we can ask what makes something a *good* will? First, as we have already seen, Kant makes a negative point: a good will is not good because the resulting action will produce good consequences.

> A good will is not good because of what it effects or accomplishes—. . . it is good through its willing alone—that is, good in itself.[4]

The good will is not good because it brings about good effects; even if your good will accomplishes nothing it intends, it is still a thing that has value in itself. In fact, if it produces no consequences at all, it can still be a good will, and if somehow the consequences turn out horrible in spite of your desires, it can still be a good will.

Using a distinction we made earlier, Kant is classified as someone who holds a **deontological** (nonconsequentialist) and not a **teleological** (consequentialist) position in matters of ethics. For Kant, the rightness or wrongness of a moral choice are independent of the consequences of behavior.

Kant will ultimately conclude that the only case of acting from good will is the case where I act out of duty, even if it runs counter to my inclinations.

Being useful or useless does not add or take away from the intrinsic value of the good will. If it is not the consequences of the intended will that make it good, then it must be something intrinsic to the will itself, something internal and not external, something about willing itself that makes it good.

But all willing is alike; all willing is of the form "Let me do A"—so it must be the *content* of the will, the A, that determines whether the will is good or not.

Human Reason Is Not the Key to Happiness

What role does reason play with the good will? Aristotle had answered that the purpose of reason is to produce happiness. As much as Kant respects Aristotle, he disagrees with him on this point. Reason doesn't work to produce happiness; reason is not designed or intended to produce happiness. Kant begins his argument for this conclusion by asserting that every organ in a living being has a function or purpose, and that those organs are well adapted to serve that purpose. Note: This is not an argument based on Darwinian evolution, because Kant died several decades before Darwin was born.

> In the natural constitution of an organic being—that is, of one contrived for the purpose of life—let us take it as a principle that in it no organ is to be found for any end unless it is also the most appropriate to that end and the best fitted for it. Suppose now that for a being possessed of reason and a will the real purpose of nature were his *preservation*, his *welfare*, or in a word his *happiness*. In that case nature would have hit on a very bad arrangement by choosing reason in the creature to carry out this purpose. For all the actions he has to perform with this end in view, and the whole rule of his behavior, would have been mapped out for him far more accurately by instinct; and the end in question could have been maintained far more surely by instinct than it ever can be by reason. If reason should have been imparted to this favoured creature as well, it would have had to serve him only for contemplating the happy disposition of his nature, for admiring it, for enjoying it, and for being grateful to its beneficent Cause—not for subjecting his power of appetition to such feeble and defective guidance or for meddling incompetently with the purposes of nature. In a word, nature would have prevented reason from striking out into a *practical* use and from presuming, with its feeble vision, to think out for itself a plan for happiness and for the means to its attainment. Nature would herself have taken over the choice, not only of ends, but also of means, and would with wise precaution have entrusted both to instinct alone.[5]

If happiness were the ultimate human purpose, wouldn't nature have provided some instinct, some faculty, some organ, for producing happiness? But no organ or faculty is adapted for achieving happiness; certainly, reason is not ideal for attaining happiness. Perhaps based on his own experience, Kant argues that reason doesn't work to produce happiness; reason is not intended to produce happiness. And people who rely on reason to achieve happiness wind up more unhappy, more frustrated than before.

> In actual fact too we find that the more a cultivated reason concerns itself with the aim of enjoying life and happiness, the farther does man get away from true contentment. This is why there arises in many, and that too in those who have made most trial of this use of reason, if they are only candid enough to admit it, a certain degree of *misology*—that is, a hatred of reason; for when they balance all the advantage they draw, I will not say from thinking out all the arts of ordinary indulgence, but even from science (which in the last resort seems to them to be also an indulgence of the mind), they discover that they have in fact only brought more trouble on their heads than they have gained in the way of happiness.[6]

You have the ability to reason, and you have will (character, intention), but the purpose of reason is not to achieve happiness. In fact, Kant argues that a person who tries to intellectually reason out a way to attain happiness seems never to attain true satisfaction. Reason is good for contemplating, for analyzing, but reason is not able to think out a plan of happiness and a plan for attaining it. Less intellectual people keep closer to instinct and do not allow reason to influence their conduct so much—this is better for the attainment of happiness.

Therefore, reason and will must have some other purpose in the "scheme of things," a different and more noble end or purpose, since it fails so miserably to achieve happiness. Some other implanted instinct would have been much better than reason for the achievement of happiness.

The Purpose of Reason Is to Influence the Will

So, what is the purpose of reason, what was reason designed to do? Kant answers that it influences the will, it influences our intentions. Since nature produces organs perfectly fitted to accomplish their goals or purposes, Kant concludes that the purpose for which reason is designed is to produce a will, "not merely good as a means to something else, but *good in itself*, for which reason is absolutely necessary." Reason was designed by nature to produce the good will.

> For since reason is not sufficiently serviceable for guiding the will safely as regards its objects and the satisfaction of all our needs (which it in part even multiplies)—a purpose for which an implanted natural instinct would have led us much more surely; and since none the less reason has been imparted to us as a practical power—that is, as one which is to have influence on the *will*; its true function must be to produce a *will* which is *good*, not as a *means* to some further end, but *in itself*; and for this function reason was absolutely necessary in a world where nature, in distributing her aptitudes, has everywhere else gone to work in a purposive manner. Such a will need not on this account be the sole and complete good, but it must be the highest good and the condition of all the rest, even of all our demands for happiness. . . . for reason, which recognizes as its highest practical function the establishment of a good will, in attaining this end is capable only of its own peculiar kind of contentment—contentment in fulfilling a purpose which in turn is determined by reason alone, even if this fulfillment should often involve interference with the purposes of inclination.[7]

Kant concludes that this good will must be the **supreme good** and the condition of every other good, including happiness. The good will is the condition for happiness. A person of good will *deserves* happiness, but happiness itself is not the ultimate good or supreme good. This explains why reason sometimes conflicts with happiness; because it was never intended by nature to produce happiness.

The Relationship between Duty and the Good Will

Now that Kant has determined that the purpose of reason is to establish a good will (the highest good, something valuable in itself), we can ask about the relationship between a good will and the sense of duty, which Kant felt so strongly in his own moral life.

> We have now to elucidate the concept of a will estimable in itself and good apart from any further end. This concept, which is already present in a sound natural understanding and requires not so much to be taught as merely to be clarified, always holds the highest place in estimating the total worth of our actions and constitutes the condition of all the rest. We will therefore take up the concept of *duty,* which includes that of a good will, exposed, however, to certain subjective limitations and obstacles. These, so far from hiding a good will or disguising it, rather bring it out by contrast and make it shine forth more brightly.[8]

Kant asks: What is the content of the ordinary will such that it becomes the *good will?* Kant answers: A good will always acts for the sake of one's duty. A good will is intrinsically valuable, and the only thing intrinsically valuable.

What kinds of reasons or motives can I have when I will to do something? Kant distinguishes two different motives. We can act from *inclination* or we can act out of a *sense of duty.* Acting from inclination is basically being emotionally motivated—your feelings or desires are your motivation—it is doing what you want to do, acting out of some desire to attain something, acting out of self-interest. But, when you act out of a sense of duty, your motivation is *purely rational*—it does not involve feelings or desires.

When you do the right thing because it is in your own best interests, you have *not* acted out of duty (acting out of duty is doing the thing *merely because it is your duty*). When you do the right thing because you are afraid that you will be caught if you don't, you are acting out of inclination, but not out of duty.

Kant argues that emotions, inclinations, and sentiment (which are subjective) *do not play any role when your sole motivation is your duty*—only abstract *reason* is relevant. Here Kant is arguing against Hume's position, because Hume had argued that inclinations (feelings of like or dislike, approbation or disapprobation) are the basis for morality.

The Motive Determines the Moral Worth of an Act

A rather startling conclusion follows from Kant's argument. If you perform some action that seems to be good for everyone, but your motive was not a sense of duty, then your act has zero moral value. If you perform a good action and your motive is that it benefits you, then your act is ultimately selfish and there

is no moral value in that action at all—you are merely following the egoistic hedonistic nature, maximizing your own self-interest. Kant asks, what moral value
could there be in doing something that benefits yourself?

Suppose I act benevolently, or altruistically. Isn't altruistic behavior unselfish, and isn't that morally good, no matter what my motive was? Kant answers, no. Moral action is not merely praiseworthy action; even altruistic behavior is not strictly moral behavior. Doing praiseworthy actions, which you do
because you enjoy spreading good will, enjoy spreading happiness and delight,
has *no true moral worth* because you enjoy doing these actions. The reason you
did them was that "it felt so good," because you felt an *emotional inclination* to
act this way; the only thing that would make them of moral worth would be if
you did them because it was your duty, not because you are naturally inclined
to do good things.

Consider this example. You do not act in self-defense to protect your life out
of duty; you do not preserve your own life because it is your duty to do so; thus,
you should not be congratulated because you've done something that preserved
your own life.

What Makes the Will Good?

With this analysis, Kant can answer the question "What makes a will good?" *A good
will always acts for the sake of duty* (it wills things just because it is one's duty to do
them). It is not the outcome of the action you willed that makes it a good will; it is
the fact that the action was your duty and this is your motive for willing it.

We act from a good will when we act out of a sense of duty—as our sole motivation. We do what is right simply because it is right, simply because it is our
duty. This factor is what makes an act of will into a *good will*.

> An action done from duty has its moral worth, *not in the purpose* to be attained
> by it, but in the maxim in accordance with which it is decided upon; it depends
> therefore, not on the realization of the object of the action, but solely on the *prin-
> ciple of volition* in accordance with which, irrespective of all objects of the faculty
> of desire, the action has been performed. That the purposes we may have in our
> actions, and also their effects considered as ends and motives of the will, can
> give to actions no unconditioned and moral worth is clear from what has gone
> before. Where then can this worth be found if we are not to find it in the will's
> relation to the effect hoped for from the action? It can be found nowhere but *in
> the principle of the will*, irrespective of the ends which can be brought about by
> such an action; for between its *a priori* principle, which is formal, and its *a pos-
> teriori* motive, which is material, the will stands, so to speak, at a parting of the
> ways; and since it must be determined by some principle, it will have to be de-
> termined by the formal principle of volition when an action is done from duty,
> where, as we have seen, every material principle is taken away from it.[9]

To summarize: An act must be done from duty in order to have inner moral
worth. Also, an act done from duty derives its moral value from the principle by
which it is determined, not from its consequences. *A good will always acts in accordance with duty.*

Two Essentials for Morality

According to Kant, two things are essential for morality: your duty, and your motive for performing your duty. Thus, the key to morality is (a) determining your duty, and (b) performing the action with the correct motive; perform the act just because it is your duty. Duty must be your only motive.

Your duty can be determined objectively and rationally. It is not subjective. And, if the reason that you perform your duty is only because it is your duty, then there is nothing subjective in that (you are not doing the act because you find it pleasurable, or useful, or because it is to your own personal advantage, etc.). There is nothing personal or subjective about morality. It is objective. Kant argues that any valid moral principle *must* be completely *independent* of experience, independent of feelings and inclinations, independent of consequences, independent of empirical data, because otherwise moral principles will be subjective and will *not* be binding upon all human beings.

The Good Will Is a Two-Step Process

So, having a good will is a two-step process for Kant: (1) first you determine your duty; (2) then, your only motive for performing the action is just respect for the moral law, respect for the fact that something is your duty. Your will is good (and intrinsically valuable) just because it never takes personal likes or dislikes into consideration. In other words, it is *never* subjective; the only motive for the good will is acting because something is your duty, and for no other reason.

Based on the previous discussion, Kant is able to isolate three key ethical propositions that form the backbone of his entire ethical system.

Kant's First Proposition An act must be done from duty to have moral worth. Only action done out of respect for one's duty has inner moral worth. As we have seen, Kant is a deontologist in ethical matters—the consequences of your action do not determine the moral worth; only the principle applied as a result of rational deliberation determines moral worth. An act done from duty derives its moral value from the principle by which it is determined, *not* from the consequences it produces.

Kant's Second Proposition An action done from duty derives its moral worth from the principle (the *maxim*) by which it is determined, *not* by the purpose that is to be accomplished or goal to be attained. Again Kant is reacting to Hume's ethical theory. Hume based morality on inclinations. Kant's Second Proposition argues that the principle is independent of your own advantage, your selfish desires, your inclinations—it is independent of anything that will lessen the moral worth of the action. There is an objective right and wrong; and you will find that you have an obligation to do what is right.*

*Note the structure: The fact that an act is your duty is what gives the action moral worth. How much moral worth? Check the maxim (an action derives its moral worth from the maxim by which it is determined).

Kant argued that an action done from duty derives its moral worth from the maxim by which it is determined. What is that maxim? Maxims are general rules or principles that we follow and use to determine our duty. We arrive at these maxims by using our reason. A maxim expresses your intention in performing an act. "When it will cause me unhappiness to keep a promise, it is all right to break my promise"—this is an example of a maxim. It is a general rule I can use to determine my duty in moral situations.

For your act to have moral worth, Kant argues that your *only motive* must be to do your duty, to do what your duty requires, *and you must have no other motive.*

Kant's Third Proposition   Duty is the necessity of acting from respect for the law. What is this "duty" that Kant stresses so much? What does he mean by "duty"? Kant explains that with his Third Proposition:

> Our third proposition, as an inference from the two preceding, I would express thus: *Duty is the necessity to act out of reverence for the law.*[10]

With this, Kant is providing us with an explanation of duty. You have performed your duty when you have acted solely out of reverence for the law; the unique unconditioned worth of a moral action derives completely from the fact it is done out of reverence for the law.

> For an object as the effect of my proposed action I can have an *inclination,* but never *reverence,* precisely because it is merely the effect, and not the activity, of a will. Similarly for inclination as such, whether my own or that of another, I cannot have reverence: I can at most in the first case approve, and in the second case sometimes even love—that is, regard it as favourable to my own advantage. Only something which is conjoined with my will solely as a ground and never as an effect—something which does not serve my inclination, but outweighs it or at least leaves it entirely out of account in my choice—and therefore only bare law for its own sake, can be an object of reverence and therewith a command.[11]

The only motives that give an action moral worth are pure respect for the law, doing one's duty *independent* of one's natural inclinations. Kant is saying that you always ought to act from one motive only: pure respect for the law—and this is your duty.

> Now an action done from duty has to set aside altogether the influence of inclination, and along with inclination every object of the will; so there is nothing left able to determine the will except objectively the *law* and subjectively *pure reverence* for this practical law, and therefore the maxim of obeying this law even to the detriment of my inclinations.[12]

If you act out of a sense of duty and not out of inclination, preference, self-love, or personal advantage, then your action will be objective and will apply to every human being.

> For duty is meant to be the practical unconditional necessity of action. It must therefore be valid for all rational beings (to whom an imperative can apply at all), and for this reason only be a law for the human will also.[13]

Kant argues that the moral law we reverence must meet the following qualifications:

Not be based on empirical facts.

Not be based on the consequences of the action under consideration.

Not be based on one's personal inclinations, desires, preferences, and so on, but instead based on reverence for the law.

Note that only rational beings could act from such motives. Thus, it would seem to follow for Kant that nonrational beings do not act morally and cannot act morally.

> Thus the moral worth of an action does not depend on the result expected from it, and so too does not depend on any principle of action that needs to borrow its motive from this expected result. For all these results (agreeable states and even the promotion of happiness in others) could have been brought about by other causes as well, and consequently their production did not require the will of a rational being, in which, however, the highest and unconditioned good can alone be found. Therefore nothing but the *idea of the law* in itself, *which admittedly is present only in a rational being*—so far as it, and not an expected result, is the ground determining the will—can constitute that preeminent good which we call moral, a good which is already present in the person acting on this idea and has not to be awaited merely from the result.[14]

There is still one additional qualification: The moral law must be capable of inspiring respect of all rational persons. Insofar as you are a rational being, you will have respect for the moral law, because it is the highest good without qualification. Question: What sort of supreme law of morality will qualify the will to be good without qualification and inspire respect in all rational persons?

> But what kind of law can this be the thought of which, even without regard to the results expected from it, has to determine the will if this is to be called good absolutely and without qualification? Since I have robbed the will of every inducement that might arise for it as a consequence of obeying any particular law, nothing is left but the conformity of actions to universal law as such, and this alone must serve the will as its principle. That is to say, I ought never to act except in such a way *that I can also will that my maxim should become universal law.*[15]

What sort of law is it that gives unconditional goodness to the will when followed? Kant answers: the universal conformity to law in general. This suggests that a rational human being should adopt the following rule (guaranteeing moral worth for actions): I am never to act otherwise than so that I could also will that my maxim (the moral principle that I am following) should become universal law.

The Categorical Imperative: The Heart of Kantian Ethics

The heart of Kant's moral theory is the rule he calls the **categorical imperative.***
The categorical imperative determines your duty and is what makes all morality

---

*Gramatically, an imperative is a demand that I act in some fashion or other. For example, if I want to get a good grade in this course, it is imperative that I read the text book and attend lectures. Imperatives often begin "You *ought* . . ." or "you *must* . . . ."

objective: Rational beings will always be guided by ethical principles (or maxims) that can be adopted by everyone or prescribed for everyone (without generating any contradiction).

We could also word Kant's categorical imperative this way: "Act only on the maxim whereby you can at the same time will that it should become a universal law."

A simple test for your moral behavior: "Is it the kind of act that everyone in similar circumstances could perform without any fear of behaving irrationally?" We might think of this as a rule that applies to everyone, universally. Can we universalize the rule or law we are following?

Kant is certain that genuinely moral persons act in such a way that they could will that the principles which describe their actions should be universal laws, and apply to everyone else as well as to themselves. The principles are **universalizable.** We do not think that individuals should make special moral laws that apply only to themselves, or moral exceptions for themselves (or ourselves), and we do not approve of people who make special moral laws that apply only to themselves, or who make exceptions for themselves; we think that this is wrong.

The categorical imperative emphasizes the *unconditional* nature of morality; morality is *categorical,* it applies to everyone. This also is completely free from empirical content because it is just pure reason.

> The conception of an objective principle in so far as it is obligatory for the will, is called a command (of reason), and the formula of the command is called an *imperative.*
>
> All imperatives are expressed by a "Thou Shalt" and thereby indicate the relation of an objective law of reason to a will which is not by virtue of its subjective constitution necessarily determined by it (an obligation). These imperatives say that something would be good to do or to omit, but they say it to a will which does not always do a thing merely because it is presented to it as being good to do.[16]

This is the implication of the categorical imperative: Before you act, consider the implications of everyone doing as you are about to do. Kant applies this categorical imperative to the question of whether one is ever justified in lying or breaking a promise. If I am in an awkward situation, is it all right for me to make a promise to someone, even though I have no intention of keeping that promise? Kant says that we should try to universalize this into a maxim, or a rule—and then ask "Would I want everyone to follow this rule that I've made up for my own actions?"

Well, what is the rule or maxim that we are using to guide our behavior? It has to apply to everyone, and not just ourselves. Perhaps something like this: Every human being may extricate himself/herself from awkward situations by making false promises; worded as an imperative, "Let me make this promise, intending not to keep it if it is not convenient."

Logic makes it clear that to follow this maxim would be irrational. This is the strength of the categorical imperative: I might think that it is OK for *me* to tell a lie in a difficult situation, but Kant thinks that no rational human being would say that he/she would have it be a universal law: "Lie when in difficult situations." If that were the universal rule, then we would never know when to believe anyone, for anyone might find it inconvenient to tell the truth.

If "Break your promise if it were inconvenient" were a universal law, no one would ever believe another's promise; and thus no one would ever make promises if they had no effect; ultimately, the very act of promising would disappear; saying "I promise . . ." would be equivalent to saying "I'll do it if it is convenient." The maxim when universalized would destroy itself. Such a universal law would be self-contradictory, illogical, and any rational human being can understand that!

Suppose I want to make a special exception for myself. Consider this example: My maxim is "Everybody except me is prohibited from initiating violence against others." If this were applied by everyone, then everyone would be the "me" mentioned in the rule. Everyone would be an exception to the rule! The rule would have no application. The rule says it applies to everyone, and then it contradicts itself and applies to no one! It is profoundly irrational to have a rule that applies to no one at all.

Imperatives Can Be Categorical or Hypothetical

Kant wants to make sure that we understand that a categorical imperative is a very special sort of imperative. It is not an imperative that uses an "if you want 'A,' then you must do 'B'." In English, we call this "If . . . then . . ." construction a *hypothetical*. If we add an order ("you must do . . .") after the "then . . . ," it is called a **hypothetical imperative.**

> Now all *imperatives* command either *hypothetically* or *categorically*. The former represents the practical necessity of a possible action as a means to arrive at something else that is willed (or may be willed). The categorical imperative would then be that which represented an action as objectively necessary of itself without relation to another end.[17]

Kant has explained how categorical imperatives differ from hypothetical imperatives. Kant says an imperative is of the form "Thou Shalt." It might also begin "Do this . . ." or "you ought to . . ." or "you must do . . ." An example of a hypothetical imperative is: *If you want to avoid punishment, then you ought to tell the truth.* That is, "If you want to attain A, then do B."

With a hypothetical imperative, there is reference to goals, consequences. If you want to accomplish A, then you *ought* to do B. "If you want to get a letter grade of an 'A' in this course, then it is imperative that you read the textbook." The imperative is conditional upon my wanting to get an A. If the imperative is being offered as a *means* to something else, then it is hypothetical.

Some hypothetical imperatives relate to technical skills, such as those of an engineer or a medical doctor ("If you want to cure a patient who has these symptoms, use this drug"): Kant calls these "Rules of Skill." Some hypothetical imperatives are simply useful rules, general pieces of advice about how to be happy ("If you want to keep your spouse happy, then do . . ."). Kant calls these "Counsels of Prudence." Here is the important point for Kant: Hypothetical imperatives are irrelevant for morality.

Now consider a categorical imperative. A categorical imperative is unconditional. There is no goal, no reference to consequences. The only thing is: *Do this.* To say that something is *categorical* is to say that it is unconditional; simply *do this.* There is no reference to wishes, wants, desires, goals. No "ifs" anywhere.

All Moral Rules Are Categorical

Kant ultimately argues that morality cannot be objective if it is hypothetical; if morality is objective, this means that "X is wrong *under all circumstances at all times*," that is, "X is categorically wrong."

Therefore, all objective moral rules must be categorical. "Keep your promises" is categorical—no "if . . . then . . ."

An example of a categorical imperative is: "All human beings ought to tell the truth" (a universalized maxim). If the imperative is conceived of as a good in itself, independent of consequences, then it is categorical. If the imperative is categorical, then it is a principle of a will which of itself is conforming to reason.

> Now, if an action is meant to be good merely as a means to *something else,* then the imperative is *hypothetical;* but if it is represented as good of itself and thus necessary as a principle of a will which is of itself in accord with reason, then it is *categorical.*[18]

A command of reason, if it seems to be obligatory to the human will, becomes an *imperative* ("you must . . ."). If the moral law expresses our duty, and if there is something necessary about our duty, then the moral law must be categorical.

The Fundamental Basis for All Morality

From the preceding discussion, Kant is ready to explain the fundamental basis for all human morality. Morality, in its essence, is acting on the basis of an impersonal principle that is valid for everyone, including oneself.

> Finally, there is an imperative which commands a certain conduct directly and which is not based on the condition of attaining any other purpose by it. This imperative is *categorical.* It has nothing to do with the matter of the action or with that which results from it, but with the form and the principle from which it itself proceeds; and its essential good consists of the state of mind irrespective of what may result from it. This imperative may be called the *imperative of morality.*[19]

A moral person wills something, not because he or she expects good consequences to result, but just because it could be willed for everyone in relevantly similar circumstances.

> For the [moral] law alone involves an unconditional and, moreover, objective and, therefore, universally valid necessity; and commands are laws that must be

obeyed, that is, must be followed even against the inclinations. . . . The categorical imperative, however, is limited by no condition and may with complete propriety be called a command as being absolutely, though practically, necessary.[20]

Understanding Kant's One Categorical Imperative

The basis of morality: a rational individual will obey a principle (maxim) that can, without contradiction, be willed to be a rule for everyone without exception. All duties (imperatives of duty) can be deduced from the *one categorical imperative:*

> Consequently there is only one categorical imperative and it is this: *Act only on that maxim which will enable you at the same time to will that it be a universal law.*
>
> Now if all imperatives of duty can be deduced from this single imperative as from their principle, then, although we here refrain from stating whether what one calls duty may be an empty notion, we shall at least be able to indicate what we understand by it and what the concept means.
>
> Because the universality of the law according to which effects are produced constitutes what we really mean by *nature* in the most general sense (according to form), that is, the existence of things in so far as it is determined by universal laws, the universal imperative of duty may read thus: *Act as if the maxim of your action by your will were to become a universal law of nature.*[21]

Kant is giving us another way to understand his one categorical imperative: Act as if the maxim of your action were to become by your will a *universal law of nature.* You must ask yourself: if I were an omnipotent being, would it be rational for me to will that the principle (maxim) I am following be made a universal law that *everyone without exception* would have to follow? This wording stresses universalizability: Moral laws must be universalizable, which means that they apply the way a universal law of nature like the law of gravity applies to everyone: universally, with no exceptions.

The categorical imperative is Kant's great contribution to Western ethics. It is very abstract, but Kant wants it to be practical. He wants you and I to be able to use it. Hence, he points out that the categorical imperative could be thought of as a twofold test: (1) maxims must be universalizable, considered a universal law of nature; (2) one must be willing to will the same thing for oneself as for others (no exceptions; the rule must apply to you as well as to others).

> . . . [A] person is in need and finds it necessary to borrow money. He knows very well that he will not be able to repay it, but he also realizes that he will not receive a loan unless he promises solemnly to pay at a definite time. He has a desire to make this promise, but he still has enough conscience to ask himself whether it is not improper and contrary to duty to relieve distress in this manner. If he should nevertheless decide to do so, then the maxim of his action would read thus: When I think that I am in need of money I will borrow and promise to repay, even though I know that I will never do so. Now this principle of my love of self or advantage may perhaps well agree with my whole future well-being; the next question, however, is, whether it is right. Thereby I change the interpretation of self-love into a universal law and arrange my question

thus: How would things be if my maxim were a universal law? Then I see at once that it could never count as a universal law of nature and still agree with itself, but must necessarily contradict itself. For the universality of a law, according to which anyone who believed himself in distress could promise anything he pleased with no intention of keeping it, would make promises themselves and any purpose they may have impossible; and since nobody would believe that a promise had been made, but everybody would ridicule such statements as vain pretenses.[22]

Applying the Categorical Imperative in Everyday Life

Are you facing a moral issue and are not certain whether your decision is right? Just apply these two tests:

1. Could I will the maxim to be a universal law of nature, as though I were an omnipotent lawgiver? Yes? Then it passes the first test.
2. Am I willing to apply it to myself as well? No exceptions for myself under any circumstances? Yes. Then it passes the second test, and it is a valid moral principle.

A Second Formulation of the Categorical Imperative

Kant believes that he has not yet exhausted the many logical implications of the categorical imperative. There is one more. Kant argues that when one understands the implications of the categorical imperative, one can see that it means that all human beings are to be treated as ends and not as means to an end.

> Assuming, however, that there is something, the *existence of which of itself* has an absolute value which, *as end in itself,* could be the basis of definite laws; then the basis of a possible categorical imperative or practical law would lie in it and in it alone.
>
> Now I say: Man and every rational being anywhere *exists* as end in itself, *not merely as means* for the arbitrary use by this or that will; but in all his actions, whether they are directed upon himself or upon other rational beings, he must at all times be looked upon as an *end.*[23]

Many things we want are useful as tools, or as means, to attain some other thing we wish, desire, or value. These things have **instrumental value,** or conditional worth. A good grade in a university course is a means to attain a degree, a scholarship, or a pay raise. The value of things that have conditional worth depends on how many people want them; their value is relative to the desires for them, and how useful the things are in satisfying desires. They wouldn't have value if it weren't for the condition that we want them to attain something else; if we didn't want to attain something else, they would have no worth.

What about human beings? Kant argues that human beings always are **intrinsically** valuable, that they exist as ends, and never are just a means to some goal, to be used by another. Rational beings are ends in themselves; they are called persons.

On the other hand, rational beings are called *persons* because their very nature distinguishes them as ends in themselves, that is as something that must not be employed as mere means and which consequently limits arbitrary action to this extent (and is an object of respect).[24]

Do not treat another human being as just a useful thing for you to use to obtain your own purposes; do not use a human being as a means only; don't think of others as a means to your own goals and ends. Never exploit another human being.

If then there is to be a supreme practical principle and in respect to the human will a categorical imperative, then it must be one which, when we conceive what is necessarily an end for everybody because it is the *end in itself*, must constitute an *objective* principle of the will and therefore be able to serve as universal practical law. The basis of this principle is: *Rational nature exists as end in itself.*[25]

The practical imperative that results from these considerations: "Act as to treat humanity, whether in your own person or in that of another, in every case as an end, and never as a means only." Kant calls this a practical imperative.

The practical imperative will then read as follows: *Act so that in your own person as well as in the person of every other you are treating mankind also as an end, never merely as a means.*[26]

Human Beings Are the Authors of Morality

As Kant understands it, the categorical imperative presupposes the absolute moral worth of all rational beings as ends in themselves. And there is a good reason for this. Kant does *not* argue that we are all important because we are created by God. He does *not* argue from the Scriptures. He has a reason that is perfectly logical. Here he explains his reasoning:

From this follows the third practical principle of the will as supreme condition of its agreement with the universal practical reason: the idea of *the will of every rational being as a universally legislative will.*[27]

Every human being is of absolute moral worth and an end in itself because every human being is a *source of the moral law;* every human being (insofar as he or she is rational) is the *author* of the moral law.

Although a will *which is subject to laws* may be bound to the law by means of some interest, a will which is itself a supreme lawgiver cannot possibly as such be dependent on some interest. . . .

The *principle* then that every human will is a will which *gives universal laws in all its maxims* would, granted that it exists at all, be very well *adapted* to be the categorical imperative because it *is based on no interest* by virtue of the very idea of universal legislation, and thus among all possible imperatives it alone can be unconditional. . . . If there is a categorical imperative (a law for the will of every rational being), then it can only command that everything be done from the maxim of a will that could also have itself as universal lawgiver as its object.[28]

The moral law comes from your own reason. When you determine your duty, you universalize the maxim. In universalizing the maxim, you are legislating the moral law for everyone! *You are the author of the moral law!*

> Now we look back upon all attempts that have been made in the past to discover the principle of morality, we can see why they had to fail. They saw man bound by his duties to laws, but it never occurred to anyone to see that man is subject *only to his own* and yet to *universal legislation,* and that he is obligated to act only in accordance with his own will, which, however, in view of the end of nature is a universally legislating will.[29]

As such, every human being deserves all the dignity and respect attributed to a "legislator of the universal moral law." Kant argues that this is merely a second version of the same categorical imperative.

> The concept that every rational being must consider himself as giving universal laws by means of all his maxims in order to judge himself and his actions from this point of view, leads to another concept which is dependent on it and very fruitful, namely, the concept of a *realm of ends. . . .*
>
> For rational beings are all subject to the *law* that each one must treat himself and every other being *never merely as means,* but *always as end in itself also.* Consequently, there results a systematic union of rational beings by means of common laws, that is to say, a realm which for the very reason that these laws are directed upon the interrelation of these beings as ends and means, may be called a realm of ends.[30]

Now we have two different formulations of Kant's one categorical imperative. They do not seem the same, yet Kant argues that the two different formulations of the categorical imperative are basically the same.

> The principle: In relation to every rational being, yourself and others, act so that in your maxim he can also be considered end in itself, is basically the same as the principle: Act on a maxim which also contains within its own universal validity for every rational being. For saying, that in the employment of means to every end I should restrict my maxim to the condition of its universal validity as law for every subject, is identical with saying, that the subject of ends, namely the rational being himself, must be made the basis of all maxims of action, and never merely as means, but as the supreme restricting condition in the use of all means, that is always an end.[31]

These two formulations are identical, according to Kant: (1) Act in regard to every rational being so that they are always treated as an end in itself and never as a means, and (2) act upon a maxim that involves its universal validity for every rational being. Kant claims that they are functionally equivalent: both of these generate the same consequences. However, we might note that others have considered these separate and distinct principles.

Kant Has Shown That Ethics Is Objective

Kant now believes that he has overcome the empiricism of David Hume and shown that ethics is objective, purely rational, as absolute as mathematics, and has not a shred of subjectivity to it. Kant's "pure moral philosophy" is not contaminated by empirical considerations.

> *Empirical principles* are never suitable as basis for moral laws. The universality which should make them valid for all rational beings without distinction, the unconditional practical necessity which is attributed to them because of it, disappears if their basis is taken to be the *particular constitution of human nature* or the chance circumstances in which he is placed.[32]

Morality is thus objective, even though it is not based upon some divinity ("it has nothing to support it either in heaven or earth").

> For since morality serves as a law for us only because we are *rational beings*, it must be valid also for all rational beings.[33]

Kant is arguing that morality itself determines its own absolute laws; it is not given to us as an "implanted sense" (Butler's conscience) or given to us by any outside source (such as God). It does not depend on our feelings or sentiments (as Hume argued). It applies to all of us equally, without exception, at all times, and at all places. In a sense, each of us is autonomous, each of us is the author of the universal moral law! And, as an autonomous legislator of the moral law, I find myself a member of a community of fellow legislators (what Kant called a "realm of ends"). Kant very strongly believed that trying to base morality on an empirical basis, as Hume did, weakens moral laws.

AN OVERVIEW OF KANT'S ETHICS

Morality, in its essence, is acting on the basis of an impersonal principle that is valid for everyone, including oneself. The moral quality of an act depends on conformity to rules, laws, or principles of action, rather than on results or goals. Duty and "a good will" are the foundations for Kant's ethical system.

A human being possesses moral worth simply by the fact that he or she uses reason to control desires and appetites for the purpose of right action, and uses reason to determine his or her duty.* To possess moral worth is more important than any other characteristic of a human being—more important than your other talents such as intelligence, strength, humor, musical ability, or artistic talent. Moral worth has *absolute* value, whereas the other talents are relative and command admiration in some people, but not in others.

Kant's test for a moral principle: Would we will that all persons (including ourselves) should act upon this moral principle as though it were the law? A rational person should not act upon a moral rule (or maxim) unless he/she can also will that others should act upon the same moral rule. Rational human beings must be consistent in their judgments.

Kant was certain that what is a right moral rule for one person at one time must also be a right maxim for any other person at any other time. This must be

---

*Do you remember that Plato argued that reason must control spirit and appetite?

so if the principles of morality are objective, if they are always and everywhere the same. Morality cannot be subjective.

These insights are all summarized in Kant's categorical imperative: those actions are right that conform to principles that are universalizable; one can consistently will these principles for everyone to follow. Wrong actions are based on maxims that a rational creature could not will that all persons should follow.

PROBLEMS TO PONDER

These are questions that any thoughtful person should think about if he or she were considering adopting Kant's analysis of ethics. Perhaps Kant can answer them. How would you answer them?

1. Kant claims that the good will is (a) unconditionally good, and (b) the only thing that is unconditionally good. Is he correct? The hedonist, like Epicurus or John Stuart Mill, would argue that Kant is mistaken; it is the pleasure that results from employing the good will that makes it good, and not the other way around, and certainly *not* the sense of duty that accompanies the good will.

2. Do you agree with Kant that the good will is the only thing that is unconditionally good? We could agree with Kant that the good will is intrinsically good, but deny that it is the *only thing* in the world that is intrinsically good. Is truth unconditionally good? Is justice? Is compassion? Is charity? Is hope? Is alleviation from suffering?

3. A common objection to Kant's theory applies to his categorical imperative. The categorical imperative overlooks individual differences in moral situations. One might argue that the duty to tell the truth is *not* unconditional. For example, I might argue that it is proper to lie to someone intending to murder another human being, because a person who wants to kill does not deserve a truth that would help him accomplish the deed, which results in such evil. Apparently Kant thinks that we need to tell the truth, even in this sort of situation.

    We can modify Kant's theory to acknowledge differences. We can agree with Kant that when an act is right for one person, it will be right for everybody *who is under the same conditions;* but when conditions (physical or psychological or cultural) change, exceptions to the general rule may be essential.

4. Because he wanted to show that David Hume's ethical theory was wrong, Kant argued that acts done out of sympathy and kindness have *no moral worth at all;* but surely this cannot be correct. Don't we all think of moral persons as people who are kind and sympathetic? Do we really think that if kindness or compassion is your motive for acting, then your act has no moral worth at all?

5. Is it really true that there is only one motive that has any moral value? Surely there could be more than one motive that motivates you to perform a moral action; Kant's restriction that the only motive that has moral value

is respect for duty ignores other equally valuable moral motives. Can I have more than one motive? Does the fact that I enjoy doing good decrease the moral value of what I do?

6. Note that Kant's entire system is grounded in the human free will and its absolute autonomy. He requires that we *freely* choose the motive of duty alone when we engage in moral behavior. This is a potential weakness. What if we could show that human beings do not have much free will? Some would argue that there is no such thing as free will, and that we cannot choose our motives. Kant's theory depends on the free will. If we cannot prove the existence of any autonomous free will, then Kant's moral vision is a complete failure. We will see that later ethical theorists move away from this reliance on free will.

GLOSSARY

Aesthetics   Aesthetics is a branch of philosophy devoted to studying art and beauty. Kant wrote extensively about aesthetics.

A priori   A priori means "prior to experience." To know something a priori is to know something to be true without needing to check the world. One simple example: "All red beach balls are red." This is true. You do not have to go to the beach to check on this. Kant might provide this example: "Every event is caused." This is true because, according to Kant, the categories of human reason impose causality on every possible experience.

Categorical imperative   In Kant's philosophy, the categorical imperative determines duty. Moral persons act in such a way that they could will that the principles which describe their actions (maxims) should be universal laws and apply to everyone else as well as to themselves. The principles are universalizable. We do not make moral exceptions for ourselves. The categorical imperative emphasizes the *unconditional* nature of morality; morality is *categorical,* it applies to everyone.

Deontological   Deontological ethics is also called "nonconsequential" ethics; consequences are not what is most important in determining the moral worth of action [*deon* = duty; *logos* = theory, "study of "]. Kant's ethical theory is deontological.

Good-in-itself   This concept is also called **intrinsically valuable.** Most things we call "good" are usefully good. A college degree is good, but it is good because it can help you accomplish some other goals in life (it is **instrumentally good**). Something intrinsically good is valuable just for itself, not for what it can be used for.

Hypothetical imperative   "Hypothetical" refers to an "if . . . then . . ." structure. An imperative says "Do this." A hypothetical imperative then is a statement that says that *if* you want some sort of outcome, then *do* this. Kant contrasts this with a categorical imperative, which simply says, "Do this." Nothing hypothetical about it.

Instrumental value   An instrumental value is something that is good and can be used to obtain something else. A reliable automobile is good instrumentally because you can use the car to obtain other things you value. The opposite would be something that is **good-in-itself,** or intrinsically good.

Maxim   Maxims are general rules or principles that we follow and use to determine our duty in moral situations. We arrive at these maxims by using our reason. A maxim expresses your intention in performing an act. "Under all circumstances, I should keep a promise" is an example of a maxim.

Metaphysics   Metaphysics is that branch of philosophy which deals with the ultimate nature of reality. For example, do time and space exist in the world, or are time and space human constructions imposed on the world? Is there more to reality than what human beings can experience?

Noumena   The term noumena refers to the way things are in themselves, apart from human experience. Things-in-themselves, the way they are independent of any observer or any sense perception. Kant argues that the way we experience the world, the appearance of things (phenomenon) is due to our subjective mental apparatus (reason), which imposes structure on external objects (noumena).

Phenomena   The term phenomena refers to the way that the world appears to human beings who know the world through their senses, their eyes, ears, noses, etc. Phenomena are the appearances caused by objects, or things-in-themselves (**noumena**). Kant argues that the way we experience the world, the appearance of things (phenomenon) is due to our subjective mental apparatus (reason), which imposes structure on external objects (noumena).

Supreme good   Some things that are good are more valuable than other goods. Which of the many goods is the highest, the supreme? Plato argued that the Form of the Good was the highest good. Kant argues that the good will is the supreme good.

Teleological   Teleological ethics is also called "consequentialist" ethics; this position argues that one can determine whether a choice is moral or immoral by examining the consequences of that choice. Actions are good because they produce good consequences; actions are wrong or immoral because they produce bad consequences. There are several different forms of teleological ethics. Kant was opposed to teleological ethical systems.

Things-in-themselves   See **noumena.**

Universalizable   To say that a maxim or principle is universalizable means that the principle applies to everyone, everywhere, under all relevantly similar conditions. Kant is certain that genuinely moral persons act in such a way that they could will that the principles which describe their actions should be universal laws and apply to everyone else as well as to themselves. In general, people do not think that individuals should make special moral laws that apply only to themselves, or make moral exceptions for themselves.

A GUIDE TO FURTHER READINGS

Action, Harry. *Kant's Moral Philosophy* (New York: Macmillan, 1970). A good study of Kant's moral philosophy.

Beck, Lewis White. *Studies in the Philosophy of Kant* (Chicago: University of Chicago Press, 1960). A standard in the field of Kant studies.

Kemp, John. *The Philosophy of Kant* (Oxford: Oxford University Press, 1968). Another good treatment of Kant.

Manthey-Zorn, Otto, *The Fundamental Principles of the Metaphysic of Ethics* (N.Y.: Appleton-Century-Crofts, Inc., 1938). Another good translation of Kant's treatment of ethics.

Melchert, Norman. *The Great Conversation, A Historical Introduction to Philosophy*, 2nd ed., ch. 20, pp. 390ff. (Mountain View, Ca.: Mayfield Publishing, 1991). A very good historical introduction to Kant.

O'Neil, Onora. *Acting on Principle: An Essay on Kantian Ethics* (New York: Columbia University Press, 1975). A scholarly evaluation of Kant's philosophy.

Ross, W. D. *Kant's Ethical Theory* (Oxford: Oxford Clarendon Press, 1954). A standard treatment of Kantian ethics.

Sullivan, Roger. *An Introduction to Kant's Ethics* (Cambridge: Cambridge University Press, 1994). A good explanation and evaluation of Kant's ethics.

Warnock, G. J. "Kant," in D. J. O'Connor, *A Critical History of Western Philosophy* (New York: The Free Press, 1964). A high-quality critical approach to Kant's philosophy.

CHAPTER 12

John Stuart Mill:

The Greatest Happiness for the Greatest Number

THE LIFE OF JOHN STUART MILL (1806–1873)

About the same time the great German philosopher Immanuel Kant (d. 1804) was finishing his rationalist and absolutist theory of ethics in Germany, a very different approach to ethics was developing in England, profoundly influenced by the empiricism of David Hume. By the time John Stuart Mill was born, two years after Kant's death, England had been influenced by three great revolutions. There was the intellectual revolution known as the Enlightenment, which put forth the idea that social institutions ought to help people to

develop themselves, to make room for liberty and happiness. There was the French Revolution, which demonstrated that the direct actions of the people could destroy the old feudal system and put in its place a republican government.[1] The third revolution was the Industrial Revolution, leading to new technology, greater wealth (unfairly distributed), unhealthy dirty factories, impossibly long working hours, child labor and unfair women labor, low wages, and dirty ugly industrial towns polluted beyond recognition.

In 1806, the year Mill was born, Beethoven conducted his Symphony No. 4 and his Violin Concerto. In 1809, Charles Darwin was born (d. 1882). In 1810, Simon Bolivar was a major figure in South American politics, and Napoleon was still active in Europe, reaching his highest power in 1810. In 1818, Karl Marx was born (d. 1883). And, as with previous generations, many significant discoveries of science were coming thick and fast in the early decades of the 1800s.

Davey Crockett was killed at the Alamo in 1836. In 1848, the *Communist Manifesto* by Marx and Engels was published. In 1856, Freud was born; in 1857, Louis Pasteur proved that fermentation is produced by living organisms. In 1859, Darwin published *On the Origin of Species by Natural Selection* (Mill was fifty-three years old). In 1860, Abe Lincoln was elected sixteenth president. In 1865, Lincoln was assassinated.

John Stuart Mill was born on May 20, 1806, the eldest son of James Mill, a philosopher, economist, and historian. John Stuart's father intended to train his son to be the leading philosopher of the followers of a leading British political thinker named Jeremy Bentham, who developed a very liberal political philosophy. Mill's father was a severe teacher, but his father could not have achieved what he did were it not for the fact that John Stuart Mill was intellectually brilliant. At age three, he was taught Greek (reading Plato) and arithmetic (in addition to reading and writing English). By age twelve, Mill was studying logic, philosophy, and economics.

His father taught him to *think and analyze,* not to merely memorize. Mill's father, James Mill, and his friend, Jeremy Bentham, wanted to develop a just political system for England that would bring about social equality, and their theories were used to support their social legislative program. John Stuart Mill was trained to continue their efforts. Mill worked hard his entire life upon both ethical theories and on political equality. Upon retirement from his position at the East India Company in 1858 (age fifty-two), John Stuart Mill was elected to the English Parliament from Westminster. While in office he worked on behalf of Irish land reform and for woman's suffrage.

John Stuart Mill was an Empiricist, like Hume before him, but Mill did not agree with Hume that morality depends on what we approve of and what we disapprove of. Instead, Mill feels that when we say that some choice is morally right, we are merely saying that we believe that particular choice contributes toward a state of affairs that is intrinsically good, good in itself. His major contribution to ethics is a small book entitled *Utilitarianism* published in 1861.

MILL'S UTILITARIAN PHILOSOPHY

The general term describing John Stuart Mill's philosophical position is **hedonism.** The Greek philosopher Epicurus was a hedonist. Hedonism refers to philosophical systems that assert that pleasure is an intrinsic good, not merely an instrumental good. What is morally good is that which produces pleasure. In ethics, there are three kinds of hedonism. One can be a hedonist who claims that all human beings, by their very nature, cannot help but seek to maximize their own pleasure. This is a psychological doctrine about how human beings must behave. We are born selfish and will always choose the option we think will maximize our self-interest. We cannot help it, and we cannot choose otherwise.

A second form of hedonism says you *can* act altruistically and not ego-centered, but you *should* always act to promote your own self-interest. The goal of one's life should be to maximize or promote one's own pleasure. An extreme form of this is: you ought to do whatever feels good! If it feels good and produces pleasure, it must be the right thing to do.

Neither of these two describes the hedonism of John Stuart Mill. Mill's position could be called **impersonal hedonism.** The standard is not your own personal pleasures. Mill will argue that one's own pleasures are *not* to count as worth more than any other person's happiness or pleasure; you are to consider your own happiness or well-being, but only as one among many. To say that an act is morally good is to say that it is an act of the sort that, on the whole, tends to enhance human pleasure (not *just* one's own pleasure). Happiness is the only thing desirable as an end (the only intrinsic good); and actions are right as they tend to produce happiness, wrong as they tend to produce unhappiness. Thus, Mill's philosophy of **utilitarianism** can be classified as a form of impersonal hedonism.

MILL'S ETHICS

Like most of the well-educated and intelligent people of his day, J. S. Mill was impressed by the power of science to understand and predict, to find regularities and describe them. Mill thought we could find such regularities in human social life as well—there are regularities of human behavior, and possibly even natural laws that describe human behavior.

Mill was raised by his father to defend the political theories of Jeremy Bentham (1748–1832). Bentham argued that the legislators of the political system ought to be concerned with the good for all members of the community, not just the wealthiest. Bentham argued that "general utility" or usefulness for all was the key insight. This was a social and a political technique: determine what is the good for the community; then determine how to make that good happen for everyone. Ultimately, the lawmakers could use empirical methods to evaluate proposed legislation and determine whether it really would benefit the public good. To do this, Bentham used his principle of utility. A legislator must ask, "Does this law contribute to general happiness or misery?" In the name of increasing happiness for everyone, Bentham (and later Mill) demanded changes in parliament, prison reform, the extension of the right to vote to women, full legal rights to women, greater democracy, ways of making government accountable, changes in punishment, and so on.

Mill revised Bentham's political utilitarianism to shift the stress from politics to ethics. For Mill, the political stress on social utility became transformed to a genuine teleological ethical system. It is the *consequences* of my act that determine its rightness or wrongness. Mill advises us to consider the alternative choices open, and their likely consequences for the interests of all those who will be directly affected by them, including your own. The morally correct action will be the one whose consequences are going to produce the greatest happiness for the greatest number.* Borrowing from Bentham, John Stuart Mill called his teleological position in ethics utilitarianism.

*Recall that Immanuel Kant denied this absolutely. He argued that consequences are not morally relevant; the only morally relevant facts are concerned with the agent's *intention* (act out of duty, out of respect for the moral law).

This causes a problem. The name utilitarianism makes it sound like Mill is talking about whether something is useful or not. But that isn't what he means. He wants to associate the term "utility" with the idea of pleasure.

> A passing remark is all that needs to be given to the ignorant blunder of supposing that those who stand up for utility as the test of right and wrong use the term in that restricted and merely colloquial sense in which utility is opposed to pleasure. . . . Those who know anything about the matter are aware that every writer. . . who maintained the theory of utility meant by it, not something to be contradistinguished from pleasure, but pleasure itself, together with exemption from pain.[2]

So what does the technical term "utility" refer to? Mill tells us: Utility means pleasure combined with "exemption from pain."

Next Mill explains how the **Doctrine of Utility** (which is also known as the **Greatest Happiness Principle**) is related to determining what is morally right and distinguishing it from what is morally wrong.

> The creed which accepts as the foundation of morals "utility" or the "greatest happiness principle" holds that actions are right in proportion as they tend to promote happiness; wrong as they tend to produce the reverse of happiness.[3]

How do we relate Mill's stress on happiness to the hedonistic philosophy based on pleasure? Mill combines the two. He writes:

> By happiness is intended pleasure and the absence of pain; by unhappiness, pain and the privation of pleasure.[4]

When you are faced with a moral dilemma, and you have two or three options before you, which one of the three is the best morally? Mill's answer: Add up the pleasures and the pains for each of the options. That action is morally best which produces the greatest proportion of happiness over unhappiness, and, ultimately, the greatest proportion of pleasures over pains. This process was first described by Jeremy Bentham, and he called it the "hedonistic calculus." Bentham suggests that we can quantify pleasures and arrange them on a continuum by considering both how strong the pleasure is (its intensity) and how long the pleasure is likely to last (its duration).[5]

Bentham's political hedonistic calculus works for Mill's utilitarian ethics in the same way. Simply add up the positive pleasures and subtract the pains, and go with the choice that has the greatest balance of pleasures over pains. Of course, we must take into account how everyone else is affected by the decision for each course of action contemplated.

Mill then goes on to justify the basic insight of his utilitarianism: the only things intrinsically desirable are pleasure and freedom from pain. He provides a lengthy analysis of happiness and pleasure, and then concludes:

> . . . there is in reality nothing desired except happiness. Whatever is desired otherwise than as a means to some end beyond itself, and ultimately to happiness, is desired as itself a part of happiness, and is not desired for itself until it has become so. Those who desire virtue for its own sake desire it either because the consciousness of it is a pleasure, or because the consciousness of being without it is a pain, or for both reasons united.[6]

All desirable things are desirable either for the pleasure inherent in themselves, or as means to the promotion of pleasure and the prevention of pain.

> . . . happiness is the sole end of human action, and the promotion of it the test by which to judge of all human conduct; from whence it necessarily follows that it must be the criterion of morality, since a part is included in the whole.[7]

This theory of Mill's clearly reveals the fundamental tension at the heart of Western philosophy, the tension between two worldviews of the Greeks and the Judeo-Christian tradition. John Stuart Mill combines Aristotle's claim that the good life is happiness, with that of Epicurus who claims that pleasure is intrinsically valuable. Pleasure is both the foundation of morality, and pleasure is the key element in human happiness. And then he adds the utilitarian insight: The morally right thing is that which produces the greatest happiness for the greatest number, with no individual counting more than the others.

Traditionally, the Christian tradition looked with suspicion upon physical pleasure and thought that self-denial, celibacy, and abstinence were the moral ways to live. Pleasure was the instrument of the devil. Someone skillful at attaining pleasure would not be rewarded by God with salvation. Mill must deal with this mistrust of pleasure and next defends himself against the notion that he is promoting some sort of immoral lifestyle.

Imagine a group listening to Mill lecture one evening and, during a question-and-answer period at the end of the evening, raising an objection to his hedonistic ethical system. A gentleman stands up and argues that utilitarianism is a mean and "swinish" doctrine if it assumes that life has no higher end or goal than mere pleasure . . . how could there be *nothing* more noble than pleasure, nothing more important to pursue than pleasure? Mill's theory is degrading to human beings and appropriate for pigs. Mill characterizes this objection in his book:

> To suppose that life has (as they express it) no higher end than pleasure—no better and nobler object of desire and pursuit—they designate as utterly mean and groveling, as a doctrine worthy only of swine . . .[8]

But Mill has an answer. In fact, the response that Mill makes is basically the same one made by Epicurus: this assumes that human beings are not capable of enjoying any pleasures except those enjoyed by pigs. It is the people calling Mill's theory "swinish" who seem to think human beings swines. Why? Because the objection assumes that the sources of pleasure are the same for humans and swine, that what makes life good for a pig would make life good for a human being. Mill denies this completely. Mill is *not* saying that any act is morally good if it produces the greatest *quantity* of physical pleasure.

Human Pleasures Are Higher in Quality Than Animal Pleasures

Mill points out that human appetites are higher than the appetites of pigs; the pleasures of a beast do not satisfy a human being. There are higher pleasures of the intellect (poetry, art, literature, music, dance), pleasures of the feelings and imagination! Clearly, some kinds of abstract and intellectual pleasures are higher and more valuable than other kinds of pleasures. Even when two pleasures total to the same amount in quantity, one pleasure can still be more valuable than the other. When evaluating pleasures, one must consider *quality* of the pleasure and not just the quantity.

So, to respond to the criticism that utilitarianism is a "swinish" theory, Mill argues that we need to consider not merely the total *quantity* of pleasure, but we need also to consider the *quality* of the pleasures. This raises another question: How can we determine the superiority of one pleasure's quality over another if they are equal in quantity?

> If I am asked what I mean by difference of quality in pleasures, or what makes one pleasure more valuable than another, merely as a pleasure, except its being greater in amount, there is but one possible answer. Of two pleasures, if there be one to which all of almost all who have experience of both give a decided preference, irrespective of any feeling of moral obligation to prefer it, that is the more desirable pleasure.[9]

Even though the two pleasures, A and B, produce the same amount of pleasure, if people still insist that they would not give up pleasure A for the other pleasure B, then there must be a superiority in quality of A over B. If people are capable of enjoying both, and are acquainted with both pleasures, and still give a marked preference of A over B, then it is because A uses the higher human faculties (not merely the "swinish" pleasures that we share with the other animals).

Mill believes it is easy to show that the human pleasures are superior to the pleasures of swine. No human being would agree to be changed into an animal just so he or she could enjoy the animal's pleasures—the reason for this is that some human pleasures are more valuable, higher in quality, than mere animal pleasures.

> Few human creatures would consent to be changed into any of the lower animals for a promise of the fullest allowance of a beast's pleasures; no intelligent human being would consent to be a fool, no instructed person would be an ignoramus, no person of feeling and conscience would be selfish and base, even though they should be persuaded that the fool, the dunce, or the rascal is better satisfied with his lot than they are with theirs.

A human being has higher faculties, and thus he or she requires more to keep him or her happy. We are also capable of more acute suffering; we are not willing to sink into a "lower grade of existence."

> It is better to be a human being dissatisfied than a pig satisfied; better to be Socrates dissatisfied than a fool satisfied. And if the fool, or the pig, is of a different opinion, it is because they only know their own side of the question. The other party to the comparison knows both sides.[10]

What are the higher pleasures that swine cannot appreciate? Objects of nature; the great achievement of artists, architects, composers. Those arts that fire the imagination, things like poetry and dance. Even contemplating incidents of history, the accomplishments and failures of human beings in the past and present, and our prospects for the future. These pleasures are not available to the beast.

Quality of Pleasures Is Determined by Competent Judges

Mill has argued that we must consider the quality of the pleasures and not just their quantity. What if we are unsure of which pleasure has the highest quality? Mill says, ask someone who can judge between pleasures. This raises another question: Who is to count as a competent judge?

Certainly, not everyone is a competent judge. Some people abandon their higher faculties—they are incapable of enjoying the higher kinds of pleasures. Men and women can lessen their ability to enjoy the higher pleasures by immersing themselves in the lower pleasures. After all, the lower pleasures we share with the animals are easier to attain, and sometimes people don't have an opportunity to encounter or enjoy the higher pleasures. Thus, one must use competent judges, and these are people who are qualified by knowledge of both—and the majority of such people is the final court.

> On a question which is the best worth having of two pleasures, or which of two modes of existence is the most grateful to the feelings, apart from its moral attributes and from its consequences, the judgment of those who are qualified by knowledge of both, or, if they differ, that of the majority among them, must be admitted as final.[11]

> From this verdict of the only competent judges, I apprehend there can be no appeal.[12]

Mill's Greatest Happiness Principle is not ego-centered; you are not to consider only your own happiness (the agent); the happiness of all other affected people must be considered. In addition, to be kind and generous, to be noble, is recommended by utilitarian ethics because such a noble character contributes to the total amount of human happiness for everyone affected by such a person.

> . . . for that [utilitarian] standard is not the agent's own greatest happiness, but the greatest amount of happiness altogether; and if it may possibly be doubted whether a noble character is always the happier for its nobleness, there can be no doubt that it makes other people happier, and that the world in general is immensely a gainer by it. Utilitarianism, therefore, could only attain its end by the general cultivation of nobleness of character, even if each individual were only benefited by the nobleness of others, and his own, so far as happiness is concerned, were a sheer deduction from the benefit.[13]

The Revised Greatest Happiness Principle

At this point, John Stuart Mill acknowledges that he has modified the simple utilitarian doctrine that he started with, and he summarizes his changes and offers his revised version of the Greatest Happiness Principle so that it now includes quality as well as quantity. According to the Greatest Happiness Principle, in its revised form:

> . . . the ultimate end, with reference to and for the sake of which all other things are desirable—whether we are considering our own good or that of other people—is an existence exempt as far as possible from pain, and as rich as possible in enjoyments, both in point of quantity and quality; the test of quality, and the rule for measuring it against quantity, being the preference felt by those who, in their opportunities of experience, to which must be added their habits of self-consciousness and self-observation, are best furnished with the means of comparison.[14]

Next, Mill acknowledges that although the pursuit of pleasure may be the ultimate goal or end for human actions, nevertheless this is also an ethical standard as well:

> This, being according to the utilitarian opinion the end of human action, is necessarily also the standard of morality, which may accordingly be defined "the rules and precepts for human conduct," by the observance of which an existence such as has been described might be, to the greatest extent possible, secured to all mankind; and not to them only, but, so far as the nature of things admits, to the whole sentient creation.[15]

Objections to the Utilitarian Ethical Theory

John Stuart Mill worked on his ethical theory for most of his life and was well aware of a great many objections that were made. In what follows, he explains several objections, and responds to the objections one by one.

Objection 1: It is impossible for human life to be happy. This world is filled with pain, despair, and tears. Life is not fair. What right do you have to be happy in such a world? The most that can be hoped for in his life is sorrow and misery. In such a world, the attainment of happiness cannot be the end of moral conduct, because it cannot be attained at all.

Mill replies: "Surely it is an exaggeration to assert that human life cannot be happy." Of course, utilitarianism does not claim that your life will be a continuous state of peak pleasurable excitement. States of exalted pleasure cannot long endure. A life of rapture is not possible.

> If by happiness be meant a continuity of highly pleasurable excitement, it is evident enough that this is impossible. A state of exalted pleasure lasts only moments or in some cases, and with some intermissions, hours or days, and it is the occasional brilliant flash of enjoyment, not its permanent and steady flame. . . . Happiness . . . was not a life of rapture, but moments of such, in an existence made up of few and transitory pains, many and various pleasures, with a decided predominance of the active over the passive. . . . A life thus composed, to those who have been fortunate enough to obtain it, has always appeared worthy of the name of happiness. And such an existence is even now a lot of many during some considerable portion of their lives. The present wretched education and wretched social arrangements are the only real hindrance to its being attainable by almost all.[16]

Mill argues that a life of many varied pleasures, with only a few and transitory pains, is achievable. In fact, he asserts that the only reason that there is so much unhappiness is the wretched educational system and social system. Make social changes, improve the lot of the majority of humans, and happiness will be attainable by almost all.

Objection 2: Human beings won't be satisfied with a life of only occasional highs and few pains. The second objection Mill considers is just the opposite of the first. The first says that it is impossible for human life to ever be happy. The second says that humans will never be satisfied with only a moderate share of happiness, the sort of serene happiness offered by utilitarianism—they require more!

Mill replies that lots of people have been satisfied with *less*. When people have lives of desperation and despair, they seek out the excitement of intense physical pleasures to help them endure the pain of life. But, if the social and educational system could be revised, people wouldn't have to live a life of desperation and despair. It would be possible to have a more tranquil life and appreciate more tranquil pleasures. With much tranquility, not so much excitement is needed to make one satisfied.

> With much tranquility, many find that they can be content with very little pleasure; with much excitement, many can reconcile themselves to a considerable quantity of pain. . . . Next to selfishness, the principal cause which makes life unsatisfactory is want of mental cultivation. A cultivated mind—I do not mean that of a philosopher, but any mind to which the fountains of knowledge have been opened, and which has been taught, in any tolerable degree, to exercise its faculties—finds sources of inexhaustible interest in all that surrounds it; in the objects of nature, the achievements of art, the imaginations of poetry, the incidents of history, the ways of mankind, past and present, and their prospects in the future.[17]

Everyone is capable of appreciating these things. That many people do not is a failure of the educational system.

> Now there is absolutely no reason in the nature of things why an amount of mental culture sufficient to give an intelligent interest in those objects of contemplation should not be the inheritance of everyone born in a civilized country.[18]

The next objection is clearly of a religious nature rather than a philosophical objection. The objection starts with the assertion that human beings have an obligation to learn to do without happiness. Mill responds that humans can learn to do without happiness, but it doesn't follow that humans should learn to do without happiness for themselves, unless it will result in an increase in happiness for other humans.

> It is noble to be capable of resigning entirely one's own portion of happiness, or chances of it; but, after all, this self-sacrifice must be for some end; it is not its own end; and if we are told that its end is not happiness but virtue, which is better than happiness, I ask, would the sacrifice be made if the hero or martyr did not believe that it would earn for others immunity for similar sacrifices?[19]

The objection continues. The doctrine of utility is incompatible with Christian morals, Christian values, and Christian culture. One of the highest virtues in Christianity is *self-sacrifice*, and if Mill's theory does not regard self-sacrifice as an intrinsic good, then Mill's theory must be wrong because it is incompatible with Christian teachings.

This objection does recognize a genuine difference between Mill's utilitarian ethic and the Christian virtue of self-sacrifice. Mill says that utilitarians do recognize that some human beings sacrifice their own good for the good of others; but utilitarians do not recognize that such sacrifice is an intrinsic good.

> The utilitarian morality does recognize in human beings the power of sacrificing their own greatest good for the good of others. It only refuses to admit that the sacrifice itself is a good. A sacrifice which does not increase, or tend to increase, the sum total of happiness, it [utilitarianism] considers as wasted. The only self-renunciation which it applauds, is devotion to the happiness, or to some of the means of happiness, of others; either of mankind collectively, or of individuals within the limits imposed by the collective interest of mankind.[20]

Mill stresses that the key to utilitarianism is not just the agent's happiness; it is the happiness of all concerned. One must be impartial when considering personal happiness versus the happiness of others.

But Mill is not so willing to acknowledge that utilitarianism is incompatible with Christian ethics. In fact, Mill argues that the Golden Rule is completely in the spirit of the principle of Utility.

> In the golden rule of Jesus of Nazareth, we read the complete spirit of the ethics of utility. "To do as you would be done by," and "to love your neighbor as yourself," constitute the ideal perfection of utilitarian morality.[21]

However, Mill has not grounded his moral system in the commands and prohibitions of a deity. Thus one objection to utilitarianism is that it is a godless doctrine, and therefore it must be false. Mill responds:

> If it be necessary to say anything at all against so mere an assumption, we may say that the question depends upon what idea we have formed of the moral character of the Deity. If it be a true belief that God desires, above all things, the happiness of his creatures, and this was his purpose in their creation, utility is not only not a godless doctrine, but more profoundly religious than any other.[22]

A utilitarian is not prohibited from using God in morality, because one can interpret the commands of the Deity as either pointing out to us what sorts of acts will increase human happiness, or else as simply some sort of absolute law having no connection with happiness.

Suppose someone were to object to utilitarianism as follows: Mill, you are wrong. Your utilitarian standard requires that we always consider the greatest happiness of the greatest number, but this standard is too high for people. People just cannot be motivated to do good by the thought of producing the greatest happiness for the greatest number; they are motivated to do good for themselves, they are selfish. Why would someone do what is right just because it would produce the greatest happiness for others?

Mill replies that the fact that people do not always find themselves motivated by social concern misses the point and is *not* an objection against utilitarianism. Mill responds that his Greatest Happiness Principle was never intended to provide a *motive* for doing what is right. Rather, the Greatest Happiness Principle is a tool to help you to pick the right act once you have already decided that you want to do the right thing.

> It is the business of ethics to tell us what are our duties, or by what test we may know them; but no system of ethics requires that the sole motive of all we do shall be a feeling of duty.[23]

Mill knew the history of Western philosophy well, and he was intimately acquainted with the ethical philosophy of Immanuel Kant. Kant argued that consequences are irrelevant to morality, that morality is objective and the only thing that is important is the *motive* of the agent (do your duty), not the consequences of the act. Mill responds to Kant's theory of good will by asserting that

> . . . the motive has nothing to do with the morality of the action, though much with the worth of the agent. He who saves a fellow creature from drowning does what is morally right, whether his motive be duty or the hope of being paid for his trouble.[24]

Mill says that if you save someone from drowning, the *action* itself is morally right—no matter what the motive. If your motive is selfish, then you've told us something about your own personal moral worth, whether you have a moral disposition or an immoral disposition, but the act is still a good act.

Why Be Moral? What Is the Ultimate Justification for Morality?

If the Greatest Happiness Principle is not intended to supply a motive for behaving morally, then how does utilitarianism answer the question, why be moral? What is the motive for embracing virtue and avoiding vice? Why should anyone want to do what is right? Why not do wrong? Mill does not rely upon the rewards or punishments of a divine creator to justify moral behavior, so what answer can he give to the question, "Why be moral?" Why obey the ethical principle of the Greatest Happiness Principle? What is its **sanction?** Mill replies that utilitarianism has the same sanctions that the other moral systems have:

> Those sanctions are either external or internal. Of the external sanctions it is not necessary to speak at any length. They are the hope of favor and the fear of displeasure from our fellow creatures or from the Ruler of the universe, along with whatever we may have of sympathy or affection for them, or of love and awe of Him, inclining us to do His will independently of selfish consequences. There is evidently no reason why all these motives for observance should not attach themselves to the utilitarian morality as completely and as powerfully as to any other.[25]

Mill replies that external sanctions work for utilitarianism as well as any other ethical system. These all work to support utilitarian morality as well as they support a Christian or non-Christian system of morals.

Are external sanctions the only reasons that we are moral? What if no one is looking, and no one will know what you choose? Not a fellow human being, or even the Ruler of the universe. Then, why be moral? Well, Mill argues that in addition to external sanctions, most people also have inner reasons within themselves for behaving morally. What are these "inner reasons," which Mill calls "internal sanctions"? Isn't it just our own sense of what we ought to do to please ourselves, our own sense of duty?

> The internal sanction of duty, whatever our standard of duty may be, is one and the same—a feeling in our own mind; a pain, more or less intense, attendant on violation of duty, which in properly cultivated moral natures rises, in the more serious cases, into shrinking from it [a violation of our inner sense of how we ought to behave] as an impossibility.[26]

We feel an inner pain if we violate our sense of duty. We are not happy with ourselves. Even if no one else knows, we feel badly, we feel we have not lived up to our highest personal values, we experience remorse. For Mill, this feeling is the essence of conscience. Mill does *not* think that one's conscience is an infallible inner guide given to us by the creator of all that exists. He describes conscience as a complex phenomenon:

> . . . though in that complex phenomenon as it actually exists, the simple fact is in general all encrusted over with collateral associations derived from sympathy, from love, and still more from fear; from all the forms of religious feeling; from the recollections of childhood and all our past life; from self-esteem, desire of the esteem of others, and occasionally, even self-abasement.[27]

Thus, the ultimate answer to the question "Why be moral?" is internal sanctions, and that complex phenomenon is basically just "a subjective feeling in our own minds."[28] Mill has argued that the ultimate reason that human beings are moral (instead of being immoral) is that we care for other human beings, and if we do not respond to them in a moral manner, we feel guilty, we feel remorse.

This idea of inner sanctions allows us to move from desiring our own individual happiness to desiring the happiness of everyone: we desire the happiness of everyone because we experience inward pleasure in doing these actions. We do feel *good* when we contribute to the greatest happiness of the greatest number.

> What is the sanction of that particular standard [utilitarianism]? We may answer, the same as of all other moral standards—the conscientious feelings of mankind. Undoubtedly this sanction has no binding efficacy on those who do not possess the feelings it appeals to; but neither will these persons be more obedient to any other moral principle than the utilitarian one. On them morality of any kind has no hold but through external sanctions.[29]

Thus, utilitarian morality is grounded in a subjective feeling and concern for the happiness of other human beings.

What About People Who Have No Inner Sense of Duty?

Suppose we make the following objection to Mill: You are wrong. There are some people who don't seem to have any inner sense of remorse or duty. Mill acknowledges that some people who behave immorally seem to lack this sense of caring for fellow human beings, but, for these people, there won't be any internal sanction no matter which ethical system they follow (whether it be Greek, Christian, or utilitarian). The only forces to guide such people will be external sanctions. Thus, a utilitarian morality works just as well as any other moral system, and, perhaps, even better. The reason Mill thinks it is better is because we do care about others, and that feeling for humanity is a sound basis for morality.

Next, Mill briefly considers the question: Is the feeling of duty innate (perhaps implanted in us by a divine being) or is it acquired as we grow up; is it learned? Mill responds that it really doesn't make any difference which it is. If you think that as human beings we simply have an intuitive feeling for what is morally right or morally wrong, that supports utilitarian morality.

> On the other hand, if, as is my own belief, the moral feelings are not innate but acquired, they are not for that reason the less natural. It is natural to man to speak, to reason, to build cities, to cultivate the ground, though these are acquired faculties.[30]

The feeling or caring for humanity itself is natural either way, whether produced from inside innately or created from outside ourselves by training and learning. Even if we learn the Greatest Happiness Principle as we grow up, it is still natural (it is equally true that we learn to speak as we grow up, but it is still natural for a human being). We cultivate this feeling for humanity and it grows stronger as we grow. So, either way, this inner feeling for humanity is a powerful natural feeling, and this is the strength of the utilitarian morality.

> The firm foundation [of utilitarian morality] is that of the social feelings of mankind—the desire to be in unity with our fellow creatures, which is already a powerful principle in human nature, and happily one of those which tend to become stronger, even without express inculcation, from the influences of advancing civilization.[31]

PROBLEMS TO PONDER

These are questions that any thoughtful person should think about if he or she were considering adopting the utilitarian moral system. Perhaps the careful utilitarian can answer them. How would you answer them?

1. Just because people do desire pleasure, this does not justify the conclusion that pleasure is worthy of being desired, that it is what we should desire. Even if it is a fact that human beings actually do desire pleasure, does it follow that they ought to pursue pleasure? Does it follow that pleasure is the highest good for a human being? Is a life of pleasure really life's highest good? Suppose we were to attach an electrode to your brain, and then continue stimulating pleasure every moment of your life—is this a life that you and I would value above all others?

2. Can we measure and compare pleasures and pains on the same scale? Are pleasurable intensities commensurable with pleasurable durations, and are intensities of pains commensurable with intensities of pleasures?

3. Not only is it difficult to make such hedonistic calculations for myself, but is it even remotely possible to do it for other people? How can I judge how happy or unhappy *you* will be because of my choice—and can I quantify *your* pleasures or pains?

4. Am I doing wrong if I do not act in such a way to maximize the happiness of everyone? If I go home and watch TV or read a book, when I might be doing something which would increase the total amount of human happiness for others, am I doing wrong?

5. The utilitarian principle seems simple, but to apply it in a real-life situation is enormously difficult. We cannot accurately predict the consequences of our actions, our choices. We cannot know the future. You may actually sacrifice yourself in the belief that your action will increase the total amount of human happiness, but then evil results.

6. In introducing quality (higher) pleasures, the hedonistic calculus (moral arithmetic) is made virtually impossible. Even if you agree that amounts of pain/pleasure can be calculated and totaled, how can you quantify (reduce to a number) the *quality*? If you could, they would just be quantities again! If you can't, then the hedonistic calculations won't work.

   We know that Mill argues that a utilitarian must consider quality and not just the quantity, but that means that the final test is not *quantity*. What happens to our apparently objective hedonistic calculus? The only standard is the *preference* of the "moral connoisseur" that determines which act to choose "From this verdict of the only competent judges, I apprehend there can be no appeal." But the preference is not based on quantity. Is the preference felt by the wise a better guide than totaling up intensities and durations?

7. How can one pleasure be "higher" than another? Pleasure itself is the yardstick by which we measure the moral worth. The only way one pleasure can be higher than another is if the first is more pleasurable than the second (higher quantity). So, if one pleasure is of a higher quality, then there must be some other factor besides pleasure to measure something's intrinsic desirability. Then, pleasure is not Mill's ultimate standard! Do pleasures really differ in quality, or is there just quantity—intensity and duration (as Bentham claimed)?

8. There is an ambiguity concealed in the phrase "the greatest amount of happiness for the greatest number." Consider this puzzle: When we talk about the greatest happiness of the greatest number, do we mean (a) the greatest *total amount of happiness* among all human beings, or (b) the greatest *number of human beings* who are happy? Are we trying to maximize the greatest number of happy human beings, or maximize the amount of happiness? Suppose I can make one person genuinely ecstatic, or I can make ten people mildly happy. Assuming that both choices total ten units of pleasure, which do I choose? Is a small amount of pleasure equally distributed morally preferable to a large amount of pleasure unequally distributed?

9. Another problem with utilitarianism is that it might not be able to explain adequately some of our strongest moral convictions. For example, consider our sense of duty. Suppose I need to make a choice between (1) keeping a promise that I made to you, which will result in seven units of pleasure, or (2) breaking the promise and doing something else that would produce ten units of pleasure. Intuitively I have a moral conviction that I made a promise, and that as a result I have a duty to keep my promise, even if that choice wouldn't produce the greatest amount of happiness for the greatest number. It would seem that Mill's theory would have us break our promises whenever some other choice would produce a greater amount of happiness, or a higher quality of happiness. Mill does discuss duty at length in his book *Utilitarianism*.

According to Mill's theory, the feeling of a sense of duty that requires us to keep promises would not be morally right; the *right* thing to do is always to produce the greatest happiness for the greatest number. The only valid test of right and wrong lies in the results, not in an inner sense of duty or obligation.

GLOSSARY

Doctrine of Utility   The Doctrine of Utility is also known as the Greatest Happiness Principle and utilitarianism. See **utilitarianism.**

Greatest Happiness Principle   This is also known as the Doctrine of Utility and utilitarianism. See **utilitarianism.**

Hedonism   Hedonism refers to any philosophical system based on the claim that pleasure is the ultimate good for a human being. Hedonism argues that pleasure is an intrinsic good, not merely an instrumental good. Some hedonists would claim that all human beings, by their very nature, cannot help but seek to maximize their own pleasure; this is a psychological doctrine about how human beings *must* behave. A second form of hedonism says you *can* act altruistically and not ego-centered, but you *should* always act to promote your own self-interest. John Stuart Mill's position is *impersonal hedonism*, which means that to say that an act is morally good is to say that it is an act of the sort that, on the whole, tends to enhance human pleasure for the greatest number and the individual performing the action does not count more than the other persons affected by the act.

Impersonal hedonism   This is the philosophical position that pleasure is the highest good, but your own individual pleasure is not more important than the pleasures of everyone else. Mill's impersonal hedonism is the view that any moral act is right in proportion as it tends to produce the greatest happiness for the greatest number. Mill calls this *utilitarianism*.

Sanction   Sanctions refer to penalties, specified or in terms of general social pressure, to ensure compliance of conformity; also permission or approval, support, or encouragement (as from public opinion or established custom).

Utilitarianism   The teleological ethical system of John Stuart Mill, utilitarianism is a method for finding the morally best choice when you have two or more choices available. That action is morally best that produces the greatest proportion of happiness over unhappiness. Happiness is defined as pleasure, and exemption from pain. Unhappiness is pain, and absence of pleasure. Ultimately, Mill's utilitarianism says what is morally right is the choice that produces the greatest proportion of pleasures over pains.

A GUIDE TO FURTHER READINGS

August, Eugene. *John Stuart Mill: A Mind At Large* (New York: Charles Scribner's Sons, 1975). Overview of Mill's life and philosophy.

Brandt, R. "In Search of a Credible Form of Rule-Utilitarianism," in *Morality and the Language of Conduct*, Nahknikian and Castaneda, eds. (Detroit: Wayne University Press, 1953). A scholarly analysis of the problem of whether we should guide ourselves by the total amount of pleasure involved in an act, or guide ourselves by general rules.

Gorovitz, Samuel, ed. *Utilitarianism: John Stuart Mill, with Critical Essays* (New York: Bobbs-Merrill Company, 1971). Several thoughtful studies of utilitarianism.

Lyons, David. *Forms and Limits of Utilitarianism* (Oxford: Oxford At The Clarendon Press, 1965). A lengthy study of the strengths and problems of utilitarianism.

Piest, Oskar, ed. *Utilitarianism: John Stuart Mill* (New York: Bobbs-Merrill Library of Liberal Arts, 1957). The basic writing of Mill on utilitarianism.

Chapter Notes

Chapter 1

1. (Appears in Part One opener.) A. E. Taylor, *Socrates: The Man and His Thought* (New York: Anchor, 1952), p. 59.
2. (Appears in Part One opener.) Garry Wills paraphrasing Bernard Knox (*The Oldest Dead White European Males and Other Reflections on the Classics* [Norton, 1993]) in his review "Hanging Out with Greeks," in *The New York Review of Books*, Vol. XL, No. 9, 13 May 1993, p. 36b.6.
3. The *Apology, Crito,* and *Phaedo.* Plato describes the death of Socrates. Socrates was charged with "corrupting the young," but this is a reference to politics, not to homosexual behavior. A. E. Taylor explains that "no such imputation was made by them [Socrates' accusers]. The real charge, as we shall see, was that of 'educating' Alcibiades and Critias . . ." students of Socrates, who were guilty of "disloyalty to the spirit of Athenian life" (*Socrates: The Man and His Thought,* pp. 51–52, fn. 3, and p. 90).
4. Plato's pupil, Theatetus, also did the first work on conic sections, and Eudoxus invented a method of finding areas and volumes of curved figures.
5. This point is emphasized in Paul Shorey, "Plato's Ethics," in *Plato II: A Collection of Critical Essays* Gregory Vlastos, ed., (New York: Doubleday Anchor, 1971), p. 21.
6. Plato, *The Republic,* Book II, 359d–360b, trans. G. M. A. Grube, *Plato's Republic* (Indianapolis: Hackett Publishing Company, 1974), pp. 31–32.
7. Plato, *Gorgias,* line 495, trans. W. C. Helmbold, *Gorgias* (Indianapolis: Bobbs-Merrill, 1952), p. 66.
8. *Gorgias,* line 497; Helmbold, op. cit., p. 68.
9. *Gorgias,* line 497; Helmbold, ibid., p. 69.
10. *Protagoras,* line 357d, trans. by W. K. C. Guthrie, *Plato: Protagoras and Meno* (Baltimore, Md.: Penguin Books, 1956), p. 94.
11. *Protagoras,* line 355a–b; Guthrie, p. 92.1.
12. Ibid., line 355b–d, p. 92.
13. Ibid., lines 357c–e, pp. 94–95.
14. *Protagoras,* line 358d; Guthrie, ibid., p. 95.
15. *The Republic* 439d–e, Grube, *Plato's Republic,* p. 103. Emphasis is mine.
16. Ibid., 444d–e, p. 108.
17. Ibid., 443d–444, p. 107.
18. Ibid., 445a, p. 108.
19. Ibid., 444d–e, p. 108.
20. Ibid., 445a–b.

21. According to Greek legend, this woman sent her husband off to his death in war be-
    cause she was greedy for a bribe, and then sent her son off to another war, again be-
    cause of a bribe. When her son learned the truth, he killed her.
22. *The Republic*, Book IX, 589e–591c, in Grube, *Plato's Republic*.
23. Ibid., Book VI, 508e–509a.

Chapter 2

Since all the Aristotle quotations come from one book, the *Nicomachean Ethics* translated
by Sir David Ross, rather than use endnotes to reference quotations, reference numbers
are utilized. The reference numbers refer to Aristotle, *Ethica Nicomachea*, translated by Sir
David Ross. Hereafter, all references to Aristotle are identified in the body of the text by
Bekker number, which refers to the original Greek manuscript page and line numbers.
These numbers allow the scholar to find the quotation in any translation of Aristotle's
Nicomachean Ethics.

1. Sir David Ross, *The Nicomachean Ethics of Aristotle* (London: Oxford University Press,
   1961), p. 8 (1096a15).
2. As was a common claim for a deity, the Macedonians claimed that Alexander was
   born of a virgin mother. There were numerous gods of the period for whom such a
   claim was made, including Mithra, Osiris, and so on. Most of those were also supposed to have risen from the dead as proof of their divinity.
3. There is an earlier text on ethics attributed to Aristotle called the *Eudemian Ethics*.
   Most scholars believe it reflects an earlier stage in Aristotle's thinking.
4. *Nicomachean Ethics* 1103b27, trans. W. D. Ross, in Richard McKeon, ed., *The Basic
   Works of Aristotle* (New York: Random House, 1966), p. 953.

Chapter 3

1. According to Diogenes Laertius's "Life of Epicurus," translated by Russell M. Geer,
   in *Epicurus: Letters, Principal Doctrines, and Vatican Sayings* (New York: Library of Liberal Arts, 1964), p. 3.
2. The following selections are taken from the Letters of Epicurus, especially the *Letter
   to Menoeceus*, and from the *Principal Doctrines, Fragments, and Vatican Sayings*. The
   sources are Cyril Bailey, trans., *Epicurus: The Extant Remains* (Oxford: Clarendon
   Press, 1926), and Russell M. Geer, trans., *Epicurus: Letters, Principal Doctrines, and Vatican Sayings* (New York: Macmillan Library of Liberal Arts, 1964).
3. As we shall see in the chapter on Chinese ethics, the Seven Sages of the Bamboo
   Grove was the Neo-Taoist response to a similar situation in China.
4. *Principal Doctrines* #5, Cyril Bailey, tr., *Epicurus: The Extant Remains*, (Oxford: The
   Clarendon Press, 1926), p. 95.
5. *Letter to Menoeceus* 129a, in Geer, *Epicurus: Letters*, Principal Doctrines and Vatican
   Sayings (New York: MacMillan Library of Liberal Arts, 1964), p. 56.
6. *Principal Doctrines* #3, Cyril Bailey, tr., *Epicurus: The Extant Remains*. (Oxford: Clarendon Press, 1926)
7. Fragment 54, from Cyril Bailey, tr., *Epicurus: The Extant Remains*. (Oxford: Clarendon
   Press, 1926)
8. *Principal Doctrines* #11–13, in Cyril Bailey, *Epicurus: The Extant Remains*, (Oxford:
   Clarendon Press, 1926) p. 97.
9. Democritus is what contemporary philosophers call a *hard determinist*: everything
   that happens in the world is controlled by the rules that describe how atoms com-

bine, hook together, and then come apart, and so there is no free will. But Epicurus argues that atoms sometimes behave randomly, and therefore human beings have free will.

10. *Epicurus Letter to Pythocles* in Geer, op. cit. line 85, p. 36.
11. *Epicurus Letter to Herodotus* 38b–c; tr. by Russell Geer, *Epicurus: Letters, Principal Doctrines and Vatican Sayings* (New York: MacMillan, 1964), p. 10.
12. Ibid., lines 60–62.
13. Ibid., line 41b, p. 11.
14. Ibid., line 45b, p. 13.
15. Ibid., line 74b, p. 29.
16. Ibid., line 63a, p. 23.
17. Ibid.
18. Ibid., lines 64–66, p. 24.
19. Ibid., lines 66–67, p. 25.
20. Ibid., lines 76b–77, pp. 30–31.
21. Ibid., lines 81–82, p. 33.
22. *Principal Doctrines* #1, in Bailey, op. cit., p. 95.
23. *Letter to Menoeceus* 123–124a, Geer, op. cit., pp. 53–54.
24. *Principal Doctrines* #2, Bailey, op. cit., p. 95.
25. *Letter to Menoeceus* 125, in Geer, op. cit., p. 54.
26. *Letter to Menoeceus* 126, Geer, op. cit., p. 55.
27. *Principal Doctrines* #8, Bailey, op. cit., pp. 60–61.
28. *Letter to Menoeceus* 131–132, Geer, op. cit., p. 57.
29. *Principal Doctrines* #29, in Bailey, op. cit., pp. 102–103.
30. Fragment #21, Bailey, op. cit., p. 109.
31. Fragment #23, Bailey, op. cit., p. 109.
32. *Principal Doctrines* #26, tr. by Hicks, R. D. Stoic and Epicurean (N.Y.: Charles Scribner's, 1910).
33. Fragment #48, Bailey, op. cit., p. 117.
34. *Principal Doctrines* #35, Bailey, op. cit., p. 111.
35. *Letter to Menoeceus*, in Geer, op. cit., 131a.
36. *Letter to Menoeceus*, 131b, op. cit. p. 57.
37. Fragment #59, in Bailey, op. cit., p. 115.
38. *Principal Doctrines* #15, #18, #20, Bailey, op. cit., p. 99.
39. *Principal Doctrines*, #26.
40. *Letter to Menoeceus* 132b, in Geer, op. cit., pp. 57–58.
41. *Principal Doctrines* #4, in Bailey, op. cit.
42. *Principal Doctrines* #6, #14, ibid.
43. *Principal Doctrines* #31–33, Bailey, trans.
44. *Principal Doctrines* #27, Bailey, op. cit., p. 101.
45. Fragment #34, Bailey, op. cit., p. 111.
46. Fragment #52 quoted in Melchert, *The Great Conversation: A Historical Intro to Philosophy* Mayfield, 1991, p. 189a.5.
47. Fragments #47–48, in Bailey, op. cit., p. 113.
48. *Letter to Menoeceus* 135b, Geer, op. cit., p. 59.

Chapter 4

1. (Appears in Part Two opener.) *Christos* is the Latin word for "messiah," the "anointed one." Jesus is the Greek spelling for the Hebrew name Joshua. So, Jesus Christ means "Joshua, the Anointed One."

2. St. Augustine, *City of God*, trans. Gerald G. Walsh, S. J., Demetrius B. Zema, S. J., Grace Monahan, O. S. U., and Daniel J. Honan (New York: Doubleday Image, 1958), Book XIX, chap. 4, p. 437.
3. These beliefs are often called "creeds" (from the Latin *credo*, "I believe").
4. Emperor Constantine was also a worshiper of the Sun-god, Mithra, who was worshiped on Sunday, and Constantine combined several of the holy days for the followers of Mithra with sacred days for the Christians. Mithra was born on December 25, a Sunday, and Constantine assigned December 25 to become the official birthday of Jesus. He also moved the holy day of the Christians to Sunday, the holy day of the followers of Mithra.
5. There are many profound similarities between Christianity and the so-called mystery religions of the Near East, especially the religions of Mithrism, Manicheanism, and Zoroastrianism.
6. At the opening of St. John's gospel: "In the beginning was the Logos . . . all things were made by him . . . in him was life, the light of men. . . ."
7. Augustine wrote 113 books, 218 letters, and at least 500 sermons.
8. Walsh et al., *City of God*, Book XIV, chap. 1, p. 295.
9. Walsh et al., *City of God*, op. cit., Book XIV, chap. 13, pp. 308–309.
10. Walsh et al., *City of God*, ibid., Book XIV, chapter 4, p. 300.
11. St. Augustine, *Enchiridion*, tr. J. F. Shaw, from *The Works of Aurelius Augustine*, Vol. IX, Reverend Marcus Shaw, ed., Edinburgh, Scotland: T & T. Clark Pub., 1892.
12. Ibid.
13. Ibid.
14. Op. cit, chap. XCVI.
15. Ibid., chaps. C–CI.
16. Ibid., chap. CI.
17. Ibid., Book XIV, chap. 11, p. 305.
18. Marcus Tullius Cicero, 106–43 B.C.E. Roman philosopher, statesman, and lawyer. He is most famous as a great orator, or public speaker. His life was involved in that of Antony, Cleopatra, and Julius Caeser.
19. St. Augustine, *City of God*, an abridged version from the translation by Gerald G. Walsh et al., Book V, chap. 9, p. 106.
20. Ibid., pp. 106–107.
21. Ibid., chap. 10, p. 110.
22. Ibid., p. 108.
23. Ibid., Book XII, chap. 7, p. 254.
24. Ibid., chap. 8, p. 255.
25. Ibid., Book XIV, chap. 11, p. 305.
26. Ibid., Book XIV, chap. 1, p. 295.
27. Ibid., Book XIX, chap. 4, p. 437.
28. Ibid., Book XIX, chap. 4, p. 439.
29. Ibid., Book XIX, chap. 4, p. 437.
30. Ibid., Book XIX, chap. 4, pp. 437–438.
31. Ibid., Book XIX, chap. 4, p. 440.
32. Ibid., pp. 441–442.
33. Ibid., Book XIX, chaps. 4, 14, and 17.
34. Ibid., Book XIX, chap. 4, pp. 439–440.
35. Ibid., Book XIX, chap. 4, p. 442.
36. Ibid., Book XIX, chap. 25, p. 479.
37. Ibid., Book XIX, chap. 14, pp. 459–460.

38. Ibid., Book XXI, chaps. 1 and 2, p. 494, 495.
39. Ibid., Book XXII, chap. 22, pp. 519–521.
40. Ibid., Book XXII, chap. 22, pp. 521–522.
41. Ibid., Book XXII, chap. 1, p. 507.
42. Ibid., Book XXII, chap. 29, p. 532–533.
43. Ibid., Book XXII, chap. 29, p. 539.
44. Ibid., Book XXII, chap. 30, pp. 540–541.
45. Ibid., Book XIX, chap. 20, p. 468.

Chapter 5

1. The description of historian Edward Gibbon of the Eastern Empire whose capital was Constantinople applied to most of Europe: "In the revolution of ten centuries, not a single discovery was made to exalt the dignity or promote the happiness of mankind. Not a single idea had been added to the speculative system of antiquity, and a succession of patient disciples became in their turn the dogmatic teachers of the next servile generation." (Quoted in Carl Sagan, *The Demon-Haunted World*, p. 9.1). New York: Random House, 1995.
2. Cambridge University was founded in the year 1200 C.E.
3. Although St. Thomas Aquinas is of central importance to Roman Catholic theology, Aquinas died in 1274 and the split between Roman Catholic and Protestant didn't become explicit until two hundred years later, after 1500.
4. The *Summa Theologae*, Article 3, trans. Timothy McDermott, *Thomas Aquinas: Selected Philosophical Writings* (Oxford: Oxford University Press, 1993), p. 200.
5. Ibid., pp. 200–201.
6. From the *Summa Contra Gentiles*, Book III, chap. 1, from A. C. Pegis, ed., *Thomas Aquinas: Basic Writings of St. Thomas Aquinas*, Vol. II (New York: Random House, 1945), pp. 3–4.
7. Ibid., p. 4.
8. Ibid., Book III, chap. 2, p. 5.
9. Ibid.
10. Ibid., Book III, chap. 38, pp. 59–60.
11. Ibid., p. 60.
12. Ibid., Book III, chap. 48, p. 85.
13. Loc. cit.
14. *Summa Theologica*, Question 91, Pegis, op. cit., p. 748.
15. Loc. cit.
16. Ibid.
17. I.e., a straight line is the shortest distance between two points, parallel lines do not intersect, etc.
18. *Summa Theologica*, Question 91, Article II, Pegis, op. cit., p. 774.
19. *Summa Theologica*, Question 91/XCI, Article II, p. 774.
20. Ibid., pp. 774–775.
21. Ibid., p. 775.
22. Ibid.
23. *Summa Theologica*, 1st Pt. of 2nd Pt., Question 6, Articles I, VI, VII, pp. 226–227, 234–236.
24. Ibid., pp. 234–236.
25. Loc. cit.
26. *Summa Theologica*, 1st Pt. of 2nd Pt., Question 6, Article VIII, p. 237.

27. Loc. cit.
28. Ibid., p. 238.
29. Loc. cit.
30. *Summa Theologica*, 1st Pt. of 2nd Pt., Question 19, Articles I, II, p. 335.
31. Ibid., Articles I, II, III, pp. 335–337.
32. *Summa Theologica*, 1st Pt. of 2nd Pt., Question 19, Articles V, VI, pp. 339–342.
33. Ibid., Question 20, Article V, p. 356.
34. Ibid., pp. 356–357.
35. For many scholars, the year 1517 marks the beginning of Protestantism in Europe.

Chapter 6

1. The Buddha says, "A being may tend the sacrificial fire in the forest for a hundred years, but for one moment if he were to pay homage to a single [living] person, one whose personality is well cultivated, that very homage is superior to the oblation performed for a hundred years."

   This is verse #107 of *The Dhammapada*. David J. Kalupahana, *A Path of Righteousness: Dhammapada* (Lanham, Md.: University Press of America, 1986), p. 123.

2. "Man is fundamentally good by nature and the evil in him is an extraneous outcome of his samsaric conditioning. . . . The Buddha states that 'the mind is naturally resplendent though it is corrupted by adventitious defilements'. . . . Even the evil that he commits is not due to his basic depravity or wickedness but to his ignorance." K. N. Jayatilleke, *Ethics in Buddhist Perspective* (Kandy, Ceylon: Buddhist Publication Society, 1972), p. 34. This is based upon the following quote: "Luminous is this thought, O Monks, and it is defiled by adventitious defiling elements" (*Anguttara Nikaya*, 5 vols., vol. 1.10). However, it is important to note that there is some doubt as to whether this is the proper interpretation of the quote. See David Kalupahana, *The Principles of Buddhist Psychology* (New York: State University of New York Press, 1987), pp. 28ff.

3. *The Dhammapada*, verse 276, quoted in Christmas Humphreys, *The Wisdom of Buddhism* (New York: Random House, 1961), p. 51. The translation has been slightly modified by the author.

4. In verse 165 of *The Dhammapada*. The translation is from K. N. Jayatilleke, *Ethics*, pp. 43–44.

5. Note that "Buddha" is a title (like "Your Honor" to the judge, or "Mr. President") and is *not* a proper name at all—the title translates to "someone who Woke Up," or "the Awakened One."

6. No early Buddhist works provide a precise date for the birth or death of the Buddha. Scholars, using clues found in various traditions, have estimated the birth and death dates of the Buddha. In Southeast Asian Buddhism and Sri Lanka, the traditional dates are 624–544 B.C.E. Indian scholars and Western archaeologists, correlating Buddhist writings with Greek evidence, use either 566–486 B.C.E., or 563–483 B.C.E. Japanese scholars, using Chinese and Tibetan texts, use the dates 448–368 B.C.E.

7. Although *duhkha* is usually translated as "suffering," it is much more than that. It is not just physical pain. It is the feeling that something is missing, even when you have more than enough. It is the feeling of frustration, the feeling of "is this all there is to life?" The statement "Life is *duhkha*" can be rendered "life is unsatisfactory." When you have more than enough and you are still not satisfied, that is *duhkha*.

8. Nirvana is the psychological and physiological state where one's actions and desires are not conditioned by selfish craving or an egocentric approach to life, not condi-

tioned by hatred or anger, not conditioned by unconscious habits and preconceptions, not conditioned by ignorance.

9. David Kalupahana, *A History of Buddhist Philosophy* (Honolulu: University of Hawaii Press, 1992), p. 26.

10. Quoted in "The Buddha's Last Words" from Humphreys, *Wisdom of Buddhism*, p. 94.

11. A very excellent book about the key Buddhist concept of causality is David Kalupahana, *Causality: The Central Philosophy of Buddhism* (Honolulu: University of Hawaii Press, 1975).

12. The Sanskrit term for "soul" is *atman*, and the Buddhist Sanskrit term for no-atman is *anatman*.

13. Kalupahana, *Dhammapada*, op. cit., p. 35.

14. Some of the later Buddhists accused the early followers of the Buddha of being selfish and even egocentric, because they put concern for their own liberation first, and compassionate concern for other suffering human beings second. This was one of the items at the core of the dispute between the *arhat* ideal and the *Bodhisattva* ideal, the dispute between the earlier Theravadins (disparagingly called "Hinayanists") and the later Mahayana tradition. Interesting as it is, this topic is beyond the scope of this book. Any book on the history of Buddhism will explain the details.

15. Inasmuch as the focus of this chapter is morality, it necessarily slights the meditative component of the Buddhist path. Any good book on Buddhism as a whole will provide further details on the methods of meditation.

16. Kalupahana, *Dhammapada*, ibid., p. 138.

17. Buddhism includes a list of the "Ten Fetters" or obstacles to happiness. The list includes such things as belief in an eternal unchanging soul, relying on good deeds, sensuality, pride, wanting to be reborn in a heavenly realm, and ignorance.

18. Kalupahana, *Dhammapada*, ibid., p. 131.

19. These are called the Three Marks of Existence: (1) everything is impermanent; (2) no permanent and unchanging soul; (3) dissatisfaction or frustration (*duhkha*).

20. As with the chapter on Christianity, we must note that we are discussing the philosophical foundations for early Buddhist ethics. That there is a popular religious Buddhism with a popular idea of morality is uncontested. That the popular understanding of Buddhist morality would place a much heavier stress on *karma* and rewards and punishments is also clear. This chapter is not on popular Buddhist religion, it is on early Buddhist philosophy.

21. It is interesting to compare this list of virtues with the Greek list (wisdom, temperance, courage, justice) and the Christian virtues (faith, chastity, obedience, hope, charity).

22. Discussed in Sutta 27 of the *Majjhima Nikaya*, 1:180. A person hears the dharma, expresses confidence in it, goes forth to a life of houselessness, governs his or her life by the moral rules, and consequently experiences joy. Then he or she controls the six sense organs, develops mindfulness and clear consciousness and enters the levels of meditative awareness. The disciple understands the Four Noble Truths, understands the causal interdependent nature of reality and ultimately attains liberation. See I. B. Horner, tr. *The Middle Length Sayings* (London: Pali Text Society, Luzac & Co., 1967).

23. The careful reader will note a similarity to Plato here. Plato argued that it is in one's own self-interest to be virtuous because unjust behavior is harmful to the soul (cf. the Ring of Gyges).

24. From the translation of Jayatilleke, *Ethics in Buddhist Perspective*, p. 4.

25. Causality has two dimensions: one that applies to the physical objects in the external world (every event is dependent upon prior causes and conditions), and a second

that applies to the human personality. The second addresses the question of free will. The Buddhists hold a position called "Soft Determinism": it is true that every action we take is caused, but as long as those causes include our own wishes, desires, and preferences, our will is free and our actions are done freely.

26. "Buddhist recognizes the importance of the hedonistic principle that man is predominantly motivated to act out of 'his desire for happiness and the repulsion for unhappiness' . . . " Jayatilleke, *Ethics in Buddhist Perspective,* p. 19.
27. Karma functions more like a descriptive law than any kind of reward and punishment system built into the universe by a deity. If you jump off the roof, you will hurt yourself; similarly, if you cause evil to happen to another, then you will have evil consequences return to you.
28. Kalupahana, *Path of Righteousness,* op. cit., p. 113.
29. Verse 239 of *The Dhammapada.* Kalupahana, ibid., p. 135.
30. To live in the world in a self-centered way, produces anger, resentment—we look to things in the world to solve our *duhkha,* and they don't do it more than temporarily. Suffering is caused by (1) greed or self-centered craving or desire/lust, (2) hatred, anger, or aversion and (3) ignorance or confusion. By eliminating these Three Poisons one can eliminate *duhkha* and attain *nirvana.*
31. *Majjhima-Nikaya,* I.283, in Horner, *The Middle Length Sayings,* Vol. I, p. 338.
32. *Digha Nikaya* III.89. T. W. and C. A. F. Rhys Davids, *Dialogues of the Buddha* (London: Pali Text Society, 1899–1921).
33. However, note that attachment to rules as though they were absolute is warned against in Buddhism. Blind attachment is one of the Ten Fetters (*samyojana*) that will bind a person to the cycle of birth and death. Rules are guides to behavior, not absolute imperatives.
34. The Buddhist literature is divided up into three sections, one of which is called the *Vinaya,* or rules or precepts imposing standards of conduct. There are 227 precepts applicable to monks, and several more for nuns. Most are procedural and not specifically moral.
35. Kalupahana, *Path of Righteousness,* #50, p. 117.
36. The earliest form of Buddhism was primarily concerned with those who had retired from the worldly life and were living the celibate life of a mendicant. It is very probable that the Noble Eightfold Path was originally intended for such people. The Five Precepts is probably a later adaptation for the use of laypersons.
37. Kalupahana, *Path of Righteousness,* #23, p. 115.
38. Kalupahana, ibid., #35, p. 116.
39. It is interesting to note that selfless detachment, love, and nonviolence are placed under the heading of wisdom. Thus, craving, self-centeredness, and violence are due to a lack of wisdom.
40. *Majjhima Nikaya,* I.415.
41. Which is to say that if you do not practice morality, you cannot attain enlightenment and nirvana. However, practicing just morality is not sufficient to attain them either.
42. These are called the Six *Paramita,* the Six Virtues or Perfections.

Chapter 7

1. (Appears in Part Four opener.) This is profoundly different from the traditional Western Judeo-Christian presuppositions. In the West we have a hierarchy: on the top is God, and below God is God's special creation, human beings (who possess divine souls). On the bottom is nature, which is decidedly inferior to human beings. In the

world, human beings are the most important with everything else much less important. We do not belong here; our true home is found elsewhere after we die.

2. (Appears in Part Four opener.) This is also different from the Western Christian assumption that without divine intercession, no human being can liberate himself or herself. For the West, a divine intermediary is essential. By ourselves, we can never attain the highest goal. No Chinese ever thought that there was an unbridgeable gulf between the realm of heaven and the realm of humanity, nor did they ever think that God had turned his back upon humanity.

3. D. C. Lau, *The Analects* (New York: Penguin Books, 1979), Book 2, Verse 4 (hereinafter listed simply as 2.4).

4. The term *Analects* comes from the Greek, meaning "Things Gathered," and the title in Chinese, *Lun-yü,* could be translated "Conversations," "Discourses," or "Dialogues."

5. Lau, op. cit., 7.1.

6. Lau, op. cit., 12.19.

7. Since no English term is equivalent, we will simply use the Chinese *li* throughout our discussion.

8. Lau, op. cit., 8.2.

9. Lau, op. cit., 4.1.

10. Recall that the Greeks argued that it was reason or intellect that separates humans from the animals; the Christians claimed that it was a divine soul that separates human beings from the rest of nature.

11. Lau, op. cit., 15.35.

12. Lau, op. cit., 4.4.

13. Lau, op. cit., 13.19.

14. Lau, op. cit., 12.2.

15. Although it was not the original intention of Confucius, the combination of *jen* and *li* worked together to serve as an instrument of conservative political and cultural policy. *Li* were turned into a standardized list of rules governing social and political situations; *li* became rigid and dogmatic. Thus, *li* were used to resist social change; Confucianism became a supporter of rigid social rules governing everyone.

16. Lau, op. cit., 4.16.

17. Lau, op. cit., 14.34.

18. Lau, op. cit., 2.5.

19. Lau, op. cit., 15.24.

20. Lau, op. cit., 2.3.

21. Lau, op. cit., 4.10.

Chapter 8

1. There is great controversy whether Lao-tzu is the real name of the author of the *Tao Te Ching,* and whether any of the facts in his biography are accurate. We shall ignore these questions here.

2. Many scholars take the term Tao to name some sort of ultimate substance, a metaphysical thing. It is possible to read the *Tao Te Ching* with that interpretation, but I feel it is less satisfactory for the *Chuang Tzu.* For a more technical discussion, see Chad Hansen, "A Tao of Tao in Chuang Tzu," in Victor Mair, *Experimental Essays on Chuang-tzu* (Honolulu, Hawaii: University Press of Hawaii, ASH 29, 1983).

3. Burton Watson, tr., *The Complete Works of Chuang Tzu* (New York: Columbia University Press, 1970), chap. 6, p. 81.

4. The author's translation from the opening four verses of the *Tao Te Ching*. The primary Chinese text used is that of Han-shan Te-ching (1546–1620), *Lao Tzu Tao Te Ching Han-shan chiai (Han-shan's Explanation of Lao-tzu's Tao Te Ching)*, p. 51.

5. *Tao Te Ching*, chap. 25. Author's translation from Han-shan Te-ching, op. cit., chap. 25.

6. Watson, op. cit., chap. 6, p. 78.

7. Author's translation of *Tao Te Ching*, op. cit., chap. 34.

8. Watson, op. cit., chap. 8, pp. 99–100.

9. Author's translation of *Tao Te Ching*, op. cit., chap. 45.

10. Tao Te Ching, op. cit., chap. 48.

11. Watson, op. cit., chap. 13, p. 144.

12. *Tao Te Ching*, op. cit., chap. 8.

13. Chapter 55 of the *Tao Te Ching* has a wonderful description that begins, "One who is steeped in virtue is akin to the new born babe . . ."

14. *Tao Te Ching*, chap. 55.

15. *Tao Te Ching*, op. cit., chap. 15.

16. In Chinese imagery, the mountain is the *yang* or masculine symbol, the valley is the feminine receptive *yin* symbol.

17. *Tao Te Ching*, op. cit., chap. 6.

18. *Tao Te Ching*, op. cit., chap. 28.

19. *Tao Te Ching*, op. cit., chap. 36.

20. *Tao Te Ching*, op. cit., chap. 22.

21. *Tao Te Ching*, op. cit., chap. 5.

22. *Tao Te Ching*, op. cit., chap. 57.

23. Chapter 60 of Steven Mitchell, *Tao Te Ching* (New York: Harper & Row, 1988).

24. Ch'en Ku-ying, *Lao Tzu: Text Notes, and Comments* (San Francisco: Chinese Materials Center, 1977), p. 60.

25. The earliest biographical entry is in the "Records of the Historian" by Ssu-ma Ch'ien (145?–89? B.C.E.). The entry is brief with no real biographical details.

26. The other two sections in the book are called the "Outer Chapters" and the "Miscellaneous Chapters."

27. Watson, op. cit., chap. 6, p. 87.

28. Watson, op. cit., chap. 11, p. 119.

29. Watson, op. cit., chap. 2, p. 44.

30. Watson, op. cit., chap. 6, p. 80.

31. Watson, op. cit., chap. 6, p. 81.

32. Watson, op. cit., chap. 3, pp. 52–53.

33. Watson, op. cit., chap. 6, p. 84.

34. A loach is a freshwater fish.

35. Watson, op. cit., chap. 2, pp. 45–46.

36. In other words, the sage freely uses the conceptual distinction between "this" and "that," between "right" and "wrong," but recognizes that there is nothing ultimate about the discrimination. From a different perspective, the judgment would be different.

37. Watson, op. cit., chap. 2, pp. 39–40.

38. Watson, op. cit., chap. 2, pp. 48–49.

39. Watson, op. cit., chap. 17 (Autumn Floods), pp. 178–179.

40. Watson, op. cit., chap. 12, pp. 127–128.

41. Watson, op. cit., chap. 2, p. 47.

42. Watson, op. cit., chap. 7, p. 97.

43. Watson, op. cit., chap. 11, p. 118.

44. Watson, op. cit., chap. 17 (Autumn Floods), pp. 180–181.
45. Ibid., ch. 22, pp. 234–235.
46. Watson, op. cit., chap. 22, p. 241.
47. Watson, op. cit., chap. 6, p. 86.
48. Watson, op. cit., chap. 6, pp. 88–89.
49. *Tao Te Ching*, author's translation, chap. 41.

Chapter 9

1. (Appears in Part Five opener.) Much of this discussion is inspired by the clever discussion found in James Burke, *The Day the Universe Changed* (New York: Little Brown & Co., 1995), especially pp. 133ff.
2. Ibid., Burke, *Day Universe Changed*, p. 311.
3. We see the influence of the Greeks and especially Plato here.
4. "Preface to Five Sermons," para. 12, from Stephen L. Darwall, ed., *Joseph Butler: Five Sermons* (Indianapolis, Ind.: Hackett Publishing Company, 1983), p. 13. All the quotes from Butler are taken from Darwall's book.
5. Preface, ibid., para. 14, pp. 14–15.
6. Ibid., Sermon I, para. 5, p. 26.
7. Sermon I, para. 6, p. 27, op. cit.
8. Ibid., para. 7, p. 28.
9. This is Sermon IV in *Five Sermons* but was originally Sermon XI of the complete text of Butler's sermons.
10. Sermon IV, para. 2, ibid.
11. Sermon IV, para. 5, 7, ibid., p. 47.
12. Sermon I, para. 8, ibid., pp. 29–30.
13. Ibid.
14. Ibid., pp. 37–39.
15. Ibid., para. 14, pp. 39–40.
16. Ibid., para. 8–9, pp. 37–38. The passages in italics were added by the author of this book.
17. Sermon II, para. 3, ibid., p. 35.
18. Sermon III, para. 5, ibid., p. 43.
19. Ibid.

Chapter 10

1. Originally reported by Hume's biographer, E. C. Mossner, and quoted in Roger Johnson, H. Paul Santmire, eds. *Critical Issues in Modern Religion* 2nd ed., (New York: Prentice Hall, 1990) p. 1.
2. David Hume, *An Enquiry Concerning the Principles of Morals,* 2nd ed. (LaSalle, Ill.: Open Court Classics, 1966), p. 2. All quotations from Hume are taken from this standard work.
3. Ibid., p. 3.
4. Op. cit., pp. 4–5.
5. Ibid., p. 4.
6. Loc. cit., p. 4.
7. Op. cit., p. 4.
8. Op. cit., Appendix I, p. 129.
9. Ibid., p. 132.

10. Ibid., p. 134.
11. Ibid., pp. 130–131.
12. Ibid., p. 8.
13. Ibid., p. 11.
14. Ibid., p. 14.
15. Ibid., p. 15.
16. Ibid., p. 16.
17. Ibid., p. 18.
18. Ibid., p. 111.
19. Ibid., p. 109.
20. Ibid., pp. 112–113.

Chapter 11

1. *Immanuel Kant: Groundwork of the Metaphysic of Morals,* translated and analyzed by H. J. Paton Harper Torchbooks, TB 1159, p. 61. All quotations from Kant's text came from this volume.
2. Ibid., p. 61.
3. Ibid., p. 62.
4. Loc. cit., p. 62.
5. Ibid., pp. 62–63.
6. Loc. cit.
7. Ibid., p. 64.
8. Ibid., pp. 64–65.
9. Ibid., pp. 67–68.
10. Ibid., p. 68.
11. Ibid., p. 68.
12. Ibid., pp. 68–69.
13. Ibid., pp. 42–43.
14. Ibid., p. 69
15. Paton, op. cit., p. 70.
16. Ibid., p. 29.
17. Ibid., pp. 30–31.
18. Ibid., p. 31.
19. Ibid., p. 33.
20. Ibid., p. 33.
21. Ibid., p. 38.
22. Ibid., pp. 39–40.
23. Ibid., pp. 45–46.
24. Ibid., p. 46.
25. Ibid., p. 46.
26. Ibid., p. 47.
27. Ibid., p. 49.
28. Ibid., p. 50.
29. Ibid., pp. 50–51.
30. Ibid., p. 51.
31. Ibid., p. 56.
32. Ibid., pp. 60–61.
33. Ibid., pp. 66.

Chapter 12

1. When the French overthrew their king, they were also beginning to discard traditional Christian values that asserted that the king ruled by the grace of God. To overthrow the king was to overthrow the Christian theory that the world existed in a hierarchy, and that God had appointed the king to rule, and God had appointed each serf to be a serf, and hence it was a sin to try to put oneself in the place of those whom God had placed above you.
2. Chapter II, "What Utilitarianism Is," in J. S. Mill, *Utilitarianism* (Bobbs-Merrill Library of Liberal Arts, 1957), p. 9. All subsequent quotations from Mill are from this edition.
3. Op. cit., p. 10.
4. Ibid.
5. J. Bowring, ed., *The Works of Jeremy Bentham* (London: Simpkin, Marshall, 1838), vol. 1, p. 16.
6. Mill, op. cit., p. 48.6.
7. Ibid., p. 49.2.
8. Op. cit., p. 11.
9. Op. cit., p. 12.
10. Op. cit., p. 14.
11. Op. cit., p. 15.
12. Ibid.
13. Op. cit., pp. 15–16.
14. Ibid., p. 16.
15. Loc. cit.
16. Ibid., pp. 17–18.
17. Ibid., pp. 18–19.
18. Ibid., p. 19.
19. Ibid., p. 21.
20. Ibid., p. 22.
21. Ibid., p. 22.
22. Ibid., p. 28.5.
23. Ibid., p. 23.7.
24. Ibid., pp. 23–24.
25. Ibid., p. 35.7.
26. Ibid., p. 36.4.
27. Ibid., p. 36.
28. Ibid., p. 37.2.
29. Ibid., p. 37.5.
30. Ibid., p. 39.2.
31. Ibid., p. 40.3.

Credits

Chapter 1

Excerpts from Plato's *Republic.*

Source: Excerpted from Plato, *The Republic,* trans. G. M. A. Grube (Indianapolis: Hackett Publishing, 1974). Reprinted by permission of Hackett Publishing Company, Inc. All rights reserved.

Excerpts from Plato's *Protagoras.*

Source: Plato, "Protagoras." From *Protagoras and Meno* by Plato, translated by W. K. C. Guthrie (Penguin Classics, 1956), pp. 92, 94–95. Copyright © W. K. C. Guthrie, 1956. Reproduced by permission of Penguin Books Ltd.

Chapter 2

Excerpts from Aristotle's *Nichomachean Ethics.*

Source: Aristotle, *The Nichomachean Ethics,* translated with an introduction by David Ross, revised by J. L. Ackrill and J. O. Urmson (1980). Reprinted by permission of Oxford University Press.

Chapter 3

Excerpts from the Bailey translation of *Epicurus.*

Source: Cyril Bailey, trans., *Epicurus: The Extant Remains* (Oxford: Clarendon Press, 1926).

Excerpts from the Geer translation of *Epicurus.*

Source: Russell M. Geer, trans., *Epicurus: Letters, Principal Doctrines, and Vatican Sayings* (New York: Macmillan Library of Liberal Arts, 1964). Reprinted by permission of Prentice-Hall, Inc., Upper Saddle River, NJ.

Chapter 4

Excerpts from the Walsh et al. translation of *St. Augustine.*

Source: Excerpted by permission of The Catholic University of America Press from Gerald C. Walsh, S. J., Demetrius B. Zema, S. J., Grace Monahan, O. S. U., and Daniel J. Honan, trans., *St. Augustine: City of God,* vols. 8, 14, and 24 of the Fathers of the Church series (New York: Doubleday Image edition, 1958).

Chapter 5

Excerpts from Pegis's *Thomas Aquinas.*
Source: Excerpted from Anton Charles Pegis, editor and annotator, *Thomas Aquinas: Basic Writings of St. Thomas Aquinas,* vol. 2 (New York: Random House, 1945). Reprinted by permission of Hackett Publishing Company, Inc. All rights reserved.

Chapter 7

Excerpts from Lau's translation of Confucius.
Source: From *The Analects* by Confucius, translated by D. C. Lau (Penguin Classics, 1979). Copyright © D. C. Lau, 1979. Reproduced by permission of Penguin Books Ltd.

Chapter 8

Excerpts from Watson's translation of *Chuang Tzu.*
Source: From *The Complete Works of Chuang Tzu* trans. Burton Watson. © 1968 Columbia University Press. Reprinted by permission of the publisher.

Chapter 9

Excerpts from Darwall's *Joseph Butler.*
Source: Stephen L. Darwall, ed., *Joseph Butler: Five Sermons* (Indianapolis: Hackett Publishing, 1983). Reprinted by permission of Hackett Publishing Company, Inc. All rights reserved.

Chapter 11

Excerpts from Paton's *Immanuel Kant.*
Source: Immanuel Kant: Groundwork of the Metaphysic of Morals, translated and analyzed by H. J. Paton (New York: Harper Torchbooks, 1964), pp. 29–31, 33, 38–40, 42–43, 45–47, 49–51, 56, 60–70. Reprinted by permission of Taylor & Francis, for Routledge (Unwin Hyman).

Index

Boldface page numbers indicate boldface terms in text.

CPSIA information can be obtained at www.ICGtesting.com
Printed in the USA
LVOW03s0408050115

421509LV00012B/76/P